Hitchcock's Moral Gaze

Also in the series

William Rothman, editor, *Cavell on Film*

J. David Slocum, editor, *Rebel Without a Cause*

Joe McElhaney, *The Death of Classical Cinema*

Kirsten Moana Thompson, *Apocalyptic Dread*

Frances Gateward, editor, *Seoul Searching*

Michael Atkinson, editor, *Exile Cinema*

Paul S. Moore, *Now Playing*

Robin L. Murray and Joseph K. Heumann, *Ecology and Popular Film*

William Rothman, editor, *Three Documentary Filmmakers*

Sean Griffin, editor, *Hetero*

Jean-Michel Frodon, editor, *Cinema and the Shoah*

Carolyn Jess-Cooke and Constantine Verevis, editors, *Second Takes*

Matthew Solomon, editor, *Fantastic Voyages of the Cinematic Imagination*

R. Barton Palmer and David Boyd, editors, *Hitchcock at the Source*

William Rothman, *Hitchcock: The Murderous Gaze, Second Edition*

Joanna Hearne, *Native Recognition*

Marc Raymond, *Hollywood's New Yorker*

Steven Rybin and Will Scheibel, editors, *Lonely Places, Dangerous Ground*

Claire Perkins and Constantine Verevis, editors, *B Is for Bad Cinema*

Dominic Lennard, *Bad Seeds and Holy Terrors*

Rosie Thomas, *Bombay before Bollywood*

Scott M. MacDonald, *Binghamton Babylon*

Sudhir Mahadevan, *A Very Old Machine*

David Greven, *Ghost Faces*

James S. Williams, *Encounters with Godard*

William H. Epstein and R. Barton Palmer, editors, *Invented Lives, Imagined Communities*

Lee Carruthers, *Doing Time*

Rebecca Meyers, William Rothman and Charles Warren, editors, *Looking with Robert Gardner*

Belinda Smaill, *Regarding Life*

Hitchcock's Moral Gaze

∾

Edited by
R. Barton Palmer, Homer B. Pettey,
and Steven M. Sanders

Cover: Publicity still from Alfred Hitchcock's *I Confess* (1953). Courtesy of Warner Bros. and the Academy of Motion Picture Arts and Sciences.

Published by State University of New York Press, Albany

© 2017 State University of New York

All rights reserved

Printed in the United States of America

No part of this book may be used or reproduced in any manner whatsoever without written permission. No part of this book may be stored in a retrieval system or transmitted in any form or by any means including electronic, electrostatic, magnetic tape, mechanical, photocopying, recording, or otherwise without the prior permission in writing of the publisher.

For information, contact State University of New York Press, Albany, NY
www.sunypress.edu

Production, Eileen Nizer
Marketing, Fran Keneston

Library of Congress Cataloging-in-Publication Data

Names: Palmer, R. Barton, 1946– editor. | Sanders, Steven, 1945– editor. | Pettey, Homer B., editor.
Title: Hitchcock's moral gaze / edited by R. Barton Palmer, Steven M. Sanders, and Homer B. Pettey.
Description: Albany : State University of New York Press, [2017] | Series: SUNY series, horizons of cinema | Includes filmography. | Includes bibliographical references and index.
Identifiers: LCCN 2016031494 (print) | LCCN 2016048537 (ebook) | ISBN 9781438463858 (hardcover : alk. paper) | 9781438463841 (pbk. : alk. paper) | ISBN 9781438463865 (e-book)
Subjects: LCSH: Hitchcock, Alfred, 1899–1980—Criticism and interpretation.
Classification: LCC PN1998.3.H58 H5755 2017 (print) | LCC PN1998.3.H58 (ebook) | DDC 791.4302/33092—dc23
LC record available at https://lccn.loc.gov/2016031494

10 9 8 7 6 5 4 3 2 1

Contents

Illustrations	vii
Acknowledgments	ix
Introduction *R. Barton Palmer and Steven M. Sanders*	1

Skepticism

1. Jealousy and Trust in *The Lodger* *Graham Petrie*	23
2. Fun with Suspicion *Thomas Leitch*	37
3. Heroic Satans and Other Hitchcockian Heresies *Nick Haeffner*	59
4. "Guilt, Confession, and . . . Then What?": *The Paradine Case* and *Under Capricorn* *Brian McFarlane*	75
5. The Forgotten Cigarette Lighter and Other Moral Accidents in *Strangers on a Train* *George Toles*	91

Immorality

6. Hitchcock's Immoralists *Steven M. Sanders*	117

7. Hitchcock the Amoralist: *Rear Window* and the Pleasures and Dangers of Looking 133
   Sidney Gottlieb

8. Voyeurism Revisited 151
   Richard Allen

Moralizing

9. Alfred Hitchcock as Moralist 173
   Murray Pomerance

10. The Deepening Moralism of *The Wrong Man* 193
    R. Barton Palmer

11. Hitchcock and the Philosophical End of Film 211
    Jerold J. Abrams

Moral Acts

12. The Dread of Ascent: The Moral and Spiritual Topography of *Vertigo* 237
    Alan Woolfolk

13. The Philosophy of Marriage in *North by Northwest* 253
    Jennifer L. Jenkins

14. "The Loyalty of an Eel": Issues of Political, Personal, and Professional Morality in (and around) *Torn Curtain* 271
    Neil Sinyard

15. Hobbes, Hume, and Hitchcock: The Case of *Frenzy* 287
    Homer B. Pettey

Bibliography 309

Alfred Hitchcock Selected Filmography 317

Contributors 319

Index 323

Illustrations

Figure 0.1	*I Confess*—Alma Keller (Dolly Haas) in moral crisis during the Logan trial.	6
Figure 0.2	Father Logan (Montgomery Clift) with the dying Otto Keller (O.E. Hasse).	14
Figure 1.1	Flashing sign, *The Lodger*.	29
Figure 1.2	*The Lodger*—Joe's (Malcolm Keen) jealousy.	33
Figure 2.1	*Suspicion*—glass of milk.	42
Figure 3.1	*Shadow of a Doubt*—the world is a foul sty.	69
Figure 4.1	*Paradine Case*—Judge Gay (Charles Laughton) advances.	79
Figure 4.2	*Under Capricorn*—anguish and atonement.	84
Figure 5.1	*Strangers on a Train*—Bruno (Robert Walker) with Guy's (Farley Granger) cigarette lighter.	94
Figure 5.2	Bruno's fingers and the lighter.	111
Figure 6.1	Hitchcock with *Rope* cast.	121
Figure 7.1	*Rear Window*—Jefferies (James Stewart) in anguish.	134
Figure 7.2	Jefferies falls.	134
Figure 8.1	Lisa (Grace Kelly) and Jefferies (James Stewart) watching.	161
Figure 8.2	Miss Lonely Hearts (Judith Evelyn).	168
Figure 9.1	*The Man Who Knew Too Much*—fake Draytons.	185
Figure 10.1	Manny (Henry Fonda) at the Insurance Office.	199

Figure 11.1	*The Birds*—birds as theater audience members.	231
Figure 12.1	Midge (Barbara Bel Geddes) leaving sanitarium.	241
Figure 13.1	Eve (Eve Marie Saint) walking down the train "aisle."	259
Figure 13.2	Thornhill (Cary Grant) and the new Mrs. Thornhill in their berth.	268
Figure 14.1	*Torn Curtain*—blackboard scene.	275
Figure 15.1	*Frenzy*—Rusk's (Barry Foster) flashback post-murder.	293
Figure 15.2	Oxford's (Alec McCowen) aural flashback of Blaney's (Jon Finch) cries of innocence.	294

Acknowledgments

R. Barton Palmer recognizes those fellow students and faculty, members of the Dartmouth College Film Society in 1964–1965, who spared neither time nor expense in mounting the first American retrospective of the films of Alfred Hitchcock, which was complete save for those then unavailable for exhibition. To an eighteen-year old undergraduate, the experience in the Hopkins Center theater, week after week, was more than enlightening and gave rise to a life-changing enthusiasm.

Homer B. Pettey would like to thank his friend and fellow admirer of Hitchcock, the late crossword genius Merl Reagle; his pals in crime, Carter Burwell and Chip Johannessen, who continually open his eyes to the magic of the industry; and especially to the loved ones who make his life better, Jennifer and Melissa.

Steven M. Sanders thanks his parents, Herb and Ruth Sanders, for bringing him and his sister Lynn to the Gables Theatre to see *Vertigo*, best friend Mike Stephans for sharing in the horror at the Trail Theater screening of *Psycho*, and his wife Christeen for aiding and abetting (to say nothing of abating) numerous viewings of Hitch's films.

Introduction

R. Barton Palmer and Steven M. Sanders

An Unrivaled Figure

IN THE WEEK FOLLOWING INGMAR BERGMAN's death, film critic David Denby wrote in *The New Yorker* that Bergman "was perhaps the most influential of all filmmakers as well as the most widely parodied" (10). Of course, Denby said "perhaps," and he supported this view by writing that "In the nineteen-sixties and seventies, antic couples quarreled in mock Swedish, film students spoofed his morbid dream sequences, Woody Allen sent the hooded figure of death from 'The Seventh Seal' stalking through 'Love and Death.'" Nevertheless, this assertion was astonishing. It was as if someone had called Nietzsche "perhaps the most influential of all philosophers as well as the most widely parodied," and had noted that in the nineteen-seventies students walked about Harvard Square in Nietzsche T-shirts, that some thinker had designated Nietzsche *the* philosopher of the twentieth century, that even the much-heralded HBO television series *The Sopranos* invoked the pronouncement for which Nietzsche is best known (at least to non-philosophers): "God is dead."

Indeed, the case for Nietzsche is considerably stronger than the analogous one for Bergman. While there may be no obvious alternative candidates to Nietzsche as the "most influential" philosopher (at least in the twentieth century)—with the possible exception of John Dewey, Martin Heidegger, or Ludwig Wittgenstein, if philosopher Richard Rorty is right (5)—there *is* an obvious alternative to Bergman in the person of Alfred Hitchcock, whose work has influenced and been imitated, parodied, and otherwise sent up by admirers and acolytes from Mel Brooks and Jonathan Demme to Gus Van Sant and Brian de Palma (see Boyd and Palmer). Has there ever been a more recognizable filmmaker, one who combined artistic achievement so thoroughly with commercial success, and whose influence can be felt in such disparate movements and subgenres as film noir, the French New Wave, the thriller, the psychological drama, espionage, romance, and horror films? Another significant indication of the continued influence and importance of Hitchcock is the ascent of *Vertigo*, his 1958 assay of the passions and obsessions of romantic love, to the top of the 2012 *Sight & Sound* critics poll, displacing for the first time in four decades Orson Welles's *Citizen Kane* (1941). While there can be little doubt about his place in the history of filmmaking, the essays in this volume provide new and compelling perspectives on Hitchcock, who worked through a "moral lens" whose contours and significance continue to provoke complex and appreciative responses.

A Philosophical Filmmaker

Irving Singer argues that Alfred Hitchcock, much like both Orson Welles and Jean Renoir, was not only a "great" filmmaker but also a "philosophical" filmmaker. Singer is one of the most prolific and respected of contemporary thinkers, so who might be more qualified to make such a judgment? And yet Singer thinks that Hitchcock himself would have scoffed at any notion that his films could be termed philosophical or, more weakly, that they even could be seen as seriously exploring weighty themes. Hitchcock, of course, would not have disputed being considered a giant figure of world cinema; he had, after all, by the end of his career achieved an unequaled record of critical and popular success. He directed more than fifty films for two different national industries, working regularly and profitably as a filmmaker for almost six decades; after making his way up the professional ladder, Hitchcock first assumed the director's chair in 1922 (with *Number 13* for Gainsborough, which was never finished); his last completed project was for Universal, *Family Plot* (1976). In addition, during the 1950s, he moved into producing a television series that proved an immediate popular and critical success. The director turned on-screen personality hosted numerous episodes of *Alfred Hitchcock Presents* with an unforgettable mixture of deadpan humor, playful ghoulishness, and cynical observations about human nature, in the process extending and enhancing his already considerable reputation as a storyteller and ironist, about which he was never too modest to feel quite proud.

Yet Hitchcock, or at least so Singer imagines, never would have considered any of his feature films or TV episodes philosophical because in them he never "pontificates about eternal verities or the analytic niceties of analytical philosophy" (3). Never reluctant to discuss his artistic aims and procedures, Hitchcock considered himself a gifted storyteller and well-practiced professional entertainer, but he was prone to slight the weightier aspects of the films he made. This self-conception emerges time and time again in his occasional writings (a precious few, but filled with interesting perceptions about the creative process and production procedures), as well as in interviews.[1] In a 1955 conversation with the director, for example, André Bazin observed that "several young French critics" (he refers to his *Cahiers* colleagues Claude Chabrol, Éric Rohmer, and François Truffaut) have found "hidden beneath the crime fiction pretexts of your films" a singularly "consistent and deep message." Hitchcock's response: "From the outset I take no interest in the story I am telling but rather only in the means I employ to tell it"; most important to him as a filmmaker, he continues, is maintaining the proper balance between drama and comedy, with at that point in his career the most successful of his works by this criterion being *The Lady Vanishes* (1938) (Bazin 29). To be sure, this film is arguably among his wittiest, remaining consistently popular with critics and his fans. But *The Lady Vanishes* has not been understood as propounding a "deep message," and, perhaps for this reason, it was never a favored text of the *Cahiers* Hitchcockians (Bazin 28–29). Chabrol and Rohmer, for example, drily observe that "it prompts little in the way of commentary" (62). To be sure, if Hitchcock's major cinematic accomplishment were a judicious manipulation of tone *tout court*, we would not be talking about him as one of world cinema's greatest directors, but as a forerunner of specialists in the contemporary dramedy, with his talents in this area measured against the likes of the similarly gifted James Mangold (*Knight and Day*, 2010) and James Liman (*Mr. and Mrs. Smith*, 2005), both of whom have produced amusingly witty comedy thrillers in the tradition staked out by *The Lady Vanishes*.

But the nature of *The Lady Vanishes* should give us some pause. Easily dismissed is the notion that all of Hitchcock's directorial efforts are necessarily informed by meaningful commentary on the human condition, broadly conceived. Or that they are uniformly profound in the sense somewhat overenthusiastically proclaimed by Alexandre Astruc in the early days of Hitchcock criticism. Engaging in these films, each of which, so Astruc says, tells "very much the same story," is to "find oneself in a universe that is simultaneously aesthetic and moral where black and white, shadow and light find their places," a universe reminiscent of the fictional worlds conjured up by a Dostoevsky or Faulkner" (Astruc 5). It is evident, of course, that not all Hitchcock films are reminiscent of highbrow fiction or provide provocative variations on some weighty ur-story. A number of Hitchcock projects, especially during the early years of his UK career, are scarcely even personal, if at all; they are studio assignments, such as *Juno and the Paycock* (1930), which is better considered a Sean O'Casey adaptation than a Hitchcock film, properly speaking. And, much like Graham Greene's "entertainments," a number of Hitchcock films (such as *The Trouble with Harry* [1955]) offer low-key, mostly comic versions of the themes the director pursues more deeply and complexly elsewhere: the dark underside that suddenly intrudes, shockingly, and sometimes violently, into the banal everyday; the often neither unpleasant nor unsympathetic face of evil; a hitherto solid identity lost to misadventure that a therapeutic double pursuit restores, even remakes; the physical struggle that inevitably closes out the confrontation between good and evil and mostly ends, if more than a little precariously, in the righteous vindication of the characters Hitchcock has convinced us to at least consider good, despite their evident shortcomings, so that we might derive pleasure from their triumphs and consequent reclamations of self. As David Sterritt puts it, films such as *Frenzy* (1972), whatever challenges they pose to interpretation, offer "evidence of a broad moral vision that runs through Hitchcock's work"; there is no doubt that he is a filmmaker who views the world he conjures into being "as a locus of substantial moral complexity"(16).

Hitchcock and Catholicism

At least these days, Hitchcock's critics find themselves largely in agreement with Singer and Sterritt—and with good reason. Despite the director's protests to the contrary and the fact that his oeuvre unsurprisingly includes productions that resist any penetrating thematic exegesis, it seems true enough that most, if perhaps not all, of Hitchcock's films are philosophical insofar as they are infused, as Singer puts it, with "a profound perception of, and concerted interest in, the human condition as [he] knew it" (3). This "infusion" (surely a useful metaphor for this aspect of the creative process) resulted not from some intent to express or promote some religious, ethical, or political message. And yet some of his early admirers, most notably Chabrol, maintained that Hitchcock had a "Catholic conception of what life is," even if he "could not envisage the direct (I mean 'living') intervention of God in that struggle whose reward is human deliverance" (Chabrol 20). Writing the first full-length study of Hitchcock's films, Chabrol and Rohmer argue that Hitchcock's central theme is the interchangeability of the guilt of each and every one of us, which is to say that his films address the collective ontology of an Original Sin whose central fact is its totalizing transference from one generation to the next. For these two critics, then, Hitchcock's films illuminate different, but equally central, forms of sinfulness: the prideful presumption of innocence, even though depravity is in us all; and the self-regarding surrender to despair once we discover our presumption of innocence to be mere illusion. The moralism of his narratives, or so they suppose, oscillates between two poles of action: an unmerited descent into madness or loss (a consequence of the unfathomable and diabolical machinations of the universe) that is balanced by the unexpected deliverance from lasting disaster or death whenever divine grace finds its salvific powers activated by the virtuous exercise of free will (Chabrol and Rohmer *infra*, esp. pp. 150–54).

Though ingenious and at times illuminating, this attempt to claim Hitchcock as essentially a Catholic artist in the tradition of a Graham Greene or François Mauriac no longer persuades many. Such a reading of Hitchcock's moralism has mostly seemed unnecessarily narrow, overemphasizing the centrality of those few films such as *I Confess* (1953) and *The Wrong Man* (1956) that deal directly with Catholic practice and institutions, with the supposed doctrinal themes of these films given perhaps unwarranted weight. As Robin Wood rather acidly puts it, this approach has "the effect of depriving the films of flesh and blood reducing them to theoretical skeletons" (Wood 62). Interestingly, even if he took a different path to understanding and appreciating Hitchcock's accomplishment, Wood was too perceptive a critic to deny that Hitchcock is a philosophical filmmaker in the sense that Singer maintains. "Hitchcock's morality, with its pervading sense of the inextricability of good and evil," he opines, "is not so simple" (63). But even in the frenzied first decade of Hitchcock enthusiasm in France, the notion that Hitchcock, the successful studio artist, was also "philosophical" found its detractors. Hitchcock, *Positif* critic Ado Kyrou dismissively observes, has served three roles in the history of world cinema: first, he was fronted by a British film industry short on talent and resources that needed to promote its productions; second, he became a successful and compliant employee in a Hollywood determined to reduce film production to a series of commercially-proven formulae, of which the Hitchcockian thriller is a paramount example; and third, taken up by critics "who wished to use him to advance their particular opinions," the director "became a canvas on which theories could be portrayed," with even his minor touches of humor or insight into character "considered to be laden with the most abstruse metaphysical meanings" (qtd in Chabrol/Rohmer 10).

Such an unsympathetic attitude toward Hitchcock's seriousness (or, more precisely, toward those who would promote him as a serious artist) is perhaps as distorting as the attempt to turn him into a didact committed strictly to exploring and propagating his religious faith. However, it bears remarking that, following the path blazed by Wood, contemporary Hitchcockians have perhaps too eagerly turned a blind eye toward what in his films occasionally bears the (perhaps inevitable) traces of their maker's Catholic sensibility. Certainly, his choice of a very much out-of-date French play largely unknown in the Anglophone world by Paul Anthelme (*Nos deux consciences*, first produced in 1902 and in Paris) as the source for what would become *I Confess* reflects an interest in specific moral questions raised specifically by the Catholic practice of private confession, in which the priestly confessor becomes a stand-in for an attentive and forgiving God. There is more of Catholicism in this film than in any of his others, at least such is the critical consensus. In part, the drama revolves around the dilemma of a priest able to identify the perpetrator of a brutal murderer but who is prevented from so doing because he has learned the truth in hearing the man's confession. Even

Figure 0.1 . *I Confess*—Alma Keller (Dolly Haas) in moral crisis during the Logan trial.

when through a set of strange coincidences he himself becomes accused of the same crime, the priest does not break his silence. But this is not to say that *I Confess* is a "Catholic movie" whose iconography and themes persuade the attentive viewer to interpret the film's crime fiction narrative as evoking the path to the Cross followed by a Jesus determined through his sacrifice to redeem a mankind otherwise condemned to eternal damnation (Chabrol and Rohmer 119). Instead, here Hitchcock's characteristically broader, and more engaging, approach to moralism predominates; the film's complex dramatization of ethical issues central to the human condition certainly includes, yet goes far beyond, its thematizing of the "seal of the confessional." On this, more below.

Moralism, Not Moralizing

Like most contemporary Hitchcockians, Singer imagines the director's "interest in the human condition" as not taking shape through "pontification" in any sense, including the promotion of Christian ethics or eschatology. Hitchcock's high seriousness is rather the inevitable result, so Singer suggests, of the ways in which "whatever elements . . . [of great art that] entertain a receptive audience" also "permeate . . . the aesthetic fabric of the work itself" (8). The more deeply they succeed in providing entertainment and delight, especially through very Aristotelian mechanisms of emotional arousal and release, the more Hitchcock films (at least potentially) become philosophical in the very general sense identified by Singer. "There is nothing in the idea of entertainment," he writes, invoking something like the Horatian ideal of *dulce et utile*, "that necessarily excludes the presentation of a meaningful perspective" (8).

Early in his career Hitchcock embraced the creation of suspense as what perhaps best defined his work as an entertainer; he became known as its "master," with his aim to leave spectators "limp as dish rags at the end," their feelings of fear and anxiety vicariously aroused only to be pleasurably purged (qtd. in Kapsis 24). Hitchcock's concern with suspense, and with affect in the Hollywood manner more generally, should perhaps be seen, Jean Douchet argues, as the key to his moralism:

> Suspense expresses the most ancient possible of all philosophical perspectives. It bears within it the primitive form of existential anguish, being connected to fundamental feelings of insecurity . . . the drawing out of a present caught between two contradictory possibilities for the imminent future . . . [and] linked to the first age of human emotions . . . Just the opposite of the hero who follows where adventure leads, the spectator

of a suspense film cannot take flight. He is rooted in his seat. Not only does he share the anguish of the character he observes, but he makes it his own. He becomes the victim of his own fascination. . . . The spectacle of the conflict between Darkness and Light guides Hitchcock's cinematic imagination (Douchet 5, 7, 11).

For Singer, the kind of great art that Hitchcock by current consensus produced becomes "philosophical when it offers probing insights into our reality that are valuable to people who have learned how to appreciate them" (8). The philosophical, in other words, is defined not only by what it communicates about the human experience, but also by the kind of value that filmgoers might find in the pleasing expression of significant ideas. Hitchcock's interest in various forms of crime narrative, primarily the thriller, meant of course that his "insights" connect most often to issues of value, and particularly of right and wrong. Hitchcock, we might say, is a moralist (an artist committed to portraying characters who find themselves compelled to choose), even if he does not moralize, that is, argue that some consistent set of values should guide or be marshalled to judge what they do. But there are those who argue, and provocatively, that Hitchcock's moralism is more narrow than "broad" (Sterritt), more *engagé* than the perceptions of a bemused observer of the human scene. In a recent study, for example, William Rothman claims that Hitchcock's moralism connects, if obliquely, to the American tradition of righteous conduct, moral perfectionism, which found its institutional home in New England Universalism and whose principal exponent was Ralph Waldo Emerson. Moral perfectionism, as Rothman describes it, emerges from "our obligation to become more fully human, to realize our humanity in our lives in the world, which always requires the simultaneous acknowledgement of the humanity of others" (4). Such an approach to the moral life was in ascendancy in Hollywood, and had thus achieved something of an international popularity during what might be called the New Deal Era of the 1930s and early '40s, eventually to be challenged by the pessimism of film noir, a contrary movement, with its inspiration more European than American, that was also influential for Hitchcock. In addition to his enthusiasm for moral perfectionism, Rothman admits that Hitchcock was drawn to an "incompatible vision" of the human condition, one that emphasized the innate depravity of original sin, especially in *The Birds* (1963) and *Marnie* (1964); however, he "overcame or transcended his ambivalence toward the Emersonian way of thinking he had longed to embrace for the sake of humanity" (8). These films, then, unambiguously propound a moral perfectionist view of human purpose.

Emphasizing the notion of artistic struggle, Rothman offers a challenging, if hardly uncontroversial view, of Hitchcock's development as an author interested in the meaning of the stories his films purveyed.

It is important, however, to remember that Hitchcock worked within an industry devoted to, and absolutely dependent on, the provision of viewer pleasure. Hitchcock's interest in the human condition was defined to some degree by his notion of entertainment, which emphasized the importance of delivering a benign shock to the audience through a heightened presentation of human experience, fabulized as a series of dangerous trials that must be endured and overcome; such a rhetoric might be considered an instrument of moralizing power in and of itself, beyond the meaning of the dramatizations that it depends on, because it forces viewers to confront their more elemental terrors. "Our nature is such," he wrote in 1936, "that we must have these shake-ups or we grow sluggish and jellified. . . . Watching a well-made film, we don't sit by as spectators; we participate" (Gottlieb 109). But, as Singer points out, echoing the arguments of poststructuralist theorists like Fredric Jameson, what might be mistakenly dismissed as simpleminded popular "entertainment is always capable of awakening our susceptibility to new ideas," becoming a vehicle that "conveys . . . artistic truth" (8) (see Jameson). One way of looking at Hitchcock's moralism takes the director at his word, emphasizing his masterful articulation of the primal anxiety of suspense through plots that characteristically can be reduced to the multiform dilemmas of souls "torn between good and evil . . . suspended miserably between the sky and the earth" (Douchet 8).

I Confess: What We Say, Whom We Tell

Among the many images from Hitchcock's films that might serve as exemplary illustrations of this inescapable predicament, consider the frame enlargement from *I Confess* on the cover to this volume. It is our first view of the film's protagonist, Father Michael Logan (Montgomery Clift). This medium shot emphasizes his priestly garb and how he is framed (or, perhaps better, contained) by the window of the rectory, a spot above from which he views the world below. Visibly reflected in one of the panes is an image of the church across the way. What he sees through that window, and it turns out to be the worst kind of evil, calls him to act, but only as a priest, providing the sacrament that makes divine grace available to others, not as a man like other men, who respond only to secular protocols. As this initial image suggests, Logan is a man thoroughly defined by inflexible institutional rules that privilege him (the camera honorifically looks at him from below, from an angle slightly slaked, in this image and others, to suggest the disorder of his world) even as those rules restrict. The obligations attendant upon his special status as a priest prevent him from doing what he can to save himself from a mistaken charge of murder. Though legally exculpated, he is unjustly found guilty in the court of public opinion of what is, if unofficially, just as serious a charge: his romantic involvement, long before taking his vows of celibacy, with a woman, Ruth Grandfort (Anne Baxter), who continues to love him even after she marries. She does not tell Logan she is married when, not yet ordained, he returns home from the war; caught in a storm, they spend the night together (only in the literal sense of that term) at a remote farmhouse. Logan, it turns out, is neither a murderer nor an adulterer. And he never violates his vows, though in the end his technical innocence does not matter.

On this most fateful night for him and others, Logan spies from his window an as yet unrecognizable dark figure who has just entered the church he serves as a priest. We have been shown that this man is a murderer fleeing the scene of his crime. But Logan does not know if he is in need of spiritual comfort or is up to no good. It does not matter, in any case, though it turns out that the man is both a religious responsibility and a threat. Logan hurriedly enters the church and realizes that the figure kneeling at a pew is someone well known to him: Otto Keller (O.E. Hasse), a refugee from Germany who, along with his wife Alma (Dolly Haas), has been looking after the needs of Logan and the two other priests of the parish. Shaken and anguished, Keller asks for Logan's help and asks to make his confession, revealing, as the ritual unfolds, that he has just murdered a rich lawyer named Villette (Oliva Légar). In the grip of an irrational desperation, fueled by jealousy and his own sense of failure, Keller determined to steal the considerable money secreted in Villette's cash box in order, so he says, to provide his wife with some relief from the domestic drudgery that now is her life. Surprised in the act by his intended victim, Keller struck the man dead when, despite all entreaties, he persists with his intention to call the police.

Logan pronounces Keller absolved of mortal sin, leaving to God the question of the man's doubtful contrition and the ultimate efficacy of the sacrament. But, as Keller shows himself fearfully aware, if God has perhaps forgiven him, restoring the promise of eternal salvation, man has not. With his guilt unquestioned, how might he escape being hanged for the killing? The priest has no answer for him, other than to tell him that he should make another confession, this time to the police. But this confessional path promises not absolution, but the merciless condemnation of a state committed to the lex talionis. God, who sees all, cannot be fooled, or so the murderer seems to believe, but his fellow men are another matter indeed. Keller thinks he might yet avoid human justice if the police fail to identify him as the guilty party. He had committed the crime incognito, having donned a cassock as a disguise to hide his identity, and to provide any passing policeman with an implicit alibi for his walking the streets of a deserted city at close to midnight.

But if this Logan, as God's representative, is the source of Keller's eternal deliverance, as a man he possesses the power, even though forbidden its exercise, to bring about his arrest and the imposition of the gruesome penalty that will inevitably follow. Will the priest break the seal of the confessional so that human justice might prevail, even at the cost of going against the explicit command of the Church? This is the film's initial source of suspense, a conflict of moral imperatives that creates a tension that is increasingly unbearable for Keller as circumstances, in a series of ironies, become more threatening. The killer was observed leaving the scene of the murder by two schoolgirls, who concluded he was a priest. Logan falls under suspicion himself when he is found to have been the only priest in the city who was out at that time of night and has no alibi to offer. Ironically enough, he had been meeting with Ruth to discuss the predicament in which they found themselves. Villette had been blackmailing her, threatening to reveal what he knew of her relationship with Logan. By killing the blackmailer, Keller had, so it seems, unintentionally put the couple in the clear, but, ironically enough, Logan now finds himself accused of an even more shameful violation of his vocation. Ruth inevitably finds herself dragged into the investigation, but she cannot clear the name of the man she loves. In the end, it does not matter that Logan is as innocent of murder as he is of adultery.

I Confess is no whodunit; its foregrounding of Villette's murder and Keller's guilt is just a typical Hitchcockian MacGuffin, the inaugural movement of plot that offers a form of initial interest and diversion that proves more or less irrelevant in the end. Predictably, Keller is eventually identified as Villette's murderer, but not by the ever-silent Logan, who remains true to his vow. It is a misreading of Hitchcock's art to complain, as does the usually more perceptive Bosley Crowther, that the film lacks suspense because "the audience is told near the start of the film that the hero is not guilty of the murder with which he is subsequently charged."[2] The title of the Anthelme play that is the source of the script (*Nos deux consciences*) suggests the way in which concerns with right behavior of different kinds inextricably links protagonist to antagonist, but the situation in which they find themselves is in the film rendered more complex than this bond of trust/distrust. It might seem that the play's original title would have appealed to Hitchcock, and he must have been impressed by its far from simplistic handling of moral issues (including the difficult one of public reputation) when he saw it on the London stage in 1930 or in a later revival. Hitchcock's work in this period especially emphasizes his fascination with doubles (in *Shadow of a Doubt* (1942), *Strangers on a Train* (1950), and *The Wrong Man*, perhaps most notably). But he has changed Anthelme's title for a phrase that evokes more generally the several moral questions that the film raises, all of which involve the making public of what hitherto had been private. *I Confess* is a literal translation of the Latin *confiteor*, the first word of the prayer required of penitents, and it suggests, in both its religious and secular meanings, the painful expression of what might embarrass, shame, or condemn, an issue that confronts all the characters in the film, not just Father Logan and the miserable, conniving sinner who is his dark other. If Keller confesses willingly, crucial confessions in extremis come later from both Ruth Grandfort and Alma Keller. Both women are compelled, if for very different reasons, to divulge secrets that are simultaneously exculpating and incriminating, meant to free a man wrongly accused, but, ironically, resulting as well in the condemnation of the men they separately love.

I Confess dramatizes characters complexly connected by secrets revealed and as yet unconfessed. The night of the murder, Keller confesses more than once; the second time to his wife Alma, revealing to her that he turned thief for her sake and was forced to kill Villette in self-defense. The priest, he tells the horrified woman, now knows the truth, and so Alma, in addition to being made the unwitting beneficiary of the botched robbery, is made to share her husband's anguish that Logan, to whom she is grateful for his many kindnesses, will tell what he knows to the detective leading the investigation, Inspector Larrue (Karl Malden). To Keller's horror, Larrue runs into the priest the next morning at Villette's, where the detective is beginning his inquiries. Logan was to meet Ruth there to confront Villette, and he keeps their rendezvous even though he knows the man is now dead. Seen by Larrue, who knows the killer wore a cassock, Logan falls under suspicion, especially when, protecting Ruth, he refuses to tell the detectives why he went to see Villette that morning. However, she is forced to tell them Logan had met with her the night before, even though this information, because of the crime's timeline, does not exculpate him. Cheered to see the priest implicated, Keller plants the cassock he wore, stained with Villette's blood, in Logan's closet, where it is found. Logan is brought to trial, and Ruth is forced to testify to their relationship, including their innocent night spent together.

The evidence is circumstantial, and so Logan is found not guilty, though he earns the scorn of both jury and judge for his presumably unpriestly behavior in continuing his relationship with Ruth behind her husband's back. Alma sees the man who offered them shelter and work when they arrived in Quebec as refugees exposed to the hatred and scorn of the townspeople assembled outside the courtroom. She feels overwhelmed by the injustice done to him and starts to proclaim in a loud voice that it was Keller who killed Villette.

His fear overcoming deep feelings of love, Keller shoots her down in mid-sentence, and she dies after Logan gives her absolution. A chase ensues, Keller is cornered, and police trick him into confessing that he murdered Villette. His freedom no longer matters, with Alma now dead by his own hand. Ruth finds reconciliation with her husband and leaves the scene, while the priest is left with a mortally wounded Keller, shot down by the police as he attempts to kill Logan. Before he does, he asks enigmatically, "Father, forgive me." Does he address Logan as a man, asking him to forgive his attempts to ruin and kill him, or as the priest who offers him once again the chance to clear his conscience? Logan hesitates for a moment as if deciding between the two alternatives (or, perhaps, uncertain whether to do anything at all for the man who has set into motion a chain of circumstances that has ruined his life). A pained look crosses his face, and he responds by uttering the Latin formula of absolution.

"It would be better for you if you were as guilty as I am," Keller had said just moments before, recognizing that only in an ironic sense has Logan lifted from him the burden of the crime Keller had committed. Better also, the bitter man says, to be killed now rather than condemned to years of suffering. Learning of Villette's death that first morning, Ruth had exclaimed to her former lover, "Now we're free," not thinking that even Logan's presence that morning at her tormentor's office would lead to making public the information that had given the lawyer power over them both. Logan's obligations to God and to the woman hopelessly in love with him do not conflict in some simple way; nonetheless, the two find themselves first trapped by suspicion, then forced to confess to or admit what publicly shames them, marking them for life. What Villette had threatened comes to pass, even though Keller accidentally does what Ruth would not have dared wish for. Ruth is forgiven for her emotional betrayal by the husband who loves her. But Logan's virtues and innocence do not prevail, and for human rather than religious reasons. For him there is no second chance. Keller is right. His supposed imperfection is simply unacceptable.

Figure 0.2. Father Logan (Montgomery Clift) with the dying Otto Keller (O.E. Hasse).

"We are creatures typified by diverse ethical loves, some of which bear uneasy relations to each other," writes philosopher Anthony Cunningham. "And, in the extreme, [these] may clash in tragic ways that can tear us apart at the moral seams" (4). He is speaking of literature when he writes the following, but the sentiment is applicable as well to great filmmakers like Hitchcock, who, in their best work, "offer us character portraits that can provide us with the right stuff for concrete, particular deliberation in all its ethical complexity" (5).

The various chapters of *Hitchcock's Moral Gaze* reconsider the concept of morality in terms of Hitchcock himself, the content of his films, and their effect on his audience. Grounding much of their discussions on traditional moral philosophy, these new essays call into question assumptions by film critics who critique Hitchcock for his perverse, fetishistic, and amoral worldview. The contributors re-address Hitchcock's morality as far more complex, ambiguous, and ironic than accepted cinema scholarship has suggested. In fact, Hitchcock's films often use moral predicaments to undercut stereotypical reactions of indignity in order to accept rather than simply debase as evil desires and misperceptions that are all too human. Hitchcock was always skeptical of over-moralizing human behavior. That he chose morally detestable acts—serial murders, kin-killing, marital violence, and degrading acts toward women—has too often been argued as evidence of his own distorted moral compass. As though filming perversions makes one a deviant, this almost puritanical logic comes under scrutiny in these chapters, not to elevate Hitchcock's ethics, but rather to humanize the fundamental fascination shared by people for the abnormal, the aberrant, the macabre, and the morbid, which accounts for the prominent place accorded such themes in popular entertainment cinema, both in Hollywood and elsewhere. The essays collected here invite readers to re-examine and re-view Hitchcock's career, from the silent era to the beginning of his mastery of suspense, with an eye to intricate visual, thematic, and narrative structures that reveal how morality, like the devil, is always in his details.

A case in point is Hitchcock's lifelong fixation with Jack the Ripper. Graham Petrie offers close readings of Marie Belloc Lowndes's novel and Hitchcock's adaptation of it in *The Lodger* (1926) as he positions Hitchcock in relationship to the audience. Critics have condemned Hitchcock for merely playing a cruel, cynical joke on his audience, but Petrie wants to explore how the director provides a moral recognition of human emotional frailty in this first true Hitchcock film. Thomas Leitch approaches the problematic ending of *Suspicion* (1941) by laying out various theories proffered by film scholars before examining how Hitchcock's deliberately ironic construction of the film eschews any "logical or emotionally satisfying" conclusion. Hitchcock provides a view "both inside and outside Lina's consciousness," so that suspicion and guilt become the overarching vantage point for the audience's need and complicity with storytelling.

Another side of complicity resonates in what Nick Haeffner attacks as the "Spoto myth," which claims that the sexual perversions of his villains are thinly veiled projections of Hitchcock's dark and diseased personality. Beginning from a Sadean perspective that immorality increases human understanding, Haeffner evaluates Hitchcock's villains, particularly Uncle Charlie (Joseph Cotten) in *Shadow of a Doubt* (1943), as Byronic, Gnostic, and aristocratic, all characteristics that are decidedly unlike Hitchcock, the man. Castigating Hitchcock for the amorality of Uncle Charlie ignores the Sadean challenge to societal hypocrisy. As Haeffner points out, the condemning of Hitchcock's morality by his biographer Donald Spoto and others might well be a veiled judgment on their own moral uncertainty and guilt. Concentrating on the play of guilt and confession, Brian McFarlane resurrects from critical obscurity two undervalued Hitchcock films, *The Paradine Case* (1947) and *Under Capricorn*

(1949). Of specific interest to McFarlane is how the complex role of feminine culpability, especially when bounded by class and patriarchal constraints, leads to either death or redemption.

Immorality often characterizes the tensions among the Hitchcock hero, villain, and audience. George Toles goes into considerable detail on the moral significance and consequences represented by the cigarette lighter in *Strangers on a Train* (1951). Dismissing the idea that the lighter is a mere Hitchcockian MacGuffin, Toles elaborates on the complex systems of doubling, criss-crossing, and exchange that occur in the film as a result of Hitchcock's visual emphasis upon this lighter, which, from a moral point of view, serves as "the repository and secret conductor of all the sinful thought energy" in the film, which is Bruno's (Robert Walker) lack of ethics. Steven M. Sanders places Bruno in relationship to Uncle Charlie and other immoralists in Hitchcock's oeuvre, all of whom demand from audiences an answer to the fundamental question of their personalities: "Why should *I* be moral?" Three immoralist perspectives—egoism, amoralism, and nihilism—generally characterize their motivations and unethical behavior. Criticizing Kantian morality as too broad and Hobbesian egoism as too narrow, Sanders finds Hitchcock's cinematic "thought experiment" suggests a judgment—more objective and impartial than the two philosophers provide—from the audience on comparative values or choices of conduct.

Sidney Gottlieb unhesitatingly claims Hitchcock to be an amoralist in his structuring of looking in *Rear Window* (1954). Gottlieb lays out seven propositions for looking by which to evaluate the pleasures and desires of the eye: the I, looking good and looking well, the gaze, the compounded gaze of people gazing at people gazing, the spectator, the attraction and distraction of cinema, and finally, the ethical warning of look, but do not touch. Such intricate analogies among the various types of visual experience in Hitchcock reveal that "optical expectations and experiences inevitably go awry." By examining voyeurism in *Rear Window*, Richard Allen offers a typology that includes sexual voyeurism, psychological curiosity, and legitimate intrusions of privacy. The personal satisfaction from seeing, for Allen, both associates Jefferies (James Stewart) with the film's audience and displaces any such analogy. Allen posits that this film in particular serves as "a moral allegory for cinema" and spectatorship, one that continually renews and rejects facile ethical categories and simplistic moralizing conclusions.

Moralizing accompanies much of the misdoubt in Hitchcock's narratives. Further investigations of Hitchcock's moral cinema are carried out by Murray Pomerance in "Alfred Hitchcock as Moralist." Pomerance contributes what we might describe as a conceptual map of, in Pomerance's words, "the ethical world of [Hitchcock's] characters, that world and its doubts, its vacuums, its labyrinths, its obscurities, its fervent hopes." In this connection he discusses at length *The Wrong Man*, *The Man Who Knew Too Much*, and *The Lodger*. R. Barton Palmer observes in "The Deepening Moralism of *The Wrong Man* that "in a number of Hitchcock films misidentification becomes the pretext for a different approach that centers on a disturbing probing of guilt, innocence, and, most centrally, the limitations of human agency." Palmer calls attention to "the elucidating and contextualizing of this significant change in tone" after the commercial and critical failure of *The Wrong Man*, a change that leads Hitchcock to focus on the life-transforming experience of profound mischance, of life-altering disasters that seem to drop out of a clear blue destinal sky . . . And cannot be entirely reversed, if at all, or even fully understood."

According to Jerold J. Abrams, philosophers since the time of Hegel have explored the idea that art in some sense passes over into higher forms of consciousness. For the contemporary philosopher Arthur C. Danto, painting passes over into philosophy and reflects on the philosophical structure of art itself. Film, too, Abrams argues, attains a philosophical end. He explains that this is especially so in the way Hitchcock's cinema "traverses the sensuous show of objects on the screen and enters into an investigation of the very medium of film itself . . . in Hitchcock film is doing philosophy." Abrams discusses *Rear Window*, *North by Northwest*, *Rope*, and *The Birds* in connection with this thesis of the self-reflexivity of Hitchcock's films in which these films "are actually *about* the experience of film itself."

Moral acts often define and plague Hitchcock's heroes. In "The Dread of Ascent: The Moral and Spiritual Topography of *Vertigo*," Alan Woolfolk writes that in this film "Hitchcock's insights extend . . . [t]oward a moral psychology that is reminiscent of the Crisis psychology of European intellectuals such as Kierkegaard, Nietzsche, and Freud." In his detailed discussion, Woolfolk depicts the psychological struggles Scottie (James Stewart) faces as he tries to deal with his vertigo and the moral costs to him as he gradually uncovers the plot of wicked, adulterous Gavin Elster (Tom Helmore) and Judy Barton (Kim Novak), costs that include depression, feelings of futility, and despair. Against the background of Bertrand Russell's treatise on *Marriage and Morals* (1929), Jennifer L. Jenkins takes up Hitchcock's philosophy of marriage. That philosophy, as it is exemplified in *North by Northwest*, "espouses a union of equals serving the greater good of domestic security won through trouble and strife." Marriage, she writes, "functions as a leitmotif: . . . The philosophy of marriage in *North by Northwest* is a singularly democratic one: a volitional Union of equals, hard-won by strife and commitment to an idea greater than themselves."

In " 'The Loyalty of an Eel': Issues of Political, Personal, and Professional Morality in (and around) *Torn Curtain*," Neil Sinyard discusses this film's "quite complex view of morality in both the personal and political sphere." He also considers issues of professional morality, loyalty, and betrayal in the context of the falling-out between Hitchcock and the distinguished composer on many of Hitchcock's films, Bernard Herrmann. In "Hobbes, Hume, and Hitchcock: The Case of *Frenzy*," Homer B. Pettey first identifies the chiasmus structure of *Frenzy* "whereby moral issues cross over to their opposite meanings," and provides the reader with a detailed account of the way *Frenzy* achieves this crossover effect. He then explains how the concepts of skepticism, causation, and moral judgment are handled by philosophers Hobbes and Hume and provides a clear explanation of the way, in *Frenzy*, Hitchcock's unique "moral gaze" offers an intriguing alternative to the approaches of both these philosophers to issues of moral conduct.

In all of the chapters, the contributors have taken new views of the master of suspense to find correlations between cinematic style and ethical issues that disclose another form of Hitchcock's signature: what Irving Singer usefully identifies as his "profound conception of, and interest in, the human condition as he knew it."

Notes

1. Consider, for example, the interview with David Brady entitled "Core of the Movie—the Chase," reprinted in Gottlieb 125–32, in which Hitchcock discusses with lucidity and energy a number of topics related to what he sees as the most characteristic narrative element of the cinema, including the advantages to emotional engagement of the double pursuit ("As the camera cuts from police to hero to real criminal, the audience has the opportunity to identify itself with both the chaser and the chased in the person of the hero without suffering the frustrations of a divided allegiance") (130); and the relationship between pure action and characterization ("In the ideal chase structure . . . the tempo and complexity of the chase will be an accurate reflection of the intensity of the relations between the characters. But I have found that even in the final physical chase, touches of characterization will embellish it") (129).

2. Bosley Crowther, "I Confess," *The New York Times* 23 March 1953 http://www.nytimes.com/movie/review?res=9B00E2D91F3AE23BBC4B51DFB5668388649EDE (accessed 12/26/2014)

Works Cited

All translations from the French are by R. Barton Palmer

Astruc, Alexandre. "Quand un homme . . ." *Cahiers du cinéma* no. 39 (1954): 5.
Bazin, André. "Hitchcock contre Hitchcock." *Cahiers du cinéma* no. 39 (1954): 25–32.
Boyd, David, and R. Barton Palmer, eds., *After Hitchcock: Influence, Imitation, and Intertextuality*. Austin: University of Texas Press, 2006.
Chabrol, Claude. "Hitchcock devant le mal." *Cahiers du cinéma* no. 39 (1954): 18–24.
Chabrol, Claude, and Éric Rohmer. *Hitchcock*. Paris: Cahiers du cinéma, 1957.
Cunningham, Anthony. *The Heart of What Matters*. Berkeley: University of California Press, 2001.
Denby, David. *The New Yorker*. August 13, 2007: 8.
Douchet, Jean. *Hitchcock*. Paris: Éditions de l'Herne, 1967.
Gottlieb, Sidney, ed. *Hitchcock on Hitchcock: Selected Writings and Interviews*. Berkeley: University of California Press, 1995.
Jameson, Fredric. *Signatures of the Visible*. New York: Routledge, 1992.
Kapsis, Robert. *Hitchcock: The Making of a Reputation*. Chicago: University of Chicago Press, 1992.
Rorty, Richard. *Philosophy and the Mirror of Nature*. Princeton, NJ: Princeton UP, 1979.
Rothman, William. *Must We Kill the Thing We Love?: Emersonian Perfectionism and the Films of Alfred Hitchcock*. New York: Columbia UP, 2014.
Singer, Irving. *Three Philosophical Filmmakers: Hitchcock, Welles, Renoir*. Cambridge MA: MIT Press, 2004.
Sterritt, David. *The Films of Alfred Hitchcock*. Cambridge: Cambridge UP, 1993.
Wood, Robin. *Hitchcock's Films Revisited*. Revised Edition. New York: Columbia UP, 2002.

Skepticism

1

Graham Petrie

Jealousy and Trust in *The Lodger* (1926)

Factual and Fictional Sources for the Film

There is almost no uncontested fact concerning the Jack the Ripper murders that, by way of Marie Belloc Lowndes's play and novel on the subject, provide a distant source for Alfred Hitchcock's third film. The number of victims, the identity of the killer, the authenticity of the two letters and a postcard that were sent to the police and signed by the name that subsequently became notorious, or the reason why the murders stopped abruptly after the last in the series—all are still matters of dispute. Most writers on the subject agree on five (or possibly six) killings that can be attributed to the same source, taking place between August 31 and November 9, 1888, though Philip Sugden, for one, extends the number to nine, beginning before August 31 and ending in February 1891. It is generally agreed that all the victims were prostitutes, living, working, and dying in a relatively small area of the then sordid and poverty-stricken East End of London, particularly in Whitechapel. All had their throats cut, and several were severely mutilated after death, with their internal or sexual organs removed and left lying close to their bodies. The letters and postcard claiming responsibility for the killings, sent halfway through the series, are assumed by many to be authentic and by others to be a hoax (they seem, incidentally, to have inspired the 1960s and '70s serial killer known as Zodiac, in California, who similarly sent letters to newspapers and the police challenging them to identify him). The list of suspects is endless and still violently debated, ranging from Polish Jews and various other foreigners, Masons, American visitors, butchers, slaughterhouse workers, insane medical students and equally insane doctors, "mad Russians," homicidal lunatics, and murderous misogynists to society figures such as the painter Walter Sickert and Queen Victoria's grandson and potential heir to the throne. And though most writers agree on one single murderer, others vote for two or even three acting in concord. The murders stopped either because the killer went totally mad and was incarcerated without anyone knowing his true identity, or he went insane and committed suicide, or he just disappeared. In short, no one knows anything for certain about Jack the Ripper.

The continuing fascination with what, in today's context, seems a relatively small number of killings, stems partly from the fact that they represented an unusual phenomenon at the period and thus created huge public interest and were extensively reported, creating in turn large-scale panic in society at large; and partly from the unspeakably sadistic and cruel treatment of the bodies and the mutilation of both external and internal organs—the face and body of Mary Kelly, generally thought to be the final victim, were so disfigured as to be almost unrecognizable. Perhaps the earliest full-length fictional treatment of the subject is Marie Belloc Lowndes's 1913 novel, *The Lodger*, which was turned into a successful stage play in 1915 called *Who Is He?*, written by H.A. Vachell and "very freely adapted" from the novel (Barr 218). Particularly the ending of the play (which was never published) differs considerably from the novel and is closer in many respects to the script that Hitchcock, along with Eliot Stannard, his regular collaborator at this period, created for the film. Two of Hitchcock's two main biographers, Donald Spoto and John Russell Taylor, agree that he saw the play, probably in its original (and only) West End run, and Hitchcock confirms this in his book-length interview with François Truffaut (30).

Belloc Lowndes's novel (developed from a short story the previous year) picks up some of the widespread speculations at the time of the murders—that the killer must be a lodger in one of the many boarding houses in the area, which would account for his ability to operate virtually unseen and then disappear, and that some of the suspects described by witnesses carried a black bag, presumably containing the knives and other tools with which the victims were dismembered.

But, apart from these details, and the fact that the eight victims mentioned in the book are all women, the novel departs quite radically from the known facts. Though the victims are not specifically identified as prostitutes, they are often described as "drunken" or "drink sodden," and their deaths appear to be random rather than part of a calculated campaign. The "Avenger," as he calls himself on notes attached to the bodies of each victim, is described at one point as "moving west towards King's Cross and the Edgware Road" (the area in which the main characters, the Buntings, live) rather than confining himself to a limited area of the East End. Though the murders are referred to as horrific, the details are hinted at rather than fully described. The events of the book are seen largely through the eyes of the landlady, Ellen Bunting, and to some extent her husband, a once prosperous middle-class couple down on their luck and in need of whatever remuneration they can get for letting out some rooms in their house. Mr Bunting is an avid reader of crime reports in the newspaper and is friendly with a young detective, Joe Chandler, with whom he exchanges theories about the Avenger's activities.

When they decide to advertise for a lodger to alleviate their financial plight, they are almost immediately contacted by "the long, lanky figure of a man, clad in an Inverness cape and old-fashioned top hat." Ellen instantly categorizes him as "a gentleman" and finds him somewhat "dreamy," quiet and polite, and is happy to accommodate him, despite some rather strange requests and his delight at finding a huge gas stove in his room. He carries a mysterious black bag (which soon disappears from public view), calls himself by the rather unusual name of Sleuth (a word that came into English via America in 1876), and announces that he doesn't eat "flesh meat." As he begins to settle in, he asks to borrow a Bible Concordance and starts to quote ferociously misogynistic extracts from it to a somewhat puzzled Ellen and turns her prized framed engravings of "early Victorian beauties" to face the wall. He purchases what seems to be an unnecessary amount of second-hand clothes and has the "funny habit . . . of going out for a walk after midnight in weather so cold and foggy that all other folk were glad to be at home, snug in bed" (45).

As these "funny habits" begin to coincide with nights on which the Avenger's killings take place, it soon becomes obvious, both to Ellen and the reader, that she is harboring a murderous religious fanatic and woman-hater in her home—yet she does nothing to denounce him, a fact that then becomes the central puzzle of the book. She systematically ignores the obvious clues to his identity that begin to pile up, displaying relief when descriptions of the Avenger by witnesses differ from his own appearance, and rebukes her stepdaughter, Daisy, who arrives to stay with them, for being interested in the reward now offered for his arrest:

"'Well, it *is* a horrible idea!' [Ellen] said sullenly. 'To go and sell a fellow-being for five hundred pounds'" (61). [In another deviation from original facts, and despite much urging from the press, no reward was ever offered for information leading to the arrest of the historical Ripper.]

Despite finding her lodger "gentle" and "grateful," Ellen feels an urge to satisfy her curiosity about him and searches his room while he is out one day, discovering that his bag is locked inside a cupboard, out of which "some dark-coloured liquid was oozing" (73). Refusing to acknowledge, even to herself, that this liquid is blood, she decides it is red ink and apologizes to him for accidentally spilling his bottle of ink, giving him an opportunity to remove the evidence. She also finds that he is using the gas stove to burn something that smells like wool, but refuses to admit to herself that this might be to remove bloodstained evidence of his crimes.

How does the author account for this odd behavior? One reason seems to be financial: even if he is a mass murderer, the lodger pays his rent on time and has relieved her and her husband from a dire financial crisis. She also has a weird fascination of her own with murder, for which she reproaches herself at one point: "It was dreadful that she, of all women, should have longed to hear that another murder had been committed last night!" (91). At the same time, she excuses her silence by reassuring herself that there must be a limit to his lust for vengeance and that it must be satiated soon, after which he would return to being "what he evidently had been—that is, a blameless, quiet gentleman" (99). The main reason, however, seems to be a strangely protective pity that she feels for him. She constantly thinks of him as "gentle . . . lonely, very, very lonely and forlorn . . . polite and . . . misunderstood," yet is tormented by the secret knowledge that she is concealing. Though Belloc Lowndes tried to generalize her behavior at one point by claiming that "[i]n the long history of crime it has very, very seldom happened that a woman has betrayed one who has taken refuge with her" (92), it is more convincingly explained through Ellen's personal psychology: ". . . in a sort of way, Mrs. Bunting had become attached to Mr. Sleuth. A wan smile would sometimes light up his sad face when he saw her come in with one of his meals, and when this happened Mrs. Bunting felt pleased—pleased and vaguely touched. In between those—those dreadful events outside, which filled her with such suspicion, such anguish and such suspense, she never felt any fear, only pity, for Mr. Sleuth" (98).

But it finally becomes impossible for her to ignore any longer what she knows full well to be the truth. First of all, while out for a walk quite late one night, Mr. Bunting encounters his lodger and accompanies him back home; as they enter the house, Bunting's hand brushes accidentally against his companion's Inverness cape and encounters something "wet and gluey," which Mr. Sleuth unconvincingly claims is animal blood. His suspicions aroused by this and by the news of yet another murder accompanied by the clue of a footprint left by a rubber boot of the kind that the lodger wears, and that he now replaces with a new and different pair, Bunting and his wife start to have fears for Daisy's safety (in the book, the killer's victims are not exclusively prostitutes) and are finally forced by this to articulate their fears openly: ". . . as they stared at each other in exasperated silence, each now knew that the other knew" (189).

Yet, when the lodger invites all three members of the family to accompany him on a visit to Madame Tussaud's, Bunting experiences a spasm of relief: "Surely it was inconceivable that this gentle, mild-mannered gentleman could be the monster of cruelty and cunning that Bunting had now for the terrible space of four days believed him to be" (191), though his wife is now very uneasy in Mr. Sleuth's company. While waiting to enter the Chamber of Horrors, they overhear a conversation among a group accompanying the new Commissioner of Police and an important police official from Paris as they discuss the murders and attribute them to a criminal lunatic "suffering from an acute form of religious mania" who had recently escaped from an asylum and had stolen a large amount of money in gold as he left. Remembering that the lodger always paid his rent from a large pile of gold sovereigns, Mrs. Bunting, irrationally perhaps, wants to warn the lodger of his danger, but he forestalls her by turning on her and accusing her of "hideous treachery" and betraying him. "But I am protected by a higher power, for I still have much to do," he hisses at her. "Your end will be bitter as wormwood and sharp as a two-edged sword. Your feet shall go down to death, and your steps take hold on hell" (196). He then makes his escape from the building, and we are given a final glimpse into his mind as he contemplates Ellen's "treachery" and her cooperation with the French official "who had entered into a conspiracy years ago to have him confined—him, an absolutely sane man with a great avenging work to do in the world—in a lunatic asylum" (197). He then disappears from the story—nothing further is heard of him, and there are no more Avenger murders.

The identification with the Ripper murders is thus made clearly enough, though the focus of the story is obviously on Ellen's ambivalent and vacillating responses to her suspicions. Whether these are always presented convincingly enough is probably a matter for debate, but the book is still of interest in focusing not on "who done it?" or even "why did he do it?" but on the reactions of a woman suspecting the truth but unable to make herself take the actions that she knows she should take to identify a dangerous criminal and put an end to a continuing series of murders.

Hitchcock and Stannard's Script

The Lodger is usually characterized as the first "true" Hitchcock film, not least by the director himself (Truffaut 30), but, as Charles Barr somewhat indignantly points out, Hitchcock throughout his career consistently denied or ignored any substantial creative input from his scriptwriters, a proceeding that has been slavishly followed by *auteurist*-inclined critics who attribute everything in his films to his own initiative ("Hitchcock decided this, Hitchcock changed that," etc.). Eliot Stannard, however, scripted or co-scripted eight of Hitchcock's nine silent films, including *The Lodger*, and must surely have been trusted by the director and had more than a minimal influence on the results. Whoever made the creative decisions, the film is an amalgam of some of the known Ripper facts, Belloc Lowndes's novel, and Vachell's play, but altering or adding to each of them in almost unrecognizable ways. There is a mysterious serial killer, whose seventh victim is reported as the film begins, who identifies himself as "the Avenger," but, though his victims are all women, they are far from being unglamorous and unattractive prostitutes, as in reality, but "golden girls' from the worlds of fashion and show business. The murders are set not in the sordid and rundown East End, but in the very center of London, and the locations move steadily along the Embankment. And, in contrast to the book, the action is focused on Daisy (here the couple's daughter rather than Bunting's daughter by his first wife), who is herself a fashion model and is present and central throughout, rather than being peripheral to the main action. A major change is that Ellen, far from being sympathetic and protective toward the lodger, despite being convinced that he is a killer, is a relatively minor character who is hostile to him almost from the start, but for reasons other than suspecting that he might be a killer.

What results, then, is less complex psychologically than the book and closer to what was to become the regular Hitchcock formula of suspense, misdirection, and—in this case at least—an unambiguous conclusion. The film places a great deal of emphasis on public and media reactions to the murders—as was the case with the original Ripper killings and in Belloc Lowndes's novel. It opens with a closeup of a screaming woman, followed by what becomes a recurrent visual motif of a flashing neon sign, "Golden Curls," shots of obviously terrified women, and then a policeman and a crowd examining a body with the Avenger's

Figure 1.1. Flashing sign, *The Lodger*.

trademark signature on it. (This is how the restored British Film Institute print begins; Lindsay Anderson, Higham, and Rohmer and Chabrol all describe it differently; see Barr 19–20 and 219.) In a pub, a witness (and there were many witnesses—almost all unreliable—in the Ripper case) describes a tall man with his face wrapped up, and we then see a montage of newspaper presses and headlines and delivery boys shouting the news of the latest murder. A group of show business "golden girls" discuss the case apprehensively, and then the blonde fashion model Daisy makes her way home past another newsboy to where her father is intently studying the latest newspaper report of the murders and discussing them with Daisy's boyfriend, Joe, who, in the film, is a complacently incompetent lover and detective, perhaps reflecting not so much Hitchcock's well-known fear of the police as his contempt for their abilities. It is only after all these indications of budding media frenzy that the lodger is introduced, in a scene dominated by shadows and intermittently flaring gaslight, wearing a top hat with the lower half of his face muffled by a scarf and carrying a bag, thus corresponding closely to the earlier description of the killer. (Though he is never named in the film, some critics call him Jonathan Drew, following the title of the American release, *The Strange Case of Jonathan Drew*.)

As in the book, he expresses distaste for the pictures of women decorating his wall and turns them to face it, pays his rent in advance, and puts his bag away in a cupboard. His misogyny and religious fanaticism, however, are reduced to a few fairly innocuous comments such as that the pictures "get on my nerves" and "Providence is concerned with sterner things [than money]." Some ambiguous scenes involving Daisy follow: he stares at her with unusual intensity whenever she appears, fingers a knife and pushes it playfully toward her when she serves him breakfast, and later plays chess with her, commenting at one point, "Be careful, I'll get you yet." In this scene he also picks up a poker, as she searches for some chessmen that have fallen on the floor, but, when Joe enters, he uses the poker only to stir up the fire. He also comments approvingly on Daisy's "beautiful golden hair." Joe, who has now been assigned to the "Avenger" case, starts to express jealousy at their growing friendship, asks her father if the lodger might mean harm to her, and is openly hostile when he hears her screaming, rushes upstairs, and finds her in the lodger's arms, claiming she was frightened by a mouse and is being comforted.

Meanwhile we see the lodger leaving the house at night, muffled up, and an increasingly suspicious Mrs. Bunting reporting this to her husband and expressing fears for Daisy's safety, while he brushes her concerns aside and remains immersed in newspaper reports of the steady stream of murders. When the lodger buys Daisy a dress, her indignant parents insist on her returning it, and Joe's jealousy intensifies, especially when he finds the couple outside at night; Joe tries to drag her away with him, but she tells him she is sick and tired of his behavior. Nevertheless, the lodger's actions are ambiguous and, in a subsequent embrace, he puts his hands around her neck as if about to strangle her, before kissing her.

The police investigation into the killings continues, tracing the Avenger's activities as he moves along the Embankment and trying to anticipate his next move. Joe's jealousy now takes the form of trying to cast suspicion on the lodger; he organizes a police search of his room, finds his concealed bag, and inside this discovers a revolver and a map of the area that corresponds to the one the police have drawn up to follow the Avenger's movements. Despite his protests of innocence, the lodger is arrested and handcuffed, but manages to escape, with Daisy's help, before being pursued and cornered by an enraged lynch mob—in another incident reminiscent of the original Ripper case, where there were several occasions of mob violence and pursuit of suspects. A repentant Joe, however, having belatedly discovered the lodger's innocence, manages to rescue him just in time. The lodger is then revealed to be an upper-class figure who has been tracking down the Avenger, who had murdered his sister, possibly intending to kill him in revenge. A happy ending sees him welcoming Daisy and her family to his home.

Jealousy and Trust in the Film

Much of the critical commentary on the film's visual style focuses on its Germanic and, in some cases, Soviet influences, both valid enough, considering that Hitchcock had spent some years working in Berlin and Munich and had witnessed first-hand F.W. Murnau filming *The Last Laugh*, and had shown interest in the work of Eisenstein and Pudovkin. The heavy use of shadows and unusual lighting effects, and high-angle shots down a staircase, though common enough in the director's later films, can be initially attributed to German influences, and the editing effects that led the audience to misread the lodger's intentions toward Daisy could be considered Soviet. Most critics single out the use of a glass ceiling to "show" what the characters "hear" as the lodger paces up and down in his bedroom upstairs as a particularly effective device.

There is less uniform agreement, however, considering the film's themes and characterization, though the "wrong man" theme and the implication of the audience in criminal or dubious activities that they would otherwise condemn, are often commented on, together with the "ambiguity of appearances" that leads the audience to misunderstand or misinterpret the motives and actions of the characters. Though the lodger is indeed "the wrong man" and is almost lynched by an angry mob, he is not entirely innocent and seems to be planning not simply to confront but to kill the man who murdered his sister, and is diverted from this aim just in time. Moreover, though we are not invited to condemn him for this, Hitchcock is on record as saying that he originally wanted his role as the Avenger to be more ambiguous and for him simply to disappear into the shadows at the end of the film—but that neither the producers nor the audience would accept the idea of matinée idol Ivor Novello as a killer (Barr 34; Spoto 1992, 9; Truffaut 30). If this is truly the case, the idea of the "wrong man" being initially central to the structure of the film is put into question, though it might have developed as the script and filming proceeded.

Lindsay Anderson has written, with respect to Hitchcock's work up to the late 1940s, that he "has never been a 'serious' director. His films are interesting neither for their ideas nor for their characters," but that this is irrelevant in films "where incident and narrative are what matters" (58). John Russell Taylor puts it rather differently in suggesting that *The*

Lodger, like most of Hitchcock's work, "takes a very dark view of human nature and traps us into accepting it by subtly but consistently distorting our moral perspectives" (76). Charles Barr argues that "It doesn't ultimately matter that much whether the lodger himself turns out to be innocent or guilty. No-one's motives are entirely pure, among participants and observers alike. . . . We all have violent and vengeful potential in us" (41), and that "We are drawn to *The Lodger* for the same kinds of reason that the public depicted in it are drawn to the stage show, and to the press and radio accounts of the horrific murders: the attraction of sex and violence, and of provocative female beauty" (40).

If this is so, where does it leave Hitchcock as moralist? Is it simply a question of the director allowing us to indulge our own worst impulses and then showing us how wrong we are in doing so? Charles Higham, in one of the most hostile articles ever written on Hitchcock's work, sees him as "a practical joker, a cunning and sophisticated cynic . . . contemptuous of the audience which he treats as the collective victim of a Pavlovian experiment. . . . The mechanics of creating terror and amusement in an audience are all Hitchcock properly understands" (3–4). Though Higham concedes that *The Lodger* "remains the best of Hitchcock's silent films" (the others being a pretty bad bunch, apparently), this is so not for any positive views of human nature but because in a film like this, "dominated by morbidity, physical disgust, and terror his gifts have usually been in striking display. . . . Whatever one might think of their internal rottenness and viciousness, their deliberate pandering to mob lust, they [a select list of some half dozen films, including this one] brilliantly succeed as cinema, and are conceived, executed and embellished by a dazzlingly clever mind" (5).

Is there nothing more positive, then, in Hitchcock's moral stance than an attempt to torment and disorient his audience? It could be argued against these charges that the changes made by Hitchcock and Stannard to the original novel raise rather more positive and complex issues than this. In the novel, Mrs. Bunting displays a mistaken, and almost perverse, loyalty to someone she knows full well is a serial killer, making herself complicit in any future crimes he may commit by refusing to make her suspicions known. Her loyalty is rewarded only by accusations of betrayal and threats of future vengeance. Mr. Bunting, a subordinate figure in the book, finally comes to share her suspicions, but is equally reluctant to act on them, though he does not sympathize with the lodger in the way that his wife does. Daisy, who enters the book at a fairly late stage, has no particular interest either way in the lodger, but is attracted to the idea of a reward for the capture of the Avenger. She has a suitor, a detective named Joe Chandler, who is part of the team searching for the Avenger, but who never suspects the lodger or sees him as a rival for Daisy's affections.

All four characters and their relationships change quite drastically in the film. Mrs. Bunting in particular is far less prominent and only quite late in the film voices a tentative suspicion that her lodger might be a murderer and that Daisy might be in danger as the Avenger's activities move closer and closer to their own area. Her husband, who is so wrapped up with reading about the murders in the newspaper that he is unwilling to pay much attention to what is happening in his immediate vicinity, brushes her concerns aside, but agrees that their daughter should not be left alone with the lodger. Yet both parents are more upset about the lodger's growing friendship with Daisy, which they see as creating a breach between her and Joe, who they consider her accepted suitor, than with worrying about his true identity, and they are quick to take offense at any unwelcome advances that he makes toward her, such as buying her a new dress.

Joe, the least attractive character of the four, is much less competent as a detective than his counterpart in the novel, and shows irrational

Figure 1.2. *The Lodger*—Joe's (Malcolm Keen) jealousy.

hostility and jealousy toward the lodger from their very first meeting: "Does the lodger mean any harm to Daisy?" he asks Mrs. Bunting fairly early on. Yet he is smugly confident of his own control over Daisy, physically indicated by his attempts to handcuff her (a motif that occurs in other Hitchcock films and which takes on a different resonance as the lodger, handcuffed by Joe, and attempting to escape, is trapped by having them caught on a iron railing and dangles helplessly there at the mercy of a furious and misguided mob). Puzzled by Daisy's increasing coolness toward him as she warms toward the lodger, and finding them together in what he considers compromising situations, Joe's jealousy takes the form of trying to get rid of his rival by assembling (or concocting) evidence against him, obtaining a warrant to search his room, and refusing to accept the lodger's attempted explanation of the evidence he finds there. His misguided obsession (though the audience is encouraged to share it by his finding a revolver in the lodger's possession) almost brings about the other man's death—he is saved at the last minute from being virtually a murderer himself.

Daisy, though tolerating rather than welcoming Joe's overconfident attentions at the start of the film, gradually develops an attraction to the lodger, which leads to an increasingly closer physical contact and a rejection of Joe ("I'm sick and tired of you") when he discovers them embracing out of doors at night and tries to pull Daisy away. It is after this scene that Joe arranges the search of the lodger's room, on no greater basis than a desire to somehow discredit him. Daisy's affections, and loyalty, now switch firmly to the lodger, who she never suspects or believes to be a murderer and, once her trust in him is confirmed by his telling her of his sister's murder and his attempts to identify and trap the Avenger, she protects and assists him from then on. Of the three family members, she is the one most disposed to believe in the lodger's innate decency and to resist submitting to unconfirmed suspicions about him.

The lodger himself, though the subject of misguided distrust (from the other characters) and deliberate misdirection of the audience's sympathies by the director, does not emerge morally unscathed. Though his behavior in the household is quiet and well-mannered and shorn of the misogynistic rantings of his counterpart in the book (he turns the pictures of young women in his room to face the wall because—as we assume later—they remind him of his murdered sister), yet he obviously has the urge for violence in his search to inflict personal justice on the Avenger—becoming, perhaps, a potential avenger himself.

Though the film's plot is based on what were to become familiar Hitchcock ingredients—suspicion, fear, jealousy, and ambiguity, along with a recurrent interest in sexual fetishism, as the killer appears to concentrate exclusively on young blondes with golden hair, rather than the often middle-aged and worn-out prostitutes of reality, or the women who arouse the lodger's warped religious hatred in the novel—it would be excessive to see the film as an overall condemnation of human nature and a denial of basic human kindness, as Higham and Taylor tend to do. Hitchcock, in Taylor's words, "is inclined to believe that people's instincts of decency and kindliness may be natural but do not often survive a severe test. *The Lodger* is just such a test, and no one comes through it with flying colours" (77). Though this may be true of Joe and of the mob, who relish every detail of the Avenger's activities and then attempt to beat an innocent man to death, it is only partly true of Mr. and Mrs. Bunting, who are weak and misguided rather than vicious, and not true at all of Daisy, who is in effect the moral center of the film and whose loyalty to the lodger is not mistaken or prompted by deliberate self-deception, as is the case with Ellen in the book.

Postscript

It is well known that the initial cut of the film was considered "unreleaseable" by its producers and the film was almost shelved, until Michael Balcon came up with the idea of asking Ivor Montagu, a leading figure in the prestigious Film Society, and someone very knowledgeable about contemporary international film developments, to attempt to salvage it. Montagu, who genuinely admired the film as it stood, persuaded a sceptical Hitchcock to reshoot several scenes, severely reduce the number of title cards—from over three hundred to about eighty—and permit a redesign of some of the cards. The result was a critical triumph, with the film proclaimed "[possibly] the finest British production ever made" (Spoto 1983, 89). As became typical for him, Hitchcock, as with his refusal to acknowledge substantial input from his scriptwriters, later attempted to downplay Montagu's contribution, telling Truffaut only, and without even mentioning Montagu, that he [Hitchcock] "agreed to make about two" changes (35).

Works Cited and Consulted

Anderson, Lindsay. "Alfred Hitchcock," in *Sequence* 9 (August 1949), reprinted in *Focus on Alfred Hitchcock*, ed. Alfred LaValley. Englewood Cliffs, NJ: Prentice-Hall, 1972.
Barr, Charles. *English Hitchcock*. Moffat, Scotland: Cameron & Hollis, 1999.
Begg, Paul. *Jack the Ripper: The Uncensored Facts*. London: Robson Books, 1988.
Brill, Lesley. *The Hitchcock Romance*. Princeton, NJ: Princeton UP, 1988.

Deutelbaum, Marshall, and Leland Poague. *A Hitchcock Reader*. Ames: Iowa State UP, 1986.
Higham, Charles. "Hitchcock's World." *Film Quarterly* 16.2 (Winter 1962–63): 3–16.
Lowndes, Marie Belloc. *The Lodger*. Oxford: Oxford Popular Fiction, 1996. [Originally published by Methuen in 1913.]
Rohmer, Eric, and Claude Chabrol. *Hitchcock*. Paris: Editions Univérsitaires, 1957. Translated by Stanley Hochman as *Hitchcock: The First Forty Films*. New York: Ungar, 1979.
Rothman, William. *Hitchcock: The Murderous Gaze*. Cambridge, MA: Harvard UP, 1982.
Ryall, Tom. *Alfred Hitchcock and the British Cinema*. London: Croom Helm, 1986.
Spoto, Donald. *The Art of Alfred Hitchcock*. New York: Doubleday, 1992.
———. *The Life of Alfred Hitchcock: The Dark Side of Genius*. London: Collins, 1983.
Sugden, Philip. *The Complete History of Jack the Ripper*. New York: Carroll & Graf, 1994.
Taylor, John Russell. *Hitch. The Life and Work of Alfred Hitchcock*. London: Faber & Faber, 1978.
Truffaut, François. *Le Cinéma Selon Hitchcock*. Paris: Laffont, 1966. Published in English as *Hitchcock*. London: Secker & Warburg, 1968.
Yacowar, Maurice. *Hitchcock's British Films*. Hamden, CT: Archon Books, 1977.

2

Thomas Leitch

Fun with Suspicion

During the closing session of the 1996 Baylor University conference on "The Late Alfred Hitchcock," six panelists were invited to name Hitchcock's greatest film. After the first panelist demurred on the grounds that it was impossible to select a single preeminent film from such a distinguished career, the other five, one at a time, all named a single film: *Vertigo*. Yet the choice, which seemed so obvious to the panelists, was met with polite bewilderment by the generally much younger audience, some of whom echoed the film's original reviewers in pronouncing it slow moving, humorless, and not particularly mysterious or suspenseful. Their reaction made me wonder if *Vertigo*, even if it is Hitchcock's greatest film, is in important ways atypical of his work because it largely eschews his trademark wit and the exhilarating changes in tone that had characterized his films since *The Man Who Knew Too Much* (1934). And that reflection led to a further question: What is Hitchcock's most typical film—not necessarily his most profound or accomplished or perfectly achieved, but his most Hitchcockian?

There are many candidates for this honor. Apart from *Vertigo*, the most obvious of them are *Psycho* and *The Birds*, the two films most likely to have been seen and remembered by viewers for whom they have come to define Hitchcock. Yet both these films, which cross the line from the suspense genre that was the director's stock in trade to the horror genre that he largely shaped without ever fully inhabiting, are metonyms rather than synecdoches for Hitchcock's work. In introducing his study of the Hitchcock romance, Lesley Brill has observed more generally the danger of "allow[ing] certain especially interesting but somewhat atypical films to distort our understanding of the larger shape of his work" (xiii). Films lodged more plausibly in the heart of Hitchcock's oeuvre rather than at its fringes include *Rear Window, Strangers on a Train, Notorious, Shadow of a Doubt, The 39 Steps, Blackmail,* and *The Lodger.* Susan Smith, who uses *Sabotage* "to establish the overall nature of the relationship between film-maker, text and audience in Hitchcock's cinema," titles her chapter on the film "A Cinema Based on *Sabotage*" (xi, 1).

Without meaning to dislodge any of these nominees, I'd like in this essay to suggest another, perhaps more surprising, candidate: *Suspicion.* Although it marked the first of Hitchcock's four collaborations with Cary Grant and the only time a lead performer in any of his films received an Academy Award, *Suspicion* has been widely accounted a compromise or a failure. Patrick McGilligan reports that "[e]veryone in Hollywood, including Fontaine, suspected that her Oscar was really for *Rebecca*" (290). And the film as a whole, with its disconcerting shifts of tone between high romance, farcical byplay, and paranoid terror, is largely accounted, along with *The Birds* and *Marnie,* as Hitchcock's most problem-ridden.

All this is true. *Suspicion* is certainly marked by the collision between the ending of the novel the film was adapting, Francis Iles's *Before the Fact* (1932), and the refusal to cast Cary Grant as a killer. In all likelihood, Fontaine's Academy Award as Best Actress probably was a belated honor of her work in *Rebecca,* which her performance in *Suspicion* largely recapitulates, as even Fontaine acknowledged in a letter to Hitchcock, offering to play the role without salary: "I'm convinced it will be another 'Rebecca'" (Leff 93). And the film, with its multiple screenplay drafts and multiple endings, is among Hitchcock's most problematic. Without arguing for the film's greatness, however, I'd like to suggest that the problems it ran into in production, like the problems it raises for latter-day critics, are quintessentially Hitchcockian. These problems arise from the taboo nature of its subject matter, a young wife's gradually dawning awareness that her charmingly impecunious husband is a cheat, a thief, and a murderer who has decided to get the money he needs to extricate himself from his latest scrape by killing her; from the dissonance between the way the characters were written, at least in the novel under adaptation, and the way they were cast; and from the director's struggle to make the film he wanted to make. All are utterly typical of Hitchcock's films, at least before he set up as an independent producer-director with *Rope,* and all help explain his determination to remain a quasi-independent after the collapse of Transatlantic Pictures sent him into a series of production deals with Warner Bros., Paramount, MGM, and Universal. My exploration of these problems is intended not to rehabilitate *Suspicion* but to clarify what sort of film it is and what it is (and especially what it isn't) attempting to do. Appreciating its typicality will ultimately provide a better understanding of Hitchcock's work as a whole, and incidentally cast new light on the peculiar nature of Hitchcock's standing as a moralist.

It is hardly surprising that "Hitchcock had mentioned Iles admiringly to interviewers" even before his arrival in America, "and said he'd like to film one of his books—they would make precisely 'his type of film'" (McGilligan 267). *Before the Fact*'s ironic portrayal of a woman married to a thief and killer is especially suited to the public persona Hitchcock would display most memorably in his appearances on *Alfred Hitchcock Presents*. Iles, the pseudonym under which detective-story writer Anthony Berkeley had already published *Malice Aforethought* (1931), strikes this tone in his famous opening paragraph: "Some women give birth to murderers, some go to bed with them, and some marry them. Lina Aysgarth had lived with her husband for nearly eight years before she realized that she was married to a murderer" (Cerf 3).

Iles begins by showing Lina McLaidlaw, the clever but unpretty daughter of General McLaidlaw, meeting Johnnie Aysgarth, the impecunious and vaguely disreputable fourth son of an impoverished aristocrat, and falling instantly for his boyish directness and cheek. Although Iles presents their courtship from Lina's point of view, his presentation of that point of view oscillates between intimacy and irony, as several stylistic devices reveal. He frequently summarizes Lina's mental reactions in twitchy one-sentence paragraphs disconcertingly at odds with the situations that provoke them, from "But she was interested" to "Everything Johnnie did was right" (4, 18). He uses the word "actually" twice (13, 17) to imply Lina's naïve surprise at Johnnie's pursuit of her. And he emphasizes from the beginning her back-and-forth ambivalence toward her unlikely suitor's physical advances: "Never had Lina dreamed that kisses could be so convincing. Johnnie kissed her till her jaw ached quite painfully. She was enraptured" (18). By the end of the first chapter, the couple has been married over the objections of "a resigned but still indignant General McLaidlaw" (20).

Lina gradually realizes that the scapegrace she has married is far worse than even her censorious father had indicated. Following a showdown in which Lina taxes Johnnie with having seduced her best friend and he responds by spitefully enumerating half a dozen other affairs and announcing that he married her only for her money—"I never cared two straws about you. After all, I do like my women to be pretty" (99)—he stalks out of their home, and Lina, on the advice of her sister Joyce, gathers evidence that will allow her to divorce Johnnie and takes a lover, the artist Ronald Kirby, with whom her affair, fueled by her neurotic uncertainty about her desirability, is quite as tempestuous as Johnnie's courtship of her. The affair ends abruptly with the return of Johnnie, who "swear[s] I'll be different if you'll come back to me" (142), as of course she does.

The discovery that Johnnie encouraged General McLaidlaw to drink too much at a Christmas dinner, urged him to exert himself fatally in attempting "the three-chair trick" (153), and left Lina providentially an heiress sends her back to Ronald, but his confession that she kept him at arm's length for so long that he became engaged to another woman forces her to return to Johnnie. She soon allows Johnnie's crime to be eclipsed in her mind by the land-development scheme in which he is joined by his old friend Beaky Thwaite. Gradually becoming certain that Johnnie plans to murder Beaky in order to steal £15,000 from him, Lina realizes that "only she could stop it" (180), but she is prevented from doing anything by Johnnie's unruffled behavior, by her reluctance to trust perceptions that can only bring her further grief, and eventually by Johnnie's role in saving Beaky from driving his car over a cliff. When Beaky dies shortly afterward during a trip to France after an unknown companion encourages him to down a full beaker of brandy, Lina, seeing herself as Johnny's pusillanimous accomplice in arranging a death that recalls her father's, accepts the similar circumstances this time as proof of his guilt but realizes that "[h]er panic was lest Johnnie be caught" (189).

Realizing that Johnnie has pressed her to insure her life so that he can more profitably kill her, she neither turns him over to the authorities nor confronts him with her suspicions:

> Lina was not frightened any longer. After the first shock she had seen how extremely simple the solution was. She had only to buy back her life from Johnnie. She had only to tell him that she knew he was in financial trouble, forgive him once more, forgive him once more too for forging her name again, and settle his debts. That was all. And that, in time, was what she would do.
>
> But somehow she never did it. . . .
>
> For of course there was always the feeling that though Johnnie might possibly be going to try to cause her death tomorrow, it was out of the question that he should be doing so to-day. (218–19)

Certain that Johnnie will never kill her but will only "try to make her kill herself" (218), Lina is confident that she is too well-informed about his intentions to acquiesce in his plan. In the end, however, her mind, which has come to "alternate between hysteria and a strange calmness which surprised herself more than the hysterics did" (225), is changed by her extreme weariness in waiting for Johnnie to kill her and the realization that, at forty, she is going to have his baby. Determined to prevent Johnnie from reproducing himself but resolving against an illegal abortion or suicide, Lina turns all her attention to helping Johnnie cover his tracks. She leaves a suicide note to be opened in the event of her death. She frets that Johnnie will lose patience and kill her under suspicious circumstances. When he brings her a poisoned glass of milk-and-soda during a spell of influenza, she drinks it willingly, relieved that her death will be assumed to be a result of her illness and ready to accept her status as "accessory before the fact to her own murder" (231).

Appealing as this tale must have been to Hitchcock, he surely knew that any film adaptation of it would inevitably undergo substantial changes. The demands of the Hays Office would eliminate Lina's affair with Ronald Kirby and the scene in which Johnnie boasted about his own conquests. The requirements of well-made melodrama would lengthen their tempestuous courtship, which is expanded from one-twelfth of the novel to one-quarter of the film, and exteriorize the conflicts their marriage engendered. In the screenplay Hitchcock filmed, for example, Lina sneaks out of her parents' home, pretending to go to the post office, and elopes with Johnnie. The imperatives of Hollywood casting, which would prevent Lina from being played by an actress whose homeliness would justify the sobriquet "Letter-box McLaidlaw," would make Johnnie's interest in Lina less obviously mercenary. The eventual casting of Cary Grant as Johnnie and Joan Fontaine as Lina had a decisive impact on the film. Their mutual lack of cordiality gave their scenes an added tension. More fundamentally, as Hitchcock told François Truffaut, "Cary Grant could not be a murderer. . . . [T]he producers would surely have refused" (Truffaut 44). Most important, the ending would require special treatment.

Just how and why *Suspicion* came to have the ending that it did has been the focal point of the film's many commentators. In the ending RKO released, based on a script credited to Samson Raphaelson, Joan Harrison, and Alma Reville, Johnnie brings Lina a glass of milk lit from within to look unusually sinister. Instead of drinking it, however, she packs hurriedly the next morning and prepares to go home to her mother. After Johnnie protests angrily, he demands to drive her. As their car hurtles along the dangerous cliffside road, Lina, convinced that he is going to push her over, screams in panic and flings open the door, causing Johnnie to stop the car abruptly and seize her roughly. In the ensuing scene, he denies any intention of killing her and tells her that, threatened with prison for his debts, he had planned to commit suicide. Although she accepts responsibility for keeping him distant and vows that their marriage will change, he is still maintaining that they can never be happy because he is incapable of change when their voices are last heard. After they get into the car, however, a U-turn seen in a high-angle long shot suggests that they have reached an accord, and a second shot from behind shows his hand curling around her shoulder, before a third, a return to same camera setup as the first, shows the car returning to their home.

The path to this ending, a virtual whitewash of Johnnie that turns Lina from a damsel in distress to an over-imaginative paranoiac, was rocky. Bill Krohn summarizes no fewer than six endings Hitchcock and his collaborators scripted, often filmed, and sometimes previewed. In an early draft excerpted in *Hitchcock's Notebooks*, Johnnie is vindicated of any intention of killing Lina and given a long monologue in which he

Figure 2.1. *Suspicion*—glass of milk.

recounts the sins of his youth and swears that he will stop gambling, cheating, and lying, even though a stage direction indicates that "we know that she cannot believe him" (Auiler 85). In a slightly later draft, Johnnie is allowed to purge his lesser sins by his heroic—and, it is hinted, ultimately self-sacrificial—duty as an RAF flier (Auiler 87–92). When Fontaine's illness delayed the filming of the scene in which she visits him as a flier incognito after the Battle of Britain, the collaborators wrote a third ending in which Lina, although she suspects Johnnie of seeking her death, drinks the glass of milk he has left her, realizes she is not dying, and goes to him just in time to prevent him from drinking poison himself. Preview audiences booed a screening of the film that included this ending, and Hitchcock said, "I don't blame them. They pronounced the girl stupid to willfully drink her possible destruction. With that I don't agree. But I did agree that the necessary half-reel of explanation following the wife's survival was deadly" (Twiggar 3). In response, Hitchcock devised a more comical fourth ending: Lina realizes that she has mistaken Johnnie's intentions when the family dog drinks the milk without suffering any harm. She accepts Johnnie's promise to reform, and he responds: "Do you know—I almost believe it myself" (Krohn 81).

But this ending was scrapped when RKO tested still another version of the film in which incoming producer Sol Lesser had cut out any suggestion that Johnnie was a killer. Not surprisingly, this print, which chopped forty-four of the film's ninety-nine minutes, also flopped with preview audiences, and Hitchcock and his collaborators prepared a sixth ending in which two scenes in which Lina suspects Johnnie of trying to kill her—the scene revolving around the glass of milk and the wild car ride along the cliffs—were transposed and partly reshot, leaving the film with the ending it has had ever since.

Nor were these the only endings the studio considered. As Krohn explains:

> RKO was not at all averse to making an adaptation of Iles's novel in which Johnnie would turn out to be a murderer: two screenplays were written before Hitchcock came to the studio in which John Aysgarth was a very bad character indeed. The fact that RKO considered casting Orson Welles and Laurence Olivier, both of whom had played villains on stage, show that we have to weigh Hitchcock's words carefully: the studio didn't want *Cary Grant* to play a murderer. (71)

In the second of these two earlier screenplays, written by Nathanael West and Boris Ingster shortly before West's death, Lady Ellen Aysgarth shoots her husband, Sir Anthony Aysgarth, dead with her father's handgun when he offers her a poisoned drink, and the story unfolds as a series of flashbacks from her trial for murder. The story has a happy ending, but not for Tony, whose murderous attempt, despite his insouciant dying quip—"Lay you three to one—it's a boy" (West 741)—utterly justifies his wife's suspicion of him.

Hitchcock's biographers offer sharply differing accounts of the history that led to the ending with which the film was released. John Russell Taylor, who describes Johnnie inaccurately as "a practiced wife-murderer," quotes Hitchcock as telling Harry Edington, chief of production at RKO, that "he will follow the novel as to story, persons, locale and sets, excepting only that he would tell the story as through the eyes of the woman and have her husband be villainous in her imagination only" (176). According to this statement, it was Hitchcock's idea to turn Iles's story of a wife's justified suspicion of her husband into a story of unjustified suspicion.

Donald Spoto contrasts this account with Hitchcock's insistence in later interviews that he had initially wanted to film Iles's ending but had been prevented from doing so. In the best-known of these interviews, Hitchcock described still another ending to Truffaut:

> I'm not too pleased with the way *Suspicion* ends. I had something else in mind. The scene I wanted, but it was never shot, was for Cary Grant to bring her a glass of milk that's been poisoned and Joan Fontaine has just finished a letter to her mother: "Dear Mother, I'm desperately in love with him, but I don't want to live because he's a killer. Though I'd rather die, I think society should be protected from him." Then, Cary Grant comes in with the fatal glass and she says, "Will you mail this letter to Mother for me, dear?" She drinks the milk and dies. Fade out and fade in on one short shot: Cary Grant, whistling cheerfully, walks over to the mailbox and pops the letter in. (Truffaut 142)

Unlike Russell, who summarizes the ending and notes that it "never actually reached the script stage" (177), Spoto forthrightly asserts that "this idea did not occur to him at the time, for it cannot be found in the first treatment he submitted to RKO, and it is contradicted by memos in which he stated emphatically that he wanted to make a film about a woman's fantasy life" (243–44).

Patrick McGilligan offers still another account of the ending's genesis. He observes that "RKO had owned the rights to Iles's novel since publication, but the studio had failed over the years to produce a script that satisfied the Hays Office" because "[s]uccessful murderers and willful suicides were taboo in Hollywood. But telling Hitchcock what he *couldn't* do exerted a kind of aphrodisiac effect on his creativity" (278, 279). McGilligan explains the conflict between Hitchcock's statement of intention to Edington and his later account to Truffaut by attributing to the director a deceptive strategy worthy of Johnnie Aysgarth:

> Now he smoothly assured RKO that he would tell *Before the Fact* "through the eyes of the woman and have her husband be villainous in her imagination only" . . . even though this turned the very crux of the novel, the springboard which so appealed to him, on its head. . . . Hitchcock figured he could develop a working script, assuage the censors with petty concessions as the drafts progressed, and then slip Grant as a murderer past the authorities just before the closing bell. (279)

Presenting the evolution of the film as its succession of reformulated endings made Johnnie less and less culpable, McGilligan concludes: "As with *The Lodger*, another book about a serial killer, in the end Hitchcock was forced to surrender the very thing that had intrigued him most about *Before the Fact*" (289).

This welter of endings has offered a field day to commentators on the film. Even though Johnnie is no longer a killer—in the release print, he is exonerated of any attempt to kill Lina, and there is no suggestion in any of the screenplay's surviving drafts that he has caused her father's death—Raymond Borde and Etienne Chaumeton, in their pioneering study of film noir, classify *Suspicion* as "a murder film" because an abrupt and incongruous ending had simply been "tacked on to a rigorous crime story" (31). Robin Wood, by contrast, contends that the shot showing Lina, dressed in black and standing in front of a window "whose framework casts around her a shadow as of a huge web," feels "the victim, the fly caught in the trap," but is here revealed as "in reality the spider, fattening herself on her suspicions in the center of the web she has herself spun" (71–72). Stephen Heath, discussing the oddly gratuitous pair of moments in which Benson, one of the two police officers who comes to ask Lina about Beaky's death, pauses on his way in and out to stare at an abstract painting in the front room that appears nowhere else in the film, notes "its effect as missing spectacle" that raises unanswerable questions about point of view, the law's authority, and the film's narrative economy and coherence (24). Ken Mogg has argued that even if he never filmed the ending he told Truffaut he would have preferred, Hitchcock planted the seeds of that ending in several earlier moments in the film he did make: "In the opening scene on the train, Johnnie 'borrows' a stamp from Lina; later, the camera repeatedly emphasises the pillar-box in the local village, and we even see Hitchcock himself posting a letter there" (79). These references might be seen as the film's transformation of Letter-box McLaidlaw, the nickname Iles had given Lina.

Bill Krohn has made the most sustained attempt to reconcile the evidence that seems to support such contradictory accounts. Echoing Mark Crispin Miller's assertion that "[t]he film's weak ending . . . is actually a necessary index of the film's extraordinary strength" (275), Krohn hails the film's peculiar indeterminacy as a strength rather than a weakness. Reviewing the available evidence, he agrees with Mogg that the final ending of the film is necessarily ambiguous, since the only dramatically satisfying ending, one that did not merely confirm filmgoers' suspicion that Johnnie was guilty, would be "an ending whose terrible ironies expose the ambivalence underlying the ambiguity" (109)—the ending showing that Lina cannot believe Johnnie's confession, the ending in which he jokes about his own inability to believe it, or the ending in which he assures his own destruction by posting Lina's accusatory letter. Krohn finds Lina's ambivalence toward Johnnie echoed in Hitchcock's equally radical ambivalence toward the story and its hero, which generates, "somewhere off to the side of the film . . . a shadow-*Suspicion* which Hitchcock seems to have been making with his left hand, whose traces remain . . . when Lina and Johnnie go driving off at the end" (108).

Despite the limited range of archival material available for the study of *Suspicion*, there is abundant circumstantial evidence to support this theory, from the remarkable variety of endings Hitchcock considered to his complaints when he was given only a month to edit the film, whose tone would have to be established by myriad choices among the alternate takes Krohn argues he must have been shooting (96–97). It seems clear that what originally attracted Hitchcock to the novel was not only its story and its gorgeously realized portrait of a criminal and ultimately lethal Peter Pan but its archly ironic tone. Iles's decision to present Johnnie from Lina's point of view, by turns breathlessly infatuated, monitory, indulgent, uncertain, and increasingly suspicious, virtually guaranteed that his presentation of Johnnie would be proof against any ending that sought to fix any single interpretation on the charming scoundrel.

Unwilling as I am to contest Krohn's powerful reading of the film's, and the filmmaker's, ambivalence, I'd propose that the question of the film's ending, which has exercised so many critics for so long, is in a fundamental sense a red herring. I do not mean that the problem of the ending is unimportant, because it does indeed illuminate the most characteristic problems of the film, but rather that trying to choose from the best ending from among the many candidates that were scripted or shot—or imagining a still better ending no one ever thought of, in the manner of Raymond Durgnat—overlooks the crucial point that the film is impossible to bring to a satisfactory conclusion. Iles's novel, an ironic study that boldly and playfully satirizes Lina's romantic fantasies from the beginning only to show her devotion to her impossible husband gradually deepening as she loses her ability to escape him, could end with her sadly but calmly awaiting her death at his hands. But Hitchcock's less straightforwardly ironic film, which lodges itself somehow both inside and outside Lina's consciousness and the generic frame of the women's film, cannot possibly reach an ending that is logical and emotionally satisfying for viewers who demand both Lina's happiness and Johnnie's guilt.

Miller, going still further, turns the case against the film's weak ending into a case for its power as an indictment of the uncritical immersion in its fictions to which the culture industry invites its consumers:

> Hitchcock simply was unable to devise a strong conclusion, and so even with a looser schedule, and therefore more attention to technique, he still could not have redeemed this ending, whose weakness was determined, not by temporary pressures or the requirements of the studio, but by the very quality that makes *Suspicion* great and challenging—its reflective subjectivity. By locating *Suspicion* within his heroine's mind, Hitchcock had written himself into a corner. He was unable to end the film convincingly because any such conclusion, answering every question and dispatching all unfinished business, demands a sudden pulling-back into the light of day, a reversion that, after our immersion in Lina's dark and too-familiar consciousness, must leave us blinking. (274–75)

Miller argues for the necessary ambivalence of any conceivable ending Hitchcock might have used for a film that had already entangled viewers far more completely than Iles's dry-eyed novel in its heroine's yearning for romance with an impossible mate. As Rick Worland has observed, "a film version of *Before the Fact* that did not make clear Johnnie's murderous intent and Lina's complacent death would in essence be a different story, one that did not reconcile with the book's title" (7). But here Worland, more explicitly but not more carelessly than other commentators, conflates two elements of Iles's novel perhaps too easily: Johnnie's murderous intent and Lina's acceptance of her own death. As Worland points out, every ending of the film that was actually scripted and shot on Hitchcock's watch shows "the couple reconciled" (7). The only two exceptions are the West/Ingster screenplay, in which Lina killed her husband, and Hitchcock's unscripted postbox ending, which would have marked them both for death. But even the different reconciliations that were actually scripted present Johnnie in such different ways that they cast very different retrospective lights over Lina's suspicions of her husband.

An even more revealing constant through all the endings except the one in which Lina knowingly drinks what she erroneously believes is poisoned milk is that in none of the others does Lina accept even momentarily the prospect of her own death. It is especially telling that, as Hitchcock told Truffaut, members of the preview audience for this ending pronounced Lina "stupid to willfully drink her possible destruction." If the film had followed the novel more closely, of course, viewers would presumably have accepted Lina's implication in her own murder as the ultimate expression of the self-sacrificing subordination of her own will to Johnnie's that she had been showing through the whole film. But Hitchcock seems never to have seen the project primarily in terms of its heroine's conscious acceptance of her death. Despite his well-publicized preference for Iles's title over *Suspicion*, a title he told George Schaefer was "cheap and dull" (Auiler 95), *Before the Fact* would have been a puzzling and misleading title for virtually every proposed adaptation of the novel, from the West/Ingster screenplay to the final release print.

Whatever possibilities Hitchcock saw in Iles's novel did not focus on the novel's most original figure—not the murderous husband, a figure Iles had already explored to considerable acclaim in *Malice Aforethought*, but the wife driven to acquiesce in her own destruction by her infatuation, lassitude, and habit. Given the vicissitudes of the film's ending, it is no wonder McGilligan has remarked that Hitchcock's initial assurance to RKO that Lina's suspicions that Johnnie had killed Beaky and planned to kill her were baseless "turned the very crux of the novel, the springboard which so appealed to him, on its head" (279). McGilligan is surely correct in identifying Lina's acceptance of her death at Johnny's hands as the crux of Iles's novel. But since he offers no evidence that this crux constituted Hitchcock's primary interest in the novel, it is quite possible that that interest lay elsewhere.

Analyzing Hitchcock's adaptation of Marie Belloc Lowndes's *The Lodger*, another novel that revolves around a suspected killer who turns out to be innocent in the adaptation, Richard Allen observes:

> Either Mrs. Bunting or Daisy may be deceiving themselves about the Lodger, but Hitchcock is not interested in exploring

motivation. Depth in Hitchcock's film is a matter or surface, as it were. Ambiguity resides not in the motivations of character but in visual narration, in the legibility of appearances. The pleasures of narrative suspense are not subservient to moral insight, as in Belloc Lowndes's novel, but become an end in themselves. A deadly serious question—"Is the Lodger a psychotic killer?"—becomes for Hitchcock a source of entertainment, a macabre joke. . . . It is fun to think that the Lodger might be a psychotic killer. (52)

This description applies even more pointedly to *Suspicion* than to *The Lodger*. In both cases, the novel under adaptation defines its heroine through her ambivalent response to a murderer who lives in her household. In both cases, the heroine becomes convinced that the mysterious man in question is indeed a killer but covers up for him. Although the mystery man is the most intriguing character in either novel, the focus in both cases is on the moral development of the heroine through her increasingly maternal and self-sacrificing solicitude. This focus vanishes in both films, to be replaced by the far more problematic suspicion of what Ken Mogg aptly describes as "men who may, or may not, be murderers" (Krohn 109)—a suspicion that can be resolved only in the sort of anticlimactic finale Hitchcock provides for both films (someone besides the lodger is the Avenger, some never-identified Englishman must have been present at Beaky's death), since any resolution will end the fun of suspecting without knowing.

The condition of suspecting without knowing—that is, of wondering—is characteristic of many more Hitchcock films. Just as Mrs. Bunting wonders whether her lodger really is the Avenger and Lina wonders whether Johnnie is a murderer who is planning to kill her, Iris Henderson and Gilbert wonder what has become of Miss Froy, the second Mrs. de Winter wonders what sort of person her predecessor was, Charlie Newton wonders why her Uncle Charlie is behaving so suspiciously, Dr. Constance Peterson wonders why Dr. Anthony Edwardes is acting so strangely, Charles Adare wonders why Lady Henrietta Flusky has descended into an alcoholic fog, Sam Marlowe wonders how Harry Warp came to meet his untimely end, Scottie Ferguson wonders what secret is accounting for Madeleine Elster's trancelike behavior, Sarah Sherman wonders what has gotten into her fiancé Dr. Michael Armstrong, and virtually everyone in *The Birds* wonders why the birds are suddenly attacking people. *Rear Window* might be described as an epitome of wondering, as L.B. Jefferies laboriously assembles the evidence that will reveal not only whether Lars Thorwald murdered his wife but what all his neighbors are really like. In practically all these cases, of course, the film eventually provides an answer, sometimes within only a few minutes of posing the question. But those few minutes, like the moment in *The Wrong Man* when the clerk at the insurance office sees Manny Balestrero reach into his coat pocket to take out his policy and wonders whether he is the man who robbed the office, are pivotal.

In each of these films, the suspicions of the characters are ultimately subordinate to the suspicions of the audience, which they are designed specifically to arouse. Even when the characters are too benighted to suspect each other or wonder how to read the sinister portents that surround them, Hitchcock still plays on the audience's suspicions. We wonder whom Hannay can trust in *The 39 Steps*, whether something will prevent the bomb from exploding in *Sabotage*, and then why it hasn't exploded already. We wonder how Rowley will try to kill Huntley Haverstock in *Foreign Correspondent* and how long it will take Alexander Sebastian to notice that his wife has pinched his key to the wine cellar in *Notorious*. We wonder when Rupert Cadell will put together the clues to David Kentley's disappearance in *Rope*. We wonder how long it will take Guy Haines to realize that Bruno Anthony really wants to kill his wife in *Strangers on a Train*, Margot Wendice to realize that her husband is setting her up to be killed in *Dial M for Murder*, and Richard Blaney to realize that Bob Rusk is using him as a patsy in *Frenzy*. We wonder whether Marnie is going to get away with her robbery of the Rutland safe and how many people will have to vanish from the Bates Motel before someone realizes that it is a dangerous place. Hitchcock's well-known preference for suspense over surprise means that viewers of his films are often far more suspicious than his unwitting characters. In fact, the audience's suspicions are primary; the characters' suspicions are only a means toward the end of arousing and shaping them, and a means that can readily be dispensed with in films that favor dramatic irony over mystery.

When Allen says that it is fun to think that the Lodger might be a psychotic killer, he does not of course mean that it is fun for the other characters to think so. Daisy scarcely suspects the lodger until the film has nearly run its course; her suspicions are finally awakened only to be swiftly reassured; and her mother's suspicions are anything but fun for her. Although characters like Bob Lawrence, Richard Hannay, and the characters in *The Trouble with Harry* and *Family Plot* may enjoy particular episodes in their adventures, it is only Hitchcock's audience for whom suspicion is generally fun. The discrepancy between the audience's pleasurable experience of the stories' vicissitudes and the generally unalleviated anxiety of their apparent identification figures is a hallmark of Hitchcock's work. His audience shares the characters' anxiety, but the wit of the film's auditory and visual exposition, the ways their anxiety is produced, makes it a pleasurable anxiety, a nightmare from which we never want to awaken. Although, as the intertitle that introduces *The Lodger*'s epilogue reminds us, "All stories must have an end," Hitchcock's films, however swiftly they hurtle to their endings, are not made for the sake of those endings. They are made for the sake of their middles, those deliciously extended second acts characterized by the fun of indulging in unresolved suspicions before they are inevitably resolved.

The single most important change Hitchcock's film makes in adapting *Before the Fact* is not in disproving Lina's suspicions of Johnnie, or even leaving them ambiguous. It is in transforming Iles's resolutely end-oriented novel, whose direction is predicted in surprising detail by its opening paragraph, into a film that could have accommodated any of a number of endings, even though none of them would have resolved its problems completely. However frustrated or disappointed Hitchcock may have grown with the project, it made sense for him to persist in it through ending after ending because he was not making it for the sake of the ending but for the sake of the middle.

Thinking of Hitchcock as a director of middles shows why the Master of Suspense had so little interest in filming detective stories, in which all the clues lead to an ending that serves as the fulcrum of the story. It illuminates his well-known impatience with "the plausibles," those inconvenient explanations that provided a rational basis for the shocks and suspicions that were his stock in trade. It helps explain why such a highly regarded film as *Vertigo* ends so abruptly and, even for many of the film's most ardent admirers, so unsatisfyingly. And it indicates why films like *The Birds*, *The Lodger*, and *Suspicion* are so central to Hitchcock's career: because they explore, more fully than any of his other films, the problems and consequences of awakening suspicions than can never be fully resolved. *Suspicion* especially casts Hitchcock as a director of entertaining possibilities rather than often climactic certainties and his world as one in which anything is possible and every telltale gesture is a potential clue.

Allen's observation that depth in *The Lodger* is a matter of surface—"the pleasures of narrative suspense are not subservient to moral insight, as in Belloc Lowndes's novel, but become an end in themselves"—opposes morality and entertainment in a way that is familiar to anyone conversant with the history of Hitchcock commentary. Even analysts who do not share Keats's view that poetry is not so fine a thing as philosophy may well share Allen's view that Hitchcock's status as entertainer inevitably compromises his claims as moralist. Yet the opposite is the case. Hitchcock the moralist depends on Hitchcock the entertainer. It is precisely because he makes it fun to suspect characters like Johnnie Aysgarth that his films provide stellar examples of morally consequential experience. The reason Hitchcock commentators have been so ready to overlook this connection is that they have persistently looked in the wrong place for the moral experience the films provide.

Reviewing *Suspicion*'s production difficulties, Donald Spoto contends that because "[n]o one had any idea how the picture would end . . . no scene or line of dialogue had a sure purpose" as it was written or shot (245)—a summary that contrasts amusingly with Samson Raphaelson's recollection that "[t]hat story broke more easily for me than anything I have ever written" (McGilligan 279). The assumption behind Spoto's assessment is the Aristotelian belief, shared alike by the authors of Athenian tragedy and detective fiction, that because the meaning of each story resides in an ending that casts a retrospective and definitive light over the whole story, every detail of the story has its own meaning only in the light of that ending. Without knowing the ending, the filmmakers cannot know the meaning of any speech or shot that precedes it. Uncertain whether Johnnie would turn out to be innocent or guilty, Hitchcock literally did not know what he was doing in making the film.

Spoto's argument has a corollary that becomes more explicit in Chapter 6 of Aristotle's *Poetics*:

> Tragedy is essentially an imitation not of persons but of action and life, of happiness and misery. All human happiness or misery takes the form of action; the end for which we live is a certain kind of action, not a quality. Character gives us qualities, but it is in our actions—what we do—that we are happy or the reverse. In a play accordingly they do not act in order to portray the Characters; they include the Characters for the sake of the action. So that it is the action in it, i.e. its Fable or Plot, that is the end and purpose of the tragedy; and the end is everywhere the chief thing. (1461)

Because actions, and life in general, are conceived in terms of their ends, it is only their ends that reveal their true moral import. The tragedies Aristotle considers often seem to be tending toward one moral conclusion, but this apparent conclusion is as untrustworthy as a Hitchcock character's suspicions until a reversal or a recognition redirects them to their true meaning. The morality of these stories is incarnated in the experiences of their characters, whose actions, because they are purposive and freely chosen, provide an idealized image of life.

This analysis of fictional characters' actions as images of moral decision and moral consequence has been so influential in Western aesthetics for the past twenty-five hundred years that it is hardly surprising to see it applied to Hitchcock as well, even by commentators like Raymond Durgnat, who complained a generation ago that "[o]ne critical trick with Hitchcock's minor movies is to suggest that the suspense is created principally out of our moral criticisms of the hero (and of ourselves), and only secondarily out of our anxiety that the hero and his conformist morality should enjoy their happy and reassuring triumph over the villain and his villainy" (32). This unfair attempt to inflate the director's reputation, Durgnat noted, treated him as a special case instead of acknowledging the ways their pleasures were simply the pleasures of mainstream commercial cinema:

> [I]t's doubtful whether Hitchcock's movies provide reflections on the duplicity or opacity of human nature any more effectively than, say, Michael Anderson's *The Naked Edge*, an efficient, perfectly unimportant thriller, in which Deborah Kerr, worried about her husband Gary Cooper, wonders, "Can you sleep with a man for seven years without realizing he's a murderer?" The answer, obviously, is Yes, though the answer matters less than the sense of alienation which it induces. (32)

Despite his sharp disagreement with Robin Wood, who pronounces Hitchcock a moralist, Durgnat largely agrees with Wood that the moral significance of a fictional story is found in the behavior of its characters. In two qualifying phrases he casually drops, however, he indicates another possibility. "And of ourselves" and "the answer matter less than the sense of alienation which it induces" both redirect attention from the characters' experience to the audience's experience. This latter experience is the focus of *Suspicion*, and indeed of all Hitchcock's films. When the director spoke, as he often did, of playing the audience like a piano or putting them through it, his language accurately reflected his paramount concern. Throughout his career, he is interested in the relations among his fictional characters only as a means of developing the primary relationship between his very real audience and himself. Lina Aysgarth's shifting attitude toward her husband, morally fraught as it may be, is never as important as the audience's attitude toward them both.

This attitude is not only more complex than that of the audience for *The Naked Edge*, whose anxieties are reducible to a simple did-he-or-didn't-he coin toss, but considerably more complex than that of

Lina herself because of the multiple and often contradictory interpretive frames we are invited to bring to the film. Despite Robin Wood's ingenious suggestion that in the absence of a definitive ending, "the only way the film could possibly be shot was to deny all access to [Johnnie's] consciousness, showing him exclusively through [Lina's]" (230), the film presents Johnnie apart from Lina's mediating consciousness any number of times. If its first sequence presented him from her point of view, the second sequence, in which Johnnie, surrounded by attendant women, refuses to smile for a photographer taking his picture at a local hunt until he suddenly glimpses Lina astride a horse, presents her, entirely unaware of his presence, from his point of view. Two brief but important scenes in the film—Johnnie's rueful salute to the dead General McLaidlaw's portrait ("You win, old boy") after he has learned that the General's will restricts Lina to a small annual income, and his ascent of the stairs with the sinister glass of milk—take place in Lina's absence. The second may well be an echo of the moment in *The Lodger* when a shot of the lodger descending the stairs seems to visualize the landlady's thoughts, but the first is clearly designed as an objective presentation of a moment to which Lina is not privy. In addition, many scenes between Lina and Johnnie emphasize facial reactions Lina does not see, like the troubled expression he makes over her shoulder in reaction to the announcement she makes from the shelter of a wing chair that the police have visited to ask about Beaky's death. Despite its much greater intimacy with Lina than with Johnnie, the film does not lock viewers inside Lina's consciousness; it places us both inside and outside.

In addition to knowing everything that Lina knows about her husband, the audience for *Suspicion* knows a great deal more. When we see a long shot of Johnnie pushing Beaky over the edge of a cliff superimposed on a closeup of Lina's fingers forming the word "MURDER" from her Anagram tiles, we can readily identify the image as subjective without being consumed by it; that is, the means by which it is identifying as Lina's imagining allows us both to identify with Lina and to detach ourselves from her. The costumes we see Lina wear not only express her sense of herself but identify her supposedly private emotions in terms of a long-standing code of Hollywood costuming, from the mannish suit she wears in the opening sequence to the artless off-the-shoulder dress she wears to the Hunt Ball to the severe pinstripe suit she dons for the final scene. The background music we hear not only telegraphs Lina's rollercoaster emotional reactions but muddles the distinction between what Lina hears and what she only imagines, most memorably in the conclusion to the scene in which Johnnie, having playfully asked permission of the General's portrait to marry his daughter, asks her, "Do you hear that music?" and the soundtrack obliges with a reprise of the couple's signature tune, the Strauss waltz "Wiener Blut," even though we cannot tell whether Lina is hearing it from the distant Hunt Ball, where it was played earlier in the evening, or merely imagining it, as she clearly imagined the interdiction of her father's portrait.

The ambiguous valence of "Wiener Blut," which many critics of the film have pointed out, is linked to a larger pattern that implicates the audience's interpretation in Lina's suspicions without making them congruent. Beginning with the first time she meets Johnnie on the train, Lina, who after the opening scene never wears glasses unless she has put them on expressly in order to read something she considers important in making sense of her present situation, typically interprets what she sees in terms of preexisting visual categories. Her initial indifference to her train companion changes to interest when she recognizes him from a photograph in a magazine she is reading. She takes the photo, which presents him as an eligible bachelor, as an index of his true nature. Later she will do the same thing with the General's portrait, which she is certain is forbidding her to marry Johnnie; with the letter tiles that spell "MURDER," which literally bring to life a photo of the proposed seaside development, to which she adds two tiny figures, one throwing the other off a cliff; with the newspaper story headlined "ENGLISHMAN FOUND DEAD," which persuades her that Johnnie has murdered Beaky; and with the letter Johnnie has written about repaying his debts in which the words "some other way" are highlighted for the audience's benefit. Hitchcock shows how images shape perceptions still further in two shots in which Lina's point of view is subordinated to the audience's: first when Johnnie suggests purchasing some cliffside land on which to build and Lina's reaction shot is a still photograph in which the crashing waves are frozen in time, then later when mystery writer Isobel Sedbusk's brother Bertram, the Home Office pathologist played by Gavin Gordon in impossibly thick eyeglasses, is first introduced by a photo on Isobel's desk that shows exactly how geeky he is.

More generally still, we know at every moment of the film, as Lina cannot know, that we are watching a movie designed to entertain us, and a movie whose allegiances to the genres of romance and suspense license us to enjoy Lina's agonized uncertainty about her husband in ways she never can. We know, as Lina never knows (although Joan Fontaine certainly does), that Johnnie is played by Cary Grant, best known as a peerless light comedian who has accepted the role in hopes of extending his range. We know that Lina is played by Joan Fontaine, who is largely reprising her role as the sorely used young wife in *Rebecca*, in hopes of stealing the picture from her better-known costar. And if we have read

Iles's novel, we know that Johnnie is a killer—know it so unshakably that many of us, like Borde and Chaumeton, will go right on knowing it no matter what the film tells us. Although Lina at no point offers herself as an accessory before the fact of her own murder, the audience is frequently in that position. True, we do not actively conspire to cover it up, as Iles's Lina does but Hitchcock's Lina generally does not. But we take a perverse pleasure in the revelation of Johnnie's unquestioned perfidy (his irresponsibility about money, his guileless determination to live off his wife, his embezzlement from his cousin Captain Melbeck, his inveterate gambling) and allow ourselves the still more perverse pleasure of contemplating the possibility of still greater crimes (the velvety moment when he ascends the stairs with that glowing glass of milk). Our demand to be entertained whatever the price to the characters' lives and happiness makes us accessories before the fact.

Our own assessment of both Johnnie and Lina therefore requires us to analyze a much wider range of clues than Lina ever considers as we shift among a number of contextual frames which are neither consistent nor logically parallel. From its opening shot, a black frame that makes many viewers wonder if something is wrong with the picture, we shift back and forth between interpreting the story of Johnnie and Lina as the history of a romance realistic enough to be compelling and our ineradicable knowledge that it is only a movie, and a romantic thriller, and a Hitchcock thriller, and a thriller starring Cary Grant. Our demand for entertainment assures us that Lina's suspicions must come to something (else the heroine would be intolerably diminished) but that the film must provide a climactic reversal or surprise (else its structure would be insufficiently dramatic). We want to see Cary Grant expand his range at the same time we want the Cary Grant we know and love. Above all, we want every clue to both Johnnie's guilt and innocence, Lina's rational detective work and paranoia, to be explained in the end. It is only on that basis that we are prepared to enjoy her tribulations. Each of the film's several endings, more or less satisfactorily, tells us that we cannot have all the things we want, not even from popular entertainment. In refusing to resolve the nature of Lina's suspicions satisfactorily within its fictional frame, these endings all force us to refer back to other frames we are used to taking for granted, ultimately indicting the complicity of our demand for entertainment.

Even in Aristotelian tragedy, moral wisdom is primarily for the audience and only incidentally for the hero whose sufferings pay the price for that wisdom so that the audience can get it at a steep discount. In *Suspicion*, Hitchcock presents a story and a heroine so resistant to rational integration that viewers are encouraged to bypass them as a source of wisdom and fall back on the primary relationship between the storyteller and his audience. Tempting as it is to claim that this model of moral instruction is bold, novel, and postmodern, it is far older than the Aristotelian model it displaces. As Walter Benjamin noted, the modern storyteller "in his living immediacy is by no means a present force" (83) because he no longer commands a breadth and depth of experience more comprehensive than our own. Hitchcock, who is neither Sophocles nor Aesop, does not end his nightmares by tendering morals that are useful or authoritative. Instead, he offers through all his films—especially through *Suspicion*, the most Hitchcockian of them all—the more archaic wisdom of the storyteller: Suspicion may be fun, especially for an audience that has paid for the privilege of indulging it, but it always carries a price.

Works Cited

Allen, Richard. "*The Lodger* and the Origins of Hitchcock's Aesthetic." *Hitchcock Annual* 10 (2001–2): 38–78.

Aristotle. *The Basic Works of Aristotle.* Ed. Richard McKeon. New York: Random House, 1941.

Auiler, Dan. *Hitchcock's Notebooks: An Authorized and Illustrated Look Inside the Creative Mind of Alfred Hitchcock.* New York: Avon, 1999.

Benjamin, Walter. "The Storyteller: Reflections of the Works of Nikolai Leskov." 1936; rpt. in *Illuminations,* ed. Hannah Arendt, trans. Harry Zohn. New York: Schocken, 1969: 83–109.

Borde, Raymond, and Etienne Chaumeton. *A Panorama of American Film Noir, 1941–1953.* Trans. Paul Hammond. San Francisco: City Lights, 2002.

Brill, Lesley. *The Hitchcock Romance: Love and Irony in Hitchcock's Films.* Princeton, NJ: Princeton UP, 1988.

Cerf, Bennett, ed. *Three Famous Murder Novels: Before the Fact, by Francis Iles; Trent's Last Case, by E.C. Bentley; The House of the Arrow, by A.E.W. Mason.* New York: Modern Library, 1941.

Durgnat, Raymond. *The Strange Case of Alfred Hitchcock, or, The Plain Man's Hitchcock.* London: Faber and Faber, 1974.

Heath, Stephen. "Narrative Space." 1976; rpt. in *Questions of Cinema.* Bloomington: Indiana UP, 1981: 19–75.

Krohn, Bill. "Ambivalence (*Suspicion*)." *Hitchcock Annual* 11 (2002–3): 67–116.

Leff, Leonard J. *Hitchcock and Selznick: The Rich and Strange Collaboration of Alfred Hitchcock and David O. Selznick in Hollywood.* London: Weidenfeld and Nicolson, 1987.

McGilligan, Patrick. *Alfred Hitchcock: A Life in Darkness and Light.* New York: HarperCollins. 2003.

Miller, Mark Crispin. "Hitchcock's Suspicions and *Suspicion.*" 1983; rpt. in *Boxed In: The Culture of TV.* Evanston, IL: Northwestern UP, 1988.

Mogg, Ken. *The Alfred Hitchcock Story.* London: Titan, 2000.

Smith, Susan. *Hitchcock: Suspense, Humour and Tone*. London: BFI, 2000.
Spoto, Donald. *The Dark Side of Genius: The Life of Alfred Hitchcock*. Boston: Little, Brown, 1983.
Taylor, John Russell. *Hitch: The Life and Times of Alfred Hitchcock*. London: Pantheon, 1978.
Truffaut, François. *Hitchcock*. Revised ed. New York: Simon and Schuster, 1983.
Twiggar, Beth. "Alfred Hitchcock, Master Maker of Mystery." *New York Herald Tribune*. 7 December 1941. Section 6, p. 3.
West, Nathanael. *Novels and Other Writings*. New York: Library of America, 1997.
Wood, Robin. *Hitchcock's Films Revisited*. New York: Columbia UP, 1989.
Worland, Rick. "Before and After the Fact: Writing and Reading Hitchcock's *Suspicion*." *Cinema Journal* 41.4 (2002): 3–26.

3

NICK HAEFFNER

Heroic Satans and Other Hitchcockian Heresies

> I authorise the publication and sale of all libertine books and immoral works; for I esteem them most essential to human felicity and welfare, instrumental to the progress of philosophy, indispensible to the eradication of prejudices, and in every sense conducive to the increase of human knowledge and understanding.
>
> —Marquis de Sade, *Juliette*

IN 2006 I COLLABORATED ON A traveling new media art installation inspired by Hitchcock's *Vertigo* (1958), called *Repossessed*. One of the aims of *Repossessed* was to reopen debate on gender and sexuality in *Vertigo* with the aid of new technologies. The exhibition also challenged some of the assumptions routinely made about Hitchcock's authorship of the films. In addition, we aimed to foreground the role of the active audience in making narrative and meaning from the raw material of a film. As part of my contribution to *Repossessed* I wrote an essay called "The Spoto Myth" for the exhibition catalogue.[1]

I use the term "Spoto myth" to refer to Donald Spoto, Hitchcock's biographer, and in particular his best-selling account of Hitchcock's life and work called *The Dark Side of Genius*, first published in 1983. It is Spoto's contention that Hitchcock's films chart the developing realization of Hitchcock's personal rape and revenge fantasies directed at a succession of blonde actresses whom the director fetishized and desired. A great deal of this hypothesis relies on reading the Hitchcock canon backward from Tippi Hedren's allegations of mistreatment and physical abuse during the filming of *The Birds* (1963) and subsequently, *Marnie* (1964). Hitchcock's penultimate film *Frenzy* (1972) is also given a key role in the prosecution's case, with its explicit scene of a murderer achieving orgasm on the soundtrack while the camera remains intently trained on the face of a woman being strangled to death. Spoto sees this late entry to the Hitchcock canon as the culmination of a trend reaching back to *The Lodger* (1927), with its storyline of a serial killer whose lust for women and for murder is kindled by "golden curls." Spoto asserts that the films are coded confessions of Hitchcock's own violent fantasies about blonde women and that *Frenzy* is the most daringly frank cinematic realization of the director's perverted fantasies.

Spoto's assessment of Hitchcock's output transformed from an earlier appreciation of the films in *The Art of Alfred Hitchcock* (1976) to a disapproving moral attack on the work in *The Dark Side of Genius*. Hitchcock the man is represented as immoral, and the films themselves are seen as unhealthy symptoms of his own diseased psyche. In my book on Hitchcock (2005) I went to some lengths to refute Spoto's reading of Hitchcock's films and to establish it as a myth.

A critique of the Spoto myth might look something like this:

1. The figure known as Hitchcock is not a consistent unified self but, like all of us, multifaceted and exists always in dynamic relation with others: to paraphrase Walt Whitman, Hitchcock is legion, he contains multitudes. Different situations and different interactions with others brought out different facets of a many sided personality.

2. Hitchcock's films are self-evidently not only the product of Hitchcock's mind. They are the intertextual and are the product of economic imperatives and social relations. Many collaborators contributed original ideas, perceptions, insights, desires, prejudices, dramatic archetypes and stereotypes (for instance, the above-mentioned scene in *Frenzy* was already in the source novel *Goodbye Piccadilly, Farewell Leicester Square* written by Arthur La Bern six

years earlier; Hitchcock didn't simply think it up). Studio executives and censors successfully exerted their will over the films, effectively setting imperatives and constraints in spite of Hitchcock's best efforts to wrest control away from the studio system.

3. The Spoto myth works to close off questioning about the moral position of the audience watching a Hitchcock film. This is something Hitchcock thematized in key scenes from a number of his films, from the opening of *The Pleasure Garden* (1926), through to a set piece chase across a cinema screen in *Saboteur* (1942) and right up to Hitchcock's most sustained meditation on the ethics of spectatorship in *Rear Window* (1954).

Nevertheless, a recent book entitled *Hitchcock's Villains* (2013) suggests that there is much life left in the Spoto myth and that the role of the active audience may still be left unacknowledged in an appeal to the apparently straightforward idea that a Hitchcock film is an unmediated expression of Hitchcock's personality and should be consumed, rather than co-produced, by audiences. The moral complexities raised by the films are flattened into a simple formula: the villains in the films express Hitchcock's own dark side, which is evil. The villains are "a tiny sliver of himself" (2013, 10). In case we miss this point, it is repeated several times. We are told, "his villains were often stand-ins for his own fantasies" and, again, that Hitchcock's villains were merely "fun house reflections of Hitchcock himself" (13). In case we haven't got the point by the end of the first chapter, it is spelled out a little more bluntly: "Hitchcock was his villains, and they were Hitchcock" (19). Alexander Sebastian (Claude Rains) in *Notorious* (1946) is subsequently described as "another example of Hitchcock's inner psyche imprinting itself on the film" (49).

In the view of the authors, it would seem that we enjoy these characters as entertainment in spite of the fact that they are the creations of an unhealthy imagination. "It's not always comfortable getting inside the heads of these characters," the authors claim. "They're not good people after all, driven by dark urges and evil intent" (2013, ix). According to this viewpoint, we are normal, and Hitchcock is pathological.[2]

What follows is an intertextual examination of villainy in Hitchcock's films that seeks to understand the characters and their actions not as expressions of Hitchcock's own morality, personality, and personal beliefs but rather as effective dramatic conventions with their own histories.

Hitchcock drew on these conventions and traditions because they catered to the desires of his audiences. Contrary to the Spoto myth, the films do not necessarily reflect Hitchcock's own personality or dispositions.

Although audiences might find it easier to make sense of art and culture through an appeal to the personality of an individual, the reality is far more interesting and complex, involving a web of associations with others, living and dead. As Hitchcock himself observed:

> Subconsciously we are all influenced by the books that we've read. The novels, the paintings, the music and all the works of art in general, form our intellectual culture from which we can't get away. Even if we want to. (Gottlieb 1997, 142)

One provocative challenge to the personality-led approach to art and culture is T.S. Eliot's essay "Tradition and the Individual Talent" (1919). Eliot controversially rejects the idea that the artist's personality is an appropriate reference point for the work. Instead, Eliot argues that great artists are those who have mastered the traditions from which their work springs. The vitality of these traditions is what animates the artist and the work: "the most individual parts of his work may be those in which the dead poets, his ancestors, assert their immortality most vigorously" (1982, 37). Most interestingly of all, Eliot challenges the idea that the work expresses the emotions of the artist. It is the "sign" (drawn from tradition), not the artist, that creates the emotion. "The emotion of art is impersonal," Eliot writes. "Poetry is not a turning loose of emotion but an escape from emotion. It is not an expression of personality but an escape from personality" (1982, 37). It follows, therefore, that from this perspective, the supposed morality of the artist cannot be used as any kind of meaningful guide to the moral content or purport of the work. Nor, indeed, can the work be used as a reliable indicator of the morality of its creator.[3]

As a commercial filmmaker, Hitchcock worked with the dominant codes and conventions of popular literature, drama, music, painting, and cinema. We still know too little about Hitchcock's relation to popular theater and fiction of the early 20th century, although Barr's study *English Hitchcock* has made a notable contribution to this area. The popular tropes, dramatic archetypes, and stereotypes of villainy that Hitchcock drew on included the figure of the villain as suave, sophisticated, and wealthy (Bruno Anthony in *Strangers on a Train* [1951] or Brandon Shaw in *Rope* [1948]); the villain as foreign other (Abbott in *The Man Who Knew too Much* [1934], Alex Sebastian and his mother in *Notorious*, and Otto

Keller in *I Confess* [1953]); or the villain as sexually perverse (Handel Fane [Esmé Percy] in *Murder!* [1930], Mrs. Danvers [Judith Anderson] in *Rebecca* [1940], Norman Bates [Anthony Perkins] in *Psycho* [1960], and Bob Rusk [Barry Foster] in *Frenzy*). Of course, there are various permutations of the above.

Hitchcock and Truffaut were in agreement that "the better the villain the better the picture," with Truffaut going on to nominate Claude Rains, Joseph Cotten, and Robert Walker as Hitchcock's best villains (Truffaut 1986). However, as Leitch notes, *Psycho*, *Vertigo*, *Notorious*, *The Birds*, *North by Northwest* (1959), *Shadow of a Doubt*, *Foreign Correspondent* (1940), *Frenzy*, and *The Lady Vanishes* (1938) do not seem to bear out Truffaut's observation:

> Apart from *Notorious* and *Shadow of a Doubt* (1943)—and of course *The Birds*—how many of them depend for their effectiveness on their villains? The villain in *Vertigo*, like the real thief in *The Wrong Man* (1956) hardly registers at all; until the last few minutes, Lars Thorwald is only glimpsed from across the courtyard in *Rear Window*; the real "Avenger" in *The Lodger* (1926) never appears onscreen. Would these films be better if their villains were more prominent? *The Lady Vanishes* (1938), *Foreign Correspondent* (1940), and *North by Northwest*, which feature Hitchcock's most polished villains, use these characters mainly to motivate threats and dangers without disturbing their films' tone of comic or adventurous melodrama. (Leitch 2014)

Given the somewhat mottled moral complexion of Hitchcock's heroes and the complex psychology of the ostensible villains, Leitch argues that the category of "villainy" is more helpful than the label "villain." It may be that Leitch is onto something more significant here. Could it be that in the drive to canonize Hitchcock as a great artist, an illicit form of order has been imposed on a far more messy and uneven corpus?

Clearly there are areas of coherence and consonance in the corpus. With respect to villainy, we can observe that very often the encounter with evil works to draw out a monstrous and/or murderous nature in the ostensible hero. For example, Devlin in *Notorious*, who behaves as a bully and a heel toward the heroine; Guy Haines in *Strangers on a Train*, who confesses that he could "break the foul stupid, useless little neck" of his wife; and Rupert Cadell in *Rope*, who misguidedly teaches the superiority of the intellectual to his two murderous charges.

As Leitch observes:

> [T]he more villainous Hitchcock can make his heroes act, the more completely he can blur the line between heroism and villainy, the more successful the picture. [. . .] The test case is *Vertigo*, whose nominal villain, Gavin Elster, is important only as Judy Barton's master and the nightmare prototype of the increasingly possessive Scottie Ferguson, who ends up treating Judy as badly, and in very much the same way, as Elster ever did. In the same way, *Notorious* isn't a great movie because Claude Rains is a great villain; it's a great movie because of the ways it allows Devlin, its hero, to act just as villainous as the villain while still retaining his heroic status. *Blackmail* (1929) and *Sabotage*, in this accounting, become two of the most fascinating Hitchcock films, since in allowing each of their leading characters—Alice, Frank Webber, the blackmailer, the artist in *Blackmail*, Verloc, the Professor, Stevie, Mrs. Verloc in *Sabotage*—a chance to play both villain and victim, it raises enduring questions about how little different those functions may be. (Leitch 2014)

Indeed, one of the most subversive ideas in *Shadow of a Doubt* lies in its tacit endorsement of Nietzsche's aphorism in *Beyond Good and Evil* warning that "Whoever fights monsters should see to it that in the process he does not become a monster" (2003, 146).[4] In this context, it is relevant that the admirable heroine of *Shadow of a Doubt*, Young Charlie, tells her uncle that he must "go away or I'll kill you myself" and that it is she who finally dispatches him.

However, this should not be taken as evidence of Hitchcock's own morality. Rather, we should read such devices as effective dramatic conventions, learned by Hitchcock from his predecessors. The idea of upsetting the opposition between good characters and bad characters is well established in both fiction and criticism, often subtended by psychoanalytic theory. William Indick's textbook *Psychology for Screenwriters* contains a good deal of advice for budding screenwriters on such topics as the "the Id as villain" and "neurotic conflict." Of the villain, he writes:

> It's no secret that audiences enjoy the unrepressed villain more than the good-goody hero. As the representative of the id, the villain is a sinner, and sinners have much more fun. (Indick 2006, 17)

It is certainly a well-worn trope of Hitchcock criticism to draw on a Freudian supposition that the uncivilized id is never far below the surface of civilized existence—a perspective established as early as 1965 in the first edition of *Hitchcock's Films* by Robin Wood. For Hitchcock, however, such a view may have come from literary, rather than a personal or psychoanalytic, source through one of his favorite novelists, John Buchan. In *The Powerhouse* (1916), the reader is admonished as follows:

> You think that a wall as solid as the earth separates civilization from barbarism. I tell you the division is a thread, a sheet of glass. A touch here, a push there, and you bring back the reign of Saturn. (Buchan 1916, 16)

In *English Hitchcock*, Charles Barr recalls Buchan's characterization of civilization as a "thin crust" that comes from the latter's novel *Augustus*: "Once again the crust of civilization has worn thin, and beneath can be heard the muttering of primeval fires" (Buchan 1937, 40). The sources of such an anxious view of the world may not be Freudian in the first instance (indeed, this fear may be seen as typically associated with Conservative politics in its constant appeals to various types of "other" as barbarians, such as immigrants, homosexuals, and the indigent, at the gate, ready to tear down the fragile walls separating white, Western culture from an imagined "outside"), but they are readily absorbed into the psychoanalytic perspective.

It has, however, become increasingly apparent that, although not necessarily mistaken, the psychoanalytic line of enquiry now tends to yield schematic and somewhat predictable conclusions. Where once it appeared subversive to explore the possibility that the hero might be villainous, it is now something of a commonplace observation. Perhaps it might be more interesting at this juncture to look at what makes the villains heroic.

If we are to talk of recurring preoccupations with regard to villains in Hitchcock films, it could be said that there is a propensity to endow them with Romantic or heroic qualities. Many of the most memorable villains can also be seen as Byronic heroes. *The Romantic Agony* by Mario Praz explains the impact that Milton's *Paradise Lost* had on the sensibilities of Romantic writers, and the image of Satan as hero that some have taken from Milton's poem has had a long and successful career in the thriller genre—for instance, the character of John Doe in David Fincher's *Seven* (1995) or Hannibal Lector (voted the American Film Institute's number one villain).[5] The novelist Philip Pullman has already made connections between Hitchcock's representations of villainy and *Paradise Lost*. At the opening of his new introduction to the poem, Pullman quotes an anonymous eighteenth-century reader, who says of Satan in *Paradise Lost*, "By God! I know not what the outcome may be, but this Lucifer is a damned fine fellow, and I hope that he may win!" (Pullman 2005, 1).⁶ Pullman goes on to draw parallels between Milton's and Hitchcock's strategy for making the audience root for the villain, noting that:

> The opening governs the way you tell everything that follows, not only in terms of the organisation of the events but also in terms of the tone of voice that does the telling, and not least, it enlists the reader's sympathy in *this* cause rather than *that*. Alfred Hitchcock once pointed out that if a film opens with a shot of a burglar breaking into a house and ransacking the place, and then, with him, we see through the bedroom window the lights of the car drawing up outside, we think "Hurry up! Get out! They're coming!" (Pullman 2005, 4)

The most obvious manifestation of the villain as romantic hero in Hitchcock's films is Uncle Charlie (Joseph Cotten) in *Shadow of a Doubt*. Not only Hitchcock, but also writers Thornton Wilder and Sally Benson, use Uncle Charlie to meld popular fictional conventions with the high romantic critique of bourgeois values. Like the Romantics, Uncle Charlie finds the modern world materialistic and dispiriting. He looks to an imagined golden age in the past when life was full of excitement and gaiety. His niece, Young Charlie (Teresa Wright), has also grasped the existential poverty of her family's relatively comfortable life through her intuition. Of her family, Young Charlie complains, "we just sort of go along and nothing happens. We're in a terrible rut." Charlie's father tries to argue with her, proudly pointing out that the bank gave him a raise last January, to which Charlie replies contemptuously, "money, how can you talk about money? I'm talking about souls." With his aristocratic air and values, Uncle Charlie enacts a similar critique of bourgeois life but from an imagined upper-class subject position—imagined, because, as we are shown, Emma and Charlie's family is not particularly grand. Indeed, Emma's family is quintessentially bourgeois—the "typical American family." The townspeople of Santa Rosa hail Uncle Charlie as a model citizen, and as John Orr (2005) observes, he is only one of a number of Hitchcock murderers with "impeccably bourgeois credentials":

Yet, in spite of his outwardly bourgeois appearance, Uncle Charlie has adopted the dandyish manners and values of an old world aristocrat. His role in *Shadow of a Doubt* is to set in motion a familiar set of Romantic oppositions which run:

> Bourgeois: ordered, repressed, sexless

Bohemian: passionate, dangerous with an emphasis on deviant sexuality (in Charlie's case, violent misogyny and an incestuous wish).

Robin Wood sees in *Shadow of a Doubt* a Catholic vision of a fallen world—an inverse of the optimism of the American Dream—but both this and his attempt to link the film with Marxism may operate to close off other pertinent considerations. First, the critical position focalized through Uncle Charlie in *Shadow of a Doubt* is recognizably a high Tory Romantic critique of the modern industrialized world as explored by Raymond Williams in his landmark study *Culture and Society* (1983), which showed how both Socialists and Conservatives in nineteenth-century Britain despaired of the materialism of capitalist society. Uncle Charlie's critique of bourgeois society is from an imagined aristocratic Conservative position. He has no affection or sympathy for the proletariat and no feeling for the suffering of others. He simply laments the lack of passion, eccentricity, and excitement in a world dominated by middle-class values. He longs for the restoration of a devil-may-care aristocratic ethic.

Second, Uncle Charlie's sermonizing could be seen as closer to Wilder's Puritan Ethic than to Hitchcock's imputed Catholicism. Wilder's upbringing imbued a strong Puritanism in his work. While they appear deeply un-Christian in a conventional sense, Uncle's Charlie's sentiments, particularly as expressed in his keynote speeches at the dinner table and in the *Til Two* bar, are delivered with the self-righteous zeal of a puritan jeremiad.

In that case we are dealing with more of an immanent critique from within North American traditions than an outside view from the Old World (Catholic, European, and cynical) looking in. Like all of Hitchcock's films, *Shadow of a Doubt* involved close collaboration between Hitchcock and his screenwriters. However, *Shadow of a Doubt* provides an especially instructive example of the way in which Hitchcock's writers were far more than hired hands.

Third, we might ask ourselves whether we can comfortably extricate ourselves from the morality of Uncle Charlie. Uncle Charlie, like Jefferies in *Rear Window*, has a way of making us complicit. Joanne Faulkner, in her essay "Jimmy Stewart: Mon Prochain: a Reading of Rear Window," reads the film alongside Pierre Klossowski's celebrated essay on the Marquis de Sade to suggest that, like the citizens of the French revolution at the time of the terror, we exist as a community partly in relation to our fascinated gaze at "gruesome and arbitrary murder":

> As we watch Jefferies watching his neighbours, perhaps we should ask ourselves a question analogous to that which Pierre Klossowski poses to himself in relation to Sade, with the title of his book Sade, Mon Prochain. While Klossowski asks "as Sade's reader, how am I related to him?" or "how do I share my humanity with Sade, who is also a product of reason?"—we might ask how we, as viewers of the film, are related precisely to whatever makes us most uncomfortable about Jefferies' voyeurism. (Faulkner 2014)

The Sadean side of Uncle Charlie is to be found in his belief that the liberties he takes with morality and the law are rationally justified.

According to Robin Wood, the frisson of subversion that many have detected in *Shadow of a Doubt* comes from the dissonant pairing of the pieties of small-town American values with those of film noir, with its echoes of European nihilism and cynicism (although, of course, those elements are also already in the small-town film to some extent). Wood wants to enlist Hitchcock as our contemporary and chastises him when his films fail in this regard. For Wood, Hitchcock does not mount a head-on critique of American patriarchal capitalism, so all he can do, as a commercial filmmaker, is to acknowledge that the American Dream is subtended by a nightmare. However, a more nuanced account might acknowledge that the origins of Uncle Charlie's transgressive villainy lie in an unstable mixture of Nietzschean, puritan, heterodox Catholic, Sadean, and Gnostic elements.

There are certainly echoes of Gnosticism in Uncle Charlie's world-view: Gnostics believed that the accepted Christian account of creation is wrong. They argued that the world was created by an incompetent and malign being called the demiurge (an aborted emanation from the goddess of wisdom, Sophia). The demiurge is, in effect, a false God who is malign and incompetent. The demiurge created a botched world, filled with wars, famine, diseases, natural disasters, corruption, crime, and murder. However, there is still a divine spark inside human beings that contains the possibility of enlightenment as to the true state of the world and provides an idea of what the true God stands for (Holroyd 1994; Jonas 2001).

As the Gnostic account of creation was driven underground, Gnostics themselves came to see themselves as elite visionaries who alone comprehended the truth of the world. Young Charlie tells her Uncle that she knows he has "a secret" he is keeping from her. When Uncle Charlie tells his niece that the world is foul sty, he reveals the scandalous truth to her and echoes the Gnostic contempt for material existence.

Heroic Satans and Other Hitchcockian Heresies 69

Figure 3.1. *Shadow of a Doubt*—the world is a foul sty.

Although Blake, Goethe, Melville, Existentialism, and Jung have all been aligned with the Gnostic worldview, perhaps film noir is the most suggestive hint of the survival of this form of heresy (e.g., Woolfolk 2006). Robin Wood is right up to a point to suggest that *Shadow of a Doubt* cannot resolve the ideological conflict that results from a collision between the small-town film and the film noir. However, as Orr (2005) and Naremore (1999) have pointed out, Hitchcock's films differ from the conventions of film noir in important respects. Orr sees Hitchcock's emphasis on the *homme fatale* as one of these key differences:

> In Hitchcock the resistant suspicious heroine faces off the *homme fatale*: personified by Grant in *Suspicion* and *Notorious* as the unreadable face of male intention that is matched by Cotten in *Shadow of a Doubt*, by Peck in the opening of *Spellbound* and at a fascinating tangent, by Montgomery Clift in *I Confess*. Yet Hitchcock's *homme fatale* is a case study in ambivalence—witness *Suspicion*. (Orr 2005, 159)

Another example of the *homme fatale* in Hitchcock would be Johnny Cooper (Richard Todd) in *Stage Fright*, who is paired off against Charlotte Inwood (Marlene Dietrich) in a classic piece of role reversal.

John Russell Taylor, author of a biography of Hitchcock, has recently revealed that Hitchcock was concerned that he would turn out gay. Hitchcock told the playwright Rodney Ackland, "I think I would have been a poof if I hadn't met Alma at the right time" (Timesonline 2008). Given this information, it would not be surprising if the attractive male tempter carried more than a little extra freight for Hitchcock. In this context, it is also significant that Wilder himself is now thought by some to have been gay (Samuel Steward, Wilder's close friend, is widely reckoned to have been his lover). If we entertain the idea that Hitchcock himself was fascinated by the idea of the Romantic hero-satan, with Nietzschean overtones, does he then apply this idea of villainy with any consistency? Certainly, we could find other examples of such hero-satans in Hitchcock's films: Bruno Anthony in *Strangers on a Train* is an obvious example. Brandon Shaw in *Rope* would make the connection with Nietzsche as explicit as it's possible to make it. Yet there is scant evidence that Hitchcock endorsed the idea of the Nietzschean superman, whose actions are beyond good and evil, with any consistency. One has only to look at the pathos with which other villains are represented to see that Hitchcock was far from rejecting Judeo-Christian morality in favour of a Nietzschean revaluation of all values. Pathos and victimhood were anathema to Nietzsche, yet in various ways we are invited to sympathize with characters such as Otto Keller in *I Confess*, Alex Sebastian in *Notorious*, Verloc in *Sabotage*, and even, of course, Norman Bates—all of them had mitigating circumstances and might be equally seen as victims. Mrs. Danvers in *Rebecca*, Lars Thorwald in *Rear Window*, Gromek in *Torn Curtain* (1966), Tracy in *Blackmail*, and Fry in *Saboteur* are not blueprints for a master race. Rather, they are sad specimens of humanity. The humanism and sentiment with which Hitchcock and his writers treat the demise of these characters is totally out of keeping with a Nietzschean worldview. It is more likely with his upbringing that Hitchcock felt the temptation or seductive quality of such ideas: certainly this is a nexus at which ideology and sexuality seem to coincide quite obviously.

An assumption now buried deep in Hitchcock studies is that Hitchcock's films form some kind of unity and that they are bound together by a consistent worldview or creative vision, or at least one whose contradictions are consistent. In place of the idea that there is a consistent worldview in the films, perhaps it would be more useful to think of themes and motifs in the films using the terminology that Antonio Gramsci used to describe common sense: "disjointed and episodic" (1971,

324). Although it would be mistaken to dismiss the ultimate centrality of Hitchcock to his films, it is notable that some kind of auteurist view of Hitchcock and his films has persisted for so long in the face of growing evidence that it obscures as much as it reveals. It is only comparatively recently that book-length studies have been dedicated to the contribution of Hitchcock's writers. *English Hitchcock* (1999) by Charles Barr is the first study to use detailed empirical research to show the extent to which Hitchcock's early films were collaborations. But the most important attempt to demolish the myth of Hitchcock's auteurism is *Hitchcock at Work* by Bill Krohn. In this study, Krohn's approach is to treat each film as an experiment and a collaborative endeavour. As such, the drift of this kind of criticism is to emphasize the singularity of each film, not necessarily what they share in common. It is quite sobering to learn that the crop duster sequence in *North by Northwest* was visually conceived by writer Ernest Lehman, and that the shower sequence in *Psycho* was at least partly the work of designer Saul Bass. If Hitchcock's authorship and the view of him as a control freak have become an article of faith, Krohn's book is an impressive work of heresy. In the last few years, it has become increasingly apparent that far too little attention has been given to Hitchcock's collaborators (producers, writers, composers, and technicians) and that Hitchcock's films can be viewed productively as quite inconsistent and contradictory.

Shadow of a Doubt, for instance, does not merely reveal Hitchcock's gaze on America, it also reveals that of Wilder. As Krohn has clearly demonstrated, others brought things to the picnic, in spite of Hitchcock's efforts to persuade us to the contrary. To explain the various strands of his work, scholars would be better off looking first at his opportunistic borrowing of conventions from popular genres, second at the ways in which his films were industrial collaborations, rather than works of art, and third at the broad cultural history of ideas itself.

To conclude, it's worth returning briefly to the Marquis de Sade, whose words open this chapter. Hitchcock lived through an era in which de Sade's work underwent reevaluation and, to some extent, rehabilitation, most pertinently through the efforts of the surrealists. Hitchcock was a keen admirer of Buñuel, who was interested in de Sade. The Sadean challenge is how to rescue conventional morality from his powerful charges of double standards and hypocrisy. Our daily consumption of coldness and cruelty dealt out by the media cannot simply be explained or excused under cover of concern for others. The supposition that we all have sadistic and masochistic desires actually makes for a more persuasive account of how, for instance, the frequent scenes of torture in a Hitchcockian suspense thriller such as *24* come to be consumed as entertainment. In seeking to judge the morality of Hitchcock and Hitchcock's films, as Spoto and others have done, we should be careful lest they end up judging us. Or, to put it another way, in the immortal words of Stella (Thelma Ritter) in *Rear Window* (scripted, of course, by the very talented John Michael Hayes): "We've become a race of Peeping Toms. What people ought to do is get outside their own house and look in for a change."

Notes

My sincere thanks to Professor Peter Evans, who suggested that I follow up links between Hitchcock, Buñuel, and De Sade.

1. The exhibition is discussed in Christine Sprengler's book *Hitchcock and Contemporary Art* (2014).

2. For an influential discussion of these terms, see Georges Canguillhem, *The Normal and the Pathological* (1991).

3. The trial of Oscar Wilde also hinged partly on the question of whether the author's works could be taken as evidence of his own immorality.

4. Perhaps, even more pointedly, Schopenhauer's insistence that "there really resides in the heart of each of us a wild beast which only waits the opportunity to rage and rave and injure others, and which, if they do not prevent it, would like to destroy them" (in Copplestone 2003, 253).

5. The literary critic William Empson wrote a book called *Milton's God* (1979) in which he interpreted God as a bully and a usurper. Also relevant here is the short story by Jorge Luis Borges "Three Versions of Judas" (1962) in which a biblical scholar hypothesizes three ways in which Judas might be considered more righteous than Jesus. In the third version, it is suggested that Judas may have been the mortal incarnation of God himself:

6. God became a man completely, a man to the point of infamy, a man to the point of being reprehensible—all the way to the abyss. In order to save us, He could have chosen any of the destinies which together weave the uncertain web of history; He could have been Alexander, or Pythagoras, or Rurik, or Jesus; He chose an infamous destiny: He was Judas (Borges 1962, 156).

I am indebted to Peter Evans for pointing out these examples.

Works Cited

Barr, Charles. *English Hitchcock*. Moffat, UK: Cameron and Hollis, 1999.
Borges, Jorge Luis. *Ficciones*. New York: Grove Press, 1962.
Canguillhem, Georges. *The Normal and the Pathological*. Trans. Carolyn R. Fawcett and Robert S. Cohen, foreword by Michel Foucault. New York: Zone Books, 1991.
Copplestone, Frederick. *A History of Philosophy: 18th and 19th Century Philosophy, Volume 7*. New York: Continuum, 2003.

Eliot, T.S. "Tradition and the Individual Talent," reprinted in *Perspecta: The Yale Architectural Journal*, vol. 19 (1982): 36–42.
Empson, William. *Milton's God*. New York: Praeger, 1979.
Gottlieb, Sidney. *Hitchcock on Hitchcock: Selected Writings and Interviews*. Los Angeles: University of California Press, 1997.
Gramsci, Antonio. *The Prison Notebooks*. London: Lawrence and Wishart, 1971.
Haeffner, Nicholas. *Alfred Hitchcock*. Essex: Pearson, 2005.
———. "From Auteurs to Digital Amateurs: Exploring Vertigo, New Media and Gender Controversies with Repossessed" http://www.re-possessed.com/watermanscatalogue/catalogue/nick_repossessed.pdf
Holroyd, Stephen. *The Elements of Gnosticism*. Dorset, UK: Element, 1994.
Indick, William. *Psychology for Screenwriters: Building Conflict in Your Script*. California: Michael Wiese Productions, 2004.
Jonas, Hans. *The Gnostic Religion*. Boston: Beacon Press, 2001.
Klossowski, Pierre. *Sade, My Neighbour*. Trans. Alphonso Lingis. Evanston, IL: Northwestern UP, 1991.
Konkle, Lincoln. *Thornton Wilder and Puritan Narrative Tradition*. Columbia: University of Missouri Press. 2006.
Leitch, Thomas, *Hitchcock's Villains*. http://www.labyrinth.net.au/~muffin/villains_c.html
McGilligan, Patrick. *Alfred Hitchcock: A Life in Darkness and Light*. New York: Harper, 2004.
———. Lecture on Alfred Hitchcock at Hillsdale College, Michigan, 2008.
Milton, John. *Paradise Lost*. Introduction by Philip Pullman. Oxford: Oxford UP, 2005.
Naremore, James. "Hitchcock at the Margins of Noir" in Allen and Ishii-Gonzales (eds.), *Alfred Hitchcock: Centenary Essays*. London: BFI, 1999.
Nietzsche, Friedrich. *Beyond Good and Evil*. Trans. R.J. Hollingdale. Harmondsworth, UK: Penguin, 2003.
Orr, John. *Hitchcock and 20th Century Cinema*. NY: Wallflower Press, 2005.
Praz, Mario. *The Romantic Agony*. Oxford: Oxford UP, 1970.
Russell Taylor, John. "Was Hitchcock a Misogynist? He Was Adored by Actresses." Timesonline, 6 September, http://entertainment.timesonline.co.uk/tol/arts_and_entertainment/film/article4666530.ece
San Juan, Eric, and Jim McDevitt. *Hitchcock's Villains: Murderers, Maniacs and Mother Issues*. Lanham, MD: The Scarecrow Press, 2013.
Sprengler, Christine. *Hitchcock and Contemporary Art*. New York: Palgrave Macmillan, 2014.
Truffaut, Francois. *Hitchcock by Truffaut*. London: Paladin, 1986.
Williams, Raymond. *Culture and Society*. New York: Columbia UP, 1983.
Wood, Robin. *Hitchcock's Films*. London: Faber, 1989.
Woolfolk, A. "The Horizon of Disenchantment: Film Noir, Camus and the Vicissitudes of Descent" in Mark T. Conrad (ed.), *The Philosophy of Film Noir*. Lexington: University of Kentucky Press, 2006.

4

Brian McFarlane

Guilt, Confession, and . . . Then What?

The Paradine Case and *Under Capricorn*

TWO BEAUTIFUL WOMEN HAVE been involved with murder. Each excites the passionate involvement of a man who is meant to be helping her to deal with the facts of her guilty past. Each will confess—one in private, the other as publicly as possible—to her crime. If there is a kind of redemption involved in each it takes widely different forms. These women are Maddelena Paradine and Henrietta Flusky, "heroines"—to use the term in its loosest sense—of, respectively, Alfred Hitchcock's *The Paradine Case* (1948) and *Under Capricorn* (1949), two of his most neglected works.

These two films, made in a comparative lull in Hitchcock's career, have in hindsight a good deal in common. Neither was notably successful at the time of its release. Those accounts of Hitchcock that treat him as a master of suspense, as though this were his chief claim to fame, will not be likely to number these two films among his greatest achievements. Such appraisals, though, fail to do justice to the often subtle moral discriminations the films exhibit. The popular view of him as an entertainer probably accounts for the comparative neglect of *The Paradine Case* and *Under Capricorn*. These are not films that trade in suspense and surprise as key elements, though that is not to say that they are wholly without moments that can shock us. However, their main interest seems to me to lie in the quite intricate play of guilt between characters, and the ways in which confession is less straightforwardly a matter of cleansing than simpler-minded philosophers might have us believe.

These films have several things in common, apart from their lack of commercial popularity and critical regard at the time of their appearance. For one thing, both are adapted from somewhat old-fashioned novels, and in this they are typical of Hitchcock's dealings with the literary. He virtually never attacks major literary fictions, those novels or plays that may be said to articulate complex moral interactions. Rather, he has characteristically addressed himself to popular novels, as if preferring to impose—or work out through them—his own moral vision. *Sabotage* (1936), his version of Joseph Conrad's *The Secret Agent*, is perhaps his nearest brush with the literary. In the instances of *The Paradine Case* and *Under Capricorn*, he has drawn on competent middle-brow fictions, by Robert Hichens and Helen Simpson, respectively, and used each of them as a basis for his own explorations of moral sensibilities.

I'd want to add here that these two novels both testify to the seductive potential of such middle-brow novels with their strong plot-lines and their distinctive character drawing. Both novels, in fact, seem to me to stand up surprisingly well to being read more than a half-century after their first publication, *The Paradine Case* in 1933 and *Under Capricorn* in 1937. Hitchcock told François Truffaut: "What I do is read a story once, and, if I like the basic idea, I just forget all about the book and start to create cinema" (49). This is typically ungenerous (not to say disingenuous) in his way of writing off his indebtedness to his sources, and in this case I'd say he has taken a good deal more than "the basic idea": in his version of *Under Capricorn* he seems to have swallowed its "Book One" (a little short of half its length) intact; and it is at least arguable that Hichens's five-hundred-page *Paradine Case* is a more subtle and demanding work than the adapted film. However, that is another issue: we are not here concerned with arguing the relative merits of novel and film, but rather with what Hitchcock has made of them in terms of constructing dramas of moral complexity.

In the latter respect, one notes that both films—and indeed the novels from which they are derived—are also concerned with cross-class liaisons. In each a woman in a superior social position is drawn into a passionate attachment with a man in her—or her family's—employ. And in each case a murder takes place in which the guilty feelings of the woman concerned will complicate the outcome of the crime. The situation in each case spirals out so that another man, not initially involved in the crime, will be drawn to the woman, and both films are concerned to make distinctions relating to the place of sexual passion in the moral spectrum, acknowledging in both the difficulty that such passion will make for a man who also wants to act honorably. My aim is to examine these two films from the point of view of how far they go beyond genre expectations to put before us works of serious moral texture. This is not necessarily to argue for overlooked-masterpiece status, but to explore the kinds of distinction they offer.

∾

In Robert Hichens's novel, as in Hitchcock's film, Mrs. Paradine's guilt leads to confession, to a kind of absolution and to a suicide. The novel—published in 1933 and out of print since the late 1950s, as far as I can discover—is extremely long, belonging perhaps to a period in which there was more time and inclination to read novels of such length. It is remarkably and absorbingly detailed in putting before us the lives of its main characters, giving a complex sense of the tensions in those lives and a minutely documented account of the trial.

Essentially, as the title suggests, Hichens is concerned with a court case and how this resonates among the principals of the novel. The title also suggests that Mrs. Paradine, on trial for the murder of her husband, a blinded World War One hero, is at the novel's center; so, from one point of view, she is. However, the book's real fascination lies in the way in which she becomes the rallying point for at least five relationships, in all of which guilt in some measure will play its part. We know of what went on between Mrs. Paradine and her husband only from what she tells us and from the testimony of Marsh (Latour in the film), her husband's valet. Hichens keeps the reader guessing as to how far either of these can be believed. She has been her husband's "eyes," and he has been sometimes difficult to deal with in the frustration of his life. Marsh, his wartime batman and now his valet, appears to have a ferocious devotion to his master and a misogynistic distaste for women. The testimonies of Marsh and Mrs. Paradine in court are, like the rest of the trial, given in engrossing detail, and only toward the end does she make clear to her counsel, Sir Malcolm Keane, that she loves Marsh and "must not be saved at his expense" (430), that theirs has been a passionate attachment. The motives for their respective statements in court are complex, partly concerned with protection of the other and partly with the urge to self-protect.

The other relationships that contribute to the novel's texture include that between Keane and his client, with whom he becomes obsessively involved personally as well as professionally. "Your case is my life," he tells her (203), but he is also in sexual thrall to her. His wife, Gay, is increasingly aware of this, and the strain on their once apparently rock-solid marriage becomes the basis for the book's main interest. She recognizes "the overmastering love" (519) Mrs. Paradine has felt for Marsh, and this acts as a parallel for Keane's passion for his client. The fifth of these relationships that feels the pressure of this case is that between the sadistic, lascivious presiding judge, Lord Horfield, and his nervous wife who fears the effect on her husband if he hands down a death sentence. There are powerful overtones of guilty feelings in all these relationships, and Hichens has the space to deal with them exhaustively, as Hitchcock will not.

Hitchcock starts his film with Mrs. Paradine herself, rather than with Keane, and is perhaps already signaling a different emphasis from Hichens's. Her "otherness" is now not Scandinavian, as in the novel, but Italian to accommodate producer David O. Selznick's star, Valli,[1] and from the outset she establishes an air of dignified breeding that invites the arresting officer, Inspector Ambrose (Lester Matthews), to treat her with respect. At once an element of class intervenes: she may be a murderess, but she is also a "lady," and she remains impressively calm both at home and in interview at the police station. Legal adviser Sir Simon Flaquer (Charles Coburn) reinforces this situation when he tells her, "You won't need to waste words telling me the police are making a terrible mistake." He can have no grounds for such confidence other than that she seems to belong to the wrong class for homicide.

The film necessarily has to pare down the strands it can afford to develop. However, the first scene in which Keane (Gregory Peck) arrives home to be greeted by his wife Gay (Ann Todd) establishes the arena for the other main conflict of the film. While Gay mixes cocktails, she talks about how "Nice people don't go about murdering other people," but Keane gently derides her for her "delusions about nice people." After he has bathed, she dries his hair, hidden in a towel, as she talks, and he pulls her on to his lap. This episode is intended to give us insight into the Keanes's marriage, but it is skimpy compared to the intense interest and detail Hichens offered. If their marital harmony is to be profoundly disturbed by his finding Mrs. Paradine "strangely attractive," there is also another teasing influence at work on it. Judge Horfield (Charles Laughton) makes advances to Gay at a dinner party, his gaze resting on her bare shoulder. He then goes to sit by her and tells her she looks "appetizing," and he takes her hand in a way that makes her uneasy and

Figure 4.1. *Paradine Case*—Judge Gay (Charles Laughton) advances.

causes her to break away from him. Hitchcock, in this brief exchange, indicates Horfield's awareness of her distaste, but oddly enough the film fails to follow up this tantalizing lead, as Hichens does, in relation to Keane's dependence on keeping on side with Horfield in the trial.

The sort of guilt the film is concerned with has several manifestations. Keane's guilty passion for Mrs. Paradine causes him to imperil his married state, almost snapping at Gay, who wants them to "get away" for a while to celebrate their anniversary. "Some things are more important than anniversaries," he replies, as he plans to travel up north to view the Paradines' house—and not to take Gay with him. "I want to keep all this ugly business away from you," he tries, his guilt growing. "But can you?" she asks. His guilt is a matter of having let his professional duties become clouded by his private feelings. Gay knows this, knows he's infatuated, but plays the only card she can: "I'll be waiting here . . . cozy, comfortable and protected" when he comes back from Cumberland. While up north (and a very Hollywood idea of rural England it is), Keane steeps himself in Mrs. Paradine's world, lingers in her bedroom, in which her portrait is found in an oval frame set in the bedstead and seems to follow Keane around the room as the camera prowls suggestively. Back in his inn room, he engages in a curiously combative scene of verbal fencing with the valet Latour (Louis Jourdan). To Keane, Latour is not merely a potentially hostile witness but is resented on the grounds of possibly being Mrs. Paradine's lover. As another element in the film's account of gender relations, Latour assures Keane "I would never have served a woman." (One notes in passing the casting of Jourdan, another Selznick hopeful, the nationality of Colonel Paradine's valet being somewhat improbably changed to accommodate the producer's investment. Certainly, though, Hichens makes much of the character's good looks, and Jourdan more than adequately measures up in this respect, though Hitchcock told Truffaut he wanted someone "horny-handed," someone like Robert Newton [Truffaut 129].)

The film's chief interest, for me at least, is in its comparison of various kinds and degrees of guilt and how these are articulated and worked through. Mrs. Paradine's is explicitly stated and will lead to her public confession in court. When she learns that Latour has "done away with himself," the camera rests on her reaction, and records her confession: "What does it matter now? . . . The man I loved is dead." Following this is her bitter rebuke to Keane: "My life is finished. My only comfort is the hatred and contempt I feel for you." As Keane leaves the court, an overhead shot stresses his desolation and exposure: his guilt and its aftermath are more complex than Mrs. Paradine's. She may be hanged; he will be alive but with no prospect of either confession or easy expiation. The sort of upbeat support, the promise of redemption, that Gay offers him in the last scene—"The most important moment in your life is now . . . I want you back on the job just as fast as ever you can"—seems jejune in the face of the moral torment he has been through. More telling is the film's penultimate scene in which Lady Horfield (Ethel Barrymore, very eloquent in her brief scenes) talks nervously to her husband about guilt and her wish that Mrs. Paradine be not punished. In her fluttering way, she has signaled a moral subtlety denied to either her husband or to Keane. Donald Spoto is right to claim that "[t]his is a powerful sequence because of its emotional content and its delineation of one man's callousness and a woman's sensitivity" (182).

The function of the women in this film is primarily that of offering support of one kind or other to men. Mrs. Paradine has been her husband's "eyes," prior to murdering him. Lady Horfield loves and fears her husband; Judy Flaquer (Joan Tetzel) is an intelligent sounding-board for her father and a close and clever friend to Gay Keane; and Gay's main purpose is to be there whenever Keane chooses to consult her. Perhaps the role of Gay is underwritten, or maybe Ann Todd fails to suggest the kind of wife Gay has been, in spite of what she told me in interview: that Hitchcock had wanted her "to be the most exciting person in the film" (561). For whatever reason, for the most part there doesn't seem to be enough at stake in the Keanes's relationship. (It is also arguable that Gregory Peck doesn't persuasively convey the torment of mind we are required to assume. John Russell Taylor claims that he was cast against Hitchcock's wishes (196). This is borne out by Peck's biographer [Freedland 90].) The one sequence in which Todd is given enough rope, as it were, is that in which she urges Keane on with "I want you to win this case. I want you to set her free." There is a moment of clear-eyed honesty as she asserts the need for the "fight"—for Keane's love—to be an even one, and the camera focuses on Keane's face furrowed with uncertainty. If, instead of settling for the more conventionally optimistic ending mentioned above, Hitchcock had pushed this kind of moral issue harder the overall film might have seemed more satisfying. The film is nonjudgmental about the matter of jealousy, whether Gay's of Mrs. Paradine or Keane's of Latour; its more compelling concern is, at least potentially, with how that jealousy is dealt with, how it is contextualized in the network of relationships.

To turn to *Under Capricorn*, one is first reminded of that remark quoted above about how Hitchcock simply took the "basic idea" from a novel. In fact, the film version of *Under Capricorn* reproduces the events and relationships of the first half of Helen Simpson's novel almost intact. Thereafter, the screenplay (the work of Hume Cronyn and James Bridie) departs quite sharply from the original, which introduces an important character (Susan Quaife) that the film dispenses with. Further, Hitchcock's film focuses much more single-mindedly on the emotional network that entraps these four: the guilty Lady Henrietta (Ingrid Bergman); the husband, Sam Flusky (Joseph Cotten), who has initially borne the burden of her guilt; the visiting sprig of an Irish county family, Charles Adare (Michael Wilding), who helps to restore Henrietta to some sort of health, while falling guiltily in love with her; and the treacherous housekeeper, Milly (Margaret Leighton), who nurses a secret passion for Flusky. As we shall see, there is some rearrangement of these quadrangular connections in the film, but whereas these four are also central to the novel the latter displays them in a much more fully realized context of the burgeoning colony.

Most obviously, perhaps, Adare doesn't leave the colony at the end, but has—in a demotic touch appropriate to the new country—found love with the daughter, Susan, of a former hangman-turned-barber. There is a suggestion that their cross-class union, a mirror reflection of the Henrietta-Flusky marriage, should be seen as offering hope for the future of a country where a person's worth will be measured by what he is and does, not by the stratum of society into which he has been born. Adare is a distant cousin of the Governor who, having adapted to the post he took up at the start of the novel, concedes: "Charles is a misfit in England, in Ireland he is lost in the crowd; but he may do very well if he lives." That final phrase, "if he lives," refers to the near-fatal expedition Adare has embarked on in search of rivers and gold, a narrative element the film omits. Its concern, as suggested above, is with the lives lived in close-up, not with the broader picture, let alone with the indigenous population that is virtually unglimpsed in the film.

Hitchcock has extracted from Simpson's tale a romantic melodrama, only vestigially concerned with historical events or verisimilitude. The opening shots of Sydney, incorporating what are clearly handsomely painted backcloths, accompanied by Richard Addinsell's lush score, set the tone for the film's generic affiliations. In brief, in the film (as in the novel), Sam Flusky has been transported from Ireland to Australia for killing in self-defense the brother of Lady Henrietta Considine. Flusky has been a groom in her family's stables; he and Henrietta have run away together; and when the brother pursues them, it is Henrietta, not Flusky, who has shot him, but Flusky has protected her by assuming her guilt. Or as much of it as can be reached by the law. Henrietta has followed him to Australia, waited for his release and married him, from reasons both of love and expiation. Adare, cousin of the colony's governor, recognizes her at a dinner at the now-prosperous Flusky's imposing mansion, and helps her back toward health and away from the grip of alcoholism, into which she has been precipitated by the self-righteous Milly, as well as by her own sense of guilt and inadequacy.

Like Mrs. Paradine, Henrietta lives with a guilty secret: each has killed; each has loved across the class divide; and each will capture the love of another man whose aim is to help her. Whereas Keane aims to save Mrs. Paradine's life through the exercise of his professional skills, Charles Adare represents a kind of saving sanity and health to Henrietta because he comes bearing resonances of the class and life she has forfeited by coming to New South Wales in her attempt to make some amends to Flusky. Flusky has made an enormous sacrifice to save her: he has been transported for seven years, been a member of a chain gang in the colony, and been flogged. As an emancipist, he has prospered and become a substantial landowner, but he has not won social acceptance in the colony, nor indeed sought it, withdrawing for the most part into his own shell, abrupt and taciturn in his social dealings.

The film makes plain in a dinner party scene that mere wealth will not buy him the position he wants as long as the old British-inherited *mores* persist. One by one the men he has invited, men of some standing in the fledgling society, arrive bearing excuses from their wives. Flusky may have some importance in the economic structure of the colony, and, in view of this, the morality of the men has been flexible enough to enable them to overcome any repugnance they may feel at his history. Indeed, very early in the film Adare has been warned: "We don't talk too much about the past here." Perhaps the men do not, but their wives, with less to occupy them and less reason to ingratiate themselves with Flusky, clearly do so, and they have their suspicions about Henrietta. Twenty-five minutes into the film, Henrietta makes her first appearance. Hitchcock takes his lead here from Simpson, who writes: ". . . her bare feet were shod with ancient red slippers that flapped as she moved. She looked like a goddess careless of human clothing, or some heroine of antiquity run nobly mad" (39). Does any other of Hitchcock's heroines make a more striking first appearance than Bergman does here, shot feet first in closeup, giving way to a sort of ravaged glamour that survives her obvious drunkenness? (It does, of course, recall fleetingly her unease in *Notorious*.) Her ease with Adare (there is an "Irish" strain to the film's score at this point as "Charlie" and "Lady Hetty" recall their earlier friendship) contrasts with the stiffness of the other guests and the pain of Sam Flusky's shame at what he has brought her to—and hers at what she has done to his life. She and Sam, she a (minor) aristocrat, he a groom, exhibit in their largely unspoken dealings with and concern for each other a subtler and more compassionate morality than anyone else in the film.

In a film of striking parallelisms, sometimes for contrast, sometimes for comparison's sake, none is more moving or more crucial to *Under Capricorn*'s emotional core than the two versions of what has brought Flusky and Henrietta to their present situation. Since each version has Adare for its audience, it is clear that we are meant to have them in mind together when we think of the film as a whole, and when Adare takes his leave of the colony at the end. Each involves a long and surprisingly moving exposition. The usually taciturn Flusky explains that he has invited Adare to the dinner party in the hope that the "ladies" of the colony might be lured by the promise of meeting the Governor's cousin. "I can buy gentlemen in packets of a dozen," he claims, but he has wanted the ladies to be present so that Henrietta can meet "some of her own sort." He speaks of the sacrifice that she has made in following him to New South Wales to await his release, a "sacrifice" that we understand is a matter of atonement on her part. With touching candor he tells Adare that, though they married, "There was nothing to talk about that we wanted to talk about," but it is plain that he has never stopped loving her, and there is generosity in his contemplation of a new life for her based on the "old times" Adare comes trailing in his wake.

Henrietta's own narrative to Adare, after the fiasco of the Government House St. Patrick's Day Ball, is one of the great set pieces in the Hitchcock oeuvre, staged in a remarkable long take, back at the Flusky mansion. Adare, trying to explain Flusky's aggressive behavior at the ball, urges: "He's jealous of your world," and jealousy of one kind or another plays its part in the film. But Henrietta is not to be swayed by the moral escape route this seems to offer her. She speaks openly of her guilt, as explicitly as Mrs. Paradine has done in court, and with real poignancy explains how she trusted Sam in the old Irish past, but how she has been "wrong to marry him" because she has not been able to give him children. Atonement is what she has intended, atonement "to make up

Figure 4.2. *Under Capricorn*—anguish and atonement.

for all that he had suffered." She has tried to make a home for him and believes she has failed, though we by now know she has been undermined by Milly's insidious malice, but "Sam is part of me forever . . . Nothing can change that." When Adare tries to persuade her to leave with him, urging that "You owe him [Sam] nothing," her reply indicates the depths of feeling and obligation between her and Sam: "If you understood, you could not talk of debts."

This scene precipitates the film's denouement when Flusky returns home and finds Adare with his arms around Henrietta, orders him out of the house, and accidentally shoots him when he returns after the horse bearing him back to Sydney has fallen. Much of the writing about the film has concentrated—and rightly so—on Bergman's performance. As Robin Wood, writing particularly of this film, claims, "The essential Bergman thematic, however complex its realization in specific texts, might be summed up in a simple formula: the attempt (usually by men) to destroy Ingrid Bergman's smile, and its final, triumphant restoration" (316). In this case, the smile is first restored by Adare and is finally in place as she stands by Flusky to farewell Adare.

And, yes, faces can be signifiers of moral and emotional states as revealing as words. This being so, I draw attention to the skillful use the film makes of the Flusky/Cotten and Adare/Wilding visages. In their first meeting, one is struck by the apparent contrast in ages and experiences as "written" in Cotten's morose, furrowed countenance and Wilding's blandly smiling, unlined face that seems indeed waiting for greater maturity to do its work. As the film proceeds, one remembers this initial contrast. In the sequence referred to above, when Flusky tells his version of the past to Adare, he ends with a quiet smile as he thinks of a happier Henrietta, while Adare has been brought to an unwonted seriousness as he listens. While Adare has an inborn ease of manner, evinced in the dinner party sequence, Flusky may lack social grace but exerts the authority of a commanding presence. The visual contrasting detail is carried through in their temperamental and moral differences and in the way their respective backgrounds have shaped them and the ways in which they deal with their experience.

In the end, they will each be marked by sacrifice. Flusky's love for Henrietta has years ago led him to make the massive sacrifice of his freedom, leaving her with a burden of guilt and gratitude; indeed, Flusky can say with some truth to Henrietta, "All along we've sacrificed ourselves for each other." Adare's love for Henrietta is in a sense a betrayal of the trust both she and Flusky have accorded him, but in returning to England at film's end he too is making a sacrifice of sorts. He will have to make a difficult moral decision and submit to the unaccustomed experience of placing the prospect of someone else's happiness before his own. Lesley Brill has argued that: "Because he is fooling himself as well as others, Charles Adare practises the most complete deceit in *Under Capricorn*. His wish to help Hettie becomes indistinguishable from his unholy desire to prize her away from Flusky . . . He leaves New South Wales with a self-knowledge and maturity that he lacked when he arrived" (252). Flusky's dilemma is that, as it seems, he can save himself only by sacrificing Henrietta. Adare's is that, if he loves Henrietta, he will exonerate her and renounce all emotional claims on her. As we have seen, this is a departure in the film from Simpson's novel, and arguably a move in a more conventional direction. However, Hitchcock is making a romantic melodrama, not a historical romance that needs to end on a note of hope for civilization in a new setting, as distinct from the film's needs to find an emotional closure for its principals.

This pattern of contrasting behaviors and appearances is not limited to the Flusky-Adare pair. Each of Henrietta and Milly is allowed a long soliloquy, the former's to Adare, as we have seen, the latter's to Flusky, to whom she makes up as overtly as she dares. Bergman's lush beauty, even when presented in *déshabille*, is used to suggest an emotional and moral openness at odds with Leighton's trim tightness and averted looks as she contemplates the effects of her words. Henrietta gives Milly her due (and the film's mise-en-scène supports this) for the smooth running of the Flusky household, whereas Milly undermines *her* with alcohol and innuendo—and the smooth expressionlessness of her face.

The class issue, highlighted in several key scenes, such as the dinner party at the Flusky mansion and the Governor's Ball, is further concentrated in the "pairings" of Flusky and Milly, Henrietta and Adare. Milly plays on the sense of class inequality as she tries to turn Flusky not only against Adare but also against Henrietta, and at one point Flusky concedes in discussion with Adare, "Maybe Miss Milly and I look at things in another way" [a "way" distinct from Adare's and Henrietta's]. While she and Flusky may share an inferior social class, they are not morally similar: where Milly works toward her own ends, Flusky has an element of the selfless, even of the heroic. There is certainly class jealousy at work in Flusky when he accuses Henrietta of wanting to return to Ireland with her "fancy man" Adare, and in his scornful references to "gentlemen" whom he sees as operating some kind of esoteric club. And yet it is Henrietta's recognition in Adare of something recalling her past life in Ireland that begins her return from the brink of alcoholism and possible insanity.

This matter of class inequity surfaces in *The Paradine Case*, in the heroine's passion for her husband's valet, but it is crudely articulated by comparison with its representation in *Under Capricorn*. Nevertheless, I think it is true to say that both these films deserve more detailed and sympathetic treatment than they have commonly received. They each deal not only in the subtleties and cruelties of class but also in those relating to the situation of women in intensely patriarchal societies. In *The Paradine Case* it is probably true to say that the women are more insightful than the men, who are too blinkered by the demands of their professional roles to understand their own most profound conflicts of mind. Even the benign Flaquer (the film dispenses, interestingly, with his Jewishness) is outflanked in a discussion with his clever daughter, who intuits more sharply than her solicitor father that Keane has gone to Cumberland for a jealous confrontation with Paradine's valet. "Tony [Keane—more solidly "Malcolm" in the novel] is in love with that woman.... The best men always end up with the worst women," she claims, and her friendship for Kay is the truest bond of affection in the film. Her father's only partly jocose rebuke to her is: "I don't know how you came by this decidedly unfeminine interest in things." As for Lady Horfield, she had been bullied into quivering verbal inconsequence by her husband, but he can't quite quell her compassionate perceptions. As Wood has written of this film, "the attitude to marriage is remarkably . . . bleak and skeptical" (244). In *Under Capricorn*, Henrietta is the only fully drawn female character but, between them, Hitchcock and Bergman (underpinned by the screenplay's density in evoking her inner world) make something very affecting about this damaged woman in a society that has allowed women little scope. There is less mitigating detail in the character of Milly for Margaret Leighton to work on, but she is able to suggest a competence which, in other circumstances, might have served her well, and invests Milly's "sanctimonious hypocrisy" with a steely urge to self-promotion (Brill 97).

 It is not my purpose to offer definitive reappraisals of these two films. What I have wanted to do is to indicate some of the kinds of interest they have to offer, even if they seem at some remove from the director's master works that would follow. Their tensions are not so much associated with the creation of suspense, which is for many the hallmark of Hitchcock the entertainer. There are striking moments in each—Mrs. Paradine's confession from the dock; Henrietta's appearance on the stairs in her ball gown—but it is apt to be the smaller effects that linger in the mind: Lady Horfield's nervous cough in court, attracting an oblique look from her husband, the judge; a closeup of Flusky's hands from behind as he quietly secretes the ruby necklace he has bought to complete Henrietta's ball costume, she and Adare having dismissed rubies as inapt adornment, not knowing Flusky has bought them. This is not to undervalue the bravura effects of, say, the play of light and dark in *The Paradine Case* (notice how neither Keane nor Mrs. Paradine is seen in full light in their early interviews, whereas her face is in full light when she denounces him in court, or the dramatic cutting in the court scenes) or of Henrietta's extraordinary self-revealing soliloquy as the camera circles her and the listening Adare. *The Paradine Case* may well be seen as an over-talkative piece—and indeed much of it is developed in duologues—but it takes an imaginative director to show us the Old Bailey from an angle that stresses postwar damage, as if to imply that the very legal system is in ruins and will prove inadequate to this case.

These are two films with guilty heroines, both of whom confess their wrongdoing, but in *The Paradine Case* the woman's guilt will lead to her death, whereas in *Under Capricorn* it leads to redemption. It brings relief to Henrietta and new hope; to Mrs. Paradine it may bring relief but also spells the end of hope. There are tougher moral challenges and dilemmas in *Under Capricorn* and it, in consequence, keeps the firmer hold on our emotional attention. Neither film, though, deserves to be passed over lightly in discussion of Hitchcock. If these are not great films in the Hitchcock canon, they have moments that are inescapably the work of a great filmmaker.

Note

1. Selznick had originally wanted Greta Garbo for the part. See Leonard J. Leff, *Hitchcock and Selznick* (232). Fell details the prickly relationship between producer and director on the film, claiming that "[d]espite producer-director meetings about major decisions, Selznick remained the employer, Hitchcock the employee" (235).

Works Cited

Brill, Leslie, *The Hitchcock Romance*. Princeton, NJ: Princeton UP, 1988.
Freedland, Michael. *Gregory Peck*. London: W.H. Allen, 1980.
Hichens, Robert. *The Paradine Case*. London: Ernest Benn Limited, 1933.
Leff, Leonard J. *Hitchcock and Selznick*. London: Weidenfeld and Nicolson, 1988.
McFarlane, Brian, ed. *An Autobiography of British Cinema*. London: Metheuen/ British Film Institute, 1997.
Simpson, Helen. *Under Capricorn*. London: Angus & Robertson, 1983.
Spoto, Donald. *The Art of Hitchcock: Fifty Years of His Motion Pictures*. New York: Doubleday & Co., 1976.

Taylor, John Russell. *The Life and Work of Alfred Hitchcock*. London: Faber, 1978.
Truffaut, François. *Hitchcock*. New York: Simon and Schuster, 1966.
Wood, Robin, *Hitchcock's Films Revisited*. New York: Columbia UP, 1989.

5

GEORGE TOLES

The Forgotten Cigarette Lighter and Other Moral Accidents in *Strangers on a Train*

> As we read, we throw aside the trammels of civilization, the flimsy veil of humanity. "Off, you lendings!" The wild beast resumes its sway within us, we feel like hunting-animals, and as the hound starts in his sleep and rushes on the chase in fancy, the heart rouses itself in its native lair, and utters a wild cry of joy, at being restored once more to freedom and lawless, unrestrained impulses. Everyone has his full swing, or goes to the Devil his own way.
>
> —William Hazlitt, "On the Pleasure of Hating"

AT THE AMUSEMENT PARK CLIMAX of *Strangers on a Train*, an elderly man operating a merry-go-round is accidentally shot by a policeman. His intended target was the film's "innocent" protagonist, Guy Haines. As the ride operator topples to the ground and (presumably) dies, he extends the accident by pushing down the lever controlling the merry-go-round, causing it to accelerate to an alarming speed. A second old man (perhaps the work partner of the first) emerges from the crowd, volunteering for the dangerous task of crawling beneath the merry-go-round, which is filled with riders, young and old, to reverse the lever and bring the whirligig to a halt. He accomplishes his goal expertly, displaying admirable poise and mettle throughout. As a result of his heroic action, the merry-go-round collapses, hurtling a large number of those trapped on it off its spinning surface. It is impossible to determine how many riders have been killed or seriously injured. Besides, the viewer is distracted at this juncture by the dramatically more pressing question of whether Guy will successfully retrieve a lost cigarette lighter from his sinister double, Bruno Anthony.

In the space between the two matching elderly amusement park operators and the double accident lies the cigarette lighter, which somehow replaces them as a locus of moral thought. The two men (victim and hero, respectively) and their equivalently harmful accidents, in effect, cancel each other out. The lighter is what permits the action to break free of this potential blankness and go forward, providing in the process a saving focus and a curiously charged ethical significance. In its taut relation to the chaotic energy surrounding it, the lighter achieves the characteristic form of Hitchcock morality, and perhaps its slippery substance as well.

Moving back to the beginning of the film, one might usefully inquire why there is so much emphasis on a formal pattern that so firmly ordains Guy's first meeting with Bruno, when the meeting itself is, strictly speaking, an accident. Hitchcock requires us to think of the movements of the two men, from the moment of their separate taxicab arrivals at Penn Station, as yoked together somehow, and headed fittingly and irresistibly for contact. The visual rhythm and close matching of mirroring shots in the opening montage make it necessary to regard the portions of the men that we are shown—carefully pressed, tailored pants and immaculate shoes—as progressing unwittingly toward an already fixed destination: the meeting point forecast in the film's title. We are urged to concentrate, for the sake of comparison, on the details of the men's below-the-waist appearances (most notably, flashy wing-tips vs. conservative shoes) and the items of luggage and gestures of service that accompany the pair in transit.

All of this preliminary detective work is justified by our swift grasp of the idea that the two men belong together, that we have strong, if as yet unrevealed, reasons to consider them in terms of each other. Before we came along, Hitchcock implies, a kinship of some special significance has been developed in their separate spheres of life, and it is our task to guess, from the visual pattern laid out for us, what the nature of that preexisting (and narratively predestined) connection might be. Even when we break away briefly from our trailing of the men's movements through the station and receive a train's eye view of the tracks to indicate that a journey is now underway, the tracks themselves in their crisscross overlapping continue the language of symmetry. We are shown, through the merging of separate lines, "like" things being brought together and forming a single entity, with one path and purpose. This shot dissolves into a train compartment where the men's feet complete their seductive search for the assigned dance partner. The as yet anonymous feet select for their respective owners seats that are facing one another. The more conservatively dressed man's leg, in the act of crossing, seems to hover indefinitely in the air for a moment, and then his shoe extends itself to touch the shoe of the man sitting across from him, by accident, as it were. The shoe's gesture slightly suggests a hand politely reaching out to tap a fellow passenger's arm or shoulder.

When Bruno, the man who has been touched, suddenly acquires a face and, by further chance, recognizes Guy (a tennis celebrity), he feels entitled to initiate conversation with him. The two men—after being named and seen "whole"—immediately take on the appearance of free agents, who have met in this fashion without calculation or any clear advance notion of what their coming into contact might accomplish. Once Hitchcock inserts the idea of accident into the midst of his rigorous formal arrangements, what opportunity is there for contingency to interrupt the flow (and forceful impression) of determinism and make its own presence felt? As Bruno works himself up to proposing an exchange of murders with this "perfect stranger," our preliminary positive assessment of Guy's character is qualified by flickering suggestions of shadiness and culpability behind his affable social mask. Nevertheless, we may well decide by the end of their exchange that Guy has not been troublingly implicated in Bruno's dark thought process. He has been a polite, occasionally stimulated audience for Bruno's wild tales and proposals, but he gives little sense of taking Bruno seriously, or giving his "murder plot" serious consideration.

Two small gestures in their scene together (one at the beginning, the other at the end) might, in spite of our common-sense evaluation of what has taken place, prompt us to consider the possibility of Guy's collusion, at some sly, unvoiced, subterranean level. We can regard both gestures as accidents if we choose, and even make a case that they are *unequivocally* accidental. And yet Hitchcock's handling of them urges us to linger over these accidents, and wonder about the likelihood of a hidden purpose. These gestures seem to link up with the deterministic flow of the opening, where any hint of contingency seems excluded. The first of these gestures is the shoe touching, which, as we have already noted, instigates their conversation. Can Hitchcock's visual pattern induce us to believe that Guy's foot instinctively knows what it is doing when it reaches out to brush against Bruno's? Is Guy's body ahead of his mind in signaling a readiness for Bruno's enamored attention and his subsequent malevolent offer? At the conclusion of their talk, after Guy gives Bruno strong behavioral cues that he is merely humoring him and has consented to no further involvement with his scheme, Guy leaves his cigarette lighter behind in Bruno's private compartment. Does Hitchcock want us to regard Guy's forgetting of his lighter as sheer absent-mindedness, or as a veiled declaration of sympathy with a psychological double, and tacit encouragement?

From the moment that Bruno catches sight of the fortuitously left behind lighter, he strives, perhaps madly, to interpret it as a coded message from Guy. He swiftly, smilingly infers that Guy has relinquished it deliberately. Guy has left the lighter expressly for Bruno to find and have, as a secret handshake and pledge. Is Bruno's view of the lighter's significance utterly mistaken? Given our growing awareness of Bruno's

Figure 5.1. *Strangers on a Train*—Bruno (Robert Walker) with Guy's (Farley Granger) cigarette lighter.

psychopathic proclivities and our judgment that he is oblivious to Guy's amused, patronizing dismissal, we have sufficient grounds to decide that Bruno is making something out of nothing. Yet Hitchcock is no more prepared to let go of this seemingly negligible object than Bruno is. He will, in fact, structure the entire film narrative around the lighter's itinerary, as it weaves its way by a tortuous, murder-lit route back to Guy's possession. Or almost possession: Guy's and the spectator's last view of the lighter occurs when Bruno involuntarily opens his hand to reveal it in the act of dying. This dead man's give-away does not result in the lighter officially changing hands.

One way of holding on to the accidental dimension of the lighter being left in Bruno's keeping is to regard the object as a "mere" plot device. We can readily categorize the lighter with many other complication-generating items in Hitchcock that the director has enticingly described as "MacGuffins." A MacGuffin is an arbitrary something that is of great concern to the characters in a story, but whose precise significance is of only slight concern to the viewer. The MacGuffin object—for example, spy plans—is a resonant blank, like the "O" that stands for nothing that fills the space of Roger Thornhill's middle name in *North by Northwest*. I am not satisfied with this tidy method of curtailing the moral importance and expressive force of the lighter. If Guy's forsaking of the lighter is reduced to pure chance—an act, that is, in which volition and accountability play no part—then his emotional complicity in the killing of his wife, Miriam, is wiped out. He becomes, simply and hollowly, a victim of circumstance. To grant him this reliable status deprives him of any weight, or suggestiveness, in the elaborate system of doubling which, like the lighter, looms large in the film's opening sequence, and establishes a dense network of imagery that parallels the lighter's journey through the entire narrative.

For Bruno to function meaningfully as Guy's double, there must be core affinities between their characters. They need to be bound together inwardly, to an even greater extent than they are bound by the machinations of the external plot. The double-spawning protagonist, whether in the spectral tales of German Romanticism or the amnesia-saturated world of film noir, is not required to acknowledge, comprehend, or actively embrace the affinities he encounters in his secret sharer. But as the double's story proceeds, the topography on which his split figure moves acquires a volatile, dreamlike shiftiness. The man-with-a-double's capacity to hold fast to personal boundaries and oases of clear intention is treacherously impaired. What once seemed safely sequestered in a knowable and private "inner life" has leaked outside somehow, where it confronts you in the guise of an alien personage—formidable, slippery, menacing, opaque, yet peculiarly intimate as well. For Bruno to expand, with the shadowing double's license, until he has infiltrated every recess of Guy's psychological terrain, Guy must at some stage say "yes" to him. He must collaborate, at least in his thoughts, in the act of self-division. He must cross a line that suggests that this dubious mirroring presence of Bruno has been summoned, and that his subterranean services are indeed acceptable: "after one's own heart," as it were.

The phrase "crossing the line" brings to mind an anecdote recounted by Alma Hitchcock in Patrick McGilligan's biography of the director. The story is offered as evidence that Hitchcock's often professed "fear of policemen" was more than a showman's spiel. Hitchcock, according to his wife, while driving in England, once "swerved slightly over the white line . . . and was stopped by a bobby who took down the particulars. Hitch drove everyone around him crazy for days, worrying whether or not he was going to get a summons" (448). The line that Guy Haines crosses in Bruno's private train compartment, barely perceptible at the time of its occurrence but adequate to forge a binding pact with Bruno, is his perverse desire to have Bruno make off with his lighter. It is an action that Guy might idly fantasize, without having to witness or explicitly sanction. If Bruno wishes, he can seize and pocket the lighter, after Guy's departure—that is, once his back is turned. Guy will not have performed a visible, incriminating act in overlooking his lighter. This gesture has a beautiful air of latency, of a vagrant, mischievous thought that can flare to life in another's possession. Forgetting the lighter has, by any outward measure, the most tenuous imaginable connection to wrongdoing.

Whatever links to *sin* the carelessly abandoned lighter insinuates exist solely at the level of thought. In movies, the most compelling use of objects is to allow *characters*' thoughts, and their accompanying feelings, to become visible. In a Hitchcock film, the viewers' thoughts, aligned with a character's, may tilt in a certain iniquitous direction, and as they do so, a material sign emerges to focus them sharply, giving form and solidity to their otherwise ephemeral existence. The type of thoughts that most fascinate Hitchcock, whether they sprout up in his characters or, better still, in his projected audience, are those that might turn out to be sins. If it is possible, as Catholic theology affirms, to sin not only in words and deeds, but (with equal opprobrium) in our thoughts, then there is no reason why movies could not afford a ripe and sticky occasion for this third, most impalpable mode of sinning. Hitchcock can pass contagious, half-formed thoughts from his own outward-looking, pattern-making consciousness—where images compose and follow each other in the clear, light, quick manner of vivid external impressions—to the more inward-looking, vulnerable consciousness of the viewer.

We viewers complete Hitchcock's thoughts by attending closely to his images.

As we absorb these thought-pictures, the most arresting may prick us or spread within us like an inkblot. They may lodge in us as our own thoughts, even if we began by "borrowing" them, and we can potentially become "guilty parties" in our means of pursuing and elaborating them. The thought transfer is as subtle and difficult to pin down as Guy's reason for losing track of his lighter. A little space of awareness bids welcome to an unsavory impulse. The mind soon enough passes beyond that space—like leaving a room—disavowing its fleeting decision to linger there and traffic in the inadmissible. But suppose this flashing impulse in its tiny mental chamber sets off kindred vibrations in other sectors of consciousness, and that these vibrations prove strong enough to form an alliance. The thought that is not dispelled, but keeps echoing, wants to verify its presence and demand closer attention. A literal object can be a kind of shorthand representation of the thought and all of the associations that have accrued to it. The object is a material reference point for the amplifying thought, and a receipt for its first emergence. Think of the cigarette lighter as such a receipt: firm, compact, ready at hand.

The lighter belongs to Guy, who has received it as a lover's gift that he may not quite deserve. The lighter also belongs to Hitchcock, who covertly passes it to the viewer (as something to notice, to take in) in a manner that resembles in its deviousness Guy's "thoughtless" delivery of the lighter to Bruno. We are like Bruno in our subsequent use of the thought-object that we have picked up after Hitchcock leaves it for us. Bruno takes the lighter to be Guy's clearest expression of authorization for Bruno to "proceed" with his ideas. After stalking Guy's wife in the amusement park, he will illuminate her face with the lighter just before strangling her. He ignites this flame in part so that he will see her by Guy's light before laying hands on her. As viewers, we employ Hitchcock's borrowed lighter as though it were our permission to transgress freely, Bruno-style, in our looking and thinking and emotional participation. As long as it is Hitchcock's lighter, not ours, we are exempt from the obligation to dwell "uneasily" on where mere thinking leads us.

The viewer becomes Hitchcock's cavalier emissary and agent, unwrapping his own sordid fantasies by the light of the director's images. But there is no automatic consequence for such indulgence. We can tell ourselves that we are doing what we are supposed to do with the images, that we are simply honoring, again like Bruno, someone else's wishes and implicit instructions. As long as we are clasping Hitchcock's lighter, as it were, we are doing *his* bidding, visually and morally speaking. The authority for any giddy thought crimes in the movie's amusement park cannot, fairly, be traced back to us. Any crime we witness is not our crime—it is borrowed from someone else. We can participate vicariously in whatever fashion we wish, or we can simply watch. It all comes down to what we might, in our real and bogus innocence, call the thoughtless simplicity of watching.

Julien Gracq, arguing for literature's incontestable superiority to film in the matter of graduated, shaded vision, deplores the fact that the "sensory distribution" in its assimilation of movie images is "strictly egalitarian":

> To grasp this singularity [and hence the superiority of written images to those photographed], just imagine a cinema where, alongside a scene unfolding right in the optical field, other scenes or landscapes, related or different, would be vaguely and simultaneously perceived, in secret or in lost profile, from the corner of the eye—now anticipating the future, now revisiting the past, and always qualifying, neutralizing, or reinforcing the scenes being played out on the main screen. This domain of margins distractedly but effectively perceived, this domain of *the corner of the eye*—in order to compensate for other infirmities, such as less dramatic efficiency, less of a sense of the present, the elastic vagueness proper to images born of literature—accounts for almost all the superiority of written fiction. (287)

Hitchcock's invariably cunning and oblique deployment of visual form—which aims for a productive ongoing tension with the surface story and its declared values—corresponds in many respects to Gracq's "domain of the corner of the eye." While the visual patterns Hitchcock elaborates are certainly noticeable—at times, as in the beginning of *Strangers on a Train*, so conspicuous as to be unavoidable—they recede from prominence as character and plot concerns move to the viewing foreground. Emotional interest more naturally flows in the direction of character activity and conflict than it does toward rhyming images. The viewer is meant to be aware, but only lightly, glancingly, of formal devices, and the continuing repetitions that punctuate and intensify character busyness. Hitchcock's play with form has an "elastic vagueness" of exactly the same sort that Gracq celebrates in literature. His patterns are designed in such a way that they dwell on the optical margin, as it were, "distractedly but effectively perceived." Images set off mysterious countercurrents, crisscrossing anticipation and retrospect, and giving off stealthy signals that reverberate in the absence of clear interpretive cues.

Gracq's phrase "lost profile" conjures up the famous Hitchcock line drawing that the director's portly silhouette moves into to complete at the commencement of each episode of his television series, *Alfred Hitchcock Presents*. Hitchcock images so often seem to give us the profile of something, elusive but naggingly familiar, something powerfully glimpsed a short time ago but now (most likely) already estranged from us. The lost image, en route to being forgotten, is like a shadow of something that briefly arrested our attention but whose place in our mind was quickly usurped, "written over," by something else. Hitchcock emphatically does not want his images to prompt a full, rational accounting. He would rather have them "tease us *out of thought*" rather than match up with and reinforce those portions of his story that are emotionally and morally definite. The cigarette lighter, in its various manifestations, serves as a model Hitchcock image. We are never in doubt about what we're looking at or what its normative, automatic associations are. It never tries to elevate itself, portentously, to the status of a symbol—a metaphor in cement shoes. But as it craves to repeat and return in the narrative, as it becomes (wittily rather than anxiously) overdetermined, it gradually drives us away from a stable frame of reference. The more we look at it, the more it invites speculation, but we are never pressed to settle what it means. It opens up possibilities without coaxing us to bear down on them. We can always let the lighter go, allowing it to be reabsorbed, once again, by its present-moment plot function.

We do find ourselves, periodically, moving closer to it emotionally, most noticeably perhaps when Bruno attempts to retrieve it through the sewer grate. We are at such times briefly caught in a kind of cage with it, through Hitchcock's montage and hypnotic emphasis, and we may be led to project thoughts and feelings onto it that seem "natural" and beyond our control. We are (as with other key Hitchcock images) on the hook with it long enough, intensely enough, to be smudged or dirtied by contact.

We are given an opportunity, when Bruno is first handed the lighter in the train compartment, to examine it in closeup from his point of view. How might it first appear to him, and to us, as we share the perspective of his shrewd gaze? Almost all of the offers in the Guy and Bruno "getting acquainted" talk come from Bruno ("I'd do anything for you, Guy"). The lighter, shared by Guy early on when Bruno is unable to locate a match, is Guy's best offer to Bruno, in fact his only tangible gesture of giving. He hands it over readily, and seems curiously unconcerned, at any point in their lengthy discussion, about retrieving it. Bruno pronounces the lighter "elegant," then correctly identifies it as a gift of some value. Inscribed on the lighter is a camouflaged declaration of love: "A to G."

The letters hint at a depth of affection that the gift giver is reluctant to express too directly. A pair of crossed tennis rackets above and to the left of the initials alludes to Guy's profession, and also transforms the rackets into an emblem of enduring attachment. Though Anne Morton, Guy's current lover, has no personal connection to tennis, she wittily insinuates herself into the game by her choice of the crossed rackets, and suggests by her "crisscross" that she is (or would very much like to be) in successful competition with his first love. She has appropriated the tools of the sport, and lightly proclaims that her romantic pairing with Guy transcends it. The tininess of the rackets perhaps reveals her hope that the game was but a fortuitous means to a higher end. Both in terms of career and marriage prospects, Guy can exchange tennis for something better.

Bruno swiftly deciphers Anne's secret message to Guy, claiming to have learned all about this well-fixed Senator's daughter and her relationship with Guy from the "society pages." But the larger task of interpreting the lighter's message to *Bruno* from Guy will take up the rest of the narrative. It is not, of course, Guy's conscious intention to re-gift the lighter to Bruno. Even if we are determined to find Guy guilty of some form of thought crime, we might reasonably conclude that he is at this point merely eager to have the legal loose ends of his relationship with Miriam cleared up and out of the way. She is an embarrassment and a source of vexation to him, to be sure, and someone who can easily rouse him to rage. However, he is still quite confident that she is willing to grant him a divorce. We can more profitably wonder what Guy's carelessness with the lighter reveals about his new relationship with Anne. His action implies that there is already something stale and disingenuous about his dealings with his replacement lover. The fact that the lighter drifts so quickly from his attention intimates that the woman who gave it to him has a meager hold on his heart.

Miriam and Anne become interestingly entangled here. The one that he wishes to be rid of and the one that he has recently taken up are alike dispensable, throwaway figures. In Anne's case he can rely on social forms and a self-deceiving habit of manipulation to do the work of loving. In some respects Anne matches Guy in coldness, and she exhibits a distress bordering on fear whenever he (in her presence) is forced to answer accusations that others have brought against him. The gift lighter, beneath its surface riddle of romantic declaration, contains a second layer of equivocation and withholding. Guy is a man spoken for but who has not fully, or convincingly, committed himself. Anne's reduction of their names to initials says, on the one hand, "we both know who the letters belong to and what they mean" and, on the other, more beseechingly, "fill me and yourself in, carry us further toward definition. You will have to light the fire, Guy, if the residual barriers between us are to be removed, if the residual stranger (in you, in me) is to become an intimate."

As Bruno, left alone with the lighter, leans back in his seat and scrutinizes it, he softly repeats the word, "crisscross." The sight of the tennis rackets no doubt provokes the utterance, yielding a satisfying image for him of the murder swap idea he had shared with Guy, in the first flush of his infatuation. But the word serves equally well to confirm for Bruno the appropriateness of the lighter passing from Guy's hand to his. "A" gave a gift to "G" as an avowal of love, and as a cunning attempt to solicit a reciprocal response. The "G" to "A" return-of-serve was not forthcoming, at least not in a binding form. For Bruno, since Guy left the not yet precious gift in his care, he has, in effect, readdressed it: "G to B." The original letters were arbitrary place markers, subject to reversal and revision. Crisscross. Bruno does not regard the lighter he now holds as a solid proof of Guy's attachment to him. He rather conceives it, perhaps accurately, as a pleasingly indefinite overture. "The gift will be more fully yours, Bruno, when you have *done* something to make yourself worthy of it. My affection, and of course my love, are as yet unsecured. Neither Miriam nor Anne has opened a passage to my heart. The lighter is my invitation to you to divine and answer my needs. I cannot (or will not) tell you what those needs are. If the name blazoned on your tie next to that gaudy lobster emblem belongs as well on my lighter, in place of these vague initials, you must discover where my heart is and show it to me."

Patricia Highsmith, author of the novel *Strangers on a Train*, describes in one of her late stories "the flaw of life" as "a long, mistaken shutting of the heart"(417). Guy's lighter, an elegantly sealed container for an unstruck flame, manages to embody, neatly and in miniature, this basic "flaw" in Guy's character. What saves the film version of *Strangers on a Train* from being an intricately heartless virtuoso exercise is Bruno's lavish perseverance in seeking to win Guy's emotional acknowledgment, and if possible, his love. (Bruno, however much a psychopath, is not wrong to regard expressions of hatred and wrath as "close relations" to love, and frequently an elaborate subterfuge.) Bruno's major aspiration, as he proceeds to murder Guy's wife without a firm agreement in place, is to furnish unassailable proof to Guy of how well he knows him, and of how much he is prepared to do to strengthen their bond of friendship. Bruno hopes to take Guy by storm, to override his reticence and reserve, his fastidious but false decorum, by making more daring gestures of "romantic readiness" than Guy has ever experienced. Nearly all of the emotion in the film is generated by Bruno's mad quest to woo Guy with the lures of danger, drastic excess, and irresponsibility. He wishes to cajole Guy, with all the rough, provocative means at his disposal, until he comes out of hiding. Bruno is repeatedly rebuffed, of course, and he responds to rejection with a courtly disappointment. (He is not patient by nature, but for Guy's sake he will try.) Now and then Bruno's fuming gives way, momentarily, to surprising gusts of tenderness.

Guy's relationship with Anne Morton and her family seem peculiarly afflicted by the malaise of smiling aloofness, an incapacity—even when honestly discussing his difficulties—to open himself up. With Miriam, in contrast, Guy is unable to contain himself. But even in his outbursts of anger and self-aggrandizing frustration, he can't seem to lose his tightness. The emotional world of the film seems, on the whole, misshapen—under a spell that has to do with Guy's heart, "its long, mistaken shutting." In other words, Guy's closed heart rather than Bruno's immoderate and savage open one is the covert source of the ailment that seems to confront us "through a glass darkly" at so many points in the *Strangers* landscape. I am reminded of Nietzsche's lament: "The desert grows; woe unto him that harbors deserts in himself." In the inverted logic characteristic of the best tales of doubling, the more cautious, socially adept, and respectable figure—wound tight with the strain of denial and the lack of self-knowledge—sets the terms for the double's conduct. Guy is the knot that Bruno is summoned to untie. Effectively divorced from the life he feigns taking part in, Guy also seems divorced from the pronoun "I," which in his case no longer quite seems a personal pronoun. Bruno, of course, cannot be said to understand anyone's feelings except his own (and perhaps intermittently his mother's), but he has a gala assortment of "personal" feelings that delight, pummel, and transfix him.

It is extremely rare in a Hitchcock film for the nominal villain to be so extravagantly caught up in feelings as Bruno is—with a child's need to give himself over completely to each one in turn, as though he were not yet master of any of them. His responses to the "rush" that emotion so often carries are inordinate, but he doesn't want to lessen the size and force of these responses, because he fears an irreversible, perhaps lethal, "grown-up" boredom is lying in wait for him. I can also think of no other male figure in Hitchcock who, for all of his depraved scheming, declares himself as fully as Bruno. Unlike Guy, he is, compulsively, and in almost every sense, out in the open. The "desert" that is Guy is policed by exacting social forms in a manner that parallels the policing in a Hitchcock film by an equally exacting visual form. Guy is pursued and supplicated by the childish, childlike Bruno, who wants to break through and flood Guy's controlled but arid spaces with his own ungovernable messiness. Bruno's love for Guy has a doglike excess. (This canine dimension of their bond might account for the otherwise baffling appearance of the dog on Bruno's staircase when Guy attempts a secret nocturnal visit to Bruno's father. The Janus-faced dog at first appears fierce and aggressive, but as Guy moves closer to him he turns, on the instant, lavishly tender, and licks his hand.) Topographically, the heedlessness (indeed, the brute thoughtlessness) of Bruno's chaotic attachment to Guy finds its appropriate home in amusement parks, to which Bruno naturally gravitates: places where straight lines begin to waver and wiggle, where wandering replaces set routes, and the workday commitment to pragmatic doing regresses to frivolous undoing.

Returning to our initial opposition of determinism versus accident, I think that Bruno initially appears to be in the service of fixed and fated action (his contract, his unstoppable plans), but that he is covertly an agent of accident. Unlike both Guy and Hitchcock, Bruno is a confident improviser, someone who could find nearly as much pleasure in disrupting his plans as following through on them. He is as eager to surprise himself as he is to surprise others. Paradoxically, while he makes meticulous preparations for incidents large and small, he typically has no idea what he is going to do next. He is, as a rule, delighted rather than alarmed by detours, indefiniteness, and unexpected developments. In brief, he makes maximum allowance for accident, and smoothly incorporates the workings of chance into his operations. The murder of Miriam, for example, is from beginning to end an antic impromptu. He has advance knowledge and control over almost none of the elements, including the time and setting. He agreeably adjusts his "plans" for the evening to the whims of Miriam, and counts on circumstances working out, unpredictably, in his favor.

Guy's lighter, once in Bruno's hands, begins to mirror its new owner, poised teasingly between the imperatives of fate and the arbitrary pranks of chance. The "current" it conducts in its early appearances flows equally from both sources. Bruno comes to get it and keep it, as we have seen, somewhat fortuitously, but the lighter carries in its engraved markings Kafka-like evidence of Guy's failings and evasions. A stern eye appraising this lighter can turn its "marks of affection" into a judgment; its first recipient was unworthy of the romantic faith bestowed on him. It feels right somehow that such a small but telling "throwaway possession" will eventually come to stand for every suspicion that is rightly or wrongly directed against Guy. Those barely perceptible Jamesian particles of guilt that might finally make legible the portion of Miriam's murder that authentically belongs to Guy (along with all his other sins of thought and omission) seem to collect, like magnetized filings, on the body of the lighter. As it becomes increasingly clear that the movement of the lighter, more than any competing plot element, will determine the course and outcome of the narrative—and will do so by *sure* design—we are obliged to dwell more searchingly on what this protean object reveals and conceals.

One might reasonably wonder whether the lighter itself might be deemed guilty or innocent. If Guy, for example, were to retrieve it without mishap before Bruno succeeded in planting it incriminatingly at the scene of the crime, would the object immediately be wiped clean? And would the accumulated implications of Guy's relationship with Bruno— including the film's heavy, relentless pattern of doubling—then dissolve like a dream? Were the lighter and the doubling subject to misreading all along? Perhaps they were empty categories from the outset, which we were pressured to interpret in the event that they might prove meaningful. Suppose that they never did become meaningful, in the way of red herrings and false clues. If that is the case, then we are invited to erase our own narrative footsteps at the end of the film, as well as those of Guy and Bruno. Guy's innocence, if accepted, trumps a delusive, guilt-projecting visual determinism (they were *never* doubles!), and makes his original meeting with Bruno a bona fide accident, after the fact. "Don't talk to strangers," as the movie's epilogue proposes, with pointedly limp flippancy. Guy is ironically confirmed, if we take the epilogue as instructive, in his instinct to share nothing real with others. Everyone (even declared intimates) should properly remain strangers, it seems, if one is to defend, and blankly preserve, one's innocence as an adult.

When Bruno dies in the amusement park, loosening his tight grip on the lighter and exposing the object to public view (moral consensus, if you like), does the thing itself prove to be a mere nothing, a matter of no further concern? To whom does the lighter ultimately belong—Guy, Bruno, or the viewer?—and does its meaning alter according to how we settle final ownership? One suspects that Guy would not want the tainted object returned to him. The gift is spoiled now; let the police dispose of it. Not claiming the lighter would make Guy resemble the vast majority of Hitchcock protagonists, who achieve their desired ends by complacent refusals of self-knowledge. The miserable business that one has been embroiled in is over, and it had no connection at all with the person one "really" is. For a murky interval others were confused or skeptical about one's vigorous assertions of innocence, but it can now be shown triumphantly that the wrong man had been accused. "From the beginning," Guy can tell himself, "I was doubted, mistrusted, held unfairly to be responsible. Privately I have always known myself, in the ways that count, to be in the right. Now others must ratify this view." And the viewer is exonerated by the same means, by the same self-validating stroke, at the same instant. We too are divorced cleanly, if we wish to be, from any further emotional, moral, or thought investment in this film experience. Guy's innocence is solidly matched by our own. Whatever we (as viewers) have given to Bruno, so he could run stirringly "naughty" errands as our surrogate self, or double, is safely returned to us at the end—or, better yet, disposed of.

Before Bruno manages to get to the amusement park, late in the film, to fulfill his intention of hiding Guy's lighter in plain view at the murder site, he experiences an accident of his own, one that nearly results in his losing control (and possession) of it prematurely. The viewer is persuaded, at this juncture, that Bruno's continued control of Guy wholly depends on his retaining control of the lighter. In a moment of blind cockiness, he is jostled while holding the lighter too loosely. It slips from his fingers, then drops through the opening of a sewer grate. For a time the lighter seems at a recoverable distance on an upper ledge, but Bruno, too impetuous in his attempt to grasp it, causes it to slide off and drop to a lower level, seemingly beyond his, or anyone's, reach. It lies, agonizingly, several stubborn inches past his outstretched arm's furthest reach. The emotional struggle to retrieve the lost object (this sleek, small-time grail) is one that would seem rightly to belong to the questing hero at this late phase of the narrative. Bruno appears to be pitted in an almost moral struggle against the dictates of accident—a malign force that has unjustly intervened to sever both his ties and claim to the lighter. His hand's outreach, and near miraculous stretching, feels like a religious act of faith.

Bruno's solitary Arthurian test is intercut with Guy's untypically reckless style of play in the Forest Hills tennis tournament. The logic of this episode, where Guy is concerned, is that Guy *deserves* to win his match, since he is altering his tightly controlled, conservative, self-protecting tennis strategy. The loosening and simultaneous sharpening of his customary mode of attack in the game, as he battles against the clock (i.e., Bruno's timetable), is meant to suggest a corresponding elasticity in his approach to the human dilemmas confronting him. If the same logic is applied to Bruno in his "crisscross" contest with the lighter, he should not be rewarded with success, since the accident was a fitting rebuke for his increasingly rigid, senseless persecution of Guy. It may be time for the double, whose harsh tutelage of duplicitous Guy has served its purpose, to be tested himself and confronted with limits. He must transform *his* tactics and reverse course, or face humiliating defeat in his steadily diminished sphere of influence. Yet paradoxically the emotional force of the scene, as opposed to its conventional ethical sense, places the viewer, with bewildering fullness, on the side of Bruno and his strong and dexterous strangler's hand.

One might convincingly argue that this sewer grate scene is one of three character-centered moments in the film with expansive, overtly emotional power, though in all three instances we can't readily identify the emotions at work. Each of them involves Bruno's hands and are linked to the lighter. The second episode of dauntingly obscure emotional power occurs during Bruno's earlier involuntary strangling of the "stand in" elderly society woman, Mrs. Cunningham, at the formal dress party. Bruno's hands shift intention there from a playful bit of theater to a deadly squeezing action as his eyes are caught by a young woman's stare across the room. This second woman is Anne's sister, Barbara, whose glasses reflect—for Bruno, if not for us—the flame of the lighter (Bruno's memory image) that had illuminated Miriam's features just before he strangled her. The third fraught moment is Miriam's actual death, reflected in her glasses once they separate from her and fall to the ground.

As in the sewer grate scene, Bruno at the party seems to be in a kind of trance as his hands acquire a will of their own. The party and grate incident both involve Bruno's hands taking their cue and strength from the lighter flashing tauntingly, menacingly from what I would term an unforeseen viewing distance. Bruno tightening his hold on the woman's throat seems in the party scene a proxy attempt to take the lighter back from his victim. The object seems to be part of the glasses that confront him. Previously a reflection in Barbara's/Miriam's lens, the lighter has now transformed itself into the substance of Barbara's gaze. It is "the thing" that looks back at him. Barbara's glasses and her half-fearful, half-accusing eyes (in a disconcerting, viewer-implicating closeup) rather than the invisible Mrs. Cunningham beside him, are what catch and hold Bruno's gaze, until he eventually passes out. When Barbara was first introduced to him in an earlier scene, her glasses immediately cued a memory of Miriam, whose eruption was marked by the reflection of his lit lighter in her lenses. In the party scene, the lighter is not literally reflected for a second time, but the viewer's memory of it is awakened by the carnival music accompanying Barbara's fearful reciprocation of Bruno's suddenly transfixed gaze. Throughout this party scene incident (which, like so many Bruno activities, is "out in the open"), the viewer seems placed at about four removes from the hypnotic object. The lighter is perhaps even more insistently "there," as Slavoj Žižek would tell us, by remaining hidden from *literal* sight: a vanishing point in the image. Mrs. Cunningham, whose neck has been eagerly offered to Bruno for his flirtatious use is, as I've already noted, unseen and forgotten once his "performance" is underway. Barbara, the woman who replaces the society woman as a potential object of vision, is equally not there—missing from view—in her own right. She is mistaken when she declares, solemnly, to her sister after Bruno's departure from the party, that he was attacking *her*. Barbara's glasses, from Bruno's perspective, were the only living aspect of her face, the point of his helpless concentration. Her eyes are visited (for the viewer recollecting, with Bruno, the lighter's earlier, spectral appearance) by the lighter flame, and mingled with it. The glasses, for their part, are a reminder of another pair of glasses with an equally blurry owner. They conjure up the amusement park, the setting of the murder, in Bruno's mind more vividly than they bring back Miriam herself. Remembered music from the amusement park returns him, as on a merry-go-round, to the spot where he killed her. Bruno's re-enactment of the murder is experienced as a set of enigmatic dream fragments rather than a clearly retrieved memory. Bruno tries to focus his attention on the lit lighter as though it beckoned to him from behind Barbara's eyes. The object, like an obscured face behind a window, acquires here the human power to look back at him, through the mediating lens of Barbara's/Miriam's glasses.

As the viewer reaches back for her own memory of the murder, the face of Miriam vanishes there as well. We recall only a pair of enormous glass lenses in the grass, in whose ghostly light the body of Miriam leans slowly back. She floats magically, in her partner's ably supportive grip, down to the ground, and comes to rest there, reduced to a dim shapelessness. The lighter, at this human endpoint, has transformed, as in the party scene, into Miriam's orphaned glasses—which is to say, into an act of disembodied viewing. The glasses are our replacement lighter, the sole available light to see by. Only the spectator is entitled to "wear" these glasses and peer through them. In so doing, our power of scrutiny, and involvement, is enhanced. We authorize this sight of death by entering into it with such rapt fluidity. How deliriously close we are to Miriam's dying, while still, it would appear, safely detached from it. The face that a short while ago belonged to the glasses, in a kind of supporting role to them, was lit up for us for a shy, surprised moment, and then extinguished. After a graceful shift in perspective, the oval frame holds the entire, now faceless victim comfortably, beautifully, within its borders, as Miriam passes from the light of life into a destitute, blind darkness. A ghostly light now literally inhabits the lens of the glasses. This soft afterglow replaces the flare of the lighter that earlier signaled Bruno's declaration of sexual readiness. The lens doesn't quite release its last touch of illumination. Dreamily ensnared still in the trance of Miriam's former arousal by Bruno, the glasses cradle the fading gleam of Eros as Miriam reclines gently deathward. As the glasses become an utter irrelevance to their even more deeply abandoned owner, they still clutch, as it were, onto the romantic prospect of her last thought: the anticipated fulfillment of an embrace. In her abrupt separation from the glasses, they become ours to put on and see through. The transfer of the glasses from Miriam to the viewer parallels the way in which Guy allows Bruno to claim the lighter that is "left for him" in the train compartment. By what authority does Bruno take hold of the forsaken object, look it over, and pocket it? He cannot be sure what he is "expected" or meant to do with it, anymore than we are. With Miriam's glasses, we take possession by accident, so it seems. They fall haphazardly into our hands, so we might as well put them to use; Miriam has no further need—of the glasses, or of us. Resting on the spot where accident has cast them, they take on the terrible calm of a sphinx in a Francis Bacon painting. Like the sphinx, they have cryptic designs on us, on our thoughts, that we may not be at liberty to consider. What is certain is that our matter-of-course viewing of the death scene is sharply disrupted at the moment we "find" the glasses. Unavoidably, our watching turns self-conscious, but to what end?

The morality of a Hitchcock film is so often tucked away in odd object places such as this one. We are suddenly given something to look at or through which we clearly recognize but have somehow lost our ability to interpret. The ease of looking—the entrancing force of our concentration—supplies a pleasure that works against our confusion. A sudden gap or tear in our normal, passive viewing perspective arrives without warning (brought about by a disrupted relation with a familiar object and its placement in space). We are temporarily put out of phase with our preferred, sanctioned thoughts, thoughts that square with our working notion of what the scene (indeed, what reality) is about—for example, a murder, involving a maniac and a hapless victim. When we enter this estranging gap, we may attempt to cure or remedy it by bearing down on the manifest beauty of the image until the confusion goes away. A potentially moral challenge is evaded by intensifying our absorption with the almost caressable visual surface. The visual surface allows a kind of "blanking out" until our initial idea of the scene's straightforward meaning returns to us.

In these estranging episodes, we bear some resemblance to Bruno watching the screen of Barbara's glasses at the party, a screen that holds a flickering memory image of a nearly forgotten murder. He can't remember, for the time being, who or where he is. He doesn't *know* that he is doing actual injury to the woman sitting next to him. He loses sight of her and of his squeezing hands because of the half-formed thoughts that grip him. Bruno also loses sight of the fact that he is himself under scrutiny. He imagines, in his spectator's trance, that he is hidden, but in fact he remains in the full glare of public disclosure. The joke strangling that he initiated "just for the fun of it" turns ghastly and real, a near-lethal *stretched* moment of blankness covering another thought that will not come clear. Bruno's buried thought gives the go-ahead to his squeezing hands. He blindly indulges their action without making it into an act of volition or avowed knowledge. Bruno does and doesn't own his own thoughts in this embarrassing seizure. The woman struggling for her life in the seat next to him attests that he *does* own them, in some fashion, in ways that tell. He does not, of course, wish them to spill forth uncontrollably here—given the risks of exposure—but the brutal thoughts are already in his memory-possession and, at this transitional moment, in his emotional possession. The thought of having genuinely killed Miriam, as opposed to a "test your strength" game of killing, was a thought not necessarily present or owned up to by Bruno at the time of the murder. It is like something he has accidentally dropped, or left behind—say, a lighter. An attentive stranger (Hitchcock) has noted this slip, this inadvertence, and at an appropriate later time, returns the thought (in the physical form of a lighter) to him. "Is this yours? I thought I saw you holding it earlier, and made the connection."

Robert Vischer, in his 1873 essay "On the Optical Sense of Form: A Contribution to Aesthetics," writes of how in actual experience "there exists a state of pure absorption in which we imagine this or that phenomenon in accordance with the unconscious need for a surrogate for our body-ego. As in a dream, I stimulate, on the basis of simple nerve sensations, a fixed form that symbolizes my body or an organ of it. . . . The way in which the phenomenon is constructed also becomes an analogy for my own structure. I wrap myself within its contours like a garment" (quoted in Fried 37). Later in this extraordinary, Hitchcock-prefiguring essay, Vischer combines the idea of projection with a metaphor of concealment, which contains (accidentally?) the notion of preparing for a killing. We have "the wonderful ability to project and incorporate our own physical form into an objective form, in much the same way that wild fowlers gain access to their quarry by concealing themselves in a blind. What can that form be other than the form of a content identical with it? It is therefore our own personality that we project onto it" (38). To extend Vischer's metaphors further, so they more closely approximate the movie-viewing situation, Hitchcock and the viewer are both concealed in their separate blinds. The viewer, like Bruno at the party, believes that he is sufficiently well-hidden from anyone's scrutiny not to be in danger of getting caught, or caught out. Bruno, in his game with Mrs. Cunningham, ventures fairly far into the open because he is confident that a deeper blind, invisible to anyone present except perhaps Guy (whom he confidently manipulates), is in place. And at the moment of maximum security, Bruno is transfixed and undone by an image form—akin to himself—that he had not anticipated. The viewer, in turn, is unmindful of the fact that he is himself the "quarry" of Hitchcock, who is concealed, almost in plain sight, in an adjacent "blind." It is we that the director (always) has his sights on, and it is by means of our involuntary projections, and physical/ emotional entanglements with what we see, that he will draw us out from cover, and catch us unawares. We can be exposed, in the full glare of his knowledge of what we are imaginatively capable of, without ever losing the illusion that we have remained invisible, and in control of our impulses. Our recognitions, our guilty thoughts connected, by projection, to our hands and eyes, will be strangers to us again almost immediately, as we blank out the particulars of what we have assented to.

Returning to Bruno reaching through the sewer grate, we see that his mental state is similar to that which he inhabited right before he finds his perfect moment to strangle Miriam. He is not yet in a trance. He is fully alert, has the lighter firmly in view, and can "feel" exactly how much distance separates his hand from the all-important object. In this situation, he has no doubt about whom the lighter belongs to. It is entirely *his* possession, and surely (as he sees it) it is only fair that he should get it back. If Bruno has some attachment to the idea of Providence, he has undoubtedly invoked its aid in this demanding endeavor. The restoration of the lighter, in fact, feels animated by a miracle. It could only be accomplished with the cooperation of some sympathetic, occult power. As we watch Bruno strain beyond his customary physical resources and bodily limitations to recover the object, our initial detached amusement at his plight is exchanged, without our conscious approval, for impassioned identification. The hand of Bruno becomes an extension of our own. As *our* fingers at last feel the first answering touch of the lighter, we may experience a sensation akin to ecstasy—the blessing of fulfillment. Bruno's quest, for that intense interval when it is nearly but not quite crowned with success, seems as urgent, honorable, and indeed meaningful as any that our actual life in the world has offered us.

Earlier, on the train, when another stranger to Metcalf, having noticed the lighter in Bruno's hand, requests a light from him, Bruno superstitiously refrains from sharing it, offering matches instead. In the sewer grate scene, Bruno is required, as a result of Hitchcock's framing and cutting, to share the lighter with *us*. It is immensely important to Hitchcock—and I would suggest for moral as well as visceral reasons—to have us both will Bruno's success as we emotionally collaborate with him, and at last to *feel* the lighter pass into our own hands. One of the small group of casual spectators gathered to watch well-attired Bruno (crouched on the dirty ground and exerting himself fiercely to reach the prize in the dark depths of the gutter), offers an offhand judgment on what transpired, once Bruno departs the scene. "It must mean a lot to him." The morality of Hitchcock, as I have argued earlier, has to do with making the lighter the repository and secret conductor of all the sinful thought energy in the narrative: everything that *feeds* the surface action illicitly and inadmissibly. Why is there so much pressure for the spectator to repeat Bruno's action in the train compartment opening, and to make the lighter her own? Hitchcock would like us, ideally, to feel its significance (though we can't articulate what it is) as we burn to have it in our grasp, and then assent to taking hold of it. In order to accomplish this goal, our hand and arm must fuse with Bruno's. We form a secret pact with him as the lighter's current flows through both of us at once. Our saying "yes" to Bruno here seems almost obligatory. I would argue that our "taking Bruno's place" in the lighter exchange is what frees Guy to win his tennis match.

All of Bruno's previous sordid handwork seems, in the sewer grate scene, carried over to us as we projectively push our own hand into his,

Figure 5.2. Bruno's fingers and the lighter.

like a familiar glove. Think of Bruno's two fingers delicately closing over the lighter in its resting place of leaves and sewer muck, and lifting it up toward the light. The impression of taint fades almost immediately as Bruno's hand fully grasps it and the lighter goes back in his pocket. Our temporary pact (this time a sewer alliance) with Bruno appears once more to be repealed or set aside, though it is subject, without advance notice, to renewal. Our hands and minds, according to the standard Hitchcock dispensation, are wiped clean as the lighter disappears from sight.

There is no penalty for our thought embrace of Bruno at the sewer grate, just as there was none in sharing Bruno's and Hitchcock's mastery (along with an odd wince of victim pain) during Miriam's murder. We were *there*, on the spot, but not precisely in our own person, not in our own right. If we give in for a time to the naughty pleasure of thinking someone else's thoughts, we will soon—as soon as we wish—find a clear and cleansed channel back to our own. The root of the word pain, Nigel Spivey reminds us in his brilliant study, *Enduring Creation: Art, Pain and Fortitude*, is the Latin *poena*, carrying the double burden of "penalty" and "punishment." The fugitive sinful thoughts that Hitchcock would have his strongest images breed in us are usually on the oscillating shadow line dividing pain and pleasure. We become discriminating wine tasters in our visual relation to others' suffering, and deny that there should be either penalty or punishment for what we divertingly take in. Where is the harm in imagining, in indulging fleetingly the power of images to carry us out of ourselves? The direction of our thought movement hardly matters. The lively, child greediness and messiness of the Bruno part of the viewer can always be disciplined and curtailed by the Guy part, with its wariness, carefulness, and social gift for saving face. As Bruno hastens away from the sewer to catch a cab, we are free to watch him, as we may imagine we always have, from Guy's distance, as though Bruno were eternally and reliably that "stranger" from the train, who has senseless designs on us, and whose actions and thoughts, in Guy's words, are those of a "crazy fool."

Hitchcock's form is the Bruno dimension of his films, artfully extravagant and irrational, though continually relying on meticulous plans. Paradoxically, the Bruno "form" dynamically generates the authentic moral thinking of the narrative, always running in opposition to the spurious, ready-to-wear Guy morality articulated in the story proper, which it both doubles and unravels. On Guy's behalf, it must be conceded that Hitchcock takes very seriously the claims and dictates and expansive shaping influences of *social* forms, which provide most of what passes for safety and stability in our much too fragile lives. Hitchcock never loses sight of the fact that social forms are substantial as well as arbitrary, and to the extent that they are substantial (comfortably so) Hitchcock believes in them and relies on them. His plots, with their typically self-conscious, artificial closure, are built in close alignment with social forms (like a novel of manners), forms whose great virtue is that they can be endlessly tested, found wanting, and then restored without undue strain or fuss.

Hitchcock *believes* then in Guy Haines, who is in a sense social form incarnate. But he is under no illusion that Guy's means of "making successful arrangements" has anything to do with self-knowledge or moral growth. Hitchcock believes in Guy in the same way that he believes in the movie spectator, arguably Guy's most abiding double. The visual form that is Bruno executes an intricate dance with the social forms of Guy's and the viewer's plot. To the extent that Bruno unsettles this structure, showing how it requires more than its own terms for adequate, grown-up, culpable thinking, he is both the parody "conscience" of social form and its exuberantly sinful tempter. If the viewer comes to acknowledge Bruno, by film's end, as deeply bound to the moral realm he flaunts and throws askew, she may gain the privilege of seeing beyond Guy, who steadfastly disavows kinship with the unseemly, unshareable world in which Bruno dwells. The lighter, as the central repeating image in Hitchcock's (and Bruno's) visual design, is tied to all the shifty knowledge in the film that counts. When Bruno shows it to us (involuntarily) for the last time in his limp, outstretched hand, it is ours for the taking.

Yet Hitchcock is properly skeptical of our desire for real knowledge at the movies—certainly at his movies. He suspects that we will refuse to grasp the lighter if it carries any hint of residual taint. That we have "taken" it so often before, for brief intervals of furtive, shady, possibly sinful pleasure, can be dismissed as a viewing accident that we, like Guy, are entitled to forget. We leave such accidents behind in exchange for the socially determined ease of our affiliation with Guy, and his determined innocence. He, after all, has been fully exonerated by the mere *sight* of the lighter's reappearance. Try as we might, it is hard to hold on to the idea that "the innermost temporal rhythms"—in Augustine's phrase—of our movie looking and thinking could result in a meaningful guilt of any duration. That being the case, Guy (rather than Bruno) will continue to be our surrogate, seeking his imitation of light and life in places where he is always a stranger to wrongdoing.

Works Cited

Fried, Michael. *Menzel's Realism: Art and Embodiment in Nineteenth-Century Berlin.* New Haven: Yale UP, 2002.

Gracq, Julien. *Reading Writing*. Trans. By Jeanine Herman. New York: Turtle Point Press, 1980.

Highsmith, Patricia. "The Trouble with Mrs. Blynn, the Trouble with the World," in *Nothing that Meets the Eye*. New York: W.W. Norton & Co., 2002.

McGilligan, Patrick. *Alfred Hitchcock: A Life in Darkness and Light*. New York: Regan Books, 2003.

Spivey, Nigel. *Enduring Creation: Art and Pain and Fortitude*. Berkeley: University of California Press, 2001.

Immorality

6

Steven M. Sanders

Hitchcock's Immoralists

The British philosopher Philippa Foot once observed that "outside of moral philosophy we would not think of the cool and imprudent, though wicked, man as specifically irrational in his conduct; outside moral philosophy we also know that there is nothing one can do with a ruthless amoral man except to prevent him from doing too much damage" (1970). Many moral philosophers are unprepared to accept such assertions, which they would regard as disquieting at best and flawed philosophy at worst. They argue that morality has a rational foundation and the moral wrongdoer can be shown to be acting contrary to reason and in this sense he is irrational. This Platonic-Kantian conception of morality has had its advocates since at least the time of Plato's *Republic* (around 380 BC) but it also has been subject to a variety of qualifications, concessions, and criticisms, as we shall see below. If Foot and others are correct, how might we convince the moral wrongdoer who asks, "why should I be moral?" As will be seen, this question implicates Hitchcock's films in some interesting and important ways and opens up a discussion of how to do things with Hitch.

Matters of Morality

One of the most important ways filmmakers contribute to the investigation of the abstract issues associated with moral philosophy is through the dramatic visualization of types of conduct and character that give rise to questions of moral right and wrong. Hitchcock's films vividly depict moral wrongdoing in ways that make for an achievement that is more than merely technical. One of Hitchcock's signal achievements is to have given dramatic representation to the *complexities* that run through the moral life in films that encompass moral wrongdoing in so many of its varieties. While his films do not challenge the authority of morality, they lead us to ask whether morality can be given an unambiguous specification and, in doing so, they furnish material for philosophical reflection on its nature, status, and justification

This is not to say that Hitchcock has given cinematic representation to all the philosophical issues that run through the moral life, or even tried to. The importance of Hitchcock "as moralist" should not be attributed to any philosophical or moral depth he may have had. But he was among the most successful in depicting the moral wrongdoer. In *Shadow of a Doubt* (1943), Charles Oakley (Joseph Cotten) is a literal as well as figurative lady-killer. In *Stranger on a Train* (1951), Bruno Anthony (Robert Walker) starts out chatty and amusing, but morally speaking he is shooting blanks when he tells Guy (Farley Granger) "Some people are better off dead." Even the affable shyness of *Psycho*'s Norman Bates (Anthony Perkins) belies what we eventually discover is so terribly wrong with him. Hitchcock's films create contexts within which one is led to ask whether morality can be justified. In doing so, they furnish material for reflection on the status of morality as a source of action-guiding reasons.

Hitchcock is not a moral skeptic. He regards morality—or more accurately, he assumes his audiences regard it—as extremely (if not supremely) important: when its dictates conflict with nonmoral dictates, such as expedience or selfishness, morality is supposed to take precedence. This is noteworthy because morality is problematic in Hitchcock's films precisely because the philosophically compelling question for Hitchcock's immoralists is why they should *refrain* from moral wrongdoing, especially when moral wrongdoing seems more conductive to their goals than morally right conduct. The person who believes he or she has a good reason not to refrain from doing something that is morally wrong is of longstanding philosophical interest and is given dramatic amplitude in Hitchcock's films, where central plot points often turn on lying, deception, betrayal, larceny, embezzlement, kidnapping, and murder. Of course Hitchcock's characters are driven to solve dramatic, not philosophical, problems; and they are not designed to provide anything like philosophically defensible answers to the moral problems they dramatize. Nevertheless, Irving Singer (2005) and Richard Allen (2007) are right to say that Hitchcock is a moralist in the sense that he has a worldview or way of thinking about moral themes and problems, even if he is not a moral philosopher in the sense of systematically articulating and explicitly defending the criteria by which we are to appraise character and judge the moral rightness and wrongness of actions. More important, Hitchcock's art of displacing human beings so that they are susceptible to such departures from moral conduct as those found in his films provides dimension and moral color to the abstractions of moral philosophy.

If the creation of suspense that underwrites audience reception is the self-described central objective of Hitchcock's art, morality is one of his central problems. His films delineate some of the most ambiguous features of morality through their imaginative reconstruction of character and circumstance: the jealous husband who plots to murder his spouse (*Dial M for Murder*); the teacher who, in his zeal for the thought of Nietzsche, leads his most gifted students to believe that they are above conventional moral constraints (*Rope*); the trusted employee who embezzles from her employer (*Psycho*); the charlatan who swindles her clients (*Family Plot*); the bickering couple whose acrimony ends in murder (*Rear Window*); the blackmailing spouse who drives her husband to distraction (*Strangers on a Train*); the beloved uncle's duplicity, betrayal, and murder (*Shadow of a Doubt*). Such examples furnish material for philosophical reflection on the grounds we have for refraining from doing these morally wrong things.

In his essays and interviews (Gottlieb 1995), Hitchcock was reticent about substantive matters of morality, as contrasted with his extensive discussions of technique, so we may be disinclined to make sweeping generalizations about his own moral beliefs, judgments, and principles. His films offer no more than ambiguous clues about such matters. Someone who depicts his antagonists as egoists, amoralists, nihilists, and psychopaths might be expected to endorse altruism, moral rectitude and realism, and an ethics of health and flourishing—not as a description of the way things are but as an ideal, an account of the way things should be. To the extent that the protagonists who prevail against Hitchcock's villains manifest such qualities of character as practical wisdom, courage, prudence, and moderation, we have the classical virtues of Aristotle. However, this is an oversimplification because Hitchcock insinuates that to some extent even his "morally average" protagonists are susceptible to morally questionable behavior, from L.B. Jefferies's voyeurism to Guy Haines's opportunism to Margot Wendice's adultery to Scottie Ferguson's incapacity for love because it is so tethered to obsession that we are left with a bitter aftertaste at the conclusion of *Vertigo*. It would therefore be a mistake to think that Hitchcock's main objective is to moralize in a simple or straightforward way. As several contributors to this volume demonstrate, Hitchcock's protagonists are often oblique in their moral character, ambivalent in their commitment to moral values, and by no means paragons of moral virtue. This leads us to come away from many of his films with the recognition that there is more to morality than the obligatory and the forbidden, that this dichotomy is not sufficiently nuanced to organize the phenomena of moral experience.

Three Immoralist Perspectives

Hitchcock's immoralists enter his universe under a variety of guises and disguises and, moreover, in ways that often are implicit, indeterminate, or multiply interpretable. While a full typology of the agents of moral wrongdoing in Hitchcock's films is beyond the scope of this essay, let us identify at least three immoralist perspectives on thought and action: egoism, amoralism, and nihilism. In *Dial M for Murder*, *Shadow of a Doubt*, *Strangers on a Train*, *Rear Window*, and *Rope*, to take some well-known instances, all three varieties have been dramatized as a preoccupation with the repudiation of moral values. Because egoism, amoralism, and nihilism are associated with the displacement of conventional morality in these films, they appear to be similar outlooks, but they are conceptually distinct. Egoists believe that morality is reducible to self-interest or definable in terms of it, where "self-interest" is often construed as expedience and selfishness rather than their more respectable distant relative, prudence. Because egoists claim that self-interest is the criterion of ultimate value, egoists are not relativists. Rather, egoists maintain that the justificational supremacy of self-interest reflects objective reality. In *Dial M for Murder*, for example, Tony Wendice (Ray Milland) extorts an old college acquaintance, C.A. Swann (Anthony Dawson), to murder his wife Margot (Grace Kelly) so he can live a life of decorous self-indulgence on her fortune. When the plan goes awry and Swann is killed in the act, Tony attempts to implicate Margo. If one were to ask Tony why he thinks these actions are morally justified, he would say (if he were imprudent enough to say anything at all) that such acts help to bring about a way of life in which things go best for himself.

Unlike egoists, nihilists insist that there are no objective moral values to ground judgments about what we morally ought to do or how we ought to live. In *Rope*, Brandon Shaw (John Dall) and Philip Morgan (Farley Granger) are proponents of values "beyond good and evil" and profess that "moral concepts of good and evil and right and wrong don't hold for the intellectually superior." Acting on this belief that "the lives of inferior beings are unimportant," they kidnap and kill a former classmate simply to experience the exhilaration of committing the perfect murder, without remorse (at least on Brandon's part). But, like egoists, nihilists are not relativists, either. Although they maintain that there are no objective moral values, this does not mean they believe there are no objective values at all. It means that if there are objective values, they will be nonmoral (and, in the cases of Brandon and Philip, *anti*-"moral" in the sense of conventional morality).

Our third type, amoralists, express indifference to morality. If they make any moral judgments at all, this is not because they care about morality but rather because they know that *others* care about it, and they realize that to feign care for others and concern about morality may be an effective means to achieve their ends. Whereas egoists believe that there is such a phenomenon as moral truth (though it consists in self-interest), and nihilists dismiss the idea of moral truth altogether, amoralists are indifferent to what people say and think about morality. These distinctions are not consistently observed by Hitchcock or his screenwriters. Hitchcock is fully capable of displaying the full range of moral wrongdoers—egoists, amoralists, and nihilists—in the same film, given his propensity to integrate alternative elements into an aesthetic whole, so it will be convenient to use the term "immoralist" as any of these three types of moral wrongdoer without further discrimination.

Figure 6.1. Hitchcock with *Rope* cast.

In multifarious and often ambiguous ways, Hitchcock's films are filled with value-laden assumptions, especially about the importance of moral reasons and moral values, which assist in the audience identification that Hitchcock regarded as an essential filmmaking goal. Needless to say, this is not a bad thing. Imagine what it would be like for a filmmaker to depict murder by multiple stab wounds, for example, in a morally neutral way.[1] Nevertheless, fastening on the psychological aspects of his immoralists' personalities allows Hitchcock to display their capacity for moral wrongdoing while leaving unanswered the question why they *should be* moral.

Two Immoralists

Charles Oakley and Bruno Anthony, two of Hitchcock's most fully realized immoralists, do not themselves appeal to anything recognizably "moral" (except in passing) in defense of their actions because neither cares enough about others to think that he *ought* to guide his actions by moral principles. If this is the case, then how, if at all, could we establish that they ought to constrain their conduct by moral considerations, especially since they themselves do not believe they should? Notice that when philosophers ask "Why be moral?" they are not asking "Why, *morally speaking*, should Charles Oakley and Bruno Anthony be moral?" Surely it would not do to point out (what is perfectly obvious) that in the contexts in which Hitchcock presents them, deception and betrayal, to say nothing of murder, are morally wrong, that there are moral reasons against doing such things. The cases of Charles Oakley and Bruno Anthony raise a far more fundamental question: why ought (in a nonmoral sense of "ought") they give moral considerations any weight in the first place? These cases illustrate the difficulties that arise when philosophers try to give a generally convincing answer to the question "why be moral?"

When serial killer Charles Oakley begins to feel the heat of a police investigation in Philadelphia, he decides to lay low by visiting his sister and her family in the small California town of Santa Rosa. "Uncle Charlie" is the favorite of his niece and namesake, Charlie Newton (Teresa Wright), who has indeed resolved to invite him to visit in order to shake her family out of their provincial complacencies. However, Charlie soon begins to suspect that her uncle is harboring a sinister secret, one made all the more terrible by the special bond they share.

Evidence of his pathological alter ego begins to accumulate even as Oakley warns his niece how dangerous it can be to inquire too deeply into things that might cause her great distress. In a character-revealing speech at the dinner table, we are given further insight into the advanced state of Charles Oakley's moral decay. He tells his sister's family that the wealthy widows he observes in fine hotels "spending their husband's money" are nothing but "fat wheezing animals." Charlie comes to understand that her beloved uncle is in reality the "Merry Widow Murderer" who is being sought back east for at least three deaths. Unrepentant, he gives full expression to his contempt for humanity when tells Charlie, "Do you know the world is a foul sty? Do you know if you ripped off the fronts of houses you would find swine?"

In *Strangers on a Train*, top amateur tennis player Guy Haines, whose career and love life are covered regularly in the newspapers, and Bruno Anthony, the dapper, spoiled son of a doting and dotty mother (Marion Lorne) and a wealthy father Bruno hates and wants to kill, meet on a train. Bruno has read that Guy is estranged from his wife, Miriam (Laura Elliott), and is seeing another woman, Ann Morton (Ruth Roman), a U.S. senator's daughter. Guy wants to divorce his wife, marry Ann, and begin a career in Washington politics. Miriam won't agree to a divorce. She tells Guy that she is pregnant with another man's child and threatens to ruin Guy's reputation if he refuses to take her to Washington and raise her child as if it were theirs.

Since they both have someone they'd like out of the way, Bruno proposes that they "swap murders." Since they are strangers, there's nothing to connect them. Consistent with his indifference to morality, Bruno offers Guy facile rationalizations ("What's a life or two, Guy? Some people are better off dead"). Guy humors Bruno as they depart from the train, telling him with irony evident to anyone but Bruno, "Sure, Bruno, sure." Then Bruno calls on Guy to inform him that he has *actually* murdered Miriam and expects Guy to keep his end of the agreement. Guy tells him he's crazy and refuses to have anything to do with him. Bruno is furious. He stalks Guy, showing up unexpectedly at Guy's tennis club, ingratiating himself with Guy's friends and chatting amiably in French. He calls Guy constantly, insisting that he carry out his part of the arrangement. When Guy threatens to go to the police, Bruno reminds Guy that he's already deeply implicated in his wife's murder. "Who has the most to gain?" Bruno asks with reference to Guy's affair with Ann. "Not me. I'm a stranger."

If Bruno is insane, this would certainly be the place for Hitchcock to show it. As Hitchcock depicts him, Bruno clearly exhibits a number of symptoms of psychopathy (Smith 1984, 189). There is the obvious disregard of Guy's wife, and insofar as Guy is an unwilling accomplice of Bruno's wild scheme, there is Bruno's manipulation of Guy as a means to his own homicidal ends. His superficially clever but erratic plan seems to be based on highly unrealistic expectations. Nevertheless, he does not appear to suffer from such significant incapacity to reason that he is incapable of purposive behavior. In fact, Bruno's behavior is motivated by a very specific purpose: he wants his father dead and to induce Guy to do the actual killing. The fact that Bruno is prepared to commit murder because his father has threatened to have him institutionalized shows an indifference to morality that is chilling to most of us, but it is not clear that he cannot actually tell right from wrong—a criterion of diminished capacity and an excusing condition of legal liability in many jurisdictions in the United States. In this respect, he is unlike Norman Bates, who is subject to extreme cognitive distortion. In cases of such severe forms of psychopathology, the resources the person has for dealing with his desires and beliefs are extremely limited. He becomes a person who, because of impaired cognitive processes, cannot "form his will" through a reflective process of self-management (Schopp 1991, 232). To have unimpaired cognitive capacities in the formation of the will is to have the psychological capacities for reasoning, comprehension, and abstract concept-formation that are missing in Norman Bates. But if we are to understand immoralists like Bruno Anthony and Charles Oakley, we must emphasize as well the importance of *normative* counterfactual capacities in the agent's motivational structure. Someone with normative counterfactual capacities in his motivational structure believes that if certain things were to happen, he morally ought to act (or refrain from acting) in certain ways. This normative counterfactual capacity is indispensable to making moral judgments from which the intention to act is derived. The indifference of Bruno Anthony and Charles Oakley to moral reasons and principles suggests that they are impervious to those considerations either because they do not give them sufficient thought to be moved by them or because they do not think of other persons in moral terms at all. In the end, it appears that neither man is insane in the legal sense. But each either lacks or is indifferent to utilizing the normative counterfactual capacities that underlie moral thinking.

Why Be Moral?

Most viewers of *Shadow of a Doubt*, *Strangers on a Train*, and *Rope*, for example, believe that Charles Oakley, Bruno Anthony, and Brandon Shaw have done grievous moral wrongs to their victims. When a person faces a conflict between his selfish interests and impulses and his moral obligation to respect the lives of others, the latter is supposed to prevail. Moral reasons are commonly thought to be "higher" or "stronger" or "better" than selfish ones. A concern for the welfare of, or respect for the interests of, others is normally thought to provide a stronger reason than a selfish regard for one's own interests. Even granting Hitchcock's depiction of Guy Haines's wife as a promiscuous shrew and a blackmailer, this does not provide Bruno Anthony with a moral justification for killing her. In the absence of good reasons to reject the common-sense belief that what Hitchcock's immoralists did was morally wrong, the more compelling and difficult question is *why should they do the morally right thing?* Can we give Charles Oakley, Bruno Anthony, and similar characters a reason to be moral—especially when they have very strong incentives *not* to be moral? As we have seen, Hitchcock's films help us to understand the practical implications of a failure to give an affirmative answer. If a generally convincing reason for being moral cannot be given, why shouldn't Bruno make such an arrangement and try to induce Guy to carry out his end of the bargain? And why shouldn't Guy reciprocate? And, by implication, why should Charles Oakley refrain from acts of lying, betrayal, and murder if these would be to his advantage, provided he had a reasonably good chance of getting away with them?

Morality and Rationality

The writings of Kant are notoriously difficult and subject to a variety of interpretations, but it is easy to state the central idea of his moral theory: people are moved by reasons to act in various ways, so their actions are governed by certain rational constraints, the most important of which is a principle that Kant (1785) calls the Categorical Imperative: "Act only according to that maxim by which you can at the same time will that it should become a universal law" (67). On the most common interpretations of Kant, the Categorical Imperative lays down either a rational procedure for determining the moral permissibility or impermissibility of an act, or the criterion of the moral rightness or wrongness of an act. (The differences between these two interpretations can be ignored in the present context.) When we are in a situation where we want to determine what we morally ought to do, we are to ask whether we consistently would be willing to have *everyone* follow the rule we would be following (Kant calls this rule the "maxim" of our action). If we would be willing, the act is morally permissible; if not, the act is morally impermissible because it is contrary to reason.

To see how this is supposed to work, let us return to Charles Oakley and Bruno Anthony. The rule that Bruno appears to be following (the maxim of his action) is: "If my happiness is in jeopardy, I will take the necessary steps to remove the obstacles to it." According to Kant, Bruno would not be willing for this rule to become a universal law—that is, a rule to be followed by everyone—for at some point Bruno might himself be an obstacle to someone else's happiness, and he certainly would not want to be killed for that reason. He would not be willing to be on the receiving end of a maxim that made him a target in the way he makes Guy's wife (whom he has nothing against) his target. Therefore, he cannot *consistently* "will the maxim" of his action and yet remain committed to his own happiness and well-being. Much the same approach can be taken with Charles Oakley, whose maxim appears to be: "If my happiness depends on seducing, betraying, and murdering wealthy women in order to obtain the benefits this may afford me, that is what I should do." Once again, the Kantian criticism would be that Oakley cannot consistently will that this maxim be adopted by everyone, since he could not will that he be on the receiving end of such conduct and at the same time remain committed to his own pleasure as his ultimate end.

Bruno and Charlie might rebut this objection by claiming that they can accept Kant's procedure. They can argue that the maxim "I should take whatever steps are necessary to achieve, or remove obstacles to, my own happiness" *can* be universalized. Both might be willing to take their chances with everyone following this rule because they believe that they themselves are sufficiently resourceful to avoid the ill effects that would result even if everyone did likewise. They might mount "charm offenses" and feign sympathetic understanding of the problems of others in order to persuade them that they are no threat to their happiness but are in fact quite decent chaps. Far from being irrational, this is a rational strategy for achieving their ends. Since there is no inconsistency in their willingness to universalize their maxim, neither Charlie nor Bruno would be acting irrationally and thus immorally in the Kantian view.

On the other hand, Bruno and Charlie might deny the legitimacy of the Kantian procedure for justifying morality in the first place. Against Kant's approach we can imagine Hitchcock putting these words into Bruno's mouth: "What makes you think I have to justify my maxims universally? I can justify them to *myself*, and that's all that matters to me. And if I become a nuisance to others, let them take their best shot. I doubt that they'll succeed." Charles Oakley, who lives by his wits, would have much the same thing to say. Or he might make outright moral appeals, as when he appeals to Charlie's sympathy once he realizes she has discovered his identity as the Merry Widower Murderer. He isn't being inconsistent when he does this because he is simply deploying moral language in the service of his own selfish interests.

Morality and Advantage

A number of contemporary philosophers, developing an approach to morality associated with Hobbes, focus on the payoffs and tradeoffs involved in being moral. They would say that "morality pays." This approach is nicely captured by the idea that everyone will do better if everyone follows moral rules such as "Do not kill," "Do not steal," and so on. As the philosopher Kurt Baier (1958, 200) puts it, the moral point of view is a standpoint from which moral rules are adopted "for the good of everyone alike." On this view, "being moral is following rules designed to overrule self-interest whenever it is in the interests of everyone alike that everyone should set aside his interest" (314). This means that everyone will do better if everyone follows the rules of morality and agrees to accept limitations on the pursuit of his or her own self-interest.

Although limiting your own self-interested actions in this way involves some sacrifice, it pays off because you stand to gain more from the willingness of others to limit their pursuit of self-interest than you lose from your own willingness to do likewise. Thus the rationale for this approach to the justification of morality is reinforced by getting you to think about which world you would rather live in: one in which everyone seeks his own advantage (even at your expense), or one in which everyone is willing to sacrifice some personal advantage for the good of everyone alike. The "morality pays" answer illustrates how it is in everybody's interest to be moral.

Unfortunately, the answer to the question "Why should *everyone* be moral?" is not an answer, for each person, to the question "Why should *I* be moral?" Bruno, for example, seeks what he takes to be in his own self-interest by murdering Miriam, thus denying her something that is in *her* self-interest. But that does not provide *him* with a reason to be moral, because he knows that he can count on *others* to comply with moral rules even when *he* does not. It may be true that morality requires each of us to restrain the pursuit of our own self-interest in return for acts of restraint by others. But, unsurprisingly, Bruno knows how to game the system: he believes that *he* would do *even better* if everyone *except him* followed the rules of morality and restrained their own self-interested actions while he placed no such limitations on his own. Bruno is a free rider, someone who exploits the willingness of others to place restrictions on their self-interested behavior without reciprocating by limiting his own self-interested behavior. The bottom line for both Bruno and Oakley is that "morality pays," by which they mean that it works to their advantage if everybody *else* behaves morally. But that does not mean that it pays *them* to be moral.

Self and Others

Steven Pinker (2007) succinctly expresses an approach to these questions that attempts to avoid the pitfalls of these Kantian and Hobbesian answers and is much in favor among contemporary moral philosophers: "The more one knows and thinks about other living things," he writes, "the harder it is to privilege one's own interests over theirs" (20). In his development of a similar approach, James Rachels (1994) writes: "We should care about the interests of other people for the same reason we care about our own interests. For their needs and desires are comparable to our own.... If we can find no relevant difference between us and them, then we must admit that if our needs should be met, so should theirs" (95). And William N. Nelson (1991) seeks to repudiate the idea that the requirements placed on us by moral principles "must be defensible in terms of individual *self-interest*" (ix) by arguing that people "are susceptible to moral considerations of various kinds. They are able to adopt the perspective of others and to care about what can be justified to them. And so, even when morality requires that we adopt an impartial standpoint, morality can still be justified, at least to most normal people" (x).

Many philosophers use these observations to delineate the sorts of considerations that are rationally relevant to, if not actually determinative of, morally right action. Their idea is that we can see things from other people's perspectives, people whose needs and desires are comparable to our own. This is designed to reinforce the point that *suffering, for example, is a moral reason for action and that* the identity of the sufferer is irrelevant to the status of suffering as a moral reason for taking action to reduce or eliminate it.

However, what impresses these philosophers as so obvious that no further support is needed is flatly question-begging to Charles Oakley and Bruno Anthony, for whom the idea that the pain others feel is comparable to their own does not establish why they should care about others in the first place. Charles and Bruno need not deny the alleged fact of interpersonal comparability of pain; but they would argue that their ability to see things from another's perspective or to see his needs and sufferings as comparable to their own does not entail anything about what they ought to do. They would argue that the fact that the suffering of others is comparable to one's own gives one a reason to try to alleviate it only if one already cares about them. Far from proving that the interpersonal comparability of needs, desires, and sufferings is rationally relevant to practical questions, Pinker, Rachels, and Nelson presuppose that it is.

Of course, most of us do not require convincing grounds for being moral, since most of us are not immoralists challenging the credentials of morality. But Hitchcock's immoralists take the perspective from which the question, "Why adopt the impartial standpoint?" can be raised, and from this perspective, it is entirely legitimate to insist on a justification of the altruistic point of view that most of us take for granted. This central question, which Hitchcock's powerful dramatizations force us to confront, is not, as Nelson would have it, "Why should I honor a moral obligation to someone I care about?" It is instead, "Why should I adopt an impartial standpoint at all?" And as it is what philosophers call a *justificatory* question, it is not an empirical psychological question about the susceptibility to be moved by altruistic reasons. The justificatory question arises in a context in which one asks himself or herself what he or she ought to do. Both Bruno and Charles would regard such requirements to impartiality as optional, and the observation that they *are capable of* being concerned with more than themselves would not alter this. Bruno, for example, would not be fazed by the suggestion that he is not "normal" in Nelson's sense, and he would rebut the claim that normal people are those who can adopt an impartial standpoint by asking: "Why should I be "normal" in this sense and adopt an impartial standpoint? Even if I *can* be motivated to treat others impartially, that's no reason why I *should*. It's only an option. Maybe what I should do is pursue my own pleasure at their expense. I think I will!"

How to Do Things with Hitch

Most of us find the behavior of Charles Oakley and Bruno Anthony appalling, but it is troubling that philosophers have been largely unsuccessful in providing a generally convincing response to the perspective of Hitchcock's immoralists. The approach of Kant and his followers ("morality is rational") is too broad. The immoralist who is willing to universalize his exclusively selfish maxims can pass Kant's test (that we must be able to universalize our subjective principles) with flying colors, which is why Bruno can say that *he* is rational too. The Hobbesian approach ("morality pays") is too narrow. Charles Oakley and Bruno Anthony can enjoy the benefits of everyone else's moral behavior without being moral themselves, which is why both can say that it doesn't pay *them* to be moral as long as others are. And the third approach ("the moral point of view is the impartial point of view") fails to provide the immoralist with a non-question-begging answer to the question why *he* should adopt an impartial standpoint even if he *can*. Nevertheless, this approach offers the most promise because it at least reflects an understanding of the basis of the problem—the immoralist's lack of concern for the wants and interests of others—and the direction a solution must take: the provision of an intersubjective justification for being moral that avoids the egocentricity and accompanying indifference or lack of understanding that motivates the immoralist's position. If we could compare a way of life in which being moral plays a central role with a way of life in which morality is rejected, much as Charles and Bruno have done, we could determine which way of life we found preferable and on this basis decide between the two. Insofar as Hitchcock is a moralist, his films help us to visualize and take to heart the psychological implications of such a preference. This suggests that what Hitchcock has done in *Shadow of a Doubt* and *Strangers on a Train* is to provide something cinematically analogous to a philosophical "thought experiment," an imaginative device that enables us to "see" that some possibility follows from certain assumptions. In both films, Hitchcock shows us what it would be like to be a person whose way of life involves treating other people as mere instrumentalities and who feels neither guilt nor remorse nor the slightest pangs of conscience. Charles and Bruno are extreme cases, to be sure, but if we want to understand what it would be like to be one (extreme) type of person for whom indifference to morality is a central fact of life, Hitchcock seems to be suggesting, we can look to Charles Oakley and Bruno Anthony. With Hitchcock's assistance (and that of his scriptwriters) we can understand the mindset of someone who rejects morality and make the comparison without dogmatically insisting on the correctness of our own moral perspective. By this means, Hitchcock gives us an impartial standpoint from which to compare the two ways of life. As spectators of his films, we can imagine that we are immoralists, either indifferent to or incapable of thinking of other people's needs and interests except as extensions of our own needs and interests. And we can further imagine that we can enter a third state in which we can remember both this immoralist-state and what we were previously like—persons who had feelings of sympathy, compassion, and benevolence, who were capable of remorse, guilt, and a sense of fairness, and who were disposed to care for the needs and interests of others just as we cared for our own.[2] From the perspective of this third state, we could compare the two ways of life objectively and decide which was preferable. We could contrast the satisfactions of human contact we initially had with those we would be missing in the immoralist-state and assess whether any compensating satisfactions could be found.

If we can make sense of this supposition of choosing one way of life over another from this neutral perspective, which would we find preferable: a life in which the needs and interests of others matter for their own sake and are relevant to our decisions about how to act, or a life in which this is not the case? When we think about the choice in these terms, at least some films of Hitchcock can be read as showing that far from being appealing, the immoralist-state represents a model of how not to live. The philosophical nerve beneath Hitchcock's portrayals of immoralists such as Bruno Anthony and Charles Oakley is that the decisions of such men are neither guided by, nor justified in terms of, agent-neutral reasons or objective values. Their decisions are not anchored in moral constraints, so all that remains of their motivational structure is expedience, opportunism, individual assertion, and will to power. And how have they fared? Charles Oakley is not hounded by pangs of conscience or feelings of guilt but by a profound moral exhaustion induced by his belief that "the world is hell so what's the difference?" This is both physically and morally debilitating. Beneath the veneer of the urbane ne'er-do-well, Bruno Anthony is alienated, isolated, and profoundly alone. Both men represent not how well one can live once he has shed the constraints of morality, but how devoid of feeling and stability such a life would be. While this is not a rational justification of morality nor a refutation of egoism, amoralism, or nihilism in the strict logical sense, it may be enough to vindicate morality for those who can make the comparison between the perspective of morality and its immoralist alternatives.[3]

Notes

1. The force of David Thomson's *The Moment of Psycho* (2009) is that Hitchcock's morally neutral, aesthetic point of view of the famous shower stabbing sequence "taught America to love murder," as his book's subtitle has it.

2. The idea of choosing from a "third state" can be found in Peter Singer (1979, 89). I have altered his characterization in several important respects.

3. An early treatment of some of the topics discussed in this essay can be found in my "Why Be Moral? Amorality and Psychopathology in *Strangers on a Train*," in Baggett and Drumin, 175–85.

Works Cited

Baggett, David, and William A. Drumin. *Hitchcock and Philosophy*. Chicago: Open Court, 2007.
Baier, Kurt. *The Moral Point of View*. Ithaca, NY: Cornell UP, 1958.
Gottlieb, Sidney. *Hitchcock on Hitchcock*. Los Angeles: University of California Press, 1995.
Kant, Immanuel. 1785. *Groundwork of the Metaphysics of Morals*, trans. H.J. Paton. New York: Harper, 1964.
Nelson, William N. *Morality: What's in It for Me?* Boulder, CO: Westview, 1991.
Pinker, Steven. "A History of Violence," *The New Republic*, vol. 236, no. 4, 809. (March 19, 2007). https://newrepublic.com/article/77728/history-violence
Rachels, James. *The Elements of Moral Philosophy*, 3rd ed. New York: McGraw-Hill, 1994.
Schopp, Robert F. *Automatism, Insanity, and the Psychology of Criminal Responsibility*. Cambridge: Cambridge UP, 1991.

Singer, Irving. *Three Philosophical Filmmakers*. Cambridge: MIT Press, 2004.
Singer, Peter. *Practical Ethics*. Cambridge: Cambridge UP, 1979.
Smith, Robert J. "The Psychopath as Moral Agent." *Philosophy and Phenomenological Research* 65 (1984): 177–93.
Thomson, David. *The Moment of Psycho: How Alfred Hitchcock Taught America to Love Murder*. New York: Basic Books, 2009.

7

Sidney Gottlieb

Hitchcock the Amoralist

Rear Window and the Pleasures and Dangers of Looking

"When you took your first snapshot—did you ever think it would bring you to this?"

—Stella to Jefferies, immediately after Thorwald looks out his window, directly at them and into the camera (Hayes 144). The film does not include this line of dialogue, but does include the images shown that unforgettably capture what Jefferies's voyeurism brings him to.

∾

*R*EAR *W*INDOW HAS LONG BEEN CONSIDERED to be one of Hitchcock's most provocative and insightful examinations of interpersonal and social life and the dynamics of what is often referred to as the "gaze." It takes us to the heart of our visual culture, our daily life of incessant watching and being watched, and catalogs the "looks" of our lives and their far-reaching psychic, social, moral, and philosophical consequences. Although it engages in a complex investigation of "rear window ethics," much of the film is structured around a somewhat conventional polarity: our "ways of seeing" are at least initially evaluated according to the categories of moral and immoral. The main character, L.B. Jefferies

134   Sidney Gottlieb

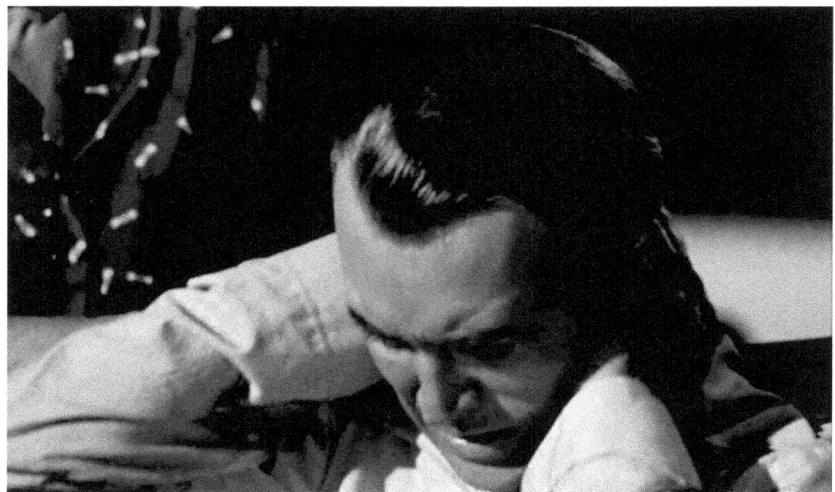

Figure 7.1. *Rear Window*—Jefferies (James Stewart) in anguish.

Figure 7.2. Jefferies falls.

(James Stewart), is both a professional and to a certain extent a psychopathological "looker," and the film traces how his gaze marks him as a justifiably punishable Peeping Tom, immature watcher rather than doer, and manipulative objectifier and victimizer of women. But his gaze is also a vehicle for a carefully negotiated relationship with an unruly world and ultimately allows for sympathetic involvement, knowledge, and the discovery of a crime and arrest of a murderer.

What is less obvious is the way in which much of *Rear Window* exposes and explores a terrain that is, to borrow Nietzsche's challenging phrase, beyond good and evil. As the film progresses, we gradually become aware that there are elements of "looking" not driven by moral or immoral impulses, or explicable by these categories, and instead of being a mechanism of control, whether used for good or bad purposes, the insistent gaze is linked to disorder and entropy. At various points Hitchcock shows that our attraction to "looking" betrays neither our wickedness nor our potentially humanizing attempt to connect with one another but a basic unconcern for or at least distance from either of those motives. Fleeting attention to the spectacle of the moment illustrates that the movements of the eye are amoral. Equally disturbing, any sense of an imperious gaze vanishes at the climax of the film, as Hitchcock shows how the "look," far from reliably establishing and managing a world of order and stability, far from serving the pleasure principle, reveals and perhaps even generates the "chaos world."

William Blake said that above all we need to be saved from "single vision," a statement that provides an apt summary of one of the lessons of *Rear Window* and a useful guide to how we should approach it. Indeed, to do justice to this film we need to take an expanded view of the wide variety of "ways of seeing" it presents. Before analyzing several key sequences that are particularly insightful, dramatic, and memorable parables about why and how we look and the attendant pleasures, dangers, and moral, immoral, and amoral consequences, it may be helpful to first outline some of what *Rear Window* surveys and proposes, organized under the heading "Seven Ways of Looking at Hitchcock's Ways of Looking," taken up not necessarily in order of importance.

First, this is a film about eyes that bind, but also eyes that blind. Rightly or wrongly, it is a commonplace notion that looking helps us connect with the world. We have a sense that to gain knowledge, of course we open our eyes, but we also have an implicit faith that by looking at people, we establish a sympathetic connection; we become more fully human, more fully social and sociable, by looking. This conventional wisdom is both dramatized and subverted in *Rear Window*. Looking can enforce rather than bridge separation and distance, and as serious writers (Sophocles and Shakespeare come first to mind) have reminded us through the years, sight is often the antagonist rather than guarantor of true vision and wisdom. "Eyes that blind" is a shorthand way of describing Hitchcock's intimation that far from alerting us to the realities and the truths of the world, looking can punish us and keep us from knowledge and human connection. *Rear Window* reminds us of numerous ways in which we look but don't see: perception almost invariably shades into misperception. The screenplay includes a humorous but telling reminder of that fact. "Unable to see much" of the dramatic action at the end, Miss Torso (Georgine Darcy) asks: "What happened?" (Hayes 159). The response of the Songwriter (Ross Bagdasarian) underscores the unreliability of all witnesses: "Somebody shot the photographer—and he fell out his window. Something like that." This exchange was left out of the finished film, but there is still much evidence throughout to confirm the likelihood that vision is untrustworthy and blank. Later in my essay I'll focus on several sequences that highlight how sight leads us away from as well as toward important things, and I'll conclude, as the film does, by emphasizing the significance of Hitchcock's stunning visualization—yes, ironies abound—of being blinded by the light.

Second, *Rear Window* is very much about the culture that we live in, tellingly described as a culture of the eye and a culture of the I, the individual self, and inevitably, although not solely, the selfish self. *Rear Window* is especially relevant and compelling because it tells us much about our contemporary society, which, even more now than it was in 1954, when the film was made and released, is a culture of looking (at ourselves as well as others) and being looked at (which also directly affects how we look at ourselves). I'll pursue these parentheses in a later discussion of the variety of looks that Hitchcock displays and analyzes, but even as brief asides here they help reinforce the connection of the eye and the I, and the ways that Hitchcock's critical presentation of a culture of narcissism—Christopher Lasch's extremely valuable book on the subject is deeply relevant to *Rear Window*—is linked with and supported by the fundamental narcissism of looking.

We need to be careful not to define narcissism too narrowly and pejoratively, as solely a negative moral judgment on selfish behavior and inordinate self-concern. Some philosophers and psychologists talk about the definition, development, and assertion of the self as inescapably oppositional. We become aware of and structure our self by recognizing the difference between the world there and the self here: outside is the Other, the essential ground that highlights and establishes the figure that we experience as inside. This dynamic is not necessarily negative, but natural, normal, perhaps necessary. We trace, confirm, and maintain ourselves by separating from what we observe: I see therefore I am. But *Rear Window* shows us the excesses and liabilities of that dynamic: the person who looks runs the risk of remaining disconnected from the

Other, and a self resting on this kind of perceptual foundation is, to say the least, limited, vulnerable, and unstable.

My third proposition is that *Rear Window* is a film about both looking good and looking well. We often use these phrases loosely and interchangeably, but *Rear Window* shows us the difference between them, and how they are gendered. Not surprisingly, at least according to the generally accepted cultural stereotype, it is Lisa Fremont (Grace Kelly), the main female character in the film, who is concerned with looking good. She introduces herself by walking across a room dressed in a stylish and expensive gown, presenting herself as though she is a model at a show. She likes being looked at, and turns on a series of lights to focus and capture Jefferies's (and our) attention. And her related concern is to make her man look good. She wants to do a makeover of him: to get him up and out of his wheelchair, change his clothes, and groom him behaviorally as well as physically. She buys him a new cigarette case, and wants to make him as stylish and accessorized as she is. Not surprisingly, that impulse keeps them apart, because he doesn't want to have anything to do with such a makeover or such a lifestyle. He is primarily concerned with looking well, which is a key part of what his job as a photographer entails. He wants to be a skillful, creative, exploring, inquisitive man, and to maintain his position as an outside observer. Hitchcock counterpoints the fundamental differences between looking good and looking well throughout the film, but not, as is often suggested, by characterizing one as passive and powerless "to-be-looked-at-ness" and the other as an actively controlling and dominating gaze. "Looking good" can be a strenuous activity and mode of power (Lisa is far from a mere mannequin, and her summary of what she does during a typical day highlights her energy and determination) and Jefferies is a compelling example of how "looking well" can be paralyzing, disempowering.

Much of *Rear Window* is set up as a romance—although a problematic romance, to be sure, that frequently edges into an anti-romance. We wonder: Are these two philosophies compatible? Will the person who emphasizes looking good and the person who emphasizes looking well ever be able to negotiate a mutually satisfying relationship? For a moment it does seem to be possible. At one point, Lisa, still dressed and made-up fashionably, goes on an adventure: she leaves the apartment that Jefferies is trapped in, climbs up a fire escape, and acrobatically makes her way through a window. He stays in his apartment and looks at her with a big smile, as though she's finally passed his test and gained his approval. She looks good—stylish and attractive—but she also looks well: she's become an inquisitor, a kind of explorer, his preferred kind of person. In the context of the romantic frame of the film, this sequence is very important and optimistic, conveying a sense of hope that they can overcome their differences and their separation: not so much because she accedes to his demands but because she can be the kind of person he admires and desires without losing or relinquishing her sense of herself. But these two contrasting orientations are not easy to reconcile; and in addition, there are other dangers that lurk in the world of the look, as I'll illustrate later, which threaten their survival, let alone their romance.

Fourth on my list of introductory propositions, *Rear Window* shows many varieties of the look, one of which I will introduce briefly but only after a short digression. Film criticism changed momentously and irrevocably after the publication of Laura Mulvey's "Visual Pleasure and Narrative Cinema" in 1975, and Hitchcock critics in particular are inescapably attuned to the prominence and significance of the several kinds of gazes that she and several generations of critics after her have so extensively analyzed. But the consensus that the gaze is at the heart of Hitchcock's cinema has not yet led to a comprehensive outline and exploration of the many types of gazes present throughout his films and their numerous expressive, dramatic, and analytical functions. We should of course continue to be alert, for example, to what Mulvey and others have defined as "patriarchal" and "panoptic" gazes of domination, objectification, and punishment, but also examine the many gazes not reducible to those rubrics, strategies, or motives: looks of conciliation, entreaty, and sympathy as well as hostility, aggression, and various kinds of judgment; vacant or inscrutable looks; distracted and averted gazes; reciprocated looks; looks of admiration, affection, assent; self-scrutiny and other kinds of intrapersonal looks, including gazes into a mirror; visual projections, dreams, and fantasies; shots of group looking; and on and on.

One of the most intriguing—and particularly Hitchcockian—varieties of the gaze in *Rear Window* is what might be call the "exponential look." In addition to instances of one person looking at another, there are frequently complex doubled, redoubled, and linked series of looks in a Hitchcock film. We see people looking, but we also see people looking at people looking, and people looking at people looking at people looking. And just when we think we've reached the end of this series we add another link: to the audience looking at a film about a person looking at a person looking at a person looking, and so on. It is a dizzying box within a box within a box kind of structure that Hitchcock loves to play with, a dazzling and witty design that provides an accurate mapping of a key part of the way we lead our lives. In the very least, it underscores the facts that a large part of what we do is look, and we are not alone in this activity, nor invisible while we do it. And the term *exponential* perhaps usefully hints at not only a numerical growth of people engaged in a chain looking, but a dramatically increasing intensity as looking generates further and further looking.

My fifth critical proposal has to do with the connection between looking and Hitchcock's mechanisms of identification: that is, how he gets us to relate to the people on screen. In a conventional film or a television show, the spectator is drawn into the drama via techniques that are somewhat simplistic and obvious but often very powerful. Attractive people do exciting things—these categories, I should add, are far-ranging and often include unexpected qualities: attractive does not always mean beautiful, and exciting does not always mean athletically active—and we not only watch but also vicariously share their emotions and experiences. Hitchcock certainly exploits these conventional techniques to a certain extent, but he has other ways of establishing complex patterns of identification. In *Rear Window*, our experiences (that is to say our engagement with and understanding of the world presented therein) are primarily mediated by looking at, with, and through the main character, Jefferies. We identify and sympathize with him and share his experiences and emotions to a large extent because we see things as he does, sometimes literally through his point of view but also more generally because he is a center of visual attention and a center of consciousness (although not the only one, as it turns out). Furthermore, the fact that Jefferies's perceptions are fallible and problematic has a ripple effect: we not only see what he sees, but make the same misperceptions and mistakes that he does. *Rear Window* is extraordinarily powerful because of the drama it depicts and also because we reenact as well as witness it.

In explaining my sixth proposition, let me begin by saying that in *Rear Window* Hitchcock creates more than the classical "cinema of attractions." Cinema from the very beginning showed exciting things and was visually spectacular in order to gain and hold our attention and interest. One of the emphases that defined early cinema was the desire to make it move, make it lively, make it "happen." Hitchcock creates a cinema of attractions but also of distractions. One of the most provocative revelations of *Rear Window* is that the excitement and interest generated by the visual spectacles can be very deceptive, and sometimes dangerously so. Watching can be an act of turning away as well as engaging, concentrating, focusing. I'll discuss later how all this is conveyed very subtly but precisely in a little film within the film that might be given the haunting title: "Whatever Happened to Miss Lonely Hearts?"

Seventh, and finally, Hitchcock subverts the conventional wisdom that you can look, but you'd better not touch. Much of the film proposes that the latter is the danger and the former is the defense: Jefferies is a photographer, and as such he wants to see lots of exciting things. But he doesn't really want to get involved. He wants to wander freely and independently through the world, and this is both a brave and a childish value and desire. He doesn't want to get married, he doesn't want to get domesticated, he doesn't want to be bound to relationships, so he looks rather than touches. He looks so that the world doesn't touch him, entangle him, and limit his freedom. This is a key "issue," often identified as one that characterizes men, particularly in American culture, and *Rear Window* dramatizes and examines it in detail, highlighting in particular that it is by no means a secure refuge from or alternative to touching and personal involvement.

Looking turns out to be arguably the most critical danger in the film. As I'll illustrate in more detail later in my essay, one of Hitchcock's basic premises, here and elsewhere, is that when you look more and more closely at the world, what ensues is not knowledge, not control, not pleasure, but confusion, chaos, and horror. *Rear Window* lets a frightening genie out of the bottle. Jefferies looks incrementally closer at the world: first he simply stares out his window, then he picks up binoculars, then he picks up a huge telephoto lens. Our first impression might be that he is successfully keeping the world at a distance, and yet still peering into it, satisfying his curiosity, and getting the "truth" out of what is there. But long before Antonioni, Hitchcock warns that an optical closeup leads inevitably to an existential blowup. As it turns out, Jefferies is looking into the abyss, with horrifying consequences. As Nietzsche says, in one of his most memorable pronouncements, when you look into the abyss, the abyss looks into you. In one of the most chilling moments in *Rear Window*, the abyss literally looks back at L.B. Jefferies, and not long after its emissary actually pays him a visit, invades his space, obliterates his consciousness, and throws him out the window.

∾

With these introductory propositions in mind, I will now turn to examine some of the details that Hitchcock uses to construct what is not only a cinematic drama but also a probing and analytical cinematic essay on the dynamics and consequences of looking. I'll focus on four key sequences—conveniently, from the beginning, middle, and end of the film—each of which is a parable about a certain aspect or quality of the look. In these parables, Hitchcock explores and ultimately challenges some of our common conceptions about the morality and immorality of looking. Ironically, his investigation of rear window ethics gradually takes us into a realm beyond right and wrong.

The opening of *Rear Window* is an establishing sequence for the film in a far-reaching way, laying out the spaces of the film and also subtly alerting us that the subject of the film is both the viewer viewing and the viewer viewed. After panning across the outside of the apartment building and yard, the camera moves inside to introduce us to the main character and tell the story of how he ended up as we see him, immobilized by broken bones. Moving from object to object, from the cast on his leg to his cameras (one of which is also broken) to the various pictures on the wall, we engage in an inferential process and figure out who he is and what has happened. The images anticipate and answer our queries: How did he break his leg? He was taking pictures and got run over by a car. What does he do for a living? Since the room is filled with camera equipment and pictures, we assume that he's a photographer. We may even guess that he has a "negative" view of women, since a reverse image of an attractive woman appears prominently in the panorama of his room. We know what we know here without any words being spoken. The opening sequence is a good example of what Hitchcock calls "pure cinema," the ability to tell a story completely by visual means. You don't need to have a voiceover explaining "Here's L.B. Jefferies, a casualty of a dangerous line of work" or conversational dialogue along the lines of "Hey Jefferies, is your leg finally healed from your accident a few months ago at the racetrack?"

But this opening sequence does far more than visually give us the backstory. It establishes that this is going to be a film about looking and also that we are going to be drawn into this activity: it sets us up as people who, like the main characters in the film, are engaged in watching, interpreting, figuring things out. Right from the beginning we experience the pleasures of such activities, and perhaps feel confident and a little self-satisfied. We congratulate ourselves a bit for being so bright, attentive, and in tune with the director's plan. But part of what Hitchcock is doing is setting us up for a fall. He establishes a brief sequence that makes us feel very confident and complacent in our position as viewers and in our ability to see the world and wrap it up in a nice little interpretive package. As the film goes on, that nice little package disintegrates almost completely, for Jefferies and also for us. It turns out that perception is unreliable, and this is not even the worst of its liabilities. What Jefferies does is dangerous in unexpected ways. We see right away that when you bring a camera in close to the action, whether at a car race or during a war (also seen in pictures in the room), accidents may happen: wheels come off, bombs explode. But we do not yet realize that these dangers go far beyond the risks faced by action photographers.

Hitchcock presents an incremental dramatic progression of different varieties of the look and thoughts about looking, and in the process he analyzes the conventional wisdom about voyeurism by presenting a case study of a professional voyeur, someone who is paid for looking and capturing this look on film. One of the first problems that Hitchcock raises is the common idea of the immorality of voyeurism, captured in part by showing Jefferies enjoying his guilty pleasures and then by calling him a Peeping Tom. As he talks on the phone, in a conversation that we might note also allows for a more conventional exposition and repetition of the information just conveyed by "pure cinema," we see him looking out at women sunbathing on the roof—with a helicopter flying overhead also trying to give the pilot a close look, reminding us that voyeurism is the norm, and giving us our first of many opportunities to look at someone looking at someone looking. We perhaps don't judge Jefferies too negatively here, but Hitchcock wants to show that voyeurism is in the very least a little bit risqué, and that it may have some worrisome consequences, confirmed by what happens as this sequence concludes. It may be that Jefferies simply needs to scratch a skin irritation inside his cast, but when he reaches a long stick with a little hand at the end of it down into his full-length lower body cast, tugs up and down on it, and then smiles, with an expression of pleasurable relief, we are fully justified in thinking that he is explicitly scratching a troublesome sexual itch that has been aroused by ogling the sunbathing beauties.

Part of what Hitchcock is suggesting here is something that probably all of us think: voyeurism is naughty, and it can lead to even naughtier things. Stella (Thelma Ritter), Jefferies's nurse, is the voice of conventional moralizing, and she reminds him in no uncertain terms about the usual harsh punishment for such behavior:

> STELLA: The New York State sentence for a Peeping Tom is six months in the workhouse. . . . and they've got no windows in the workhouse. You know, in the old days they used to put your eyes out with a red-hot poker. Any of those bikini bombshells you're always watching worth a red-hot poker? Ah, dear, we've become a race of Peeping Toms. What people ought to do is get outside their own house and look in for a change. Yes, sir. How's that for a bit of homespun philosophy?
>
> JEFFERIES: *Reader's Digest*, April 1939.
>
> STELLA: Well, I only quote from the best.

This is Stella talking, not necessarily Hitchcock. I don't think of Hitchcock as endorsing that morality, and I don't think of him as a moralizer, here or elsewhere (in fact, he is a thoroughgoing critic of moralizers). I do think of him as a moralist, which is quite a bit different: he's concerned with issues of morality, but very skeptical about and often very critical of everyday morality. (Godard's well-known comment about politics and cinema is easily adaptable to morality and cinema: the point is not to make moral films, but to make films morally.) Hitchcock presents Stella's response to Jefferies's naughtiness, and allows us to have a good-natured laugh at what he risks by indulging in such things. But this and other related assertions of the conventional wisdom about the immorality of being a voyeur are juxtaposed with insinuations of another conventional but contrapuntal idea, this time in defense of voyeurism, asserting that sometimes it is morally useful as it allows us to connect with other people and is a sign of our sympathy and engagement with the world. The film ends with at least some kind of positive affirmation of the uses of voyeurism: as a result of Jefferies's relentless curiosity, a murder is discovered, a murderer caught, and Jefferies's relationship with Lisa is solidified because of their shared activities in looking into the crime. Even before the end of the film, Hitchcock presents voyeurism in a positive manner. For example, at a key moment near the middle of the film, a woman screams and nearly everyone in the apartment building rushes to see what's happening. These are all people that Jefferies has been looking at throughout the film; now they become the spectators. They are aroused by the cry, and they look out, curious but perhaps also at least momentarily concerned. They see the body of a dog lying on the ground, and hear an impassioned speech by the distraught woman whose dog has been killed, berating the neighbors for being so unneighborly:

Which one of you did it? Which one of you killed my dog? You don't know the meaning of the word "neighbor." Neighbors like each other, speak to each other, care if anybody lives or dies. But none of you do. But I couldn't imagine any of you being so low that you'd kill a little helpless, friendly dog, the only thing in this whole neighborhood who liked anybody. Did you kill him because he liked you? Just because he liked you?

This episode is set up in some ways as the moral center of the film, structured around a lengthy, uninterrupted speech (rare in Hitchcock's films) that is deeply felt and very moving, and alerts us to a key change that has taken place. Far from suggesting that the look is immoral, the emphasis through much of the early part of the film, now the argument is that we need to look to be moral: to be fully human and establish a true community, people need to look at and care more for one another. Interestingly enough, the only person who doesn't look at this point is Lars Thorwald (Raymond Burr), the suspected and, as it turns out, the actual murderer. Voyeurism, far from being immoral and naughty, is now a moral requirement, or at least a key signifier of moral engagement, and the truly immoral and villainous person is identified as the one who doesn't look.

At the same time as this sequence is set up as a serious attempt to educate us to our responsibilities, Hitchcock complicates things. I hope I don't seem insensitive, especially to those readers who have pets, if I say that there's something disproportionate as well as moving (Hitchcock frequently has it both ways) about the seriousness and hysteria that shroud this dramatic sequence. The victim is, after all, not a person but a dog, certainly worthy of concern, but perhaps not entirely compelling as a symbol of where the heartfelt sympathies of the world should be directed. In addition, Hitchcock subtly undermines the claim that a show of attention is a sign of real sympathy and good citizenship. The fact that these people go to their window to hear a woman cry out doesn't necessarily mean that they are acting morally or that they're good people. As soon as "the show's over"—a phrase specifically uttered by an unidentified onlooker—they go back into their apartments, and there is no indication that they are changed in any way by this spectacle and this experience. Looking at by no means translates easily into looking out for one another.

These first two examples illustrate that Hitchcock presents the most common thoughts about voyeurism basically to suggest that they are predictable but insufficient explanations of a very complicated aspect of our behavior. We need to examine and analyze this activity far more deeply than by simply labeling it as immoral or moral. Hitchcock tries to reckon with the complexity of the look in several ways. One is to illustrate not the immorality of the look, not the morality of the look, but the amorality of the look. Looking at something doesn't necessarily qualify you as naughty or vain or detached, nor does it necessarily qualify you as moral, engaged, and sympathetic. Hitchcock's unsettling point is that looking is beyond morality, not an index of right or wrong. And, even more ominously, Hitchcock shows a deep connection of the look with a world that is chaotic and threatening. Much critical commentary on Hitchcock has examined how the look in his films is a strategy of power, especially a man's power over a woman, who becomes fixated and manipulated by a dominating gaze. But little attention has been paid to how the look, especially in a film like *Rear Window*, testifies to a more basic powerlessness, how, as I mentioned briefly earlier, the look discovers, reveals, and generates what Joseph Conrad so memorably calls "the horror, the horror."

The amoral center of *Rear Window* is the sequence, the film within a film, that I have titled "Whatever Happened to Miss Lonely Hearts?" Miss Lonely Hearts (Judith Evelyn) is one of the neighbors that Jefferies looks at through a window across the courtyard as his eyes move from one attraction to another. Hitchcock is remarkably prescient in giving Jefferies this habit: we now live in an age of attention jumping and splitting that testifies to our love of visual spectacle but also our basic disinterest and short attention span. As Stella and Jefferies are preoccupied with their plot to trap Thorwald, they notice Miss Lonely Hearts laying out a handful of sleeping pills, evidently ready to kill herself. The circular mask visible in this shot, one of many such masks used in the film, highlights Miss Lonely Hearts as an object of redundant attention: we are looking through a telescopic device with Jefferies, increasingly our alter ego.

But at this moment Lisa returns, and all attention goes to her. In particular, Jefferies is shown in a prolonged medium closeup staring at her with an enraptured expression. He only has eyes for her. They talk excitedly about Thorwald and plan their next move to get him out of his apartment so they can have free access to it while he is gone. But haven't they forgotten something? And, equally important, haven't we forgotten something? What about Miss Lonely Hearts? A new spectacle and object of attention has arisen, and for nearly three minutes after she somberly lays out the pills and sits down holding a Bible, contemplating last things, Miss Lonely Hearts is out of sight and out of mind.

With his usual impeccable sense of timing and slyness, Hitchcock inserts a quick cutaway of Miss Lonely Hearts lowering her blinds, as if to remind us that we have indeed forgotten about her. It is important to note that the cutaway is not to anything that the characters in the film see. At this point, Jefferies does not turn his eyes again to Miss Lonely Hearts, nor does Stella. But we do, and are jolted by the awareness that we and they have been distracted from something important. The true promiscuity of vision is not so much that it gravitates toward forbidden subjects but that it is fluid, not guided by or securely linked to compassion or moral concern.

The sequence gets even more complex and dramatic as it continues. It is not only Miss Lonely Hearts that we get distracted from and lose sight of. She is a secondary character, the eccentric, aging lady that lives across the way. Although earlier in the film we witness her on a disastrous misadventure with a gentleman caller and at least momentarily feel her disappointment and hurt, we never really get to know her, and perhaps do not develop a great deal of interest in or concern for her, thus—alas—making her eminently forgettable. But the same perceptual habit that leads us to forget about a person we don't really care much for can also distract us from the fate and fortune of someone we do care a lot about. As the sequence proceeds, Lisa climbs into Thorwald's apartment, looking for evidence that he is what they suspect him to be, the murderer of his wife. But as Lisa is discovering an important clue, Miss Lonely Hearts comes back into the picture, taken in by Jefferies's perpetually wandering eye. Four minutes after the cutaway to her that we see, Jefferies at last notices her again, and somewhat blithely and dismissively says that "Stella was wrong about Miss Lonely Hearts." This is a misperception: she is not yet out of danger, but he is unconcerned and returns his attention to Lisa.

Within a few minutes, though, there is another shift. Stella looks again at Miss Lonely Hearts, appreciates how close she is to taking the pills, and urges Jefferies to call the police, which he does. Ironically, at this moment Miss Lonely Hearts is saved by the wonderful music from the musician's apartment nearby, enchanted by the completed version of the song that the musician has been composing throughout the film, titled "Lisa." Even more ironically, all this attention to the song and to Miss Lonely Hearts takes us away from the real Lisa. Jefferies is supposed to signal her by phone when Thorwald returns, but at a critical moment he is otherwise occupied. Hitchcock shrewdly cuts to a long shot that emblematizes exactly what we are normally unable to sustain, all-embracing attention: a split-screen shows the two competing dramas at once, with Miss Lonely Hearts at the bottom of the screen, now out of danger, but Lisa at the top, with Thorwald just about to enter the apartment. The jolt we get from this shot comes not only because of our sudden awareness of Lisa's vulnerability but also because of our realization that we, like Jefferies, are complicit in it. By diverting our attention, we have put Lisa at risk. Jefferies's tormented expression as Lisa is not only threatened but throttled by Thorwald is thus a characteristically Hitchcockian mixture of sympathetic pain and guilt, and is an image of the strain on the film's main character and perhaps the film's spectator as well (see photo at beginning of essay).

Jefferies's expression here foreshadows what is to come as the film concludes, the revelation of the horror of the world, a horror that is generated by the act of looking. Despite the discomfort caused by it—Jefferies seems to be in even more pain than the person he is watching who is actually being beaten, and James Stewart expertly registers this pain almost to the point of disintegration—he simply can't stop. Once the police arrive and Lisa is safe, both Jefferies and Stella pick up their viewing devices and look out the window again. The desire to look is inexhaustible, and, as we are about to find out, the difficulties this causes accelerate. The emphasis on Lisa's vulnerability gives way to a sudden awareness of Jefferies's even greater danger. Raymond Burr, the actor who plays Thorwald, was known later in his career primarily as the gruff but genial television character on *Perry Mason* and *Ironsides*, but early on he played mostly film noir heavies, and here he is the embodiment of menace. Thorwald sees that Lisa is pointing behind her back to the wedding ring—which Mrs. Thorwald presumably would never have left if she were alive—and he then looks up and out the window, not only at Jefferies, but directly into the camera and at us. It is one of the most shocking moments in the film, perfectly capturing what I described earlier as the philosophical proposition that when you look into the abyss, the abyss looks into you, and our reflexive response is the same as Jefferies's: to instinctively recoil.

This feeling of menace intensifies, and leads to the climax of the film, which is not only one of almost palpable brutality, where Jefferies is assaulted by Thorwald and tossed around and then finally out of the room, but one of metaphysical horror as well. The action during this part of the film is deeply ironic: a puzzling murder mystery is resolved, but the veil is ripped off a much deeper unresolvable and perhaps even more frightening mystery. (Shakespeare is a useful reference point here: we have not delved deeply enough into *Macbeth* if we think that the utmost horror it dramatizes is murder, even "murder most foul." The same can be said of *Rear Window*—and *Vertigo* and *Psycho*.) What Jefferies's inquisitive look discovers or establishes is not primarily the truth about a crime; not sympathy or connection or knowledge; not any sense of the world commanded by an imperial and controlling gaze. Instead, the revelation is how horrifying and chaotic, how cognitively and physically threatening the world is, and we see this quite concretely, not abstractly, when the monster from and representing the abyss leaves his lair and enters ours. (This scenario is of course a generic convention, but I think that *Nosferatu* is for Hitchcock the archetypal horror film, and there are several intriguing parallels between it and *Rear Window*, including the fact that the residences of Count Orlok and Jonathan and Mina Harker face each other across a short space, and that at a key moment building toward the climactic home invasion, Orlok stares out his window into the Harker's, shown in extreme long shot in contrast with the telescopically enhanced close shot of Thorwald at a similar moment, but still shocking and menacing. Hitchcock's films repeatedly reveal that Nosferatu lives nearby and is always ready to visit us.)

Jefferies tries to defend himself the best way he can, with flash bulbs. He's a photographer, so according to Hitchcock's logic, he would of course defend himself by the means at his disposal. But this proves to be pathetically ineffective, yet another reminder in the film that one can wield the photographic apparatus and still not be a "director" in any meaningful way, and adds to rather than defeats the welling up of chaos. Instead of keeping Thorwald more than momentarily at bay, the flash bulbs serve as an opportunity for a dazzling and deeply significant repeated special effect: red suffusions that momentarily disturb but also reinforce the dominance of Thorwald's point of view and obliterate Jefferies's. The flashes meant as protection illuminate Thorwald and then give us glimpses of the world as seen through his eyes. This shift in point of view is often used in horror films: as the drama intensifies, we see things from the perspective of the approaching monster. But *Rear Window* complicates that tried and true convention. What we see primarily is not the victim from the monster's point of view, but a supersaturated explosion that is an image of chaos, discomfort, and confusion. A border has been crossed: to this point, vision has kept us safely distanced, but the safe separation vanishes and we are now inside the consciousness of another person, the ultimate act of penetration and dissolution. Jefferies literally turns away, but cannot avoid the consequences of his all-too-human actions: looking becomes a portal to an enveloping blankness and bleakness.

This is the second of the sequences in the film, besides the death of the dog, that brings the spectators out. We now see from outside Jefferies's window rather than looking through his window. Jefferies the spectator has become the spectacle, and in the last special effects shot of the sequence, a disorienting matte shot, we see him falling into chaos (see photo at beginning of essay). Unlike in *Vertigo*, here the person falling survives, but we wonder what kind of life he survives into. To me this sequence is one of Hitchcock's most intense and meaningful cinematic renderings of what critics refer to as the "chaos world" that is never far from us. And, again, as I've tried to emphasize throughout my essay, it is a world that is revealed and released by looking. We've come a long way from the early moments in the film where we get a presentation of what seems to be a kind of venial sin of voyeurism. We've come a long way from the complacent and confident hope of the morality of the look, the belief that it will socialize and humanize us. The film climaxes with an unmooring and shattering look into—and a final reminder of how deeply the look is connected to—"the horror, the horror."

∾

One of the guiding impulses of filmmakers from the very beginning was memorably captured by the great early film director D.W. Griffith, when he said, "The task I'm trying to achieve is above all to make you see" (quoted in Jacobs 119). Be careful what you wish for, Hitchcock might well say. He adopts Griffith's credo, but with a characteristic edge as he attempts to alert us to the subtleties, complexities, responsibilities, and not entirely pleasurable consequences of seeing, in film and in life. Hitchcock's dramatization of our ways of seeing is delightful and ominous, endlessly fascinating and endlessly disturbing. We should be charmed but also haunted by *Rear Window*. After watching it, we might well, as Hitchcock often envisioned, return home and stand around the icebox, cold chicken in hand, talking about the film. Our cue might be Lisa's determined statement to Jefferies at the almost exact midpoint of the film, borne of her new awareness that there is indeed a deep mystery afoot and her confidence that it is fathomable: "Tell me everything you saw, and what you think it means." But much of what we see in *Rear Window* explodes our complacency: it is difficult to feel confident that we can ever see something and talk comfortably about what it means after watching a film that so memorably reveals how the act of looking releases the genie of chaos and meaninglessness.

This is not to say that overall the film is a counsel for despair. *Rear Window* flirts with genres that may console us and, despite Hitchcock's own admission that he did not feel obliged to "drag" one in (see his article "*Rear Window*"), gestures toward a happy ending: the film is in part a comedy that concludes with at least a veneer of healing and restored order (although counterpointed in true Hitchcock fashion with new injuries and incipient disorder), a romance that allows for the possibility of survival and partnership, and a detective story that solves at least the whodunit part of a murder mystery (deeper and even more troubling mysteries remain), purges the murderer from our midst, and reestablishes moral and emotional equilibrium. But the brief sigh of relief conveyed by a concluding tableau of the couple coupled and the protagonist smiling, with eyes wide shut, to coin a phrase, does not balance what the film fundamentally, repeatedly, and disturbingly dramatizes and evokes: a shudder—in fact, a metaphysical shudder. That term is directly applicable to many of Hitchcock's works, although it was coined by George Williamson to describe the "peculiar intensity of feeling" characteristic of John Donne's poetry, which was preoccupied with describing and analyzing the ways in which even our most capable and sensitive look at the world around us shakes rather than strengthens the firmament, torments rather than sustains us, and calls everything into doubt. One of the powerful revelations of *Rear Window* is that our optical expectations and experiences inevitably go awry. Jefferies's camera with a telescopic lens, like Galileo's telescope that Donne contemplated with much uneasiness, is emblematic of modernity, and though it promises pleasure and power, it is more fundamentally linked with a frightening vision and unforgettable experience of "all coherence gone" (Donne, "An Anatomy of the World" l. 213).

Note

This present essay is a much revised version of a talk I gave as the inaugural Honors Program Lecture at Sacred Heart University in March 2006. I have not removed all traces of the occasional looseness and informality of that talk, in the hope that the revised version may still be accessible to the audience it was initially aimed at. Barton Palmer's enthusiastic response to an earlier revised version gave me much-needed encouragement to continue my work, and I am also extremely grateful to John Bruns and James MacDowell for additional detailed comments on this earlier version, which have been enormously helpful as I tried to expand, clarify, and in some cases modify my original thoughts.

Works Cited

Donne, John. *The Complete Poetry of John Donne*, ed. John T. Shawcross. Garden City, NY: Doubleday, 1967.

Hayes, John Michael. *Rear Window*, final white script, December 1, 1953.

Hitchcock, Alfred. "*Rear Window*." *Take One* 2, No. 2 (November–December 1968): 18–20.

Jacobs, Lewis. *The Rise of the American Film*. New York: Harcourt Brace and Co., 1939.

Lasch, Christopher. *The Culture of Narcissism: American Life in an Age of Diminishing Expectations*. 1979; rpt. New York: W.W. Norton and Co., 1991.

Mulvey, Laura. "Visual Pleasure and Narrative Cinema." *Screen* 16, no. 3 (Autumn 1975): 6–18.

Williamson, George. *The Donne Tradition: A Study in English Poetry from Donne to the Death of Cowley*. Cambridge: Harvard UP, 1930.

8

Richard Allen

Voyeurism Revisited

Hitchcock's very first film, *The Pleasure Garden* (1925), on which Alma Reville worked as assistant director, opens backstage on dancing girls descending a spiral staircase onto a stage that we view from the wings. Hitchcock cuts to a medium shot of a female dancer performing in front of a line of scantily clad dancing girls, and then to a reverse field lateral tracking shot across a row of ogling gray-haired men in entranced appreciation of the show. The camera alights on one man who adjusts his monocle for a better view, and Hitchcock cuts back to an out-of-focus point-of-view shot of the performers. A pair of binoculars then rises in the foreground, and a match on action reveals that the old man has traded in his monocle for a pair of binoculars. A new point-of-view shot through a circular mask, now in focus, laterally tracks in closeup the legs of the chorines until alighting on the female protagonist Patsy Brand (Virginia Valli) tilting up her figure to her face. The old man reacts with enjoyment to what he sees and ogles afresh with his monocle. The girl, for her part, is initially perceived wearing a genuine smile of enjoyment as she participates in the performance. However, when she realizes that the old man is leering at her, she returns his gaze with a blank stare, as if to say "and what do you think you are staring at?"

This scene at once establishes Hitchcock's preoccupation with staging themes of male voyeurism toward women in the cinema and the complexity of that staging, and it also serves to reflect indirectly on the relationship between voyeurism in the theatrical setting and voyeurism in the cinema. The scene establishes a parallel between the female performer on stage and the female performer on screen and the audience for both as a public viewer. However, from the beginning, Hitchcock reveals how cinema departs from the theater by taking us behind the scenes to the labor of the female performer. The power of cinema is further revealed as Hitchcock individuates a single spectator from the audience and aligns the spectator of the film with his perceptual point of view. The eyeglass and the binoculars explicitly link cinema to prosthetic devices of vision that allow the spectator, like the character, to ogle the bodies of the female performers. At the same time, far from establishing the authority of the male gaze, Hitchcock also suggests the unsavory nature of this front-row voyeur, whose gaze is "returned" in no uncertain terms by the blonde performer.[1]

Hitchcock's preoccupation with voyeurism and what it might tell us about cinema and, in particular, the representation of gender relationships in cinema, is among the most well-trodden ground in the literature on film. Yet in spite, or perhaps because, of the influence of Christian Metz's book *The Imaginary Signifier*, there remain several fundamental questions about voyeurism and its relationship to the cinema that appear unresolved. One set of questions has to do with what exactly is voyeurism. Is voyeurism a pathology? Is there one kind of voyeurism, or several kinds? Is cinema really a voyeuristic medium, or is it simply used to represent fictions that stage voyeurism? The second set of questions pertains to the moral status of voyeurism. Is voyeurism morally reprehensible, and if so, why? If cinema is a voyeuristic medium, is cinematic voyeurism morally reprehensible? Is there a gender bias in voyeurism? Hitchcock's practice, I believe, continues to shed light on these issues. I begin this essay by exploring the conceptual and moral issues surrounding voyeurism outside and inside the cinema with reference to Hitchcock, and I conclude with an analysis of *Rear Window* as a moral allegory of film spectatorship.

Defining Voyeurism

Within psychoanalysis, the concept of voyeurism is closely linked to that of scopophilia or *schaulust*. Freud discusses this concept in "Three Essays on Sexuality" in relationship to the so-called "polymorphous perversity" of children where the sexual "instinct" is not focused on the genitals but distributed across the body and its organs (109). In the case of scopophilia, this instinct is "attached" to sight and drives children's uninhibited visual curiosity about sexual matters. The growing male child represses polymorphous desire, to which shame is attached, as his sexuality becomes entirely focalized through his genitals and toward the goal of penetrative sex. However, this sexual reorganization raises the threat of castration, of the loss of sexual potency, concentrated, as it is, within the male sexual organ. While the male child overcomes this fear by assuming the symbolic, castrating, social authority of the father, the pathological voyeur is someone who refuses, in this way, to psychically grow up. He obsessively seeks sight of human sexual organs and sexual activities that prompt castration anxiety in order to attempt to gain mastery over the fear of loss of potency that their sight portends.

The classical psychoanalytic account of voyeurism has several important characteristics. First, although voyeurism is clearly defined as a pathology, there is no sharp distinction to be drawn between the pathological and the normal. Second, voyeurism is a normatively male activity to which women are subjected: all men are subject to castration anxiety and to the allure of voyeurism which, *per impossibile*, holds that anxiety at bay. Finally, as Jonathan Metzl has emphasized, voyeurism is defined in classical psychoanalysis not simply by sexual satisfaction through sight, but by its underlying cause as a defense against the vulnerability and impotence that it at once serves to register and occlude (417). It is, therefore, easy to understand the appeal of psychoanalysis to feminist psychoanalytic theorists, such as Laura Mulvey, who in her classic essay "Visual Pleasure and Narrative Cinema" used Freudian theory to diagnose the gendered asymmetry of looking relations in the cinema—that is, the way in which "classical cinema" enacts the displacement of male anxiety onto the fetishized figure of woman. Mulvey sees *Rear Window* as exemplifying this displacement, though it is perhaps better understood, as Robert Stam and Roberta Pearson suggest, as a "critique" of male voyeurism (208). L.B Jefferies, formally active, is now confined to his wheelchair, his leg in a cast. He is physically unable to make love to Lisa and symbolically if not literally impotent. He compensates for this incapacity through becoming a Peeping Tom and using the extended telephoto lens as a phallic prop, while Stella, his nurse, and Lisa explicitly criticize his visual fixation and his lack of appropriate desire toward Lisa.

Drawing on, but not limiting ourselves to, or presupposing the truth of, psychoanalysis, we can discriminate at least three distinct though related uses of the term "voyeurism." The first sense of voyeurism, loosely derived from the technical concept of scopophilia, suggests the pursuit of sexual pleasure or enjoyment through looking. Mulvey herself defines voyeurism as "pleasure in looking at another person as an object of sexual stimulation through sight" (18). This definition, while helpful, is limited in the sense that the class of erotic objects is surely broader than another person. It includes sexual organs, sexual activity, and perhaps also symbolic substitutes for those activities. Furthermore, it would seem that the class of erotic objects that might satisfy scopophilia might include a suitably composed painting, photograph, or film. In addition, certain qualities that we might attribute to an individual's looking behavior such as being transfixed, fixated, leering, obsessive, and ogling, may contribute, in context, to our recognition of the voyeuristic gaze, as it does in *The Pleasure Garden*.

Voyeurism also has a more precise sense that is attached to the idea of the Peeping Tom, who looks unseen and hence unauthorized by the person being looked at. Thus the *Diagnostic and Statistical Manual IV* defines voyeurism as the "act of looking at unsuspecting individuals, usually strangers, who are naked, in the process of disrobing, or are engaging in sexual activity" (532). There is a critical ambiguity here. Is the point of voyeurism in this sense to gain sexual pleasure from looking on unsuspecting strangers, and therefore remaining unseen, or is the condition of remaining unseen somehow necessary to sexual arousal itself? Freud suggests that it might be the latter. He argues that one way that children may grow into adult voyeurs is where their sexual pleasure in looking is overridden by disgust. The shame attached to the sexual pleasure in looking requires the viewer to be hidden from view in order to be satisfied. However, as Metzl points out, the *DSM IV* definition of voyeurism does not presuppose this Freudian diagnostic etiology, just a practice of concealed sexualized viewing that renders the sexual arousal impersonal and ensures that touch or intimacy is avoided. L.B. Jefferies's voyeurism in *Rear Window* also meets this condition: he spies upon Miss Torso unawares.

Voyeurism, considered as unauthorized looking into something private, does not necessarily involve erotic enjoyment. The term "voyeurism" may imply looking unseen and unauthorized at the private lives of others. This kind of voyeurism has a kinship with spying, but for the voyeur, unlike the professional spy, the activity of looking on the lives of others unobserved is undertaken for its own sake. I will term this kind, or perhaps aspect, of voyeurism, psychological voyeurism as opposed simply to sexual voyeurism since the interest here is more in the mind of others—their thoughts and feelings—than it is with their bodies. This kind of voyeurism is intimately connected with eavesdropping or listening in, unawares, on the lives of others. Like voyeurism, eavesdropping may be linked to sexual thrills, as in the telephone chat room, but it need not be. Eavesdropping is a very common feature of Hitchcock's work. L.B.

Jefferies in *Rear Window* is not only a sexual voyeur; he is a psychological voyeur and eavesdropper as he spies on the activity of his neighbors.

What is the moral status of voyeurism? The term *perversion* implies a moral evaluation, a deviation from what is natural and therefore right. In Freud, sexual perversion extends to all sexual activity outside the category of heterosexual genital sex whose aim is sexual reproduction. This is too broad a category on which to base moral evaluation. While few of us would wish to view nonprocreative sex as immoral, there are surely some kinds of sexual activity that we still unhesitatingly condemn, such as pedophilia and necrophilia. The grounds of this condemnation have to do with the absence of human reciprocity or mutuality involved in these activities, or what Thomas Nagel terms "self-reflexive recognition" (Nagel 47). There is no possibility of mutual acknowledgment, authorization, and participation when the child's body or the adult's corpse is used as a source of sexual satisfaction. Following Nagel, we might therefore define those forms of sexuality as perverse where there is a distortion or erasure of reciprocal mutual awareness between individuals in the sexual act.

This absence or distortion of mutual understanding, awareness, and participation is built into sexual and psychological voyeurism where the viewer's gaze is unseen and therefore unauthorized. As Nagel points out, a voyeur "need not require any recognition by his object at all, certainly not a recognition of the voyeur's arousal" (49). It is this lack of recognition or authorization by the other that lends Jefferies's voyeurism in *Rear Window* a morally unsavory quality. Voyeurism, in the stricter sense of sexual or psychological voyeurism, is a violation of privacy, and hence it is immoral, though arguably we attach a greater moral sanction to sexual voyeurism, since it combines unauthorized intrusion into the life of another and unwanted sexual objectification. Psychological voyeurism is also immoral. However, it is given moral license when its *prima facie* immorality is trumped for some supposedly higher moral purpose, as in practices of surveillance, which is state-sanctioned voyeurism. The practice of surveillance forms an important cultural background to *Rear Window*. The dilemma expressed by L.B Jefferies in the film as to whether their activity of spying is a moral one, even if it turned out that they proved that the object of their investigation was innocent, speaks very directly to the morality of surveillance in McCarthyite America.

If voyeurism is simply considered as sexual pleasure that is sought through looking, voyeurism need not be considered immoral when the sexual objectification is matched with exhibitionism on the part of the person who is observed. However, as the scene from *The Pleasure Garden* highlights, whether the kind of "exhibitionism" displayed by Patsy in the dance revue warrants the lurid, lascivious gaze of the male spectator is open to question. There is a space of uncertainty and a place for misunderstanding in this highly gendered transaction. A similar ambiguity arises in *Rear Window*, where ostensibly L.B Jefferies is portrayed as a voyeur in a nonreciprocal gaze as he watches Miss Torso perform her daily exercise routine. Yet, there is something "exhibitionist" in that routine and the way in which she performs it in front of the window, as if inviting the voyeuristic gaze. Or perhaps it is Hitchcock who sets up the scene: Miss Torso appears as an exhibitionist in such a way that provides an alibi for Jefferies's voyeuristic gaze.

Cine-voyeurism

Many critics have suggested that *Rear Window* offers an analogy between the character of L.B. Jefferies and the film spectator, as Jefferies confined to his wheelchair spies on the activities of his neighbors through his rear window in the manner that the film spectator looks upon the world of the film through the film screen. But how seriously should we take this analogy? In what sense is cinema a voyeuristic medium? If we simply define voyeurism as sexual pleasure in looking, then clearly cinema may offer these pleasures, but it is not special or unique in doing so. Poussin's *Nymph with Satyrs* and Corbet's famous painting of female genitalia, *The Origin of the World*, offer eminent pleasure for the voyeur, and so too does the *Folies Bergère*. The more interesting question is whether or not cinema affords sexual voyeurism, or sexual looking at a person unseen. This condition cannot be met in representational painting since we see the painting of a person's body rather than the body itself. It is only marginally met in a theatrical situation. The actor performs in the presence of a general audience. Even though, as in the scene from *The Pleasure Garden*, the individual voyeur may shelter under the general anonymity of being an audience member, his gaze may be returned.

What about the case of cinema? The first rung of support for the idea that the film spectator can be a voyeur lies in the sense in which we can be said to look at the body of an actor when we look at a photograph or film. When we watch the film *Rear Window* we are not simply looking at the visual representation of James Stewart and the set of a West Village apartment, we are arguably, via the medium of photographic moving pictures, looking at James Stewart on set. This might seem to entail that when we watch a movie we are looking at something that happened in the past and no longer exists; and the idea that we can see something that no longer exists may seem paradoxical or nonsensical (outside the context of looking into the past by looking into space). However, we should not forget here that what we are seeing is an image of something, not the thing itself. The object photographed is not in fact bodying forth before us. We do not see the actor's body rather than seeing an image of it; rather, we see the actor's body via the image.

Kendall Walton characterizes this distinctive feature of the photograph as "transparency" (Walton 252). He claims that in photography and cinema we look through the image upon what is depicted in a way that is like looking through a telescope or other prosthetic device upon an object, except in the case of photography or cinema the image of what is seen is preserved through an image. Walton's transparency argument is based on the idea that there is a sharp distinction to be drawn between what we see in a representational painting and what we see in a standard photograph or film image. Following Richard Wollheim, we may understand what we perceive in a painting as something that is formed out of the intentional configuration of marks on its surface in such a way that prompts us to "see in" those marks that which is represented (213). We cannot, however, if Walton is correct, look through a painting and gaze upon its representational contents, for paintings lack transparency.

The idea that we look through the photographic and cinematic image gives *prima facie* support to the idea of voyeurism in the cinema. First, it gives a meaningful sense to the idea that we are actually looking at someone, though we are looking at him or her indirectly via the medium of a photographic image. Second, as many film theorists have observed, while we are looking through the cinematic image at the body of a person on the screen we are necessarily looking at it from a position that is unseen. The fourth wall in cinema cannot be broken in the manner that it is broken in the theater of *The Pleasure Garden*. Even if a film actor looks back at the implied audience, he cannot actually apprehend the spectator in a mutual gaze. Thus, when it occurs in the cinema, voyeurism is never simply an erotic gaze, for it also always involves the idea of being hidden from view or looking unseen. This gives rise to the analogy between L.B. Jefferies and the film spectator who, as he looks unseen on the body of the actor, may take pleasure in looking at that body for its own sake.

However, while these analogies between the film spectator and the voyeur might justify calling cinema a voyeuristic medium—that is, a medium that facilitates voyeurism—there are two fundamental dis-analogies that force us to discriminate the cinematic situation from everyday voyeurism. The fact that the spectator is necessarily hidden makes the sense of our looking unseen in cinema distinctive, for the film spectator is "protected" from the possibility and consequences of exposure. The film spectator is necessarily rather than contingently unseen. This takes away the risk involved in voyeurism and therefore changes the quality of the experience: it guarantees the voyeur anonymity and affords him impunity. Yet, while the spectator is necessarily unseen by the actor he observes, his look nonetheless receives a general authorization. Actors in a fiction film and, sometimes, the subjects of documentary footage, are appearing before the camera with the knowledge that they are going to be looked at. They cannot know who is looking, and unlike the theater performer, they cannot control to the same degree the way they are being looked at, because the filmmaker shapes the ways the spectator sees them. Thus, while the spectator who is looking at the body of an actor in *Rear Window* may share the impersonal, voyeuristic gaze of the character played by James Stewart, his position is different in two senses. First, the cinema spectator is necessarily rather than contingently unseen. When Lars Thorwald, the known murderer, looks back at L.B Jefferies from his apartment, giving him a taste of his own medicine, this "look back" is experienced very differently by L.B. Jefferies and the spectator. Second, the gaze of the spectator, unlike that of the character, is, in a general sense, authorized.

At this point the skeptic is free to conclude that cinema is not a distinctively voyeuristic medium at all. However, one could equally argue that because cinema affords the possibility of mediated sexual looking at another, unobserved, it creates a new and hitherto unprecedented mode of voyeurism that I shall call cine-voyeurism. Cine-voyeurism manifests a further important feature that Hitchcock brings to our attention in *The Pleasure Garden* through the binocular-motivated closeup, and also in *Rear Window* through the prosthetic device of the camera with which Jefferies gets closer to the objects of his sight. This is the capacity of cinema, through what Noël Carroll has termed variable framing, to bring us close to what is seen, and to do so from a multiplicity of different perspectives. Cinema not only gives us a distinctive kind of perceptual access, it allows for a close examination of what is seen from multiple viewpoints, as classical film theorists were keenly aware of. Cinema can thus satisfy a desire to see the human body, sexual acts, and sexual organs in ways that are actually sometimes impossible to see with the naked eye. Pornography, in particular, exploits this voyeuristic dimension of cinema, but all cinema partakes of it.

Four interlocking features thus characterize voyeurism in the cinema. First, the mode of looking is indirect (via a representation), which corresponds to the distinctive mode of looking that characterizes cinema in general. Second, the onlooker is necessarily rather than contingently unseen. Third, looking has a general, though impersonal, authorization.

Fourth, the voyeuristic gaze is potentially unrestricted and ubiquitous. Whether sexual voyeurism is prompted in the cinema depends on both how cinema is used and the proclivities of the spectator, but all these conditions together help promote its occurrence. From the moral point of view, film spectatorship creates the formal conditions for sexual pleasure in looking to be exercised in a manner that is free from inhibition or shame. The voyeuristic spectator is protected from exposure by being unseen, and thus his gaze is an impersonal one. The impersonal nature of the transaction also affords protection to the actor who is engaged in self-display. At the same time, the actor's general assent to being seen endows an element of qualified reciprocity to the transaction. Even though it is impersonal, the viewer's gaze is not unwanted. Finally, the nature of variable framing allows an extreme sense of visual intimacy without the actual violation of personal space. Because the medium has historically afforded the possibility of uninhibited sexual looking, the scope and contexts of permissible representation in the cinema have historically been hedged with constraints in the form of censorship.

Of course, the moral questions arise here not simply from the fact of looking unseen but from the public display of the body, usually the female body, that prompts the sexual gaze. Patriarchal societies have long held taboos against women performing in public, and those women who did were considered on the same level as prostitutes or courtesans. However, because the display of the body in cinema is not live, but indirect and impersonal, the responsibility of the participant is lessened for that display and thereby given further license. In this respect, in spite of censorship regulations, it could be argued that cinema has actually contributed to easing the constraints on the public and impersonal display of sexuality. Cinema and other adjacent media isolate the participants from direct responsibility for the voyeuristic transaction. Furthermore, with Reality TV and the Internet, forms of what Clay Calvert calls "mediated voyeurism," which require their own separate analysis, have metastasized (2). Beginning with cinema, technological modernity has arguably helped to lead a shift in public morality toward accepting voyeurism, although the terrain of what is permissible remains morally and legally contested.

The Fictional Voyeur

Thus far I have been concerned with voyeurism only in a very limited sense of the actual actor's body as it appears on film, and therefore primarily with sexual voyeurism, since the thoughts and feelings of the actor are not themselves salient when watching a film. However, although this broad approach has been very influential in thinking about voyeurism in the cinema, it turns out to be a rather narrow and distorting lens through which to understand cinematic voyeurism and its moral implications. For, as I have argued, there is broader sense of voyeurism that is not restricted to the sexually informed, unseen gaze, but pertains to intruding on privacy and is connected to eavesdropping. Voyeurism in this sense is concerned less with looking at the physical body than in apprehending the thoughts, feelings, and motives of another. In fiction cinema, thoughts, feelings, and motives are apprehended through the performance of the actor as a character in a fictional setting. It is thus impossible to talk about the significance that voyeurism might have in the cinema without reflecting on how we engage with fictions in film and how our sensory involvement in the film world is linked to our imaginative response to fiction in general

I have followed Kendall Walton in arguing that moving image spectatorship is characterized by an indirect mode of looking, in which film allows us to gaze through the moving image at the physical bodies of the actors and props in a film. However, what is the relationship between what it is we see indirectly, and our apprehension of the fiction? We may sometimes speak of looking at a character when we are looking at a motion picture, especially when the character, say Superman, is known to us better than the actor, or when the character is actually a model, such as King Kong. Yet there is an inherent and insuperable paradox involved in the claim that we can see something that does not exist. Most thinkers reject, on these grounds, the idea that we can give any sense to the thought that we can see fictional characters and fictional worlds. However, the problem with such rejections is that they do not seem to acknowledge the distinctive experience of going to the cinema as opposed to, say, reading fictions, where we seem not only, or even primarily, to look at actors performing, but apprehend visually the actions of characters and the fictional worlds they inhabit.

The theory that best preserves the intuition that in cinema we, in some sense, perceive a fictional world is the theory of imagined seeing. George Wilson first proposed a systematic theory of imagined seeing in film, and more recently he has defended the theory at length. He argues that when we are watching a film, what we see and hear indirectly are the actors, the props, and the sounds they make, but what we justifiably imagine, or "make believe," is that we are "watching from within the space of the story" (1988, 56). "In viewing classical narrative films under standard conditions of movie spectatorship, viewers normally do imagine seeing (in the image-track) and hearing (in the sound-track) the objects and events depicted in the movie. Further, in normal cases they are justified in so imagining" (2011, 55). In *Rear Window* we indirectly

Figure 8.1. Lisa (Grace Kelly) and Jefferies (James Stewart) watching.

see James Stewart and Grace Kelly on the film set, but we imagine seeing and hearing L.B. Jefferies and Lisa Freemont looking out on the courtyard of a West Village apartment building.

As Wilson points out, what gives immediate plausibility to this idea is that there is a clear difference between an event in the fictional world of the film that we are prompted to imagine and events in the fictional world that we apprehend through sight. Thus, when in *Rear Window* Lars Thorwald (Raymond Burr) is enticed by L.B. Jefferies to leave his apartment to meet with him, we are invited by the film to merely imagine his arrival at the rendezvous and his realization that he has been duped. We do not see the event occurring. In contrast we actually see, or rather, we imagine seeing, his departure and arrival. However, the idea of imagining seeing has proven surprisingly difficult to defend. The central problem lies in where the spectator who imagines that he or she is seeing the fiction is located, for presumably if the spectator is imagining seeing the fiction he or she must imagine seeing it from somewhere. Gregory Currie dubbed Wilson's original formulation of the theory of imagined seeing the "imagined observer hypothesis" and argued that in order to be true, this hypothesis seems to require a spectator who, implausibly, imagines herself flitting from observational viewpoint to observational viewpoint as we cut from scene to scene, or, absurdly, imagines herself potentially subject to physical impingement by fictional events (167).

In response to Currie, Wilson proposes and defends two possible explanations of imagined seeing. His "modest" or minimalist claim is that the spectator imagines seeing the contents of the fiction from whatever visual perspective it is presented, but it is actually indeterminate how the spectator has access to what she imagines seeing. We are mandated by movies to imagine seeing or hearing what they depict, yet we are not mandated to imagine where we see or here them from. We can imagine having a visual perspective on the fiction without imagining occupying a particular point of view. The reason for this is that our imagination, logically speaking, just has the character that we can imagine something without imagining what it normally entails. Since the viewer does not imagine occupying an observation point in the fictional world, she thus does not move from vantage point to vantage point in editing. Nor does she imagine herself impinged upon by fictional events. However, for several reasons, Wilson endorses a stronger "mediated version" of imagined seeing in which not only does the spectator imagine seeing the fiction, she imagines seeing the fiction via the imagined seeing of "motion-picture like images." In other words, while we are actually looking through the film image at actors on sets, we imagine that we are looking through the film image at a fictional world. This does not mean that we imagine that some camera is actually recording the fictional world. Only certain films, such as *This is Spinal Tap*, mandate this. We are not required to imagine how it is possible for us to be seeing a fiction via a moving image for exactly the same reason that we are not required to imagine ourselves, in the "modest" thesis, occupying a point in space.

I am not going to attempt to adjudicate between these two positions. The issues are quite subtle, and Wilson's own arguments are not decisive. Yet, taken either way, his proposal is an important one in the context of understanding the role of voyeurism in the cinema. As Berys Gaut has argued, a strong connection between the idea of voyeurism and imagined seeing can be forged: "The idea of the invisible observer is the notion that it is make-believe that the spectator sees the events happening in the fictional world. It is also make-believe of many of these events that they are private events, and that the characters, not intending them to be seen by anyone else, would be deeply embarrassed were they to be the object of another's gaze. . . . [I]t is often make-believe that the spectator views private actions, but it is not make-believe that his gaze is returned" (7). Gaut himself rejects the thesis of imagined seeing and hence the concept of make-believe or fictional voyeurism, but if we do indeed imagine seeing and hearing fictional worlds when we watch movies we are, fictionally, voyeurs and eavesdroppers upon those worlds in a manner that allow us to imagine that we can have intimate access to the minds of others without them being aware. Cinema, as Colin McGuinn has suggested, enables us "to look in on the most private thoughts and feelings of the people we observe" (57).

While in the case of the "modest" thesis, the relationship of imagined seeing to cine-voyeurism is more complicated to explain, if we adopt the thesis that we imagine seeing the fictional world by imaging seeing through a film image of it, fictional or imagined voyeurism appears closely congruent with its counterpart in cine-voyeurism. First, it is indirect: we imagine seeing the fiction by imagining that we look through a motion-picture image. Second, the spectator who imagines seeing in cinema is necessarily unseen because he imagines looking at the fictional world indirectly through the one-way device of the motion-picture image. Third, the general institution of cinema authorizes imagined voyeurism, though here the characters we imagine seeing are unsuspecting, unlike the actors that we see through the image. Fourth, the gaze of this imagined voyeur is as unrestricted and ubiquitous as the fiction itself. In this way, the imagined looking of the spectator at the characters in the fiction supervenes upon the actual gaze of the spectator at the actors. However, fictional voyeurism, whichever way it is construed, is crucially distinctive. The spectator who imagines seeing apprehends the thoughts, motivations, and feelings of another, and thus he apprehends the mind, not merely the body, of another. When we imagine seeing fictional worlds, we see the body of the actor, which we imagine as the body of a character in the context of our overall apprehension of the character and his role in the fictional world.

The manner in which the institutional authorization of voyeurism receives its rationale from the broader institution of dramatic fiction in cinema has significant implications for understanding the nature of cine-voyeurism. The institution of fiction allows us direct and immediate access to the thoughts and feelings of others in a manner that would, in actual contexts, appear morally intrusive. For this reason, it has at least the potential to tutor us in how to understand the thoughts, feelings, and emotions of others in a manner that, as many authors have argued, may have a socially civilizing effect, even if this effect is incapable of clear empirical measurement or proof. Of course, this possibility is true of other kinds of fiction, not merely cinema. But the distinctiveness of cinema, which Hitchcock's *Rear Window* among other films constantly remind us of, lies in its particular position on the borderline between the real and the fictional and between visual, voyeuristic attraction and psychological identification. The cinema has often been condemned by moral arbiters for encouraging superficial fascination with the human body, yet, by the same token, it allows us to understand the relationship between those surface features of experience and a deeper sense of self and personhood that extends beyond our apprehension of the body. For me, this is a central reason why cinema is such a fascinating art form. Indeed, even if my characterization of imagined seeing as a form of voyeurism is questioned, on grounds similar to those used to criticize the concept of cine-voyeurism, I believe that the structure of the experience I have sought to describe remains central to the medium and to Hitchcock's exploration of it.

Rear Window Ethics

As I have already noted, *Rear Window* has often been considered an allegory of the film spectator as voyeur: L.B Jefferies confined to his wheelchair looks out across the courtyard, unseen, at the activities of the courtyard inhabitants—just as the film spectator looks unseen upon the world of the film. Furthermore, as noted, *Rear Window* has been taken to exemplify (Mulvey) and critique (Stam and Pearson) the male voyeuristic gaze in the cinema. *Rear Window* has also been construed by David Bordwell as a self-conscious enactment of how we "construct a story on the basis of visual information" (41). Here, drawing on Paula Marantz Cohen's astute commentary on the film, I will suggest that *Rear Window* provides an allegory of the role of fiction in film viewing. In *Rear Window*, male sexual cine-voyeurism is revealed as merely one register of film spectatorship whose significance is transformed once it is embedded in the broader institution of imagined seeing or fictional voyeurism, where the gaze functions as a conduit to the thoughts and feelings of the characters who inhabit the fictional world. In *Rear Window*, as Cohen writes, we come to appreciate the potential power of our own look and "to recognize its connection to the way we generate meaning and feeling" (105).

The film opens with two panning and tilting camera movements across a courtyard surrounded by apartment buildings after a window curtain has been raised on the scene. The first movement establishes the overall setting as we begin to see people asleep or waking in distant view. The second movement gives us a closer view: a man in a penthouse shaves while we hear a male voice intone on his radio: "men over forty, are you tired and rundown, do you have a listless feeling," before the man changes the station to jazz; an alarm wakens an older couple sleeping on the fire escape; a fit young woman does her morning exercises, one of which includes unhooking her bra with her back to the spectator as she bends down, and hooking it up again once she is erect, to the cooing of doves flitting on her roof; we hear the voices of children playing;

and finally we see a pair of love birds being uncovered on the left of the screen, before the camera returns us inside to the sleeping Jefferies and shows us his broken leg, his name on his cast, and photographs that reveal how his accident happened. It is only the third time we see the courtyard, with Jefferies on the phone to his editor, that we see the events across the courtyard from his point of view. We are introduced to him as a sexual voyeur. He watches as a helicopter buzzes above topless bathers, and he observes Miss Torso's extensive exercise routines that are so noisy they draw the attention of the female sculptor who lives below. He turns to look at the composer and, then, for the first time, we see, from his point of view, the future murder suspect, Lars Thorwald, coming home and entering his wife's bedroom, only to be scolded by her.

This sequence is critical for several reasons. First, it introduces the general parallel between the position of Jefferies and the position of the film spectator. Second, it introduces the idea of sexual voyeurism by presenting the topless bathers and the performance of Miss Torso. In both cases, Hitchcock conveys by suggestion what he cannot actually show: the topless bathers are perceived only by the helicopter that hovers like a predatory insect, and Miss Torso's nifty movement with the bra creates a crude sight gag, as if she has to release the bra as she bends down in order to accommodate the size of her breasts. Third, it introduces sexual voyeurism in the context of psychological voyeurism or unseen access to the intimate lives of others that serves to foster our interest in finding out about those lives. Fourth, Hitchcock's narration clearly introduces the gaze of the spectator to the world of the courtyard and demarcates that gaze as distinct from that of L.B. Jefferies, because Jefferies is asleep. There may be a parallel between the point of view of Jefferies and the spectator, but there is also a distinction that Hitchcock is at pains to articulate. Finally, as Cohen points out, we are introduced to the story of Thorwald through the gaze of Jefferies that singles out this particular story as one that is going to be central to his development as a character.

When the spectator initially views the scene, he is not positioned as a sexual voyeur; rather, he is oriented on the threshold of a fictional world, waiting to be introduced to the characters within it. To be sure, we are invited to be sexual voyeurs as we watch Miss Torso do her routines. However, our incipient sexual voyeurism here is contained within the broader compass of apprehending the fictional world and, in particular, the lives of the characters it contains. In sharp contrast to the spectator, Jefferies is clearly involved in a morally dubious act of sexual voyeurism. To underscore the illicit nature of his viewing, the scene of Jefferies looking at Miss Torso as he speaks on the phone is framed by the shot of the helicopter pilot buzzing above the topless women, and the shot dwells inordinately on his look at Miss Torso in repeated point-of-view shots and reaction shots, even suggesting that he licks his lips while doing so.

Of course, the introduction of Jefferies's sexual voyeurism is capable of being read in different ways. As I have argued elsewhere, Hitchcock often aligns us with characters who are engaged in perverse acts of looking in order to create an alibi for the spectator to enter a scene of perverse enjoyment (Allen 68). Our perceptual alignment with Stewart allows us a greater indulgence to view Miss Torso in closer view, by enjoying what the character enjoys; but, at the same time, we can also readily distance ourselves from that character, especially when prompted to do so by other characters in the fiction, such as Stella (Thelma Ritter), who roundly chastises him for being a Peeping Tom. While we are aligned with Jefferies's point of view, we are never simply aligned with his psychology. Perhaps, too, as I have already suggested, there is a sense of self-conscious exhibitionism in Miss Torso, certainly an unalloyed pleasure in bodily self-expression, which, like the performance of Patsy in *The Pleasure Garden*, invites appreciation but abjures visual predation. Or maybe this is a setup by Hitchcock, who presents Miss Torso's ostensible exhibitionism as an alibi for Jefferies's voyeurism in a manner that renders it more palatable.

From the outset, appearing alongside Miss Torso in rear windows of the courtyard are other figures who expand the field of the fiction as the film unfolds and provoke a different kind of interest: Miss Lonely Hearts, the newlyweds, the composer, the childless couple with the dog, the Thorwalds, and the spinster sculptor. As a number of critics have pointed out, it is as if each window suggests a different perspective upon the story of the central couple. In this respect, *Rear Window* highlights the way in which, when watching fiction films, as in all fiction, the spectator is invited to reflect on behavior of the protagonists by apprehending different kinds of characters in different stories or subplots. At the same time, if Jefferies begins the film as a detached voyeur, which mimics the detachment manifest in his relationship with Lisa Freemont, over time, he begins to enter into the lives of the characters whom he initially observes only from a distance, understands them more sympathetically, and sees himself as part of a broader community. The film spectator is thereby taught about the nature of an apprehension that is based on a superficial and surface gaze. He is taught how superficial understanding must be revised and integrated if a deeper knowledge of how to live with others is to be achieved, and how cinema itself affords a means of reflection upon the relationship between surface and depth perception. *Rear Window* functions as an elegant allegory of the moral education of the viewer, in particular the male viewer, from a detached sexual voyeur to an empathic spectator through his engagement with the story-worlds of film.

The fact that Jefferies solves a murder, develops sympathy for his neighbors, and falls in love might seem a conveniently self-serving moral sleight of hand, given the fact that *Rear Window* starts from the premise of an intrusive voyeurism. Deep into his investigation of the murder, Jefferies stops to ponder: "I wonder if it's ethical to watch a man with binoculars and long focus lens . . . do you suppose it's ethical even if you prove that he didn't commit a crime?" As we have seen, there is certainly a moral paradox to ponder here about real-world voyeurism and surveillance, but Jefferies is redeemed by the fact that he has evolved enough as a viewer to actually pose the question. The moral paradox of voyeurism in the film receives its echo in the residual moral paradox attached to the institution of cinema itself, with its potential for a frank display of the human body and human sexuality. It is as if fiction film, for Hitchcock, perversely, provides an alibi for the staging of voyeurism.

Gender plays a fundamental role in *Rear Window's* moral allegory of spectatorship. Lisa wishes for domesticity, intimacy, and attachment. Jefferies is a voyeuristic adventurer whose attitude to Lisa is governed by skepticism, distance, and detachment. This places them at odds and renders them incompatible. Jefferies behaves as a sexual voyeur toward Miss Torso, self-servingly confirms his prejudices about the course of domestic relationships in his negative evaluation of Thorwald's nagging wife, and manifests his facile view of sexual relationships when he opines that Miss Torso picks and chooses her men at her leisure. However, his view changes as he begins to see Mrs. Thorwald as a murder victim, as he comes to empathize with the character of Miss Lonely Hearts, and when Lisa, by joining his quest, helps tutor his understanding as she offers her own contrary judgment on Miss Torso as a woman who is engaged in "juggling wolves" and lacks interest in any of the men. Her hypothesis is confirmed when Miss Torso's husband arrives home near the conclusion of the film. While Jefferies develops a more feminine, empathic gaze, Lisa herself demonstrates a masculine sense of agency when she enters Thorwald's apartment in search of his wife's ring. When she places her life at risk, as Jefferies has consistently done as a photojournalist, she draws out from Jefferies a deeply empathic response that finally expresses his love for her.

The figure of Miss Lonely Hearts plays a critical role in fostering the education and transformation of the male gaze. During the first evening of the story, as they prepare to sit down for dinner and at a moment when Jefferies continues to react critically and negatively toward

Lisa, Jefferies watches Miss Lonely Hearts enact a ritual of entertaining a phantom suitor to dinner to the refrain of Dean Martin's "To See You is to Love You:" "To see you is to love you/And I see you everywhere/ In the sunrise in the moon glow/Any place I look you're there." The song's celebration of bringing the loved one into sight is the antithesis of sexual voyeurism. It celebrates an inner gaze in which love brings to mind the beloved so intensely that he or she seems to appear. Miss Lonely Hearts, with pathos, seems to enact the lyric of the song as she imagines entertaining her dream lover over dinner. Jefferies, across the courtyard, not only appreciates her performance but also empathizes with her lonely suffering and forms an imaginary connection to her through a shot/reverse-shot across the courtyard as he raises his glass to toast her.

Later, Lisa and Jefferies, their gazes now attuned, share their discomfort and apprehension as they watch Miss Lonely Hearts fight off the assault of a young man she has picked up from a bar. Finally, Jefferies watches with Stella as Miss Lonely Hearts decides to take her life. The response of Stella and Jefferies to the plight of Miss Lonely Hearts parallels their empathic response to Lisa's assault, and Stella's prompt to Jefferies to call the police to save Miss Lonely Hearts actually serves to rescue Lisa. Miss Lonely Hearts herself is saved, it turns out, by the composer's song, Mona Lisa. Lisa had earlier opined that the composer's inability to write the song reflects on her relationship to Jefferies. The completion of the song now accompanies Jefferies's empathic gaze and

Figure 8.2. Miss Lonely Hearts (Judith Evelyn).

presages the realization of their love for one another, and Jefferies's seeming retreat from skepticism and indifference.

Yet, as I argued in *Hitchcock's Romantic Irony* and have intimated here, there is a powerful undercurrent of human perversity in Hitchcock's vision that is also at work in *Rear Window*. Jefferies seems to bring into being across the courtyard a story that ideally expresses, indeed vindicates, his own darkest impulses toward Lisa and aligns him, imaginatively, with the figure of Lars Thorwald, his ostensible antagonist. As he imagines what it must be like to cut up a body, he looks at Miss Torso through the cross hairs of her window. At the very moment of his greatest empathy for Lisa, Jefferies, and the spectator alongside him, watch as Thorwald assaults her to the strains of the lushly romantic tune of Mona Lisa. Even the "happy" ending of *Rear Window* is, characteristically for Hitchcock, ambiguous, as Jefferies lies not with one but with two broken legs, and Lisa puts down her adventure novel *To the High Himalayas* to read *Harper's Bazaar*. This undercurrent of skepticism does not undermine Hitchcock's moral vision but is in fact constitutive of it. There is no easy triumph of communitarian values over skepticism or human isolation in Hitchcock, but a continued struggle, renewal, and reversal that rejects facile resolutions, especially in gender relationships. The aesthetic power of the voyeuristic gaze in cinema is that it can, through the entwinement of actuality and fiction, dramatize both extreme detachment from or objectification of another as well as empathic connection. Hitchcock's cinema in general, and *Rear Window* in particular, articulates the full moral power and amplitude of that gaze.

Note

1. I thank Leo Goldsmith for reminding me about this sequence.

Works Cited

Allen, Richard. *Hitchcock's Romantic Irony*. New York: Columbia UP, 2007.
Bordwell, David. *Narration in the Fiction Film*. Madison: University of Wisconsin Press, 1985.
Calvert, Clay. *Voyeur Nation: Media, Privacy, and Peering in Modern Culture*. Boulder, CO: Westview, 2000.
Cohen, Paula Marantz. *Hitchcock and the Legacy of Victorianism*. Knoxville: University of Kentucky Press, 1995.
Currie, Gregory. *Image and Mind: Film, Philosophy and Cognitive Science*. New York: Cambridge UP, 1995.
Diagnostic and Statistical Manual of Mental Disorders 4th Edition. Washington DC: American Psychological Association, 1994.

Freud, Sigmund. "Three Essays on Sexuality." *On Sexuality*. Trans. James Strachey. London: Pelican Books, 1977.
Gaut, Berys. "On Cinema and Perversion," *Film and Philosophy* 1 (1994): 3–17.
McGuinn, Colin. *The Power of Movies: How Screen and Mind Interact*. New York: Pantheon Books, 2004.
Metz, Christian. *The Imaginary Signifier: Psychoanalysis and Cinema*. Trans. Celia Britton, Annwyl Williams, Ben Brewster, and Alfred Guzetti. Bloomington: Indiana UP, 1982.
Metzl, Jonathan M. "From Scopophilila to Survivor: A Brief History of Voyeurism." *Textual Practice* 18(3) (2004): 415–34.
Mulvey, Laura. *Visual and Other Pleasures*. Bloomington: Indiana UP, 1989.
Nagel, Thomas. "Sexual Perversions." *Mortal Questions*. New York: Cambridge UP, 1979.
Stam, Robert, and Roberta Pearson, eds. "Hitchcock's *Rear Window*: Reflexivity and the Critique of Voyeurism." *A Hitchcock Reader*, 2nd ed. Eds. Marshall Deutelbaum and Leland Poague. New York: Wiley-Blackwell, 2009.
Walton, Kendall L. "Transparent Pictures: On the Nature of Photographic Realism," *Critical Inquiry* 11.2 (Dec 1984): 246–77.
Wilson, George. *Narration in Light: Studies in Cinematic Point of View*. Baltimore, MD: John's Hopkins UP, 1988.
———. *Seeing Fictions in Film: The Epistemology of Movies*. New York: Oxford UP, 2011.
Wollheim, Richard. *Art and Its Objects*, 2nd ed. New York: Cambridge UP, 1980.

Moralizing

9

Murray Pomerance

Alfred Hitchcock as Moralist

There is no such thing as an isolated man or woman;
we are each of us made up of a cluster of appurtenances.

—Henry James, *The Portrait of a Lady*

∾

Wrong Men

Writing with a keen and Catholic eye for shadow, Claude Chabrol and Eric Rohmer describe the conclusion to Alfred Hitchcock's *The Wrong Man* (1956) as including a moment when the falsely arrested Manny Balestrero (Henry Fonda), "on his mother's advice," prays to God, "and as he contemplates the image of the Sacred Heart, a superimposition shows us the true criminal walking along the street and moving toward the camera until his face dissolves into Fonda's" (148). (What we see, in fact, is the eyes of this stranger swelling up as he walks toward the camera until they occupy the space of Manny Balestrero's eyes.) Soon later, this unknown man will be apprehended and Manny, with whom we have bonded, will be free. Or, "free." It is hard not to love this leap, this swift and assured annunciation of the stranger as "true criminal" produced by his "miraculous" appearance onscreen after the prayer. When we see him, we have plenty of reason for fervently hoping that he is the thief "in truth"—that is, in legal as well as moral truth—since we want our beloved Manny, who has all along seemed innocent in our eyes, to find a way out of the Château d'If of the New York justice system in which it seems he may be condemned to spend the rest of his days for a series of robberies we earnestly believe he did not commit. Before proceeding, I must now pause, not only because all moral debates require pause but also, more importantly, because the story of Manny is more elusive than many viewers take it to be.

How do we know Manny committed no robberies? We did not see him rob anyone, and by convention when watching a film—certainly a Hitchcock film—we take the entire universe to be contained in what we see. Also, he says so, to more than one person in the story. The "he" in this case is Henry Fonda, a star we almost always like to like for his calm reasonability, his affable good humor, his dignified gaze, his yeoman humility. Manny is appropriately conventional and decent: he has a wife and two adoring children, a nice brother, and a sympathetic mother. His devotions are circumspect and honest: he makes his living by playing, of all instruments, the friendly, uncompromising, and modest double bass. He seems confused to be labeled a thief, sincerely so (and yet any professional thief might feign such confusion at such labeling). But to be rigorous in summation, as we were not present to watch the robberies we can only surmise that Manny's statement of innocence is a verity. A witness, the clerk at the insurance company (Doreen Lang), claims to be absolutely certain she saw him. Could she be wrong? She could be wrong, of course, but the point is that she utters her accusation with total conviction, the same conviction with which Manny seems by his manner to proclaim his innocence. We see that this witness is trepidacious when she must look into his face. Does this mean her memory and judgment are ultimately not to be trusted, or else that Manny is in fact the robber, and when he comes to borrow money for his wife's dentistry has once again terrified her? (What might make us wonder about this clerk is the fact that in the United States nowadays, "eyewitness misidentification is the single greatest cause of wrongful convictions nationwide, playing a role in more than 75 percent of convictions overturned through DNA testing" [Innocence Project].) Yet, still, how could the sweet and gentle Manny, Manny the loyal son whom we believe to be innocent, terrify anyone the way he is terrifying this poor woman? At the very beginning of the film we saw that he is an accomplished musician, that is, a subject of the Muse: how could an accomplished musician be a criminal, bad, immoral? We will return to these questions.

Manny, at any rate, will go free at the end of the film, and a second man will be arrested in his place, a man who looks remarkably like him yet whose features seem darker, less amicable. This second man we do not immediately like when we set eyes on him, and so we do not root for his release. We are eager and willing to accept the proposition that he is guilty. But is he really guilty? Has he really done the deed we were not present to watch him doing? True, *after* his face and body take over the face and body of Manny in the superimposition we see him attempting a *new* robbery and being caught in the midst of it. But is it not true as we see this "guilty" man striding down the sidewalk toward us, and as his "guilty" face is superimposed—almost perfectly—over Manny's, that the most we can say is that his presence forms a strange and wondrous duplication, that he has the "look" of guilt—just as Manny apparently had? That whatever "look" Manny had (that impressed the witness so powerfully with certainty) another man has, too? Is it not true that in some strange way as this man approaches on the street we have been transformed into the nervous insurance company clerk, hot to make an identification? For Hitchcock, the look of evil is not idiosyncratic. Many men can exhibit it; perhaps any man can. This second man is initiated into, and trapped within, the justice system only *after* we already come to a conclusion about him, a conclusion that he is certainly and inevitably *the one*, and we come to this conclusion even though we have as yet no evidence, no basis in material fact (the material fact of Hitchcock's images). Does he, too, not simply appear to fit the requirements of the role we are in the process of casting? And, more basically: in assigning him moral value, are we not indeed casting a role?

Howard Becker wrote in 1963—as it turns out about men like Manny Balestrero (the character of Manny was based, indeed, on a real man of the same name who underwent the same torture)—that, theoretically speaking, correct accusation is only one of four possibilities in labeling deviant behavior. False accusation is equally possible, if not exactly likely to happen, also not a complicated situation to produce. An accuser with some social weight need only point a heavy finger (and indeed the verity of the accusation might ride with the intractability of that social weight). Given that rule-breaking either does or does not happen as a result of an action, and that rule-breaking either is or is not perceived to have happened, one distinct possibility is the person who does not break a rule but is perceived to have done so, in our case, Manny Balestrero. And only one of the four possibilities—not engaging in rule-breaking, and not being perceived to have done so—leads to what social authorities, lay and professional, would call "innocence" (Becker chap. 2). Not as many people are called "innocent" as we might suppose. Or, there is no preponderance of innocence in the social world.

When they mention *"the true criminal* walking along the street" (my emphasis), Chabrol and Rohmer display a certain conviction about the stranger who is "guilty" at the end of the picture, this founded on their ability to know instantly when evil is before them, to sense its rhythms and gestures, to recognize its subtle glow. The ability is part of their commitment to Original Sin as a fundamental principal on the basis of which their own thought, and Hitchcock's (as they would like to paint it) stands. Hitchcock's work, they believe, repeatedly demonstrates "the *interchangeable guilt* of all mankind" (149): that a good and an evil man—one who is not bad, and another who definitively is—could change places, or that the goodness of a man could be replaced by another man's evil—this "goodness" and this "evil" being inherent and essential (and this transfer being a strange and wondrous form of contagion). Humans in their inextricable essence can be polluted, infected, besieged, and devoured, and the deep structure of character can be altered to tragic effect. To put this obversely, and I hope with more light: tragic changes in behavior, falls from grace, may be understood as invasions or transmogrifications of the soul, as the stuff of deep drama. It is possible that beyond Chabrol and Rohmer, French critics in general moved (in their own Catholicism) to find themes of guilt and redemption in Hitchcock's work, weighing heavily the importance of the plight—read inner turmoil, sacrifice—of the falsely accused person in a social press that has little time or patience for delicacy, gentleness, civility, or kindness as it metes out punishment and reward. Martin Jay writes of the "disenchantment of the eye," for example, linking it to a history of anti-ocularcentrism in French thought: the moral world transcends appearance, even denies it, and the riddling complexities of what the eye can see do not account for a moral summation of social life. The Hitchcockian problem, then, for what I would term "Catholic criticism" is that presumption of guilt either accords with some fundamental "interchangeable guilt of all mankind"—that man is flawed—or else resounds against some fundamental (and intrinsic) innocence that the falsely accused somehow—and horribly!—cannot demonstrate; that man cannot avoid the predicament of being read as flawed. This concentration on an inner, necessarily mute fundamental state is typical, say, of Truffaut's approach to the undeniably moral film *I Confess* (1953): "Father Michael, bound by his holy vows on the inviolability of confession, makes no move to clear himself . . . In this picture . . . although the defendant has been legally cleared, he will remain under a cloud" (200n, 206). For the Catholic thinker, a man's appearance in society must always evidence a deeper state of affairs, an innate condition, and should not be taken seriously *in itself* as a facet of the ever-shifting articulation that is modern moral life.

Natural Expression

Consider, as a radically different way of looking at this issue, an argument of Erving Goffman's:

> It is, of course, hardly possible to imagine a society whose members do not routinely read from what is available to the senses to something larger, distal, or hidden. Survival is unthinkable without it. Correspondingly, there is a very deep belief in our society, as presumably there is in others, that an object produces signs that are informing about it. Objects are thought to structure the environment immediately around themselves; they cast a shadow, heat up the surround, strew indications, leave an imprint. . . . *We take sign production to be situationally phrased but not situationally determined.* (*Advertisements* 6; emphasis mine)

The system of belief that Goffman terms the "Doctrine of Natural Expression" would account for the "truly" guilty man in *The Wrong Man* inexhaustibly, unavoidably, "naturally," and spontaneously "casting a shadow" of guilt as he walks toward the camera, "heating up the surround" with his past criminal actions, which stick to him like labels; "strewing indications" by his furtive glance; "leaving an imprint" with every step he takes. Given this logic, the story of *The Wrong Man*, seen very simply (and incorrectly, in my view), is that the "truly guilty" man happens not to show up early enough to prevent another man, "truly innocent," from being arrested in his place and undergoing the tribulations of justice. The pain of these ineluctable tribulations is the meat of the film. Further (and as elaboration): the innocent man's innocent wife is also wrapped up in the trial of his soul, and succumbs. (At the very end we learn that she is on the road to recovery, but that she has not yet recovered.)

I am not especially interested here to develop an argument about *The Wrong Man*. Instead a certain critical fascination fascinates me, specifically the unwavering attention to an undeniable, inner state of being and its relation, in an exemplary way in Hitchcock's work, to the moral life. What the Doctrine of Natural Expression, as Goffman has it, can never account for—yet what must surely be accounted for in contemporary culture since at least the turn of the twentieth century—is, first, the importance of what is around us, what is beyond the self, indeed, the context we address in our expression, this vital surround made quintessential in the act of performance, which implies and invokes the world of fakery, verisimilitude, theater, and conning; and, too, a key allied circumstance, mistaken appearance. In *The Portrait of a Lady*, Henry James has Madame Merle say,

> When you have lived as long as I, you will see that every human being has his shell, and that you must take the shell into account. By the shell I mean the whole envelope of circumstances. There is no such thing as an isolated man or woman; we are each of us made up of a cluster of appurtenances. What do you call one's self? Where does it begin? where does it end? It overflows into everything that belongs to us—and then it flows back again. I know that a large part of myself is in the dresses I choose to wear. I have a great respect for *things!* One's self—for other people—is one's expression of one's self; and one's house, one's clothes, the book one reads, the company one keeps—these things are all expressive. (287)

As I have tried to argue in depth in *An Eye for Hitchcock*, Hitchcock knows that a performance, if it is to be successful and even brilliant, need not be intentional (14–57). Further, the sign production that we (perhaps far too) casually take "to be situationally phrased but not situationally determined" may be situationally determined in fact, situationally structured, indeed—although in Manny Balestrero's case it is not—by the dramatic necessity of mounting a certain appearance in such a way as to address the expectations of a particular audience. (Manny, who wouldn't see himself as mounting a performance, suffers from sincerity, and thus has significant troubles understanding how his view of himself might not be shared by the police.) While a set of signals may be *interpreted* as flowing without interruption or contrivance from the "true" self of a performer, performers may also not regard themselves as performers and may or may not be aware of the signals they are apparently emitting. (The grounds for signaling may be established by others.) The issue, finally, is an audience's ability to successfully read intent, not an actor's desire or capacity to show it. The actor, indeed, may do very little. Writing of the epic theater in 1939, Walter Benjamin noted that the actor's task "is to demonstrate through his acting that he is cool and relaxed," and when we regard performance we attend to these qualities of coolness and relaxation as significant even if this amounts to noting that they are absent. For the actor, cool and relaxed self-awareness is thus in part—in important part—a matter of knowing what others are likely to see when one makes an entrance, regardless of what one hopes for. In playing Manny Balestrero locked up in jail, for example, Fonda at several moments produces a benignly passive gaze, a gaze that does not presume to ask for consideration or benevolence from his captors. In this way he caused Manny to sign openly that he knows he is not in control of the way his identity and appearance are interpreted and, thus, yields signally to his fate.

A Surface Life

Such a dramaturgical approach as I follow Goffman in taking resists considering "inner," or emotional, states of affairs as central in the elaboration of human interaction, and focuses instead on what might be called "outside views," such as the views an audience has of dramatically staged action (in the theater, for example, or on film). Writers discussing morality, or moralism, tend not to be dramaturgical in method, however. They have a very particular thing in mind when they say "morals," namely the relation and difference between Good and Evil, perhaps the dualism in human spirituality and experience engendered by the co-presence of Good and Evil in the world, and sometimes even the interchangeability of the two (as is demonstrated in, among other films, *Strangers on a Train* [1951], when the "good" Guy Haines is influenced [or inspired] by the "evil" Bruno Anthony to do a killing [I leave for another occasion a discussion of whether either of these men is what the canonical appreciation claims him to be]). Associated with this central, rather Manichean, focus is a concern with sin, guilt, darkness, spiritual decrepitude or decay, and doubt, and with the struggle for virtue, goodness, or happiness in a world where, as Donald Spoto has suggested, sounding not a little like Hamlet, "Respectability and luxury are not sufficient" (22) because "evil sprouts round us like demonic weeds" (535).

Two weighty conditions obtain for adepts of this version of morality, morality as an attribute of the soul: two vexing problems that become, inevitably, obsessions. First, there is a possibility of a kind of doubtful twofoldness, not at all of the kind rejoiced in by William Blake, when he prays, "Twofold always. May God us keep/ From single vision and Newton's sleep" ("Letter to Thomas Butts") but of the kind adduced by Montaigne, when he writes, "We are, I know not how, double in ourselves, so that we believe what we disbelieve and cannot rid ourselves of what we condemn" ("Of Glory," qtd. in Spoto 278). And then, there is a call for eternal (and eternally uncorrupted) vigilance. Spoto, for instance, says, "The Catholic sensibility triumphs. Everyone is capable of sin. Vigilance is *always* called for" (536, my emphasis). Ending *Shadow of a Doubt* (1943), the kindly detective Jack Graham (MacDonald Carey) intones, "The world has to be watched very carefully," a statement, we could say, about optical devotion and the performance of organized life, yet for most critics writing about it, a prediction of the theme, apparently generic in Hitchcock, that returns powerfully in *Vertigo* (1958) and that suffused *D'Entre les morts*, the novel that inspired it (see Pomerance *Eye*, 237–41), wherein Scottie Ferguson's *surveillance* is born of his ancestor Flavières's recollections of a childhood religious trauma:

> That third day.... When I was a kid, whenever I thought about that third day.... I would sneak out to the quarries and let out a great shout, and my shout ran off far underground, but nobody answered.... But it was still too soon.... Now I think my cry was heard. I want so much to believe it. (Trans. mine)

In his early criticism of Hitchcock—in this case discussing *Lifeboat* (1944)—the Catholic Truffaut, himself already concerned as a writer— and soon to be concerned as a filmmaker—with the simultaneous presence of Good and Evil, points out, "If Good and Evil are not named, it is precisely because they are in the center of the discussion, which deals with nothing else" (qtd. in Dixon 93). (The discussion in *Lifeboat* is, of course, not at all confined to Good and Evil, but also wanders at great length into social space and confinement.) Later, watching *The Trouble with Harry* (1955), Truffaut sees (among the "Fall shades" that "disclose a poetry that offers a mischievous contrast to the gruesome text and action") that the characters, "as soon as they think they are or might be guilty, start behaving as if they actually were guilty, thus creating the misunderstanding on which the whole plot is built. *This shows how much Hitchcock remains true to himself*" (qtd. in Dixon 98, 97; emphasis mine).

Perhaps, however, even if in his personal life he was the "rigid moralist" that Spoto declares him (277), Hitchcock can be understood as having screened a quite different moral vision, one that may be less focused on the innerness of dualism and the rigorous need for surveillance than his critical admirers have forced themselves to see in his films, and that points out articulately and consistently the fact of incessant moral judgmentalism in human affairs, even its impotence. When, late in his life, he told a schoolboy from his alma mater St. Ignatius, "I have a conscience with lots of trials over beliefs" (Spoto 590), he may well have been summarizing a lifelong concern not with the weeds in the garden but with our proclivity for weeding and the difficulty for fallible humankind in detecting the weeds that should be pulled. Morality gives an appearance, and as a filmmaker—a man more interested, in the end, to make pictures than to frame moral pronouncements—Hitchcock's interest naturally lay with precisely the way in which a face might attract the attribution of good or evil. It was the face, I think one could argue, that caught his fascination—the face that could present itself to a camera, the face that could cover something the camera could never see—and not the essence moralists might claim lay beneath. Then, Hitchcock was no moralist. He wanted to show the problems that confounded moralism, the state of affairs that prompted civilization to invent morality as a way of safeguarding itself against what cannot be foreseen.

In the summer of 1965, while Hitchcock was closeted with Brian Moore writing *Torn Curtain*, Phi Beta Kappa convened a symposium on morality, including such luminaries of the time as Daniel Bell, René Dubos, and Henry A. Murray. Shortly afterward, a small panel was asked to make comment on it: Robert Coles, Joan Didion, Roger Shinn, Theodore Sizer, and the young psychiatrist Kenneth Keniston, whose noteworthy book on alienated youth, *The Uncommitted*, was on the verge of publication. Keniston's contribution, "Morals and Ethics," for all its slimness, is a richly lambent jewel of meditation and analysis that repays considerable study. His primary drive is to make a particular distinction about morality—as regards its psychological function and its place in social evolution—that his fellow discussants, who "use the terms 'morality,' 'morals' and 'ethics' more or less interchangeably" are neglecting to make: what we might call "morals" and what we might call "ethics" are positioned at "opposite ends of a continuum of morality that runs from specific to general, and from reflexive to reflective and from primitive to civilized" (628). More precisely, the word "morals" refers to

> the socially learned, largely unconscious, relatively specific and apparently self-evident rules of right conduct in any community. When an individual violates his moral code, he feels guilt, the pangs of conscience experienced as a part of the "not-me," as an alien force that acts upon the conscious and experiencing self. Moral codes tend to be specific and situational: they tell us how to behave ourselves . . . in defined kinds of situations. (628)

"Ethics" refers to something rather different, something that seems to me akin to what most observers deem the "moralism" or "moral focus" to be seen in Alfred Hitchcock's films:

> the individual's thought-out, reflective and generalized sense of good and evil, the desirable and the undesirable, as integrated

into his sense of himself and his view of the world. When an ethical man violates his own ethic, he feels not guilt but a sense of human failure, a kind of existential shame that he has not been who he thought himself to be. . . . While morals tell us how to behave, ethics tells us what to aspire to. (628)

It seems clear to me that when we look at a film like *The Wrong Man* and watch the inner turmoil suffered by Manny and Rose Balestrero, particularly toward the end of the film, when it seems at once that Manny will go free but that Rose will perhaps always live now in the shadow of despair, we are watching an ethical drama play out. And also that most arguments about "Hitchcock's morality" are in fact arguments about what Keniston would call the "ethical" world of his characters, that world and its doubts, its vacuums, its labyrinths, its obscurities, its fervent hopes.

It seems at least as fruitful to consider what we may learn from Hitchcock's screen if we take it to be, exactly as the traditional critics have claimed, the locus of a "moral" drama—but "moral" in the more operational sense that Keniston has framed. Morality is thus connected with propriety, duty, social obligation, the maintenance of front, and the systematic (predictable) production of what Goffman terms "normal appearances" (*Relations* 238 ff.); it is much a feature of navigational activity, making possible the determination of who our co-actors are in life and what their alignment and intent—more this play of surfaces, indeed, than an issue of religious, metaphysical, or otherworldly aspirations and dreads. Masquerade, professional or amateur, has the potential for moral disruption. By wearing an identity that is provisional, the individual manifestly brings into play the importance of stage lines in social interaction, shows in which what we understand to be going on becomes a function of what we are in a position to perceive in the actions of those who make undertakings in our presence (and of how much social power any perceiver might be able to use). Whether or not the masks people wear can be, or ought to be, considered genuine or false (in relation to some presumably perduring deeper self) is far from the central problem—more urgent is the moral scheme that attaches to a given role performance, a specified mask, and that is limited not by the capacities and intents of he who engages in action but by the limits of the situation in which the action occurs.

Morality in The Man Who Knew Too Much (1956)

In this light let us consider the moral status of Edward Drayton (Bernard Miles) in Hitchcock's *The Man Who Knew Too Much* (1956), assuming, for the sake of a straightforward, clean argument, a point of vantage entirely proximate to that of Ben McKenna (James Stewart), another protagonist in the film, as he meets and then engages with this man. They are in a posh restaurant in Marrakech, on a balmy evening, hungry and at adjacent tables. Drayton charmingly presents himself as a wholly credible, indeed ingenuous, former "big noise in the Ministry of Food during the War," who was "quite happy farming my bit of land down in Buckinghamshire when these United Nations fellows started worrying me." Now, here he is, with his charming, even bubbly, wife Lucy (Brenda De Banzie), the two of them having "pulled ourselves up at the roots" in order to become United Nations Relief. Drayton is "preparing a report on soil erosion at the moment," he tells the McKennas, as they sit together over a Moroccan dinner. Genteel without being stiff, Edward has the kindliness to offer Ben and Jo some instructions on one-handed eating, and the grace to stutter a little when he does it. As to Jo, she is a famous popular singer who has commanded Lucy's fandom for some while, it seems, although the Draytons don't go to concert halls, Edward being "such an old stick-in-the-mud" who isn't one for "this terrible *bebop*, or whatever you . . ."—meaning most of what the popular venues offered to aficionados' ears in those days (Elvis Presley released "Heartbreak Hotel" in January of the year this film was released). The man may be a bit of a clod, but in this he is nothing if not utterly charming, and soon later, when the McKennas are involved marginally in a horrid murder in the marketplace and must go to the commissariat to file a report, Edward shows himself to be linguistically accomplished to some degree by offering graciously to be Ben's interpreter.

The situation in the marketplace is far more complex than it can first have seemed to Ben, however. The victim of the slaying, Louis Bernard (Daniel Gélin), has whispered a message to McKenna with his dying breath, thus making the arriving gendarmes suspect the two men are linked and leading to Ben's being asked sternly to come to the commissariat. Lucy Drayton steps forward with the offer that she can take Hank—Ben and Jo's ten-year-old (and rather precocious) son—under her care until they return from the police. "You . . . don't want your little boy to go, do you?" While the police inspection is in process, Ben is called out to take a telephone call. A mysterious voice informs him that his son will be harmed if he utters a single word of what Louis Bernard said to him in the market. With Drayton at his side, he quickly phones the hotel for Lucy, but she has not arrived back. Ben returns to be questioned further, but now, riddled with anxiety—and forcing Jo to go along with him—remains strictly mum about Bernard, even when he learns that the dead man had been an agent of the Deuxième bureau.

Back at the hotel, Ben learns that the Draytons have checked out, and realizes that these two proper middle-class English folk have kidnapped his son. They are "proper," not proper. At this point, and in absentia, Edward Drayton gains a new identity altogether: gone is the chummy, bumbling, educated but subservient civil servant's mask, once taken as a genuine personality but now clearly visible in retrospect as only a makeshift covering, replaced with what appears to be something far less provisional, and certainly more nefarious: a man associated in some way with a brutal slaying, a man cool enough to pretend to be one's helper in order to eavesdrop on one's conversations to the police, a man, further, so artful in performance that he was able to hide all of these "true" traits—as they now seem—under the mask of the genteel farmer who appeared last night at the restaurant and in the marketplace this morning. If Drayton is not a killer, he is at least a kidnapper, and either way he lacks the regard for the sanctity of the family, for the courtesy due to travelers in a foreign land, and for the fragility of human feeling and life that he gave the impression of having before. As for his chirrupy wife: near the end of the film, we find her guarding the kidnapped child in an upstairs salon of an embassy, as downstairs in the ballroom, in front of dowdy dignitaries and their diamond-studded wives, Jo puts on a performance of "Que Sera, Sera" in hopes of catching the ear of her son. "That's my mother's voice!" yells Hank, waking out of a dream, but Lucy, the supposed fan of Jo McKenna, can only reply, "Is it?" The fandom was a cover, too, intended to excuse the fact that, in the restaurant, Lucy Drayton had been keeping an eye on the McKennas (just as, seeing her watching them outside the hotel earlier, Jo suspected).

The Draytons, at any rate, are bogus, and perhaps Edward Drayton especially so. At a shabby little nondenominational church in London, we soon discover him to have a different personality still, one which makes any imagination of him that McKenna could have had in Marrakech quite inadequate. He is the pastor of the tiny Ambrose Chapel, a man who can boast a congregation all his own and some real powers of sermonizing. And, as we discover in his living quarters above the sanctuary, he is also a criminal mastermind hiding behind the façade of this pastorship, a slimy and insulting creature who is arrogant and haughty with the suave European (Reginald Nalder) he has hired to perform an assassination. Nor in his arrogance does he ever pause to stammer, so his restaurant vocalization was also faked. His elocution is flawless as he rehearses the assassin for the timing of the cruel act and, further, it turns out that more than being a modest untrained listener he has a serious musical background—the rehearsal involves finding a precise moment in a cantata during a performance of which, tonight, the marksman is

Figure 9.1. *The Man Who Knew Too Much*—fake Draytons.

to make his shot, and Drayton has no trouble putting the needle down on his LP recording with elegant accuracy three different times, and, indeed, pretending to conduct the piece for the assassin's benefit and his own pleasure.

I will forego some further modifications of Drayton's personality that are developed later in the film in order to concentrate a little more on the rehearsal scene. Suffice it to say that in each of the iterations of the Drayton character, a moral schedule attaches to him, and that each moral schedule differs from the one that preceded it. As a charming English husband from Buckinghamshire, he must show politeness to his wife, attentiveness to strangers she wishes to meet, and the gentility expected of the (superior) British gentleman abroad. Drayton has no trouble manifesting all of these directly and clearly. As a kidnapper, he must be purposive and swift, a man who can deftly capitalize on momentary opportunities. While the Buckinghamshire farmer was loath to leave his landholding and move to Morocco—in short, a man who does not move easily—the kidnapper of Hank McKenna was able inside an hour to arrange that a child should disappear, procure an airplane to move his cargo to England, make the necessary arrangements to get the boy across British customs, and see to it that no trace was left behind. The proper moral stance for such a person is opportunistic adaptation, and Drayton shows himself expert at this.

At the chapel, he must show the moral purity of a man of the cloth at one moment (in front of his congregation) and the brutal willingness to keep a family separated and to orchestrate a political killing at another. The killing itself is a model of the moral flexibility and masquerade Drayton has been using throughout. A piece of classical music, the "Storm Clouds" cantata by Arthur Benjamin, will cover a shooting. Not only will the shooting be invisible and inaudible—because it occurs during a performance of the music—and thus unknowable to the audience who take the music to be the central feature of their present reality; but also, the music, which appears to be a source of pleasure and enlightenment for the audience, is at one and the same time being used as a timing system for the kill, the assassin having been briefed to make his shot in a particular bar of the score and on a particular downbeat (indeed, at a tactically perfect moment, when the orchestral and choral forces will be performing at maximum amplitude). Just as the horrid kidnapper seems to be a gentle pastor, the blueprint for killing (the musical score—shown in closeup) seems to be a recipe for cultural apotheosis. While it might be convenient to regard high art as the "true" and "central" function of the cantata, and by corollary, preaching to a congregation as a "true" and "proper" aim for the human spirit, nevertheless Hitchcock's mise-en-scène does not work to privilege traditional morality in these ways. The cantata performance sequence is a brilliant tour de force in which the magnificence of the art is contrapuntally juxtaposed against the meticulous machinations of the assassin in gauging the environment, measuring space, positioning himself, taking aim, and so on, all while Ben McKenna races through the hall against the obstructions of the Metropolitan Police to try to head the assassin off (see Pomerance, "Finding Release" 224–42). In short, culture is the killer—a veritable moral twist. Drayton as kidnapper is living in a power relationship where if he controls the assassin whom he has journeyed to Marrakech to find, still he is controlled by the as-yet invisible forces behind the assassination plot, forces to which he owes obedience if not allegiance and which act to substantiate the transformations of identity that Edward must continually effect. As a kidnapper, he is playing in front of an audience just as much as he does when he gives a sermon; it is a different audience, with different expectations, but it judges how "good" he is in his actions like any other audience does. When the assassination fails, Drayton is judged to have done "bad" work—not, that is, to have entertained the "bad" thought of killing a man but to have entertained the "good" thought badly.

What Hitchcock beautifully shows is the intensively performative nature of Drayton's identities, and thus their moral equivalence. He is continually an actor mounting a character, but it is a matter of arbitration to decide which, if any, of the identity positions are fundamental and stable enough to underpin the others. Is a criminal kidnapper/killer pretending to be a preacher, after all, or is a preacher pretending to be a kidnapper/killer for the quick money his shabby congregational employment clearly doesn't bring? In focusing this way on performance and performative capacity, Hitchcock works as a modern filmmaker, aware that he lives in a social world where all is in motion, all is provisional—indeed, aware that cinema itself bespeaks this modern condition. The search for belief, for holiness, for innocence, for certainty in such a world of continual fluctuation really is an agony. As, watched by the smirking assassin who sees him as a "wolf in sheep's clothing," Drayton regards himself in the mirror, brushing the last hairs into place to become the pastor of his flock, he sees—as, looking over his shoulder, do we—two selves simultaneously, the actor/kidnapper slowly disappearing brush stroke by brush stroke, and the pastor appearing at the same time. In a culture of mobility, where moving from situation to situation and moral requirement to moral requirement is the standard business of life, what fixed truth can one possibly see evidenced in a mirror?

All of Drayton's actions, relatively incoherent as they may seem when viewed in light of one another, are appropriate for the situations in which they are enacted: all of them are "socially learned, largely unconscious, relatively specific and apparently self-evident rules of right conduct in a community" although, to be sure, the community of which the kidnapper Drayton takes himself to be a member operates according to rules incommensurate with those that govern the community of his congregation, or the community of fellow travelers to which he belongs in the Marrakech restaurant. Appeals to "the morality of good and evil" indiscriminately posit a centralized moral universe, with a single implicit community and a single scale of value; in short, appealing to broadly shared notions of "good" and "evil," while appealing to sentimentality and fear, operates by globalizing human relations and thus simplifying them, and neglects consideration of situated community, of power imbalance and conflicts of vested interest, of organized human interaction (such as crime) that works to achieve ends contradictory to what the dominant class supports and encourages. Drayton's collapse at the end of the film may well be a direct consequence not of his clearly discernible "immorality," as so many readers of *The Man Who Knew Too Much* aver explicitly or implicitly, but of the stress of moral conflict he has had to bear in constantly shifting from behaviors that would please his superiors in the kidnapping/murder scheme to behaviors that would seem logical to his (more conventional) wife and congregation. When he behaves "badly," he feels guilt, but given that Drayton shifts from orientation to orientation, in a way consonant with the shifting demands and constant mobility required of the modern personality, his guilt is itself manifold.

Who knows but that guilt might be riddling him as he chats amicably over squab in the restaurant, since he knows he is being false, at least to some degree, to his true purpose in Morocco, which is to hire a killer.

This more complex reading of Drayton requires a complex understanding of the film. Even though Hitchcock punishes Drayton in the end, he takes pains to show the many conflicting sides of his character, and the subtle transformation he must undergo as he sheds one self to don another. As Drayton looks into the mirror in the rehearsal scene, we see two persons, one, as it were, on either side of the glass: the pastor/farmer/husband (who doesn't know much about music) and the kidnapper/planner (who does). Later, during the assassination attempt, we see that the assassin himself knows music—he reads a score. Thus, symphonic orchestration is not obviously and naturally benign in this film, but takes its moral nature from the situation and the usage to which it is put. Or: the music is good for the audience because is gives them acoustic pleasure; and it is good for the assassin and his director because it gives them a logic whereby to artfully succeed in their work. Hitchcock goes to pains in this film to avoid sending any signals whereby we can decisively align the Prime Minister, who is the intended victim of the assassination attempt, with one or another moral universe; and he does the same with the Ambassador, who (*spoiler alert!*) is plotting the assassination. The Prime Minister seems jolly, the Ambassador stern, but there are many rationales that could explain either of these attitudes in men who hold such positions.

Lodging in Guilt

A mirror also functions to split a character in *The Lodger: A Story of the London Fog* (1927), a film for which Hitchcock himself had high regard. Here, rather than a villain being divided into contradictory personalities, the sensibility of the audience is divided regarding the moral status of a central character. London is being terrorized by a "Ripper" who is murdering girls in a systematic and brutal way. A dark stranger (Ivor Novello) appears in a boarding house and takes a room, soon striking up a friendship with the landlady's daughter (June), who is affianced to the chief police officer on the case (Malcolm Keen). Suspicion begins to fall on the boarder with increasing gravity until it seems all but obvious that he is the killer in question, his brooding, secretive, almost delirious behavior being interpreted by the many "conventional" bourgeois protagonists as prima facie evidence of his shadowy guilt. There is finally a chase sequence in which he flees from a mob, which succeeds in penning him against a fence and almost skewering him there, but suddenly news comes that the real criminal has been caught elsewhere. Tempting as it is to think of this as an early iteration of Hitchcock's repeated theme of the wrong man being accused and suffering torment—evidence, that is, of the filmmaker's Catholic attitude—the boarder, we must remember, appears only ambiguously as the wrong man throughout the story. He appears definitively as the wrong man only in retrospect. At this point, having "suffered a severe nervous strain," he lies in recovery in a hospital, having identified himself as the brother of one of the Ripper's unfortunate victims. The landlady's daughter comes to his side to affirm her love for him.

The room into which the boarder is shown after he makes his first entrance is hung with framed pictures, most of which are portraits of female faces roughly in a Pre-Raphaelite style. One of his first acts as resident in the landlady's house is to declare that he does not like these, and he turns the pictures to face the wall. Soon after, she comes up and carries them all away to storage downstairs, after which point the room presents itself as a constant reminder of this business, because on the walls, where each of the pictures had hung, there remains a pale patch, like a perfectly rectangular wound or scar. It is as though an effacement has been made to the representative presence of "girls" in this room, much as in the "real" world of the diegesis an effacement had been made to the living girls who through the act of murder are being removed from social life, their serial victimizations functioning as gouges in the social body. In the redemptive hospital scene at film's end, however, behind the patient's bed, a framed picture hangs on the wall, also turned away from view. On the surface, we know that his frail condition as the sibling survivor of a murder victim brought on his debility to regard and appreciate pictures of other young people, hence his censorious actions in the boarding house and presumably also here. But the missing picture, or the picture turned from view, also enunciates effacement, and here the single turned frame suggests the absence of the sister for whom he has been grieving, and at the same time the absence of the nefarious persona that had been attached to him by virtue of circumstance. Is his debilitated condition in hospital the result of overflooding guilt? Well, what could he be guilty of? He has killed no one. He could be guilty of failing to prevent the killings, of having failed to protect his sister. Thus, even ethically innocent and in love, he is morally culpable—culpable in seeming culpable—and must endure this status until some resolving force or event, beyond the limits of this scene and moment, change him. His embrace with the beautiful heroine in the finale has the power to be immensely redeeming, to cure and restore him even more wholly than the hospital stay has done. We may also read the recuperating lodger as suffering a deeper, more imprisoning guilt that flows from a deeper, more imprisoning effacement. The social world has set upon him and replaced his face with an imagined one. Desperate to find the killer, the population has created one out of an innocent man.

It is by means of a mirror that we first establish the boarder's gaze upon the problematic pictures in the boarding house. He stands at the left of the frame, gazing directly off at something disturbing directly in front of him that we cannot see except by looking in the mantelpiece mirror that is behind his back. It is a demure girl posing with slanted shoulders. As his hand catches at his heart, his eyes open and we see the back of his head and shoulder appear in the mirror. He approaches the image on the wall, now more fully visible in the mirror, and virtually disappears offscreen at left. From the side, we see him stare at the picture and then approach a window, through which the camera now peers directly into his face. His eyes are intense, glazed, dark. His lips are tightly pursed. We are in a position to read him as a warped and murderous personality, just the commodity Londoners are poised and hungry to find, fixated—because of the inspiration of the pictures—on the thought of finding a new victim; indeed, controlled by some dark and deeply buried urge that is triggered by the framed images on the walls, it is an urge he is powerless to control (and in the face of which, therefore, he is innocent!). At the end of the film, however, we are able to think back on this image and see that young man's face as having been filled with unbearable grief.

For its drama to unfold successfully, *The Lodger* thus requires the audience to be capable of entertaining two diametrically opposed views of the same character, yet not at the same time. Whereas in *The Man Who Knew Too Much* Drayton flipped back and forth in front of our eyes, using a mirror to achieve movement from role to role much as an actor would do in preparing for a part, the lodger has always been a dutiful brother but has been misperceived as a killer. For the lodger, the mirror shows us a vision we are to believe in order to experience the flow of the film, yet also to disbelieve, since in its dark and forbidding nature it is a vision of what he is not. In *The Wrong Man*, it is evident to us throughout the film that the accused man is innocent, but it is not evident to us that the man finally presented as the "actual" thief is "actually" a thief; in short, we are lured into pegging him as guilty just as the police were lured into pegging Manny. All three films, made over a span of thirty years in this director's august career, pivot on the theme of provisional goodness and evil, of moral status applied through judgment that is subject to fallibility, or through judgment enacted by official agents of the dominant culture upon others who are relatively powerless and whose motives, therefore, have a *likely* impertinence. In his sensitivity to the situated and unstable nature of the moralities and immoralities, the struggles and the guilt, that he puts on display lies Hitchcock's modernism, his dramatic springboard, and his genius.

Note

With gratitude to Nellie Perret and John Turtle.

Works Cited and Consulted

Becker, Howard S. *Outsiders: Studies in the Sociology of Deviance*. New York: Free Press, 1963.
Benjamin, Walter. "What Is the Epic Theater? (II)," in *Selected Writings* Vol. 4 1938–1940. Trans. Edmund Jephcott and others, Ed., Howard Eiland and Michael W. Jennings. Cambridge: Harvard UP, 2003, 302–09.
Chabrol, Claude, and Eric Rohmer. *Hitchcock: The First Forty-Four Films*. Trans. Stanley Hochman. New York: Ungar, 1979.
Dixon, Wheeler Winston. *The Early Film Criticism of François Truffaut*. Bloomington: Indiana UP, 1993.
Goffman, Erving. *Relations in Public: Microstudies of the Public Order*. New York: Harper & Row, 1972.
———. *Gender Advertisements*. New York: Harper & Row, 1976.
Innocence Project, online at http://www.innocenceproject.org/understand/Eye-witness-Misidentification.php. Accessed July 4, 2008.
James, Henry. *The Portrait of a Lady*. New York: George Scribner and Sons, 1908.
Jay, Martin. *Downcast Eyes: The Denigration of Vision in Twentieth-Century French Thought*. Berkeley: University of California Press, 1994.
Keniston, Kenneth. "Morals and Ethics," *The American Scholar* 34: 4 (Autumn 1965), 628–32.
Pomerance, Murray. *An Eye for Hitchcock*. New Brunswick: Rutgers UP, 2004.
———. "'Finding Release': Storm Clouds and *The Man Who Knew Too Much*," in James Buhler, Caryl Flinn, and David Neumeyer, eds., *Music and Cinema*. Hanover: Wesleyan UP, 2000, 207–46.
Spoto, Donald. *The Dark Side of Genius: The Life of Alfred Hitchcock*. New York: Ballantine, 1984.
Truffaut, François. *Hitchcock*. Trans. Helen Scott. New York: Touchstone, 1985.

10

R. Barton Palmer

The Deepening Moralism of *The Wrong Man*

"Let's just say," Alfred Hitchcock conceded to François Truffaut in speaking of *The Wrong Man* (1956), that "it wasn't my kind of picture. But the industry was in a crisis at the time, and since I'd done a lot of work for Warner Brothers, I made this picture for them" (Hitchcock/Truffaut 181). Asked to evaluate what he had accomplished, the director opined: "Let's file *The Wrong Man* among the indifferent Hitchcocks" (183). Interestingly, he refused to come to the film's defense even when gently provoked by his young admirer, who provided him with the obvious explanation for why the project must have seemed attractive: "I can see why it appealed to you: a concrete, real-life illustration of your favorite theme, the man convicted of a crime committed by someone else" (183). Truffaut was surely correct in this assumption, which is supported by how the film presents itself and by the unusual elements of its production history.

It is important to remember that the 1962 interview with the world-renowned Truffaut, who had been one of his most fervent acolytes for some years, in turn marked a crucial moment for Hitchcock in the construction of his artistic legacy; he had for almost a decade been lionized by the young cinephiles of the *Cahiers du cinéma*, including Claude Chabrol, Éric Rohmer, Jean-Luc Godard, and Truffaut. In

1967, when the transcript of this famous encounter was first published in English translation, Hitchcock was still active in an industry increasingly wracked by financial difficulties and experiencing something of an identity crisis, which he himself unsurprisingly reflected. In a cultural era that was becoming increasingly dominated by the practice of art cinema, Hitchcock certainly embraced how his French admirers had identified his works as morally profound and thus fundamentally distinct from the entertainment industry in which his authorship had otherwise played out. As Robert Kapsis notes, Hitchcock thought that "American highbrow critics would be impressed to learn that François Truffaut, one of the most esteemed directors associated with the new international art cinema movement, viewed him as one of the supreme geniuses of the cinema" (Kapsis 91). The famous interview would popularize the view of Hitchcock's seriousness propounded more than a decade before by Chabrol:

> I should say that his moral ideas point toward the metaphysic that subsumes them. It is clear enough that in human terms Morality in capital letters constitutes the only workable metaphysic, and that man's deliverance, which is the very stuff of Hitchcock's artistic fabric, in the end is closely connected to his sense of dignity. (18)

In the event, Hitchcock was proven correct that the Truffaut book would change the minds of those critics who had remained hitherto unconvinced that he was anything more than a skilled entertainer: according to Kapsis, his supporters were convinced that the interview "almost singlehandedly converted many 'Hitch*kn*ockians' to Hitchcockians" (71). With Truffaut's endorsement, Hitchcock would be understood across the Atlantic and in his own country as a director who, as Rohmer (Maurice Schérer) had so well put it in 1955, had the rare ability to take "popular themes" and "confer upon them a literary dignity" (Schérer 9).

The essence of Hitchcockian narrative, Chabrol had maintained, was its focus on the central convention of the thriller genre: a "trial, deliberately chosen because it is supremely difficult and because it represents the most disorienting situation in which anyone can be put" (Chabrol 18). In Hitchcock's films, the trial of the protagonist's physical and psychological strength is often set into motion by false accusation or misidentification; this blow is delivered by some inscrutable destiny that at first means nothing and yet comes to be everything. Misidentification was the pretext for an exciting, varied narrative of improbable adventure that Hitchcock found in the fiction of John Buchan, author of

The Thirty-Nine Steps, who was one of Hitchcock's most admired novelists. And the filmmaker used it to good effect in his reshaping of other narratives, including the gothic thriller by Saunders and Beeding that became *Spellbound* (1945) and Patricia Highsmith's *Strangers on a Train*, film version released in 1951. Starting with *The Wrong Man*, however, in a number of Hitchcock films misidentification becomes the pretext for a different approach that centers on a disturbing probing of guilt, innocence, and, most centrally, the limitations of human agency. Truffaut's comment about *The Wrong Man* went right to the heart of Hitchcock's conferring of a kind of "literary dignity" on "popular themes," his reconfiguration of the falsely accused adventurer as a suffering protagonist, Manny Balestrero (Henry Fonda), who, in the telling phrase of Jean Douchet, is "set firmly to face the true emptiness" of his life, forced to confront a self that has been objectified by others in ways that are totally estranging to him (101). This victim of fate is by a miscarriage of justice "fully installed in the day to day, but in a fashion that banishes intrinsic reality," as the ordinary facts of his life (his work, his relationships with wife, children, and mother) are replaced by his "desires or his fears" (Douchet 91).

Why did Hitchcock, interested in being acclaimed as the artist he certainly was, refuse to engage with Truffaut's observation about the thematic center of *The Wrong Man* and its relevance to the Hitchcockian thriller in general? A likely explanation is that he remained acutely aware that the film had been a critical and commercial disappointment, if not exactly a flop. Though in his onscreen introduction to the film Hitchcock specifically refers to *The Wrong Man* as a thriller, it had seemed strangely ungeneric to filmgoers, who were not pleased by its lack of drama and suspense. In his review for *The New York Times*, A.H. Weiler showed little enthusiasm for a Hitchcock release that managed to only "rarely stir the emotions or make a viewer's spine tingle. Frighteningly authentic, the story generates only a modicum of drama."[1] Such a view continues to shape critical opinion. One of the most prominent of contemporary Hitchcockians, Patrick McGilligan, complains that *The Wrong Man* is "slow, somber, remarkably restrained, it's one Hitchcock film that doesn't hold up very well for modern audiences" (538). In responding to Truffaut, this was the kind of judgment Hitchcock was eager to explain away, if not contest, suggesting that he now realized how he could have made the film more appealing, more "Hitchcockian," at least in the sense of how he had taught his public to understand that term.

With its quality in dispute, he was eager to insist that *The Wrong Man* should not be memorialized as a personal film, but rather filed away among the other slightly misfired projects for which he was willing to take little if any authorial responsibility. Hitchcock hinted to Truffaut that he was obliged to remain more or less faithful to the material in the form in which it had come down to him. It would have been more suspenseful, he went on to add, had he told the story in a different way, not focusing on the suffering of the eponymous protagonist, but on the investigation that eventually proves him innocent. In a moment of uncharacteristic modesty, he was not inclined to admit that in making the film he had been anything more than a useful *metteur-en-scène*, fulfilling his contract to the studio that had supported him in the past by taking on "their" project, and thus doing all concerned a favor in a period of widespread "crisis." Perhaps sensing his subject's discomfort, Truffaut declined to press the issue.

As Truffaut stated, however, the making of *The Wrong Man* can hardly be seen as other than signaling a shift in Hitchcock's approach to the existential issues raised by the thriller genre, as self-evidently fictional forms of adventure-promoting misidentification give way in this film to a real-life failure of the justice system that exemplifies a harsh truth of the human condition. The elucidating and contextualizing of this significant change in tone will be the focus of this essay. Hitchcock's French critics (especially Jean Douchet) recognized early on that *The Wrong Man* is by no means an "indifferent" film since it offers an important assaying of the deepening moralism that characterizes the four works that are generally considered to be his most artistically successful and intellectually challenging: these include *The Man Who Knew Too Much* (1956), released some months earlier, and subsequently *Vertigo* (1958), *Psycho* (1960), as well as (most strikingly and disturbingly) *The Birds* (1963).

These films all focus on the life-transforming experience of profound mischance, of life-altering disasters that seem to drop out of a clear-blue destinal sky (literally in the case of *The Birds*) and cannot be entirely reversed, if at all, or even fully understood. Like *The Wrong Man*, in one way or another these narratives question the efficacy of human action, the powers we believe we possess to explain, transform, and restore. Even when they manage to save themselves or solve the mystery, Hitchcock's protagonists here lose their trust in the persistence of the everyday. They must go on living in a world where they are now supremely aware that the next disaster might be just around the corner. Sudden, inexplicable misfortune has forced them to expect the worst; surviving terrible trials, they henceforth endure an irremediable state of uncertainty, best exemplified perhaps by how *Vertigo*'s Scottie (James Stewart) is left bewildered and directionless at film's end, perched at the top of the tower from which his beloved nemesis (Kim Novak) has just stumbled to her death, and with no obvious path forward beyond emulating her grim example.

A child can be abducted by apparently friendly acquaintances; a walk up to one's front door after a hard night of work can be interrupted by false accusation and wrongful arrest; a well-meaning attempt to deprive obsession of its power to kill can go horribly awry; psychopathic violence can explode from an unlikely source, mocking the ultimate insignificance of other sorts of malfeasance; and a charming flirtation can be interrupted by the sudden, murderous revolt against human presence launched by a hitherto indifferent nature. What seems to be true and solid is shown to be not; the world acquires an unexpected, unfathomed depth, known now to be concealing unknown unknowns. The disturbance in the expected order of things can sometimes be put right, and injustice made good after a fashion, but the damage that has been done endures. The world never seems the same again. An apocalypse of one kind or another may be in store, as suggests the ending of *The Birds*, with its surviving characters in full retreat toward some supposed safe haven that likely no longer exists.

The tale Hitchcock sets himself to tell in *The Wrong Man* is thoroughly undramatic, true to the often strange and improbable nature of the actual experience it attempts to delineate. As Michel de Certeau points out, such a character as the film's protagonist, in the unexceptionality of his expectations and refusal to acknowledge the fact of inevitable death, "makes plausible the universal character of the particular place in which the mad discourse of a knowing wisdom is pronounced" (de Certeau 2). The ordinary man, de Certeau goes on, channeling Freud, is "accused of yielding . . . to the 'illusion of being able to solve all the riddles of this world' and of being 'assured that a Providence watches over his world' "(3). *Homo ordinarius* believes in the perdurability of the routines that have come to define his life, even as he trusts in his apparent power to shape its course when trouble appears on the horizon. Without thinking, he believes in, and expects to be guided by, some simple metaphysics of justice. He unreflectively assumes that "things will work out." *The Wrong Man* exposes the self-serving fragility of this assumption, even though a fortunate chance effects a last-minute deliverance. To be sure, Manny washes up on the shore of a happy ending, but he is half-drowned and gasping for breath.

Manny lives the most banal of quiet lives as a nightclub musician in New York City. His problems are ordinary problems: money they don't have is needed to pay for dental work for wife Rose (Vera Miles); his two young sons squabble and must be reconciled by a father patient enough to impart moral lessons; his desire for routine-breaking excitement must be satisfied by perusing the morning paper's racing form and placing imaginary bets. After visiting the neighborhood insurance office to see if he can borrow money on her policy in order to pay the dentist, Manny finds himself suddenly, and for no reason discernible to him, accused of robbing the agency some weeks before, a crime he did not commit or is even aware has been committed. Misidentified first by eyewitnesses at the agency (who bear no grudge and do not seek his harm) and then by delicatessen owners robbed, it seems, by the same gunman, Manny's guilt seems confirmed by striking, if inconclusive, circumstantial evidence. Arrested for the crimes, Manny is subjected to a succession of low-key institutional horrors as he is arrested, questioned, paraded before those he is thought to have victimized, charged, booked, imprisoned, arraigned, and eventually brought before the bar to answer for the crimes. In the grip of forces (by no means malevolent) that it would be pointless to resist since they offer him no purchase, he struggles to construct an alibi. Bad luck haunts him. The actual witnesses to his life, those who would recognize him as himself and fix his presence in time and place, ironically enough elude his attempts at contact. Disastrously, some are no longer alive to testify. Even his time in court proceeds inconclusively, as a procedural mistake forces a declaration of mistrial. No dark conspiracy is at work here, of course, just the simple fact that things do not always go as we have come to expect, and sometimes, if unpredictably and following no knowable pattern, they go to our unwilled and unmerited destruction.

In the face of unremitting misfortune, Manny is brought to recognize his utter inability to establish who he is—that is, an innocent man with no connection to the criminal other than the unfortunate coincidence that both men entered the same insurance office seeking money, one legitimately and the other not. Though not especially religious, Manny resorts to prayer after his anguished mother prevails upon him to ask for divine assistance. We are shown him praying, but do not hear the prayer. What follows immediately can, but need not, be interpreted as a heavenly intervention; Hitchcock does not encourage, even as he allows, the viewer to take spiritual refuge in *post hoc ergo propter hoc* thinking. In any case, this much is clear: by calling upon God to help him, Manny is acknowledging his own helplessness. At this very moment, the actual criminal, who bears him an uncanny resemblance, is arrested while robbing the delicatessen for a second time. He is immediately recognized by the owners as the one who robbed them months before. There is no question of the guilt of this man, caught in the act. The police quickly realize their error, and in a second lineup, the other witnesses identify him as the perpetrator, acknowledging that they were mistaken in their previous testimony.

The Deepening Moralism of *The Wrong Man*

Figure 10.1. Manny (Henry Fonda) at the Insurance Office.

Released, Manny goes "free," as they say. But the experience of an undeserved misfortune that nearly destroys their family has unhinged Rose, who is reduced to mute despair and must be hospitalized. It is Rose who takes to heart the lesson that life seems intent on teaching them: count on nothing. A final title insists that she eventually recovers enough of her equilibrium in order to overcome her depression. Tellingly, however, her recovered trust in the everyday is not dramatized, only suggested by the closing shot of a sunny Florida city to which the Balestreros are said to have moved, leaving behind what the film has depicted as a much grimmer New York City. At this point, Bernard Herrmann's score sounds light and airy for the very first time. This is a happy ending that perhaps protests too much its strained sense of pleasingly restored order.

The "true story" that Hitchcock set himself to tell in *The Wrong Man* unleashed (or reflected?) a growing interest on his part in what can only be called a psychological moralism, with issues of character, guilt, and responsibility coming to the fore, even as a darker vision of human possibility dominates the action. In the first movement of *The Wrong Man*, Manny exchanges a comfortable home, replete with a warm and loving family, for the isolation of a prison cell, whose confining solitude is both disorienting and instructive, a place to learn about life's unfairness and the dead-end to which all human hopes and intentions must eventually come. Losing for a time all that has defined him as a person, Manny is forced to confront himself on the most basic existential level, wondering what he has done to provoke such an avalanche of disaster, questioning whether his life has value. "I wonder if you all would be better off without me," he confesses to his mother (Esther Minciotti), and the despairing sentiment has a force beyond the forgivable self-pity that prompts him to voice it.

Manny must find some way to deal with the apparent randomness of events in a universe seemingly indifferent to notions of justice and innocence. At a particularly dark moment, when his case is still very much in doubt, his lawyer (Anthony Quayle) asks: "Can you take it, Manny?" This appears to be the question the film as a whole poses, and in response he barely murmurs a weak: "I'll try." In the end, restored by circumstances, Manny seeks to identify an enemy on whom blame can be heaped for his misfortune, but there is none. At the police station, the now-identified robber, leaving the lineup that has established his guilt, walks by Manny and looks quizzically at the man who resembles him so closely. Manny angrily says "Do you realize what you've done to my wife?" But this absurd accusation falls on uncomprehending and unsympathetic ears. The meaning seems clear enough: no one can fault experience for what it proves to be. We can call it bad luck or good, but it is just what happens. It is possible, as Jean Douchet argues, to see Manny's misfortune, at least in the sense of material loss, as the most ultimately positive of experiences, in the tradition of Boethius's *Consolation of Philosophy* (sixth century):

> The test imposed on Balestrero—an example for us to consider in relation to ourselves—consists in making him come to understand by their successive loss that the only true goods of this life are emotional, spiritual, and moral ones, and that these cannot, in any circumstance, come to depend on material possessions; and that, of all these goods, the most precious is that of the spirit, whose force and vigilance alone permit us to triumph. (Douchet 100)

Such a positive reading, however, ignores the film's complex treatment of loss. Manny does arguably win through in the end because of the "force and vigilance" of his spirit; he never gives up the fight to prove his innocence despite a seemingly unending succession of reversals, and he is saved by the same chance that earlier seemed to seal his fate. Something else happens, and this time his luck is good. But the situation with Rose is quite different. Unable to cope with the persistent mystery of it all (why did this happen to us?), she retreats into a self-flagellating despair from which the film only reports she has in the end been delivered.

Earlier, after visiting the dentist, she had complained to Manny that "Every time we get up something comes along and knocks us right back down again." His response asks to be understood as "normal," but is it? "That's life, honey," he cheerfully affirms, "That's the way it is. I think we're pretty lucky, mostly." The disaster that immediately follows belies Manny's optimism. The irony fairly drips when Rose happily coos: "You make everything all right again. Oh Manny, sometimes I'm so frightened waiting for you to come home at night." Manny comforts her: "I always do." With its unquestioned certainty about a future that is both unknowable and unpredictable, this promise of unending devotion is dangerously self-deceptive, a promise thoroughly unkeepable, as it turns out, despite Manny's best intentions.

Rose comes to embody and express most deeply the lesson the story has to teach about the essential fragility of those structures we build to guide and validate our daily forms of living. Depression is an irrational state of mind, modern medicine asks us to believe, brought on and sustained by a physiological disorder that can be alleviated by the mood-altering drugs of an ever-advancing pharmacology. By this definition, Rose is not depressed. Her sadness, emotional withdrawal, and immobility of spirit and body are instead understandable reactions to what she and Manny have experienced. Manny can take what life can dish out; Rose cannot, at least for a long time, and then we have only the flimsy evidence of the film's closing shot, which tellingly does not allow us to see Rose's face.

In the previous sequence, she had been shown by Hitchcock's camera to be filled with seemingly bottomless and contradictory feelings of disappointment and disengagement. Rushing to the hospital to give her the good news of his release from custody and complete exoneration, Manny is met by her pained, distant refusal to take heart. "We can start our lives all over again," he excitedly proclaims, telling her that they can move to another city that promises anonymity. "Nothing can help me," Rose distractedly responds, "No one. It doesn't matter where I am." In an earlier scene, Rose had blamed herself for what happened. Had she not needed dental work, Manny would not have made the visit to the insurance office that started all their troubles. Had she managed their affairs more carefully, nothing bad would have happened. Disaster forces first Rose, and then Manny, to turn on themselves in desperate attempts to provide the inexplicable with some moralizing rationale. It seems likely, in fact, that his continuing slide into despair is halted only by the fortuitous appearance and subsequent arrest of the man that others thought he was.

Misidentification in such characteristically Hitchcockian thrillers as *The 39 Steps* (1935) and *Saboteur* (1942) propels "wronged" protagonists on rapid journeys through a variety of distinct, often exotic, social landscapes; in order to survive, they must call upon strength, energy, cunning, and, most important, resolution as they achieve both their own deliverance and satisfying romantic connections. Misidentification proves that they are men of action and romance who are right and do right; protagonists such as Richard Hannay and Barry Kane closely conform to stereotypes drawn from nineteenth-century melodrama, staples of the conventional fiction or drama that was Hitchcock's favored, if not only, source of material. In *Secret Agent* and *Sabotage* (both 1936), the director had attempted telling darker tales, devoid of uplift and drawn from literary not middlebrow sources (W. Somerset Maugham and Joseph Conrad), but these productions had not proved successful with audiences (see Palmer 2011 for further details). Chastened by his public, Hitchcock turned away from material of this type, especially in the early years of his American career, but with *The Wrong Man* he again attempted something similar. A previous project (*I Confess*, 1953), while more suspenseful if in an uncharacteristic fashion, was also something of an anti-thriller, with a quite different twist put on Hitchcock's standard themes, notably romance (see the introduction for further discussion). The film had failed at the box office and received the kiss of death from *Times* reviewer Bosley Crowther, who was the era's most powerful tastemaker; Crowther pronounced it "an entertainment that tends to drag, sag and generally grow dull."[2] Nonetheless, Hitchcock soon proceeded (and eagerly, as we will see) with a similar project that offered even less of the screen excitement to which he had accustomed filmgoers. His persistence in occupying himself with more of the same can only be seen as "personal," as Chabrol and Rohmer suggested early on when they said that this film was made from the heart, "selon son coeur" (147).

The Wrong Man, in fact, proceeds even more radically in its deconstruction of commercial common sense. In *I Confess*, Father Logan (Montgomery Clift) still disposes of an ability to act, even if the most important thing he does is refusing to act; he has been falsely accused of a murder whose perpetrator has confessed to him, barring Logan from revealing his identity to the police. Logan, it turns out, had motive enough to murder the man, who was blackmailing the woman, Ruth Grandfort (Anne Baxter), with whom the priest had been in love before taking holy orders, and who, though now married, is still very much in love with him. In a typically Hitchcockian twist, *I Confess* thus suggests that the actual murderer is in some sense Logan's secret sharer, the double who does what the protagonist, perhaps not even consciously, wishes done, which is to keep the secret of the affair that will embarrass now not only Ruth, but him. In *The Wrong Man*, the robber is merely Manny's physical double, bearing the man a close resemblance that can only be ascribed to genetic happenstance. Misidentification, in any case, immediately deprives Manny of freedom, indeed of motion itself; unlike his Hitchcockian predecessors, including Logan, he is never able to hazard his chances between the police and the villains in a complexly orchestrated and double pursuit. Unlike Father Logan, he never becomes the agent of his own fate; indeed, there is no villain for him to reveal or apprehend since he utterly lacks the resources to track down the actual criminal, who in any case has intended him no harm.

Released pending trial, Manny is charged by his lawyer with the responsibility for proving his innocence in the face of what seem to be unshakable accusations. Through no fault of his own, he fails to establish his innocence, that he was in another place (the meaning of "alibi") and thus could not be the man who committed the robberies. Both the men who could establish his whereabouts at the time of the crime have since died in what seems a final and fatal stroke of bad luck. In the end, he gains nothing but restoration of a sort as the district attorney declines to continue his prosecution of the case. However the film makes it clear that no one has the power to give him back what misfortune has taken from him. Committed to the delineation of a true story that is anything but spectacular, *The Wrong Man* avoids the picaresque journey of the typical Hitchcock thriller in which the hero, suddenly jerked out of his everyday pattern of living, is launched on an often-delightful journey of therapeutic self-discovery, exculpation, and heroic accomplishment.[3] Fabulation of the most *outré* sort seems a guarantee of the hero's safety and eventual happy ending; a bible in the pocket of a borrowed coat traps a fatal bullet; the hero's plane crashes into the Atlantic, but he is speedily rescued; a New York mansion fortuitously reveals a fire alarm that, when pulled, effects the hero's escape from bondage, just in time to foil the villain's plans. *The Wrong Man* utterly lacks adventure—the unexpected that with predictable unpredictability fortuitously comes the hero's way—as well as the rapid twists and reversals that sustain what-happens-next interest in the narrative. Focusing on the experiences of Manny and Rose with overwhelming misfortune, Hitchcock has even thrown away a chance to make suspenseful the capture and subsequent identification of Manny's double. The film resolutely avoids the cross-cutting that might make his apprehension "spine-tingling" (consider the finale of *Strangers on a Train* [1950] where this technique is deployed to perfection), but offers instead a speedy, largely de-dramatized version of the innocent man's release by the authorities following the perpetrator's uneventful apprehension, which features only the bare minimum of physical action. It is in the scene between Manny and Rose in which he reports the good news that Hitchcock spends his talent designing, with Rose's manner and body posture, as well as the artful framing and chiaroscuro lighting, suggesting her thoroughly numbed withdrawal from Manny and their children.

If *The Wrong Man* has been largely dismissed by Anglo-American critics, and not much appreciated by the current generation of Hitchcock fans, the film was seen as significant and artistically successful by Hitchcock's early French admirers. Their views bear revisiting. Douchet sees the film as marking a turning point in Hitchcock's artistic development:

> The issue that at this point seems to have preoccupied Hitchcock is less that of the double as such but rather the process of doubling. It's no longer a question of dramatizing an external treason from some hellish shadows. Now the need is to reveal an internal treason that is much graver and more insidious. The hero is no longer at the mercy of his double, who uses blackmail to control him [as in *Strangers on a Train*]. He is forced instead to assume an identity, an outer shell, a way of being that does not belong to him, to become someone who he is not . . . it's truly with *The Wrong Man* that our director begins to explore this new path . . . the hero then finds himself more of a prisoner than in the films that preceded. (86, 89)

In their monograph devoted to Hitchcock, Chabrol and Rohmer opine that the film is a "manifestly ambitious work" that marked a turning point on Hitchcock's part toward material he knew would not prove terribly commercial (147). As they point out, he was at the time financially secure because the films he had just made for Paramount had proven so successful, having, *mirabile dictu*, recently become as well one of the most popular figures on American television (*Alfred Hitchcock Presents* premiered to immediate acclaim on CBS in the early fall of 1955 before planning for *The Wrong Man* began in earnest).

So, Chabrol and Rohmer conclude, the director could risk commercial failure by altering his approach, finding himself free for the time from worries about deviating too far from the commercial formulas (romance, intriguing narrative, and crowd-pleasing finales) upon which both the industry and Hitchcock had based their success. An earlier period of success culminating in *The 39 Steps* had perhaps enabled a similar turn toward both *The Secret Agent* and *Sabotage*. For Chabrol and Rohmer, *The Wrong Man* adumbrated themes that, hinted at in his earlier productions, now found fuller expression:

The fundamental abjection of the human being who, once deprived of his freedom, is nothing more than one object among many others; the idea of an evil at one and the same time merited and unjust . . . the idea of culpability, also fundamental, in the sense that it is a theme of Kafka's *The Trial* . . . Here the extraordinary, as not in Hitchcock's previous works, is more than a simple pretext to be spectacularly developed. It appears here as itself, becoming the object of analysis. (149–50)

The project that would become *The Wrong Man* lacked not only romance (an industry convention that Hitchcock had usually observed and had shown considerable talent in offering), but also "suspense of every kind" (147). As Chabrol and Rohmer affirm, in "ce film de nuit, d'hiver," the hero (if that is the proper term to describe this main character) finds himself thrown into the "boue de mépris" (154, 148). Hitchcock condemns no other protagonist to inhabiting a wintry world of night as he makes his way through a pervasive scorn that clings to him and marks his shame like mud. It is indeed true that misidentification here is transformed from a narrative pretext into the film's subject. Manny is humbled in the etymological sense of the word when he is brought down to the very ground by the reification upon which the criminal justice system must depend if it is to work when faced with the inevitable large-scale violation of the law that characterizes life in the modern metropolis. What is "concrete" (to quote Truffaut again) about *The Wrong Man* is that it constructs misidentification as an authentic, low-key descent into dehumanization and abjection, the kind of misfortune that can, and does, happen to anyone. Viewers are made to share Manny's bewilderment, and the experience is more painful than engaging. Suddenly thrown into a world dominated by accusations that make no sense, Manny doesn't know what he doesn't know, and neither do we. Instead, we are, like Manny, sure of only one thing: his innocence. Our experience with this grim tale is not softened by any distancing effect of fabulation. The moral of this story is not easily stated. But it cannot be: watch your step! We have to go on living even if *The Wrong Man* demonstrates that danger lurks even in the seemingly bright spaces where we go about our everyday business.

Hitchcock here does not offer us a fiction in which, following the usual protocol for our engagement, we are invited to invest only a limited amount of belief; the film does not construct some nonaffirmed place, a world that is merely supposed and from whose discontents and injustice we are somewhat shielded. Instead, *The Wrong Man* is a scrupulously faithful chronicle of the world we share with Manny that the director instructs his audience to endorse as true. It is most emphatically not presented to us as "just a story," and many in the audience of the initial release would have known something about the case since it had been featured in *Life*, one of the era's leading news magazines. Rehearsing these nonfiction accounts, Hitchcock's film is thus yet another rendition of a disturbing case then enjoying widespread notoriety, an event that was grimly fascinating because it exposed the evil (however banal rather than either malefic or persecutory) that can without warning fracture the seemingly solid routines of ordinary living.

Here was a story, as the director informed viewers in the brief stand-up that served as a prologue, that, even though "every word of it is true," contains elements "stranger than all the fiction that has gone into many of the thrillers that I have made before." The change from glamorizable fiction to authentic factual re-creation is suggested by the choice to film in black and white, with a cinematographic style and use of real locations that made it obvious to audiences at the time that Hitchcock was offering them a semidocumentary film similar to the many others that Hollywood (especially Twentieth-Century Fox) had been offering the public for the last decade. Not emphasizing either stars (Henry Fonda and Vera Miles play "character" roles) or exotic visuals, from the outset, *The Wrong Man* flaunts instead its connection to a director who seems very much the auteur. Contrary to usual audience-grabbing trickery in inserting a cameo of himself in the story world, Hitchcock is here present in an aestheticized form (standing on a stage blank and dark, except for a decorative shaft of light that frames him in long shot). This striking image, in which the director is not seen in closeup, suggests his identity with the world of the film he has constructed. In a self-reflexive moment, *The Wrong Man* identifies its paradoxical implausibility, its purveyance of a truth that is in fact stranger than, if consonant with, the fictional structure that had preoccupied him (if not exclusively) since at least *Blackmail* (1929). At the same time, Hitchcock as Hitchcock (not as an image humorously inserted into the world of the story) takes ownership of the tale he is about to tell, explains its signal quality: a truth that goes beyond the mere plausibility in which fiction trades, partaking instead of the unimaginableness of the actual, which in its infinity of forms never loses the power to surprise or shock.

This performance of the director *qua* director belies the impression he gave Truffaut that this project was not "his kind of picture," with his participation explained only as a favor to the studio that had served him well. He did "owe" Warner's a picture to complete his contract, but all evidence suggests that he was hardly reluctant to undertake a project that fit so neatly into the most important trend of postwar Hollywood realism, the so-called "factual film" that emphasized pictorial journalism and had been developed at Fox during the previous decade by producer Louis de Rochemont (working with directors such as Elia Kazan and Henry Hathaway), under the close supervision of studio head Darryl F. Zanuck. McGilligan reports that

> Warner's was actually ambivalent about *The Wrong Man* until Hitchcock offered to waive his salary, an offer calculated to win him the go-ahead to make the picture. It's hard to think of very many other directors in Hollywood history who have volunteered to work for free this way, at the peak of their success. (532)

The 1950s in Hollywood were an era of changing, often contradictory trends, with Hitchcock cannily signing up for projects in two of the most prominent: pictorial films, shot on exotic locations in widescreen (*To Catch a Thief* [1955], *North by Northwest* [1959], and *Vertigo* most notably) and gritty true stories shot on locations that were far from exotic and generally made more obvious claims for serious themes. Against all odds, the Best Picture Award for 1955 went to Delbert Mann's *Marty*, based on a Paddy Chayefsky teleplay that, according to its author, was designed to dramatize "the most ordinary love story in the world . . . the way it literally would have happened to the kind of people I know" (183). With its source in an actual event rather than a commitment to a social realist approach of this kind, *The Wrong Man* makes an interesting companion piece to *Marty*—both films focus on the everyday in a fashion customarily eschewed by Hollywood.

Hitchcock's narrative centered squarely on the experience of Manny and his family. Thus *The Wrong Man* followed closely the way in which this story had been being told by the time it came to Hitchcock's attention. In speaking to Truffaut, Hitchcock suggested that it might well have been a miscalculation to keep the "subjective" focus on the "wrong man." To be sure, the other films in the semidocumentary crime cycle to which Hitchcock suggests that this film belongs are structured from the point of view of those seeking to solve a case and then arrest the guilty party. They are journalistic not only in the sense that, like *The Wrong Man*, they recount a true story, whose outlines they are committed to only minimally fictionalizing. Unlike Hitchcock's contribution to the semidocumentary, their rhetoric is dominated by revelation, either the proper assigning of responsibility for a heinous crime or the production of evidence required to exculpate the mistakenly convicted. Reflecting a wartime collectivism that was often jingoistic, they celebrate the power and importance of government institutions, especially the FBI (subject of the cycle's first successful release, Henry Hathaway's *The House on 92nd Street* [1945]). *The Wrong Man* is hardly this kind of story. Truffaut appropriately called Hitchcock's attention to the focus on *The Wrong Man* on moral experience: first, the unexpected incursion of thoroughgoing disaster into a life that could hardly be either more ordinary or more innocent; and second, the reversal of fortune that brings about his deliverance even when the efforts of his lawyer, and his own, prove futile (180–81).

Investigations, the director suggests, supposedly lend themselves more readily to effective dramatization, a doubtful proposition given his characteristic, and largely successful, focus on the misidentified, on the "wrong men" that Truffaut correctly identifies as stock Hitchcockian characters. In support of this odd self-criticism, Hitchcock names two of the most relevant releases, the Louis de Rochemont productions *Boomerang* [Elia Kazan, 1947] and *Call Northside 777* [Henry Hathaway, 1948], both of which are in some sense re-creations of "true stories," but his observation would hold true for many similar films of the period as well (see Palmer *Shot on Location* [2016] for a full discussion of this postwar tradition). It is difficult to see, however, how telling the story from the viewpoint of Manny might have made for insurmountable problems of dramatization; the last third of the film, as I have already suggested, could certainly have been made more suspenseful had Hitchcock cross-cut the various events leading to the reappearance of the robber in the neighborhood with those that end with the declaration of a mistrial. Surely Hitchcock could have found several ways to make the film more suspenseful if he had been interested in doing so. We should also take with a huge grain of salt his observation that the scenes depicting Rose's breakdown and then hospitalization were undramatic, even anticlimactic (180). These are carefully constructed and provide—as they were surely meant to do—an effective counterpoint to the film's more conventional narrative, its depiction of Manny's deliverance. Rose's breakdown, to be sure, is an important part of the story whose truth Hitchcock was determined to tell in full, but surely the emphasis he gives it at the end of the film provides irrefutable proof of the interest it had for him at the time. We need to be very careful in crediting his testimony about a film he has for his own reasons considered after the fact to be "indifferent."

Perhaps Hitchcock, as he says, was concerned just with truth in the journalistic sense and the kind of realism that de Rochemont, Kazan, and Hathaway had been successfully practicing successfully for some years when he determined to make his own contribution to the semidocumentary tradition. But the film's prologue suggests a different, complementary approach, with its striking chiaroscuro design more abstract than realist, something closer to Expressionist-inspired film noir than the plain-style realism of journalistically inspired re-creations. With Hitchcock standing at the apex of shafts of light and dark, we might contrast the on-scene reportage of producer Mark Hellinger delivering the voiceover introduction to *The Naked City* 1948) from a helicopter circling Manhattan. One of the more striking details of the Herbert Brean account in *Life* of Manny's trial concerns the identity and background of the robber, who is identified as Charles James Daniell. Once arrested, Daniell admitted to over forty robberies in the Jackson Heights area, and, even more remarkably perhaps, said that he had followed the Balestrero trial closely in the papers, thinking that he would turn himself in if Manny was convicted of crimes he had in fact committed. Though the film is otherwise committed to using the real names of those involved in the story, Daniell remains deliberately obscure. A dark figure given only a few lines to speak, he seems more an embodiment of luck both ill and good than a character, properly speaking, perfectly fitting the film's need to embody vaguely what it is that shadows our lives. He is a double who is no villain but, as Douchet suggests, an image of what Manny is and is not, the representative of that dark underside that can emerge to swallow our identities and freedom, only—in response to some unfathomable logic—to reappear and demonstrate that we are not those guilty selves we were for a time mistakenly thought to be. But by then, as *The Wrong Man* suggests to our horror, such vindication might well be beside the point in the light of those hard truths disaster has lain bare.

Notes

All translations from the French are my own except as noted.

1. "Hollywood or Bust," *The New York Times*, 12 December 1956.

2. "I Confess," *The New York Times*, 23 March 1953. http://www.nytimes.com/movie/review?res=9B00E2D91F3AE23BBC4B51DFB5668388649EDE (accessedm11211/2014)

3. His direct source seems to have been Herbert Brean's article for *Life* magazine, appropriately titled "A Case of Identity" http://books.google.co.uk/books?id=CkgEAAAAMBAJ&lpg=PP1&pg=PA97#v=onepage&q&f=false, based in part on Maxwell Anderson's novelization of the widely reported events, *The True Story of Christopher Emmanuel Balestrero*. Anderson and Angus MacPhail prepared the screenplay, following closely Brean's artful summarizing of the key elements of the case, discussed at more length and less dramatically in the novel.

Works Cited

Chabrol, Claude. "Hitchcock devant le mal." *Cahiers du cinéma* no. 39 (1954): 18–24.

Chabrol, Claude, and Éric Rohmer. *Hitchcock*. Paris: Cahiers du cinéma, 1957.

Chayefsky, Paddy. *The Collected Works of Paddy Chayefsky: The Television Plays*. New York: Applause Books, 2000.

De Certeau, Michel. *The Practice of Everyday Life*. Translated by Steven Rendall. Berkeley: University of California Press, 1984,

Douchet, Jean. *Hitchcock*. Paris: Éditions de l'herne, 1967.

Kapsis, Robert. *Hitchcock: The Making of a Reputation*. Chicago: University of Chicago Press, 1992.

McGilligan, Patrick. *Alfred Hitchcock: A Life in Darkness and Light*. New York: HarperCollins, 2003.

Palmer, R. Barton, "*Secret Agent*: or Coming in from the Cold, Maugham Style," in Palmer and David Boyd, eds., *Hitchcock at the Source*. Albany, NY: SUNY Press, 2011. 89–101.

———. *Shot on Location: Postwar American Cinema and the Exploration of Real Place*. New Brunswick, NJ: Rutgers UP, 2016.

Truffaut, François. *Hitchcock*. New York: Simon & Schuster, 1967.

Schérer, Maurice. "A qui la faute?" *Cahiers du cinéma* no. 39 (1954): 6–10.

Wood, Robin. *Hitchcock's Films Revisited*. Revised ed. New York: Columbia UP, 2002.

11

JEROLD J. ABRAMS

Hitchcock and the Philosophical End of Film

> But just as art has its "before" in nature and the finite spheres of life, so too it has an "after," i.e. a region which in turn transcends art's way of apprehending and representing the Absolute. For art has still a limit in itself and therefore passes over into higher forms of consciousness.
>
> —Hegel, *Aesthetics: Lectures on Fine Art*

IN THE NINETEENTH CENTURY, HEGEL argued that art evolves toward a limit, completes itself, and passes over into a higher form of consciousness. In the twentieth century, Arthur Danto draws on Hegel and claims that painting achieves its end and passes over into philosophy with the work of Andy Warhol because his works reflect on the philosophical structure of art itself. A catalyst to the final ascent of painting is the rise of cinema, which, according to Danto, also develops and passes over into philosophy, especially with certain camera techniques (used, for example, by François Truffaut): the camera breaks continuity with human perceptual mechanics, by jostling or jolting, thereby detaching the viewer's immersion in a story, and causing her to reflect on the film as an object to be examined in relation to herself. I agree with Danto that film attains a philosophical end, but that end emerges early on in Buster Keaton, especially *Sherlock Jr.*, and later recapitulates in clearer form with Alfred Hitchcock's *Rear Window*, *Psycho*, *North by Northwest*, *Rope*, and *The Birds*. The genius of Hitchcock's cinema lies in how it traverses the sensuous show of objects on the screen and enters into an investigation of the very medium of film itself. Like the maturing human mind that turns from the world viewed to examine its own formal structure of viewing, cinema turns to itself and attains a form of self-awareness, and, in attaining self-awareness, cinema finally comes to an end. Of course, many films since Hitchcock have been made, and many more will continue to be made. New styles and technologies will continue to be made. But with Hitchcock film transcends representationalism, and, as Hegel writes of art, film thereby "passes over into higher forms of consciousness." In Hitchcock film is doing philosophy.

Danto on the End of Art

Danto conceives art history as a philosophical *bildungrsroman* (an education story) on the model of Hegel's *Phenomenology of Spirit* in which human consciousness develops through history toward complete self-consciousness. "Hegel's hero, Geist," writes Danto, "goes through an ingenious sequence of states, through which he (she?) arrives at last an idea of his or her own nature" ("The End of Art" [EA] 135). Art, according to Danto, also goes through an ingenious sequence of states by which it arrives at last at an idea of its own nature: "I have certainly presented the history of art as a kind of *Bildungsroman* in which art struggles toward a kind of philosophical understanding" (EA 135).

Two historical developments, according to Danto, especially mark the growth of art: Plato and film. In the *Republic*, Plato "disenfranchises" art from truth, as mere representation (or imitation), which causes art to enter a struggle for recognition to attain its own philosophical self-identity—a struggle that will occupy art for the remainder of its history. Much later, with the rise of cinema, art's identity crisis confronts a new challenge: faced with a superior representational medium, painting must prove itself against seemingly perfect moving pictures. Reflecting on his own thesis on this antagonism, Danto writes: "I had in mind moving pictures, pictures which directly represent motion by means of moving images, thus facilitating narrative representation in a way closed off to painting. Painting was therefore required to redefine itself or collapse into a secondary activity" (*Philosophical Disenfranchisement of Art* [PDA] 118). Movement after movement and style after style emerged and faded, each one more self-reflective than the last of its own historical struggle to define itself and redefine itself to and against film—with all the "astonishing convulsions that have defined the art history of our century" (*PDA* xv)—until, at last, painting broke free of the *artistic* language of representation and began to speak in the distinctly *philosophical* language of self-interrogation and the metaphysics of the identity of indiscernibles. What began in Greece in the fifth century before Christ would finally come to an end in New York in the spring of 1964 with replicas of boxes of grocery store dishwashing pads.

> As I saw it the form of the question is: what makes the difference between a work of art and something not a work of art when there is no interesting perceptual difference between them. What awoke me to this was the exhibition of *Brillo Box* sculptures by Andy Warhol in that extraordinary exhibition at the Stable Gallery on East 74th Street in Manhattan in April of 1964. (*PDA* 35)

The brilliance of Warhol's *Brillo Boxes* is that they look exactly like actual boxes of Brillo, and with this perfect resemblance they achieve a form that does not *represent* (or attempt to represent) anything at all. Their effect, instead, is to raise a serious philosophical question: namely, *what am I?* One set of boxes *is* art, and the other is *not* art, and the one that is art is asking—as it looks into its own philosophical mirror—why the one that is *not* art is *not* art, and the one that *is* art *is* art—or *not* art. "My thesis," writes Danto, "was that once art raised the question of why one pair of look-alikes was art and the other not, it lacked the power to rise to an answer. For that, I thought, philosophy was needed" (EA 134). At this point, painting passes over into philosophy, and engages the philosopher in art's own self-examination. Painting thus become self-interrogating and in becoming *self-interrogating* it becomes *self-conscious* and in becoming self-conscious it finally comes to an end (EA 134).

Of course, to say art becomes self-conscious does not mean that the Brillo boxes themselves literally developed minds of their own. Art's "self-consciousness" refers to an analogy with human self-consciousness. Art, like human knowledge, evolves from a representational form to a self-reflective form. Like the human mind examining its own form and its own relation to the external world, art also turns from its representations of the world and examines its own form and its own relation to the viewer viewing it. Once that turn is achieved, art may not be literally self-consciousness, but it is no longer art, either: instead, art is now doing philosophy, the only discipline whose subject matter actually includes itself; the only form of inquiry that asks what it is doing while it is doing it.

Danto and the Philosophical End of Film

Meanwhile, cinema—having caused the final crisis of painting—would itself undergo a similar (though certainly shorter) evolution toward philosophy. Danto articulates this view in his essay "Moving Pictures." Cinema begins in a detached representational form: "It would be wholly natural to treat the camera in essentially Cartesian terms, as logically external to the sights recorded by it—detached and spectatorial" (*Philosophizing Art* [*PA*] 229). The director presents the film as a representation of the world for a passive spectator who freely immerses her imagination in the film: she identifies with the protagonists and becomes part of the story. Eventually, however, the director alters the representational form. Danto writes: "It is as though the director became jealous of the characters who heretofore had absorbed our artistic attention to the point that we forgot if we had ever thought about art as such, and at his ontological expense" (*PA* 230). The effect can be seen when, for example, "the camera is, as it were, 'jostled,' or when, more archly, the camera literally climbs the stairway with an eye and a lubricity of its own and pokes into one bedroom after another in search of the lovers, as in one of Truffaut's films" (*PA* 230). At one moment, the viewer lives imaginatively within the story (provided the camera perceives as we do), but at another moment (when the camera perceives as we do not), then we become acutely aware of our position in relation to the object of the film *as a film*—as a *thing* in front of us. The screen draws us into its world and then suddenly expels us: almost as if it knew what it was doing. "In such cases," writes Danto, "the movement of the camera is not our movement, and this has precisely the effect of thrusting us outside the action and back into our metaphysical Cartesian hole" (*PA* 230)—because we become aware of it, the film, as a film. "When this happens, however," Danto continues, "the subject of the film changes; the story is no longer one of young lovers, rather, it is about their being observed and filmed, as though the story itself were but an occasion for filming and the latter is what the film is about" (*PA* 230). Herein lies the transition to the Hegelian cinema, according to Danto: early film was exclusively about the world it represented (the young lovers), but now (with some exceptional works) film becomes *about* the spectator/object relation, that is, about the film experience itself. And when film reflects on its own nature, film, like painting, passes over into philosophy and comes to an end. Danto writes:

> Film becomes in a way its own subject; the consciousness that it is film is what the consciousness is of. In this move to self-consciousness cinema marches together with the other arts of the twentieth century in the respect that art itself becomes the ultimate subject of art, a movement of thought which parallels philosophy in the respect that philosophy in the end is what philosophy is about. (*PA* 230)

Now I agree with Danto's main thesis that film achieves a philosophical end once it becomes about itself. But that end, I think, is achieved very early on with Keaton and then later repeated in Hitchcock. Before getting to Keaton and our analysis of Hitchcock's particular films, however, I want first to turn to Gilles Deleuze's view of the philosophical relevance of Hitchcock, because what Deleuze says about Hitchcock clarifies the idea of an end of film (in Danto's sense), as I see it.

Deleuze on Hitchcock

Like Danto, Deleuze also develops a philosophical view of the history of cinema: "The great directors of the cinema may be compared, in our view, not merely with painters, architects and musicians, but also with thinkers" (*Cinema 1*, ix). The historical progression of philosophers reappears in film as a progression of directors. And like Danto as well, Deleuze also sees in the history of film a developmental movement that parallels the history of philosophy—with a turn in the middle. "Over several centuries," Deleuze writes, "from the Greeks to Kant, a revolution took place in philosophy" (*Cinema 2*, xi). The revolution in Kant is known as the Copernican Turn (Kant 22). As Copernicus reversed our view of planetary rotation, Kant reversed our view of knowledge of objects. Prior to Kant, many philosophers like Hume described the mind as a passive spectator: senses receive impressions and the mind forms corresponding copies as ideas (Hume 3). As Richard Rorty argues, this model permeates the history of philosophy: the mind is like a "mirror of nature." Kant reversed this view: the world becomes a mirror of the mind. Concepts like space, time, and causality cannot be copied from the world because they cannot be perceived. Instead the mind imposes them on experience. The mind, then, is involved in the construction of its own experience.

Now Deleuze seems to suggest that a similar revolution occurs in film with Hitchcock, who creates a new kind of character based on the viewer in the theater, whose job is to watch and then examine his own "mental relations" (C1, x). Before Hitchcock, for example in Griffith and Eisenstein, the viewer could identify with the protagonist whose actions move the story forward with causality, created with montage. According to Deleuze, "Hitchcock had begun the inversion of this point of view by including the viewer in the film" (*Cinema 2*, 3). The inversion takes place in two ways: teleological montage becomes causal fragmentation, and the protagonist (once a man of action) becomes a spectator who inquires into the fragmented causality all around him. Deleuze writes:

> The character has become a kind of viewer. He shifts, runs and becomes animated in vain, the situation he is in outstrips his motor capacities on all sides, and makes him see and hear what is no longer subject to the rules of a response or an action. He records rather than acts. He is prey to a vision, pursued by it or pursuing it, rather than engaged in an action. (*Cinema 2*, 3; see also *Cinema 1*, 205)

The simplest way to understand Deleuze's point about "including the viewer in the film" is to imagine the activity of inclusion in a thought experiment. Imagine a spectator in a movie theater watching a film. The film action appears fragmentary. What is missing from the film is unity (for the viewer) of the objects within the film. Suddenly the spectator levitates (still in a theater chair) and hovers over the heads of the audience, then he disappears into the screen, and finally he reappears within the film. The film *viewer* has become a film *character* and that character is *still* (like the theater viewer) a spectator, who observes and attempts to unify the action in the screen, and in observing the action, he also comes to observe his own "mental relations": his ideas of himself in relation to the actions of the other people (or things) in the film.

When we turn to Hitchcock's cinema to compare Deleuze's analysis we find many such spectator characters: Jefferies (Jimmy Stewart) in *Rear Window* seated and watching, Norman Bates (Anthony Perkins) in *Psycho* peering through a peephole, Scottie (Stewart) peering into the abyss in *Vertigo*, Roger Thornhill (Cary Grant) in *North by Northwest* viewing Mt. Rushmore through a monument viewer, Rupert (Stewart) examining the strange actions of his students in *Rope*, and Melanie Daniels (Tippi Hedren) watching the sky filled with birds in *The Birds*. In each film, a spectator examines an object, finds him- or herself confused, attempts to unify a perspective, and, in attempting to unify a perspective, perceives his or her own mental relations and limitations.

Deleuze is right: Hitchcock does include within the film the viewer who examines his or her mental relations. But a few points need to be added. The ultimate effect of the inclusion of the spectator and the revealing of mental images (as opposed to action images) by Hitchcock is the *opposition*—not the *identity*—created between the viewer in the theater and the viewer in the screen. By identifying with a viewer who is confused by moving actions immediately in front of him, the viewer in the theater is thrust from her immersion in the film, back into her "metaphysical Cartesian hole" (as Danto puts it), and forced to examine her *own* mental relations to the film as an object before her. To clarify this point, we may contrast it with Peter Bogdanovich's analysis of *Rear Window* and its place in Hitchcock's filmography:

> *Rear Window* is sort of Hitchcock's testament film—I mean, it's a French term—meaning that in *Rear Window* perhaps you see the best example of what Hitchcock's cinema, at its best, stood for, which was essentially the use of the subjective point of view. You have a shot of Jimmy Stewart. You show what he is looking at. You see his reaction. Basically the entire movie is based on that. He looks. You see what he sees. He reacts. That is kind of the heart of Hitchcock's filmmaking. And he has an incredible ability to put you in the point of view of the leading character or whatever character. ("*Rear Window* Ethics: An Original Documentary")

Bogdanovich is correct: the identity of spectator and viewer *is* what Hitchcock's cinema is about (which is the same point in Deleuze). But just as Hitchcock "has an incredible ability to put you in the point of view of the leading character"—indeed, *because* he has this ability—Hitchcock also has an incredible ability to *take you out of* the point of view of the leading character, and thrust you back into the self-conscious position of the viewer in the theater. This effect is what Danto thinks (rightly) is so essential to the development of self-reflective cinema.

But how does Hitchcock do this? How can he so absolutely immerse the mind in a character (as Bogdanovich points out), and then so forcefully eject it from the film? Hitchcock seals the identity of the viewer and protagonist with an objective perspective of the world viewed from the protagonist's position. The protagonist looks out at the world, and the viewer looks with him. Now, in two ways, Hitchcock uncouples that identity. First, Hitchcock forces the viewer so deep into the perspective of the protagonist that the viewer's suspension of self-consciousness cannot be maintained. For example, in *Rear Window*, the viewer in the theater imagines being Jefferies. Like Jefferies, she imagines herself to be seated, in a very dark room, isolated, facing directly forward, in an immobile chair, staring across a large empty space, at a massive rectangular object filled with people whom she voyeuristically watches, but who cannot see her. The deeper the viewer immerses herself in this perspective, the more she tries to imagine being like Jefferies, the more forcefully does her own actual position come into view. For her imagined character and her own position are identical. She is *exactly* like Jefferies: seated in a dark room, isolated, facing directly forward, in an immobile chair, staring across a large empty space, at a massive rectangular object filled with people whom she voyeuristically watches, but who cannot see her. Once she becomes self-aware of her position outside the film, the film itself also comes plainly into view as a film. (I'll return to this technique in *Rear Window* shortly.)

Second, Hitchcock seals three identities: the viewer's perspective, the protagonist's perspective, and the camera's perspective. We look out as the protagonist, Jefferies, looks out (through the camera). The viewer fully immerses herself in this first person subjective point of view on the objects before her (just as Bogdanovich notes). But because Hitchcock has sealed these perspectives, and the viewer instinctively identifies with the protagonist, she has also laid open her imagination to Hitchcock's uncoupling of the two perspectives of Jefferies and the camera, and the turning of the one (the camera) upon the other (Jefferies), and thus the turning of her own perspective upon herself. The camera and viewer look *out* through the protagonist's perspective *and* the camera's perspective—both at once—and then she follows the camera that detaches from Jefferies (as one of her identities) to look directly at Jefferies (another of her identities) who is also looking directly into the camera at the viewer herself, wondering what he (she?) is actually looking at—and wondering what to think while looking at it. The effect is to force the self-reflective stance of the viewer (first person looking at the third person's point of view looking at the first person's point of view); and once the viewer is aware of herself as a viewer in the theater, the film comes into view as a film rather than a story. (I'll return to this technique shortly with *North by Northwest*.)

In both techniques, Hitchcock achieves the end of ejecting the viewer's imagination from the story, and initiating a self-reflective inquiry into her own experience. Yet, paradoxically, the more self-conscious the viewer becomes of her own position in relation to the film—that is, the more she assures herself of her own detached identity from the screen— all the more she sees herself objectively mirrored within the screen (for *that* is precisely what Hitchcock's films are about). And the more she sees herself objectively mirrored in the screen, the more she comes to realize that this film in front of her has very little to do with a simple (and not even particularly interesting) murder mystery. This film is about her, the viewer, sitting right there, watching a film. And once she grasps this point, she has understood the truth of Danto's thesis: "Film becomes in a way its own subject; the consciousness that it is film is what the consciousness is of." But once she grasps the idea of self-reflective cinema, the history of cinema also comes into view. For self-reflective cinema not only reflects on itself—it reflects on its own history: namely, the history of cinema as *not* self-reflective, the history of cinema as representational up until precisely this point of self-reflectivity. And on further investigation into this remarkable history, the philosophical viewer also comes to realize its complexity and its repetition. For the end of cinema by the time of Hitchcock has already come, as Hitchcock appears only too aware—in the form of Buster Keaton.

Keaton's Spectator Cinema

Roger Ebert calls Buster Keaton (1895–1966) "the greatest of the silent clowns" (Ebert xx). Keaton was a truly great physical actor (known for his daring), a radically experimental director whose effects still are jaw-dropping, and the man who achieved the philosophical end of film in 1924 with *Sherlock Jr.*, which, along with *The Cameraman* (1928), is essential for understanding Hitchcock's *Rear Window*. The opening frame of *The Cameraman* reads: "When acclaiming our modern heroes, let's not forget *The News Reel* Cameraman . . . the daredevil who defies death to give us pictures of the world's happenings." In the next shot a daredevil photographer takes pictures on a battlefield. Then a new text frame reads: "And there are other types of photographers." Keaton (as a character) now appears as a different kind of cameraman: not a brave daredevil but a common man who takes pictures of normal people at a reasonable rate: "TINTYPES 10¢." Both cameramen are spectators within the film. But the war cameraman not only *photographs* action, he *is* a man of action. The tintype photographer, however, is much more of a spectator: "he records rather than acts," as Deleuze writes of Hitchcock.

Keaton again inserts the spectator into the film in *Sherlock Jr.* A man works as a projectionist in a movie theater while studying to become a detective (like Sherlock Holmes). The first frame reads: "While employed as a moving picture operator in a small town theatre he was studying to be a detective." The first cinematic shot of the film establishes confusion between the spectator and object. The first shot is taken of a movie theater from the perspective of the screen looking out on the audience, with Keaton himself (the actor and director)—playing both a viewer and a film projectionist—seated alone in the theater, not watching a film but reading a book, *How to Be a Detective*.

Later he gets his chance. While visiting The Girl, his girlfriend (Kathryn McGuire), another man, The Sheik (Ward Crane), steals her father's (Joe Keaton) watch, pawns it and buys her a gift, then plants the pawn receipt on Sherlock Jr.—the aspiring detective who gets caught red-handed with the receipt while presuming to solve the case of the missing watch. Having failed and lost the girl, and now an apparent thief, Sherlock Jr. gives up detective work and returns to film. The text frame reads: "As a detective he was all wet, so he went back to see what he could do to his other job." Not particularly good as a projectionist either, Sherlock Jr. falls asleep in the middle of showing the film *Hearts and Pearls* (the story of stolen pearls) and begins to dream. In his dream he steps out of his sleeping body and notices the film rolling and examines the screen. He sees the same film *Hearts and Pearls*, but now Sherlock Jr. sees it anew. The two leads in the film have become the two leads in his own life: The Sheik and The Girl. In one of the most stunning sequences in the history of cinema, Sherlock Jr. (still out of body in the screen) walks down the aisle of the movie theater and steps right into the film itself—only to be quickly tossed back out into the theater by The Sheik. Frustrated but undeterred, Sherlock Jr. waits for a scene change (without The Sheik) and jumps back in and sits on a bench to rest. But the scenes suddenly start to change around him: the bench disappears, and he falls down in a bustling street. Now he finds himself on a mountain cliff and nearly falls. Now he is surrounded by lions, now in the path of a speeding train, now in the ocean, now in the snow, and now he falls over the original bench. To quote Deleuze on Hitchcock's viewer-protagonist: "the situation he is in outstrips his motor capacities on all sides." Sherlock Jr. struggles to impose concepts of substance and causality to anticipate and schematize what might happen in the next frame given the last—just as the viewers in a theater do. Finally he gains control (within the film within the film) and assumes his new character: he becomes "the world's greatest detective—Sherlock Jr.!" Sherlock Jr. now proceeds to solve the case and gets the girl. Meanwhile Sherlock Jr.'s girlfriend has undertaken her own investigation and discovered him to be innocent and The Sheik a criminal; so she returns to Sherlock Jr. in the projection booth, who upon waking has the same inference in hand. The two lead characters in the film *Hearts and Pearls* embrace as Sherlock Jr. and his girlfriend also embrace in the projection booth.

Sherlock Jr. is only marginally a detective story: it's true power lies in its self-reflective form. And the real detective story lies in Keaton's own

Holmesian investigation into the representational structure of film itself. By examining the film from all sides, Keaton discovers (and creates) an entirely new kind of self-reflective cinema. The impact of this film, and, Keaton's cinema in general, on Hitchcock should not be underestimated. For Hitchcock not only rearticulates the end of film, but does so self-consciously, knowing the end has already come. He thereby achieves a cinema of even greater self-reflectivity than Keaton because Hitchcock's cinema is at once *formally* and *historically* self-conscious—and nowhere is this self-consciousness more evident than in *Rear Window*.

Rear Window and *Sherlock Jr.*

Jefferies is a combination of three of Keaton's characters: the newsreel war cameraman, the common man tintype photographer, and Sherlock Jr. Jefferies begins as a daredevil cameraman (like Keaton's war cameraman): "a daredevil cameraman who defies death to give us pictures of the world's happenings." But he breaks his leg taking a dangerous shot and sits confined to a wheelchair. So, just as Keaton transitions from action cameraman to passive spectator cameraman, Hitchcock also turns Jefferies into a pure spectator, who observes through his camera common lives like Keaton's tintype photographer. Yet Jefferies does not observe people's everyday lives from the street like Keaton's photographer. Rather, like Keaton's projectionist in *Sherlock Jr.*, he observes from a rear window. Jefferies sits relatively immobile (like a man in a theater or a projectionist) and stares straight ahead across a gulf of inaction at a massive wall whose proportions mirror a movie screen; and the windows themselves also appear in letterboxed proportions: each window frames the action of an individual like a movie screen. Examining these windows, Jefferies also examines himself, just as Sherlock Jr. examines his own mind as he watches a film from his own rear window. As Deleuze puts it, "The hero of *Rear Window* has access to the mental image, not simply because he is a photographer, but because he is in a state of immobility: he is reduced as it were to a pure optical situation" (205).

Within the windows of the wall, people's private stories unfold, and Jefferies observes and analyzes. He sees in their lives representations of his own life because he imposes the categories of his own mind upon the empirical givens of the apartment building windows and discovers relations among the objects and himself. Miss Torso, for example, represents the isolation of Jefferies's own girlfriend Lisa Carol Fremont (Grace Kelly), whom Jefferies holds at arm's length. The newlyweds represent the future Lisa wants. The feuding couple represents Jefferies's fear of marriage. The struggling artist represents Jefferies's own struggles with his photographic art (which have put him in a wheelchair). And Miss Lonely Hearts represents Lisa in the future without Jefferies: both women serve dinner for the men they love, but Miss Lonely Hearts only pretends someone is there with her. Jefferies and Lisa discuss the various rooms and compare them to Jefferies's own. Speaking of Miss Torso's apartment, Lisa says to Jefferies, "You said it resembled my apartment, didn't you?"

Again the influence of *Sherlock Jr.* is striking. Sherlock Jr. in the dream sequence also sees in the film *Hearts and Pearls* representations from his own life: the leads become his girlfriend and the villain. He sees from his rear window a crime take place (a theft). Hitchcock repeats this story in *Rear Window*: Jefferies also sees from his rear window a crime take place (a murder)—and, like Sherlock Jr., Jefferies—who is also no master detective—must become a master detective in order to solve the case. Jefferies, however, has a problem. He remains immobile in his wheelchair, much as Sherlock Jr. remains (sleeping) in his projectionist chair. So he must project his imagination and identity into the object viewed, just as Sherlock Jr. the projectionist also "projects" his own imagined identity into the screen, and just as a film viewer projects her own identity into the film screen. We want Jefferies to enter the screen, but he can no more enter than we ourselves (the viewers) can enter a film screen. But Jefferies, like Sherlock Jr., also has a girlfriend, and he sends her into the object (the opposing apartment building). So, like Sherlock Jr.'s girlfriend, Fremont *also* becomes a detective, and, like Sherlock Jr.'s mind, she traverses the space between the rear window and the spectator object. Once across the space between spectator and object, Fremont looks back at Jefferies and at the viewers, who identify simultaneously with both Jefferies and Fremont as spectators and objects of spectation.

The opposite traversal of the theater-like distance also occurs as the murderer catches Jefferies spying on him. Fremont finds the ring of the dead woman, puts it on her own finger (note the symbolism of what Jefferies himself might be capable of), and then, facing backward to Jefferies from the murderer's apartment, she puts her hands behind her back and points to the ring on her finger. But the murderer sees her silent code to Jefferies and looks across the courtyard to see Jefferies spying on him. And when he looks out, he looks directly out in the second person at the viewer—and indeed, Hitchcock's point is strikingly clear, as the murderer catches the film viewer (previously in a one-way blind spectatorial position) spying on him as well. Now he leaves his apartment and shows up in the dark to meet Jefferies (and to meet the viewer)—who, remember, is also in a dark room (the theater)—as if to say, I see you seeing me; now see yourself seeing you seeing me.

Sherlock Jr. also looks into and out of the screen after entering it, and once he has solved the case, he also returns from the screen to the rear window. Keaton and Hitchcock spend the entirety of these two films alternating the sides of the spectator/object opposition. As a consequence, negotiating the complexity of *Rear Window* (and *Sherlock Jr.*) is no easy task. A series of spectatorial convulsions keeps the mind off balance and unable fully to immerse itself within the film. Before the film, the spectator sits quietly in a theater aware of her position. The film begins. She identifies with the protagonists, Jefferies and Fremont. The protagonists peer out at a screen-shaped object (the letterboxed wall of apartments filled with windows that are also letterbox shaped). The more the viewer identifies with a seated viewer in the dark peering voyeuristically across a space at a letterboxed shape, the more she becomes aware that that is precisely her position in the theater. The deeper her identity with the character, the more the identity uncouples from the character, and at a certain point the uncoupling becomes strikingly conscious and the viewer is simply jolted from her vicarious adventure to see immediately before her the film as a film about the viewer herself watching the film right in front of her. She may continue to enjoy the story unfold, but an entirely new line of inquiry has opened up. For she is now actively engaged in examining herself examining an object that appears to be about what she is doing right now. The genius of *Rear Window* lies in how it simultaneously opens these two dialectical lines of inquiry at once: one by the film about a murder mystery, and the other by the film about itself. To clarify this point about two lines of dialogue, a brief analysis of Noël Carroll's view of film narration will be helpful.

Two Forms of Film Dialectic

In *Mystifying Movies*, Carroll (drawing on V.I. Pudovkin) develops the view that films narrate by raising and answering plot questions. An initial scene raises a question, and later scenes answer it. The scenes move forward in time by means of this dialectic: "The basic connective—the rhetorical bond between the two scenes—is the question/answer" (171). Carroll gives an example:

> If a giant shark appears offshore, unbeknownst to the local authorities, and begins to ravage lonely swimmers, this scene or series of scenes (or this event or series of events) raises the question of whether the shark will ever be discovered. This question is likely to be answered in some later scene when someone figures out why all those swimmers are missing. (171)

Carroll's example comes from Steven Spielberg's *Jaws*, but the same dialectic can be found in virtually any film, and certainly in Hitchcock's films. In *Rear Window*, for example, once Jefferies suspects a murder, a question arises: Will Jefferies (in a wheelchair) catch the murderer? That story unfolds according to a narrative dialectic. But in addition to a *narrative* dialectic—to build on Carroll's analysis—a *phenomenological* dialectic between viewer and viewed also unfolds within the film. These two dialectics have some common features: both rely on a relation of the viewer to the film; both take place in the form of question and answer; and both are unspoken. On this last point, we do not, for example, need a voiceover in *Jaws* for certain questions to arise in the mind of the viewer: Will the shark kill again? Will the shark be discovered?

Nor do we need a voiceover for certain questions to arise in the mind of the viewer about the relation of the film to itself. For example, the viewer asks: Why am I suddenly so vividly self-aware in viewing *Rear Window*? Why does the architecture of the set look exactly like a film theater? Is it my failure of will to immerse in the film, or does this film seem purposefully to throw into relief my own relational position to the screen? Is this film somehow actually *about* the experience of film itself? And, if so, what would that mean for the history of film? Just as a film asks questions about its characters, a film can also ask questions about itself and about the nature of film in general. These questions can also be uttered in the second person and first person self-reflexive: *Rear Window* asks the viewer: Do you see yourself reflected isomorphically in the screen? Do you understand that this film is not really about a murder mystery? Have you grasped what is really going on? And what exactly am I, if I am not a representational film?

Questions of this film-phenomenological form differ from narrative plot questions because plot questions are not self-reflective, and reflective phenomenological questions about the film as a film are not narrativistic: the two kinds of questions have almost nothing to do with each other. Narrativistically, a viewer watching *Jaws* wonders what will happen *next* within the story (but no phenomenological questions arise). Phenomenologically, a viewer watching *Rear Window* (as a self-reflective film) wonders what is going on *now* within the film/viewer relation (and narrative questions are backgrounded). Once one becomes aware of the second dialectic arising from the first, the film experience may become increasingly confusing and difficult: for the film seems to be both narrativistic and non-narrativistic. This confusion only compounds as the viewer continues to inquire into the self-reflective structure of the film. For upon viewing *Rear Window* as a self-reflective (and, in some sense, non-narrativistic) film, a new and *second* narrativistic dimension emerges within the film, one that tells the story of film itself, just as Warhol's *Brillo Boxes* tells the story of painting (from its own perspective). One cannot fully understand the philosophical dimension of the *Brillo Boxes* without some grasp of the prior movements of representationalist painting that precede it, and against which Warhol reacts. Similarly one cannot fully understand the self-reflective dimension of *Rear Window* without some grasp of the history of representationalist cinema—beginning with its most primitive forms such as the praxinoscopes and magic lanterns—and then its first historical self-overcoming in Keaton. This second narrative (told by the self-reflective film) has the genre form, as Danto points out in his discussion of Hegel and Warhol, of a philosophical *bildungsroman*: a narrative of the ascent from primitive representation to mature self-reflectivity.

Psycho

This formal and historical self-reflectivity is the defining feature of Hitchcock's work and can be seen throughout his films. While not all can be discussed here, a few do stand out. In *Psycho*, for example, Hitchcock again inserts the spectator into the screen—only this time as villain rather than hero. Norman Bates lives in a house on a hill and runs a motel below it. He spies on his guests from his house through a window and from a hole in a wall of a motel room. The house window and the motel room hole create the same one-way blind, detached spectator point of view of the window in *Rear Window*, the same one-way blind spectator point of view in a movie theater, and the same rear window spectator view in *Sherlock Jr.* Through the hole, Bates sees a world, but not the world as it is in itself. Like Sherlock Jr., he sees a world made from representations of his own mind that he projects onto the world. He sees a world made from the simply givens of his guests and the mad categories he imposes upon them—categories of a man who keeps the corpse of his beloved dead mother in a bed in his house, because he believes she is still watching him, because he has internalized her spectator's gaze as an additional spectator within his own mind. As Bates spies on a woman, he knows his mother will punish him for his attraction to the new motel guest. He begs her for his freedom, but she punishes him in the form of Bates himself dressed as his mother.

Of course, at first we do not know about Bates. In fact, we intuitively identify with him. Bates appears to be a reasonable and mild-mannered motel owner who helps a woman—who, we know, is on the run. The identification with Bates, however, is short-lived and soon uncouples as we discover Bates to be a voyeur who spies on the private lives of others. But in the moment of that uncoupling a new identification simultaneously arises with Bates: for the viewer sees herself reflected in the character of Bates as a Peeping Tom, and is promptly thrown back on herself as a detached spectator watching the screen. She, like Bates, is also a voyeur looking in through a Cartesian peephole with its one-way blind perspective—peering in on the unsuspecting individuals and imposing her own projected imagination onto the objects before her. The viewer now examines herself as an object, yet simultaneously finds Bates himself equally examining himself as an object, spectating on himself (as his mother) about his spectation on the woman. He watches himself watching others from the rear window in the house and the hole in the wall. The identity of the film viewer with a psychopathic voyeur now uncomfortably tightens. That she, the viewer, like Bates, is a conflicted human being whose self-consciousness lies precisely in her capacity for self-interrogation, and no less subject to madness, cannot be lost on the reflective viewer for whom the Hegelian divided self is an epistemological fact.

The reflective viewer now suspends the narrativistic dialectic of what will happen next to Bates, as the phenomenological dialectic comes plainly into view, and she inquires into her own relation to the film, and the film's relation to itself. The viewer asks herself: What exactly is going on here, besides the story of a killer? For she senses *something* self-reflective is taking place. The film appears to be about her, the viewer, another conflicted spectator who takes great pleasure in voyeurism and imaginatively projecting her identity into an object. And once this inference is in hand, the film appears anew. *Psycho* is no more about Bates-the-killer than it is about the viewer's relation to herself and to the screen in which the killer appears. *Psycho*, like *Rear Window*, and like *Sherlock Jr.* is a philosophical meditation *by* film on the representational form *of* film. *Psycho* is about itself.

North by Northwest

In *North by Northwest*, Roger Thornhill is mistaken for a spy (George Kaplan) and kidnapped. The spy/spectator must impose order on his confusion by conceiving himself within the manifold. He is not a spy but must become a spy to discover the plot around him. His investigation ultimately takes him to Mt. Rushmore National Park, a spectator visitation site. Upon arrival, he stands facing the grand overwhelming rectangular object, just as we face the massive rectangular object of the screen, containing the stone monument that looks back at the viewer. The camera pans in on the monument and then zooms through a circular viewing hole. Suddenly the camera pulls back from a first-person perspective and reveals that what the spectator (in the theater) had actually been viewing was the monument from Thornhill's perspective, through a monument viewer (like mounted binoculars). Now we see the relation from a third-person perspective: we see Thornhill looking through the freestanding monument viewer at the monument.

This shot series occurs quickly but is important for understanding the film. Thornhill's perspective resembles that of Jefferies in *Rear Window* and Norman Bates in *Psycho*. A detached spectator views (through a glass) an object whose proportions resemble a cinema screen from across a large empty space, and like Jefferies and Bates, he is confused by the object and his own relation to the object—an object that appears to look back at him and calls into question his own spectatorial position. Talking to the professor at his side, Thornhill says: "I don't like the way Teddy Roosevelt is looking at me." The four faces on the massive wall, like a movie screen with their letterboxed proportions, look back at the viewer as well.

The camera by this point has moved from in front of Thornhill looking at the monument (first person), to the side of Thornhill looking at Thornhill looking at the monument (third person), and now to the back of Thornhill (first person again), looking once again at the monument with Thornhill in front of the monument (facing the monument like the film viewer). The first transition reveals that what we *were* watching is someone else's perspective, while the second transition reveals to us our own self-conscious perspective. We look at Roosevelt, but then are forced to reconsider who is doing the looking. We then look at Thornhill looking at Roosevelt and are invited to reconsider what other viewing relations occur. Now we look forward at Thornhill looking forward at Roosevelt looking back. This third perspective forces the viewer's awareness of her own perspective—and not only her own perspective, but her own perspective on Thornhill's perspective on Roosevelt's perspective—of her perspective.

To take this series once again from the top, we begin with deep immersion in the protagonist's perspective. We do not even know we are looking through a glass, and we see no other characters. But then through two crucial perspective transitions, Hitchcock quickly expels the viewer from the screen. By the time the camera is behind Thornhill, we are no longer in the film as projected identities. We are squarely and uncomfortably back in our self-consciously spectatorial position: examining ourselves examining a film in which a spectator is examining himself examining an object through a glass and wondering whether the seemingly inert object (the monument) is somehow reflecting on him. In this moment, we know that the film itself is looking back at *us*—not literally but conceptually, and looking into itself as well. The film's subject matter is not the case of mistaken identity (Thornhill's), but its own self-identity in front of a reflective viewer. For the film is actually *about us* watching it. Instinctively, the mind attempts to reinsert, and Hitchcock allows it, as he slingshots the imagination directly into the monument, with Thornhill trekking across the faces of the spectator site. The re-immersion, however, is temporary, to say the least, as Hitchcock portrays on the screen in conceptual form the very idea of the immersion of the spectator from detached Cartesian position—into and out of the object again.

Rope

In *Rope*, Rupert Cadwell is a scholar who studies the world from a detached perspective—he is a kind of spectator. Two of Rupert's students, Brandon Shaw (John Dall) and Philip Morgan (Farley Granger), murder their friend and fellow student David Kentley (Dick Hogan) in cold blood for art's sake. They put him in a long wooden chest and serve dinner on top of the chest at a party for his father and aunt and his fiancée. Brandon and Philip accept Rupert's Nietzschean view that murder is immoral for the common man but permitted for superior individuals. Brandon thinks himself superior and David inferior. Rupert arrives late (which further detaches him as a spectator). He soon senses something wrong. Sitting in the middle of the manifold, he unifies the strands of action by determining causality within the party. Rupert schematizes the objects around him by means of conversation on Nietzsche's philosophy of crime and the superman and discovers the killers in the form of his students.

Brandon admits to the crime but accepts no moral culpability. He simply repeats back to Rupert what Rupert has always told him and held true. Rupert hears, in horror, his own lectures taking life as though they had leapt off the chalkboard, picked up a yard of rope, and strangled David themselves. Rupert says, "You've thrown my own words right back in my face, Brandon." Just as Kant finds the subject looking back at itself through its own construction of reality, Rupert finds himself at the center of a crime he didn't commit. The constructive activity may be unconscious to the mind (as the constructive imagination is largely unconscious on Kant's view)—but the *product* of the mind's construction is there to be seen nonetheless. Rupert, however, cannot and will not accept his own construction in the form of Brandon. His ideas about morality were merely a parlor game played with Nietzsche's texts to entertain the young on the careless assumption that no one would believe what was being said in class in the name of truth. But the spectator in the theater who performs her own investigation sees the matter otherwise.

The relation of viewer to viewed once again appears in the film and renders the film self-reflective. The viewer in the theater identifies with Rupert, a relatively passive, seated, detached spectator who watches a context unfold. The identification can be maintained more or less while Rupert is part spectator and part guest. But the two roles fall apart once Rupert realizes what he is viewing: the aftermath of a murder; and with that uncoupling, the viewer achieves a new measure of aesthetic distance. In identifying with a perspective of what is right in front of her eyes in the form of a large rectangular object, the attention contracts from the screen (as itself a large rectangular object), and the relation to the screen is thrown into relief. The relation becomes increasingly difficult as the viewer forcefully attempts to reinsert herself into the protagonist's perspective (because the story is not over). But the character of Brandon will not allow it, as he casually holds up a philosophical mirror to Rupert (with whom we identify), and shows Rupert his own reflection. Brandon seems to say to Rupert: You are more involved in this than you think are; look at yourself and see; you are not a passive spectator.

At this point, the viewer is forced again to examine her position in relation to the screen and the theater. But no sooner does she contract (again) her view and examine the phenomenological content immediately before her, than that content appears complete within the film itself. Often noted, *Rope* takes place almost entirely within one room, which gives the film continuity. But the one room film also reflects the one-room structure of the theater. In the film, a back row of seats faces out directly toward the seats in the theater. In viewing the film, we are looking at a kind of conceptual mirror image. The spectator Rupert sits with the other guests in a row before a large rectangular object that fills a large portion of the room and concentrates the attention of the room upon it. But all except Brandon and Philip are oblivious to the rectangular object for what it actually is (a coffin)—just as all in the theater are oblivious to what the large rectangular object is immediately in front of them (and which concentrates their attention): namely, a film screen. We do not think of the screen as a screen. We sit unconscious of what lies before us as we lose our sense of self inside the party at Brandon's and Philip's apartment. Hitchcock has once again immersed the spectator in a narrative, promptly expelled the imagination from the object back into a self-conscious spectatorial position, and then forced the mind to examine itself examining the object, only to find the protagonist (with whom it originally identified) doing exactly the same thing: examining himself examining the object immediately in front of him. Indeed, *Rope* is only marginally a murder mystery—like *Rear Window*, like *Psycho*, like *North by Northwest*, and *Sherlock Jr.*, *Rope* is about itself.

The Birds

In *The Birds* we're introduced to a quiet coastal town, as Melanie Daniels (Tippi Hedren) our protagonist, delivers a gift of lovebirds in a small motorboat. Like Jefferies in *Rear Window* (and the film viewer herself), Melanie sits confined, detached and isolated, in a purely observational position. Like Jefferies who sits opposed to the apartments, and the film viewer who sits opposed to the screen, Melanie sits opposed to a massive sky, whose objects, the birds, seem passive and harmless (like the distant objects on a theater screen). They can be caught and caged and given as gifts to be kept as pets. Melanie, however, has made a mistake. For seated calmly in her boat, the once passive objects of the sky begin to descend and attack. They attack Melanie and the entire coastal town.

Some think this film to be a philosophical study in how the powers of nature—seemingly passive and under human control—can erupt at any time without warning. The artifice of culture is an unstable illusion and a temporary mask on what lies beneath as sex and violence and the irrationality of the unconscious. Camille Paglia develops this view in her book *The Birds*: "*The Birds* charts a return of the repressed, a release of primitive forces of sex and appetite that have been subdued but never fully tamed" (10). There is something to this point, but it should not be taken too far. For the age-old story of the unstable polarity of reason versus nature seems to be only the occasion for Hitchcock's underlying philosophical interrogation of the film experience itself. Hitchcock achieves this form in the same way he achieves it in the other films discussed. He begins by immersing the viewer in a story; the viewer soon finds that the protagonist is a viewer who questions what she is viewing; the viewer steadily becomes aware of herself in the theater; and in becoming aware of herself she sees anew that same relational awareness mirrored in the screen.

What is most interesting about *The Birds*, however, is how, as the film unfolds, the subject/object poles reverse: from human-spectators watching bird-objects to bird-spectators watching human-objects. The transition is achieved by the birds themselves overtaking the position of the seated spectator (through violence). By the end of the film, Hitchcock has sealed the identity of the viewer with Melanie, dislodged that identity, and resealed the viewer's identity with the birds. The final sequences complete the reversal, beginning with the gas station scene. After the gas station explodes in flames, the camera moves to the perspective of the birds. The shot here is from the sky, among other birds in flight, all looking down at the flames. They are spectators in a row viewing a cinematic object, and we the viewers view the same flames from this bird's-eye point of view. This same perspective also closes the film, which Hitchcock considered the film's most difficult shot (as he explains in an interview with Bogdanovich in "All about the Birds"). The key to this last shot is its identity with the architectural space of the inside of a movie theater. From the back of the theater, we can (if we detract attention from the screen) look out and down on other film viewers in the theater. In the final shot of *The Birds*, Hitchcock shows us precisely this image on the screen. For the birds now appear as though they were seated in their own theater inside the film—hundreds of them, perched in rows, seated quietly in the dark, like film viewers watching objects across an empty space—objects that happen to be the same people with whom we originally identified in the film. In the moment the viewer realizes she is viewing a conceptual mirror image of her own position in the theater, the entire film (as a film) comes perfectly into view, and she grasps that what Hitchcock is doing in *The Birds* has little to do with birds: what he is doing is philosophy, and what he is examining philosophically is the self-reflective structure of his own representational art form.

Figure 11.1. *The Birds*—birds as theater audience members.

After the End of Film

To this day, Hitchcock remains one of the world's greatest directors—perhaps *the* greatest. His stories of the complexities of the human soul captivate the imagination with some of the most beautiful and sublime and suspenseful moving images ever put to the screen. But Hitchcock's genius far transcends his own mastery of the ultimate medium of representation. His true genius lies in the completion of a cinematic and philosophical *bildungsroman* that entered its own Hegelian struggle for recognition in the mid-nineteenth century with primitive projectors. What began as the quintessential representational medium of art, and which would speed painting to its philosophical conclusion, would itself also speed to its own philosophical end in self-reflectivity (twice): once in Keaton and then in Hitchcock—each of whom is every bit as much philosopher as filmmaker. Hitchcock's cinema not only raises questions about plot but equally raises questions about its own medium, and thereby transcends its fundamentally representationalist form and becomes self-interrogating—thus passing over from cinema to philosophy. Yet in completing the form of film, Hitchcock's cinema equally reflects its own historical self-consciousness, and its recapitulation of the end that has already come in the work of Keaton, a fact of which Hitchcock in *Rear Window* as a study of *Sherlock Jr.* seems all to aware. Yet Hitchcock is able, in the final analysis, to transcend even Keaton (if only to a very limited extent). For whereas Keaton's cinema self-interrogates and tells the story of its own medium, Hitchcock's cinema not only self-interrogates *and* tells the story of the its own medium, but it *also* reflectively tells the story of how Keaton tells the story of how cinema evolved from representationalism to self-reflectivity (from a later historically self-reflective perspective)—thereby rendering Hitchcock's cinema even more historically self-conscious, more self-reflective, and, in a certain sense, tragic as well: confined as it is to reflect on an epic end that has already come and gone. Beyond this end, no significant philosophical development in film is possible—any more than painting has a philosophical direction after Warhol. Film continues on, of course, but these post-historical films can do no more than to portray philosophical ideas on the screen or to recapitulate the same lines of development already traced out from early representationalism to the later self-interrogating and historically self-conscious cinema of Keaton and Hitchcock.

Note

I am very grateful to Elizabeth F. Cooke, Steven Sanders, and Barton Palmer for helpful comments on this chapter. Of course, any mistakes that remain are my own.

Works Cited

Abrams, Jerold J. "Cinema and the Aesthetics of the Dynamical Sublime." *Film and Philosophy*. 2003. 60–76.

Bogdanovich, Peter. Rear Window *Ethics: An Original Documentary*. DVD. 2000.

Carroll, Noël. *Mystifying Movies: Fads & Fallacies in Contemporary Film Theory*. New York: Columbia UP, 1988.

Danto, Arthur. *The Philosophical Disenfranchisement of Art*. New York: Columbia UP, 1986.

———. *After the End of Art: Contemporary Art and the Pale of History*. Princeton, NJ: Princeton UP, 1997.

———. "The End of Art: A Philosophical Defense." In *History and Theory*, vol. 37, no. 4. Theme Issue 37: *Danto and His Critics: Art History, Historiography and After the End of Art*. December 1998.

———. *Philosophizing Art: Selected Essays*. Berkeley: University of California Press, 1999.

Deleuze, Gilles. *Cinema 1: The Movement-Image*. Trans. Hugh Tomlinson and Barbara Habberjam. Minneapolis: University of Minnesota Press, 1986.

———. *Cinema 2: The Time-Image*. Trans. Hugh Tomlinson and Robert Galeta. Minneapolis: University of Minnesota Press, 1989.

Ebert, Roger. "The Films of Buster Keaton (1923)." *Rogerebert.com*. November 10, 2002.

Hegel, G.W.F. *Aesthetics: Lectures on Fine Art*. Trans. T.M. Knox. New York: Oxford at the Clarendon Press, 1975.

———. *Phenomenology of Spirit*. Trans. A.V. Miller. New York: Oxford UP, 1977.

Hume, David. *A Treatise of Human Nature*. 2d. ed. Ed. L.A. Selby-Bigge. Rev. P.H. Nidditch. New York: Oxford UP, 1990.

Kant, Immanuel. *Critique of Pure Reason*. Trans. Norman Kemp Smith. New York: St. Martins, 1965.

Paglia, Camille. *The Birds*. London: British Film Institute, 1998.

Pudovkin, V.I. *Film Techniques and Film Acting*. New York: Grove Press, 1960.

Rorty, Richard. *Philosophy and the Mirror of Nature*. Princeton, NJ: Princeton UP, 1979.

though a detailed
Moral Acts

12

ALAN WOOLFOLK

The Dread of Ascent

The Moral and Spiritual Topography of *Vertigo*

> Neither the therapeutic complacency of *Spellbound* nor the therapeutic agitation of *Vertigo* can question the essential grounds on which the "triumph of the therapeutic" is wrought—the primacy of a historical unchanging, indeed a historically transcendent, unconscious. Indeed, in this sense, *Vertigo*'s therapeutic pessimism only confirms the essential claims it seems to question; the *triumph* of the therapeutic may be called into question, but the essential conceptual structure that underlies its social hegemony—the "terror before the abyss of the self" that Adorno describes and *Vertigo* literalizes—is not. But this critique, while important to bear in mind, is also limited: In the name of historical specificity, it bulldozes into oblivion the historicity of the gesture it claims to question. To understand both *Spellbound* and *Vertigo* as historically specific acts is to inquire in not only about the historical blinders of *Vertigo* but also its powers of historical insight. Swimming against the mainstream, Hitchcock crafts a critique of American therapeutic culture as startling and passionate as those that were to follow his in the 1960s and the early 1970s.
>
> —Jonathan Freedman, "From *Spellbound* to *Vertigo*: Alfred Hitchcock and Therapeutic Culture in America" (96)

> But the mirror of possibility is not an ordinary mirror, it must be used with the utmost precaution. For of this mirror, it is true in the highest sense that it is a false mirror.
>
> —Søren Kierkegaard[1]

∾

In his incisive analysis of *Spellbound* and *Vertigo*, Jonathan Freedman contends that as Alfred Hitchcock advanced from the psychological shallowness of *Spellbound* (1945) to the psychological depths of *Vertigo* (1958) he took full advantage of the rapid institutionalization of psychology in American society during the postwar years to develop not only a relevant and compelling psychological drama, but also a devastating critique of what Philip Rieff soon thereafter called "the emergence of psychological man" in his influential work, *Freud: The Mind of the Moralist* (329–57). In fact, as Freedman suggests, Hitchcock was a moralist in his own right in *Vertigo* insofar as he illustrates through images, as much as through words, the poverty of American institutional and popular psychology when faced with serious moral questions and fateful moral choices. However, Hitchcock's insights extend beyond a critique of the manifest content of what Rieff would later call "therapeutic culture" toward a moral psychology that is reminiscent of the crisis psychology of European intellectuals such as Kierkegaard, Nietzsche, and Freud. Indeed, Hitchcock depicts in *Vertigo* the crisis of individuals afflicted by the ills of both a dying ascetic culture *and* an emergent remissive culture in a startlingly synoptic and effective manner across a variety of topics—individual freedom, despair, eroticism, and interpersonal domination, among others. However, Hitchcock concentrates on the inner crisis of a remissive, therapeutic culture, a culture which in Rieff's formulation has "nothing at stake beyond a manipulatable sense of well-being" (*Triumph of the Therapeutic* 13). He analyzes the fate of individuals in a world of too many freedoms, rather than studying the defeats of those who inhabit a symbolic and social world with too few options. He prefers to describe the deficits of the self in a culture with a dearth of spiritual and moral demands, rather than the inner conflicts of one with too many. Even so, Hitchcock portrays a world in transition that is laced with contradictions and ironies: a protagonist who fears moral heights, but is blind to the spiritual topography of everything about him; a *femme fatale* who is socially constructed by males and deadly to herself; a culture that is saturated with psychological references but which is incapable of understanding psychic ills; even a cyclical conception of time that is, in the first version, represented as transparently false and then, in the second version, re-presented as symptomatically true.

Therapeutic Dead-Ends

The best analytical entry point into *Vertigo* is through the abundant references to psychology. As Freedman points out, these begin with the first full scene of the film in which Midge Wood (Barbara Bel Geddes) consoles former police detective John "Scottie" Ferguson (James Stewart) over the circumstances surrounding the onset of his vertigo, which was triggered by his own near fatal accident during a rooftop chase that caused the death of a uniformed officer, as depicted in the opening scene.[2] Invoking therapeutic language, Midge explains to her guilt-ridden, former fiancé that "the doctors explained it to you. It wasn't your fault." Shortly thereafter, Midge explains that she has also consulted with her own doctor, who has in so many words said that "you've got it [vertigo] and there's no losing it. . . . Only another emotional shock will do it and probably won't." In short order, not taking Midge seriously, Scottie proclaims that he "won't crack up," and then proceeds to do precisely that, symptomatically fainting into the arms of Midge as he attempts to execute his own self-help therapy by climbing the steps of a kitchen height chair, while looking "up and down," just prior to experiencing a paralyzing flashback to his rooftop trauma.

Similar therapeutic clichés and dead-ends are encountered later in the film under the auspices of the official psychiatric establishment, which, as Freedman notes, "fares little better" in its curative efforts (88). The narrative of the first half of the film draws to a close with Scottie believing (and the viewer being led to believe) that his vertigo has prevented him from saving (the false) Madeleine Elster (Kim Novak), whom he believes to be the real wife of his old college acquaintance, Gavin Elster (Tom Helmore), from suicide, as he falls into a depressive catatonic state. Once again, Midge is present to help execute a therapy, but this time under the guidance of expert advice. Midge informs the catatonic Scottie, in what is the beginning of an ironic yet serious monologue, which presages the failure of this and all professional therapies, that "the lady in musical therapy" has prescribed Mozart as "the broom that sweeps the cobwebs clean." In the next scene, the pattern of therapeutic failure is once again made clear in an exchange between Midge and the nameless psychiatrist in charge of Scottie's case, who tells her that Scottie is "suffering from acute melancholia, together with a guilt complex . . . he blames himself for what happened to the woman." After Midge responds that "I can give you one thing—he was in love with that woman and still is" and inquires about how long it will "take to pull him out of this," the doctor's response becomes even more hopeless and banal: "Well, it's hard to say. At least six months, perhaps a year. It really could depend on him." At this point, Midge prepares to exit the doctor's office and the film and, by implication, Scottie's life with her response, "And you know something, doctor, I don't think Mozart is going to help at all." The last camera shot of Midge's lonely exit down the barren hospital corridor accents not only the failure of all professional therapies but also, as Freedman states, "the power madness exerts over Scottie for the rest of the film" (90). Indeed, the two points are inseparable: no therapy can adequately address the nightmare specter that haunts Scottie.

No therapy can offer a cure for Scottie's madness because the specter haunting his nightmare is, as we learn in the dream sequence that leads to his madness, a terrifying image of his own death. In this dream sequence, Scottie superimposes his own fears onto the imagined fears of Madeleine (i.e., the false Madeleine Elster) as the dream concludes with Scottie's disembodied head and body plunging toward the grave of Madeleine's supposed great-grandmother, Carlotta Valdes. No therapeutic technique can offer a solution to this nightmare because the twentieth-century therapeutic thought-world, which is itself symptomatically depicted in *Vertigo*, is by its very nature simply incapable of addressing such extraordinary problems, of which the greatest is death.

Prior to the rise of the therapeutic thought-world, the extraordinary problems of the human condition were addressed within the context of

Figure 12.1. Midge (Barbara Bel Geddes) leaving sanitarium.

religious and philosophical systems that were predicated on unconditional communal commitments and less practical forms of coping with such problems than we have grown to expect today. The rise of a therapeutic thought-world has changed all of this. In American, European, and other postindustrial societies, the triumph of the therapeutic has meant the defeat of older moralities of self-denial based on the assumption that the path to individual perfection is through submission to doctrines of communal purpose and adherence to narratives of spiritual ascent. And it has meant the victory of moralities of self-affirmation that proclaim the sovereignty of the self, which have broken the historic link between mandatory membership in the community and a therapeutic sense of well-being. Whatever the costs in terms of human suffering of earlier "commitment therapies," the development of a full-blown therapeutic culture in the twentieth century with all of its shortcomings is presciently and symptomatically depicted in *Vertigo*" (66–78). Just as no stand-alone therapeutic technique can heal Scottie's fractured existence, so therapeutic culture has proven incapable of mending what Rieff has called "the brokenness of existence," which is another way of referring to what has "been called the problem of nothingness, of the void, of nonbeing" that the religious and philosophical thought-worlds of the past have all addressed (*Feeling Intellect* 314). In short, Scottie's existence is irremediably broken because he finds himself trapped within the enormity of the present without spiritual guidance and with no symbolic resources at his disposal on which to rely.

Psychological Adolescence

The cultural and psychological complexity of *Vertigo* is not initially apparent. In fact, *Vertigo* can easily be read as the last of the classic noir films with Scottie Ferguson as the last in a long lineage of American noir protagonists with progressively decreasing powers of agency that begins with the inestimable Sam Spade (Humphrey Bogart) in John Huston's *The Maltese Falcon* (1941) and continues through the likes of the doomed Walter Neff (Fred MacMurray) in Billy Wilder's *Double Indemnity* (1944), Ole 'Swede' Andreson (Burt Lancaster) in Robert Siodmak's *The Killers* (1946), and Jeff Markham (Robert Mitchum) in Jacques Tourneur's *Out of the Past* (1947). Nonetheless, even if *Vertigo* is read as a noir film, it highlights the triumph of psychological thinking in the 1950s.

"The issue of destiny in noirs," according to Robert Pippin, "is largely framed in psychological or social or existential terms, and the relevant possibilities are severely constricted. The standard picture is of people 'trapped' either (somewhat paradoxically) by themselves (by whom they have become), or by an anonymous and autonomous social order or societal machine, or by a vast purposeless play of uncontrollable fortune, chance" (11). In the first half of *Vertigo*, Scottie appears to be "trapped" by an inexorable fate when he is hired by Gavin to follow his apparently suicidal wife, Madeleine (who is supposedly possessed by the spirit of her dead great grandmother, Carlotta), falls in love with her, and then watches helplessly, paralyzed with vertigo, as she seemingly jumps to her death at the Mission San Juan Bautista. In the film's second half, we quickly learn, of course, that Gavin has masterminded the murder of his real wife by using the *femme fatale* Madeleine/Judy (Kim Novak also plays Judy Barton) as a stand-in for his wife and that he has intentionally exploited Scottie's psychological condition. But, significantly, the revelation of the murderous actions of Gavin rapidly recede into the background of the film as Scottie's obsession with the re-creation of Madeleine through Judy and (on learning of the deception) his fateful effort to break "free of the past" by returning to the scene of the crime, move to the forefront of the narrative. That is, *Vertigo* represents the dubious triumph of psychology at the end of the classic noir period. The fate of the protagonist is framed entirely in terms of psychological entrapment.

Theoretically, Scottie does have one chance: he is by vocation a detective who prides himself on his analytic abilities. But, as Freedman notes, where Hitchcock played a decisive role with *Spellbound* in making "the process of the psychoanalytic cure . . . fully available as a narrative resource for the Hollywood cinema only when its central activity—the discovery or recovery of the meaning of a past event—was translated into the homologous narrative of the detective plot," with *Vertigo* Hitchcock subverts and severs this link (83). Unlike Dr. Constance Peterson (Ingrid Bergman) in *Spellbound*, Scottie does not cure himself or anyone else upon solving the mystery of the terrible deception perpetrated on him by Gavin Elster (Woolfolk, 129–37). Indeed, Scottie, if anything, is presented as a parody of the analytic attitude made famous by Freud (as seen, for instance, when Scottie is seated on the all-too-obvious symbol of the analyst's couch in the opening "fainting scene" with Midge). Initially, Scottie is skeptical of Elster's story about Madeleine's possession by the spirit of Carlotta Valdes, responding that Gavin should "take her to the nearest psychiatrist, or psychologist, or neurologist, or psychoan . . . or maybe just the plain family doctor. I'd have him look at you too." But even with this response, we know that Scottie is no master of analysis because it is evident how thoroughly he is imbued with an uncritical psychological worldview and, therefore, vulnerable to being taken in by Gavin's preposterous tale. The first weakness foreshadows the second weakness. Accordingly, Scottie is then, as planned, seduced by Elster's elaborate scheme with Madeleine at the erotic center of the plot, as he desperately searches for "the key" to Madeleine's feigned madness. In the end, Scottie "has indeed solved the crime, but he has done the very opposite of curing himself," as Freedman argues, thus severing the parallel between detective work and psychological analysis (94).

In addition to the fact that the psychological problems of *Vertigo* are much more profound than those of *Spellbound*, Scottie is represented as having limited analytical skills because he is anything but a model of psychological maturity. In fact, Scottie falls far short of the analytic attitude that Freud advocated and Rieff describes as necessary for surviving with a sense of self intact in a therapeutic age:

> To reserve the capacity for neutrality between choices, even while making them, as required by this new science of moral management, produces a strain no less great than choosing itself. The analytic capacity demands a rare skill: to entertain multiple perspectives upon oneself, and even upon beloved others. A high level of control is necessary in order to shift from one perspective to another, so to soften the demands upon oneself in all the major situations of life—love, parenthood, friendship, work, and citizenship. Such conscious fluidity of commitment is not easily attained. In fact, the attainment of psychological manhood is more difficult than any of the older versions of maturity; that manhood is no longer protected by a fantasy of having arrived at some resting place where security, reassurance, and trust reside, like gods in their heavens. The best one can say for oneself in life is that one has not been taken in, even by that "normal psychosis," love. (*Triumph* 66–78)

By this measure, Scottie is a case study in immaturity—at first glance, a man approaching middle-age, who is unmarried and without children, yet maternally attached to his former college girlfriend; retired early from his profession because of a trauma induced case of vertigo; and "taken in" by an old acquaintance who sets him up to be "taken in" by a carefully contrived *femme fatale*. In short, Scottie is, if nothing else, a model of psychological vulnerability and adolescence.

Symptomatic Conflicts Out of the Past

That Scottie is no master of psychological analysis and unaware of his own deeper problems is made clear from the opening scene of the film with Midge overtly depicted as both the former fiancé of Scottie *and* a maternal figure to him. Later, this association is made even more explicit when Midge tells a catatonic Scottie at the sanitarium that "Mother's here. You're not lost." That is, from the first full scene of the movie forward, we, as viewers, are given plenty of reasons to suspect that Scottie's problems did not begin with the rooftop trauma that triggered his vertigo. In addition to the opening banter about Midge's "love life" and the revelation that she broke off their engagement after only three weeks, Midge's troubled glance over her glasses during the exchange signals that she knows that something is awry with Scottie. To begin with, she is obviously in love with Scottie, but Scottie seems incapable of understanding and returning that love. One does not have to be Freud to figure out that Scottie has most likely come up against the incest taboo in his intimate life. Midge's maternal image has inhibited his erotic response. Whether Midge was maternal from the beginning of the relationship, or she assumed that role later in response to Scottie's immaturity, is a critical question that can be inferred only as the film unfolds. But it appears that Scottie is a classic case of arrested development and suffering from a deep-seated psychic conflict.

According to this reading, Scottie's hysterical episodes brought on by his acrophobia are a symptom of an unresolved repressed conflict from his past. In Freud's classic formulation, "hysterics suffer mainly from reminiscences" (7). On the surface, Scottie's acrophobic episodes are directly related to his rooftop trauma; however, he reveals in the opening scene with Midge that it was during the rooftop incident that he found out that he *had* the condition. In other words, Scottie implies that his vertigo preceded the incident—that it had been latent and deep seated, even unconscious. He is depicted as time-bound, unable to escape from something in his past. Likewise, much of the content and structure of *Vertigo* emphasizes the time-bound nature of human experience and, especially, mental disturbance, once again evoking the classic model of reminiscence. However, Madeleine's trance-like states, unconscious visits to historical and cultural locales, and apparent possession by the spirit of her dead great grandmother are all, of course, fabricated. They are parodies of reminiscence. On the other hand, Scottie's attempts to recreate and recapture the image of Madeleine in Judy in the second half of the film are clearly an authentic, desperate exercise in reminiscence, a sort of acting out of his reminiscence of Madeleine. But Scottie's acting out of his reminiscence of Madeleine may be read in at least two ways.

In the first, and less convincing, reading, Scottie's attempts to recreate Madeleine point back to his original erotic response to her as an act of liberation from the crippling inhibitions of the past. Beginning with the spectacularly choreographed and mirrored scene in Ernie's restaurant, and then continuing with the rescue of Madeleine from her plunge into San Francisco Bay and the embrace at Seal Bay with the crescendo of crashing waves in the background, Scottie's attraction to the false Madeleine may be seen as a paradigm of romantic love in which he is finally able to fall in love with a woman, but only because she conforms to a set of very specific criteria and a series of obstacles enhance his passion.[3] Specifically, Madeleine conforms to certain upper-class standards of beauty and taste (e.g., her restrained, physical poise and conservative suit and hair), comes from a social background above Scottie's, and she is married. In addition, Madeleine's madness creates yet another obstacle that must be overcome, as Scottie desperately searches for "the key" that would allow her to escape from the past. After losing Madeleine through the apparent suicide, Scottie is only then able to recapture his original romantic experience and erotic response by remaking Judy, an obviously unsophisticated, working-class young woman from Kansas, into Madeleine (unknowingly in the same manner as Gavin Elster). In this reading, Scottie's romantic reminiscence with Madeleine/Judy, however colored with obsession and gross insensitivity, is an attempt to escape once again from the neurotic conflicts of the past and to leave behind his guilt over Madeleine's apparent death. The fact that these efforts end in the disaster of Madeleine/Judy's real death does not gainsay the point that Scottie's problems *may* be interpreted as manifestations of psychic conflicts past and present associated with the neuroses of a dying ascetic culture.

The False Mirror of Possibility

Yet, there is abundant evidence to support the contention that Scottie's deeper problem is not psychic conflict but depression, that his difficulties concern a failure of self-definition rather than an inner conflict between individual desires and the moral demands of society. According to Alain Ehrenberg, depression is the successor to neurosis in a therapeutic age characterized by the relaxation of moral demands and greater tolerance toward the self:

> Depression began its ascent when the disciplinary model for behaviours, the rules of authority and observance of taboos that gave social classes as well as both sexes a specific destiny, broke against norms that invited us to undertake personal initiative by enjoining us to be ourselves. These new norms brought with them a sense that the responsibility for our

existence lies not only within us but also within the collective between-us. . . . Depression is the opposite of this paradigm. Depression presents itself as an *illness of responsibility* in which the dominant feeling is that of failure. The depressed individual is unable to measure up; he is tired of having to become himself. (4)

Scottie certainly does not appear to be in conflict with conventional norms, such as those defining marriage, sexual identity, and social class. In fact, Scottie's erotic interest in Madeleine is notable for his lack of concern with class barriers and her supposed marriage to Gavin. However, Scottie is a self-described "free man" who repeatedly characterizes himself as "wandering" and "wandering about," after his departure from the police force. Initially, these references to freedom and wandering seem to be of little significance, but they take on added significance as they are repeated and the narrative of Scottie's life comes into focus.

This narrative is bivalent, it unfolds at two levels—the first is a narrative of aimless freedom; the second is a narrative of what may be called transgressive freedom. The first narrative begins, as so much else does in the film, with the opening scene of Midge and Scottie when Scottie declares that tomorrow he will be a "free man" because the corset which he has been wearing for his injured back will come off. Aside from throwing off the obvious gender identity confusion and Midge's utilitarian approach to sexuality (she is busy designing a "cantilevered" brazier), this is also Scottie's un-self-conscious declaration of freedom from his mundane life, his apparently unconscious openness and vulnerability to what Kierkegaard called unlimited possibility—specifically, a life lacking in necessity, ungrounded in a personal synthesis of necessity and possibility, in which "everything is possible" (170). As this narrative unfolds, Scottie tells Gavin, then Madeleine, and then Midge in succession that he spends his time "wandering." But this narrative of aimless freedom also unfolds as much visually as verbally, beginning with the mirrored scene in Ernie's, and then continuing with the very next, second mirrored scene in the Podesta Baldocchi Flower Shop. In both of these scenes, Scottie catches surreptitious, reflected glimpses of the poised and beautiful Madeleine—artificially created images, as we soon find out. In addition, both scenes are devoid of any self-reflection on Scottie's part. Scottie's voyeuristic gaze is grounded in no self-awareness, no self-knowledge, let alone any knowledge of who Madeleine is as a person. Both scenes offer brilliant visual representations of Kierkegaard's false "mirror of possibility" (170).

Both Scottie and Madeleine are defined by Scottie's voyeuristic gaze, which in turn is controlled by Gavin, who in his role as Pygmalion has transformed the ordinary Judy into the extraordinary Madeleine. Under Gavin's direction, Madeleine/Judy is able to exploit Scottie's voyeuristic tendencies and secure his unintended role in the scheme to murder his wife and inherit her fortune. Scottie's very lack of self-identity and deficiency of agency allow the execution of Gavin's fantastic scheme to be successful. Without Scottie's vulnerability and voyeuristic tendencies, Madeleine's plunge into San Francisco Bay would not have resulted in Scottie taking the supposedly unconscious Madeleine back to his flat, removing her wet clothes, and placing her into his bed. Indeed, the entire scene in Scottie's flat is effective precisely because it forces the viewer to consider exactly what has transpired and fully reveals Scottie's voyeurism and, in the hindsight of later revelations, his susceptibility to erotic manipulation. Furthermore, it sets up the next, critical "wandering" scene outside Scottie's flat in which Scottie suggests to Madeleine that they go wandering together. In this scene, it becomes clear that Scottie's pursuit of possibility initially goes astray in what Kierkegaard describes as "the wishful, yearning form," at the same time that this pursuit grows increasingly fantastic because he imagines that he can save Madeleine from possession by the suicidal spirit of her dead grandmother (170). In his aimless freedom, Scottie attempts to avoid the necessity of becoming a responsible agent by escaping into an impossible romanticism, which serves to fend off the depression that must inevitably ensue once that fantastic romanticism collapses.

Madeleine's staged suicide triggers Scottie's depression, what Ehrenberg calls "the tragedy of inadequacy":

> In the same way that neurosis threatened the individual divided by his conflicts, torn between the allowed and the forbidden, depression threatens the individual apparently freed from his taboos but certainly torn between the possible and the impossible. If neurosis is the tragedy of guilt, depression is the tragedy of inadequacy. It is the familiar shadow of a person without a guide, tired of going forward to achieve the self and tempted to sustain himself through products and behaviors. (11)

For Scottie, the tragedy of his inadequacy prior to his depression takes the form of his vertiginous dis-ease, which is perhaps best understood as not so much a fear of falling as a fear of moral heights. In Ehrenberg's language, Scottie fails "to measure up." That is, Scottie suffers from a dread of moral and spiritual ascent. He prefers to remain a psychological adolescent in an age of psychological adulthood who sustains himself through ambivalent "wanderings" and an impossible romanticism, which keep him focused on the immediate horizon.

Circles of Futility

Scottie's ambivalent, wandering life after the onset of his vertigo comes into even clearer focus under the second narrative of transgressive freedom, which is introduced in the second full scene when Scottie meets Gavin in his executive office at his wife's ship building company. At this meeting, Gavin provides important clues to a much darker side of existence to which Scottie is unconsciously attracted in his references to a painting of San Francisco on his office wall depicting the city before it had "changed." According to Gavin, this old San Francisco was a city of "color," "excitement," "power," and "freedom." In an apparently innocent remark, Gavin informs Scottie that he "would like to have lived then." But Gavin's references take on much more sinister connotations a few scenes later, when Scottie and Midge visit the Argosy Bookstore run by Pop Leibel (Konstantin Shayne) to learn about the story of Carlotta Valdes, only to find out that the old San Francisco of Gavin's imagination was a city in which rich and powerful men dominated women and could discard them at will. With reference to Carlotta, they learn that she had gone mad after a rich and powerful man had taken her in and then "threw her away," while keeping their child (Carlotta's grandmother). When Pop Leibel informs Scottie and Midge that a "man could do that in those days," the repeated references to freedom suddenly become much more ambiguous and bivalent. At this point, the viewer learns that freedom can take the form of aimless wandering, but that it can also become criminal, that freedom can be remissive, but that it can also grow transgressive.

In Scottie's case, he begins to move from remissive to transgressive freedom once he recovers from his depressive breakdown and attempts to remake the newly discovered Judy into Madeleine. After recovering, Scottie initially sights Madeleine's 1957 Jaguar Mk.VIII, and then retraces his voyeuristic visits to Ernie's, the Legion of Honor Museum, and the Podesta Baldocchi Flower Shop before spotting Judy outside the Empire Hotel, thereby repeating the classic symptomatic pattern of reminiscence discussed earlier. However, once Scottie discovers Judy at the Empire Hotel, this classic pattern is radically altered, even broken. To begin with, Hitchcock employs the established noir technique of a flashback: upon being discovered, Judy composes a letter to Scottie revealing that he has been the victim of Gavin's plot and that she has fallen in love with him (and then destroys the letter), thus revealing to the viewer, but not to Scottie, the truth about the deception. This unusual plot device serves to raise not only the dramatic tension, but also to accent the fact that Scottie's dominance and control of Judy commences before he learns the truth about Gavin's exploitation of him and Judy's role in this exploitation. More important, Scottie's ignorance and the viewer's knowledge of the crime allow the viewer to understand that Scottie begins his Pygmalion imitation of Gavin prior to learning of Gavin's makeover of Judy into Madeleine.

Scottie's forced makeover of Judy into the image of Madeleine may be represented as the actions of a desperate man, but these actions also reveal a pattern of exploitation that becomes increasingly severe as Scottie descends into a world of primordial possibility. Instead of accepting Judy as an irreducible individual, Scottie strips her of every last shred of self-respect as he badgers her into conforming to his ideal of romantic perfection. Indeed, the only scene shown from Judy's perspective occurs the morning after he establishes initial contact as the two of them walk along the San Francisco waterfront, when Judy still has some hope that she will be able to make Scottie love her for herself. But this is a forlorn hope, as Scottie proceeds to enact a strange version of the "crystallization" theory of love, according to which, in the words of Ortega, "we fall in love when our imagination projects non-existent perfections onto another person" (22). In Scottie's case, the projections are conscious and take on material reality as the clothes, shoes, jewelry, hair, and makeup of Madeleine are imposed upon Judy in the vain hope that he can repeat or circle back to the past in order to make a new beginning. But Judy's eyes, more than anything else, betray the futility of Scottie's efforts. Even though she may look like Madeleine, her eyes reveal that she is still the same insecure Judy. Judy cannot be inwardly remade, turned into something that she is not.

Spiraling circles are everywhere in *Vertigo* and are closely linked at points with images of eyes. Indeed, the film opens with a closeup of Kim Novak's eyes, apparently portraying Madeleine, followed by a series of spiraling geometric images and then another eye closeup. Both the eye and circle motifs are reminiscent of the opening of Emerson's essay "Circles": "The eye is the first circle; the horizon which it forms is the second; and throughout nature this primary picture is repeated without end" (212). However, Hitchcock's circles are anything but the circles of Emerson defining the horizon of some new beginning. For Emerson, "our life is an apprenticeship to the truth that around every circle another can be drawn; that there is no end in nature, but every end is a beginning" (212). For Hitchcock, the circle is an image of futility. There are no new beginnings for either Scottie or Judy.

In order to signal that there are no new beginnings, Hitchcock's circles spiral figuratively and sometimes literally downward: Scottie's surveillance of Madeleine leads him in disturbing downward circles through the streets of San Francisco; the bell tower stairs of the Mission San Juan Bautista form a dizzying spiral; his nightmares are filled with images of downward spiraling falls; the retracing of his voyeuristic visits to Ernie's, the Legion of Honor, and the Podesta Flower Shop lead to the beginning of the second, fatal relationship with Madeleine/Judy; Judy's fatal fall at the close of the film repeats the psychologically fatal plunge of Madeleine and brings Scottie full circle. More generally, as Scottie "looks up" and "looks down," his vertigo takes the form of a dizzying downward spiral as he is terror stricken by the abyss that opens up at his feet and from which he is incapable of looking away, let alone up. Of course, Scottie imagines that he has escaped from the futile circularity and terrifying dizziness of his life once he has consummated his relationship with the recreated Madeleine. Indeed, the bedazzling 360-degree kiss scene bathed in the blue-green light of Judy's hotel room is supposed to signify for Scottie the circle of a new beginning, the anima of a new life. But the very experience of stripping Judy of her identity and dressing her up as Madeleine has only prepared him to delve more deeply into the abyss of possibilities that he has opened up, which, in Kierkegaard's words, he now approaches with "anguished dread" (170).

Once Scottie is directly confronted with the elaborate fraud that has been perpetrated against him, upon discovering one of Madeleine/Judy's "souvenirs of a killing"—the necklace—he heads straight down Highway 101 to the Mission San Juan Bautista in pursuit of yet another Emersonian end with a new beginning. Just as Scottie had imagined that he could break free of the past in his embrace of the transformed Judy, so he now imagines that he and Judy can "both be free" by going "back into the past once more" and returning to the scene of the crime, where he proceeds to drag Judy forcefully up the spiral stair case of the mission bell tower. In taking advantage of his "second chance," Scottie in effect stops wandering and resolves his ambivalence, but at a very high moral cost: the climb up the bell tower is no vertical spiritual ascent, but rather a spiritual descent. For the first time he is able to overcome his vertigo, the "tragedy of his inadequacy," but only by identifying downward with the transgressive figure of Gavin. Scottie solves the crime and temporarily cures himself, but only at the cost of consciously recognizing how closely he has emulated Gavin, in the absence of other guides. Hence, the emphatic and angry tone of Scottie's rhetorical comments to Madeleine/

Judy comes from a very personal, even intimate, knowledge of Gavin's transgressions. They have shared the same erotic object and engaged in a sort of erotic competition that Gavin has won and Scottie has lost. "He made you over just like I made you over. Only better . . . you were a very apt pupil, too, weren't you?" Likewise, Judy has also lost, and Scottie cannot resist reminding her that "with all of his wife's money and all that freedom and that power" that Judy has been "ditched." In a world of transgressive freedom, there are only winners and losers, and Scottie now recognizes how much he desires to be a winner. But in reducing Judy to nothing, just as his predecessor Gavin has done, Scottie sets her up to be scared out of her wits by an imagined apparition and fall to her death, thereby ensuring that one final circle of futility will throw him into a definitive, irrevocable despair.

Notes

1. Søren Kierkegaard, *Fear and Trembling and the Sickness unto Death*, 170.
2. Freedman, "From *Spellbound* to *Vertigo*," 88–89. The analysis of the next few pages draws heavily from Freedman's argument. I am indebted to him for his keen insights into the links between therapeutic culture and *Vertigo*.
3. See the classic text by Denis de Rougemont, *Love in the Western World*, trans. M. Belgion (New York: Harper & Row, revised and augmented edition, 1974).

Works Cited

Breuer, Josef and Sigmund Freud, *Studies on Hysteria*. Trans. J. Strachey, in collaboration with Anna Freud. Basic Books, n.d.
de Rougemont, Denis. *Love in the Western World*. Trans. M. Belgion. New York: Harper & Row, revised and augmented edition, 1974.
Ehrenberg, Alain. *The Weariness of the Self*. Montreal: McGill-Queen's Press, 2010.
Emerson, Ralph Waldo. *Essays by Ralph Waldo Emerson*. Intro. by I. Edman. New York: Thomas Y. Crowell Company, 1951.
Freedman, Jonathan. "From *Spellbound* to *Vertigo*: Alfred Hitchcock and Therapeutic Culture in America." *Hitchcock's America*, ed. by J. Freedman and R. Millington. New York: Oxford UP, 1999.
Kierkegaard, Søren. *Fear and Trembling and the Sickness unto Death*. Trans. with intro. and notes by Walter Lowrie. Princeton, NJ: Princeton UP, 1968.
Ortega Y Gasset, José. *On Love: Aspects of a Single Theme*. Trans. T. Talbot. New York: Meridian Book, World Publishing, 1957.
Pippin, Robert. *Fatalism in American Film Noir*. Charlottesville: University of Virginia Press, 2012.
Rieff, Philip. *The Feeling Intellect: Selected Writings*. Ed. and with intro. by J. Imber. Chicago: The University of Chicago Press, 1990.

———. *Freud: The Mind of the Moralist*. 3rd ed. Chicago: The University of Chicago Press, 1979.

———. *The Triumph of the Therapeutic: Uses of Faith After Freud*. New York: Harper & Row, 1968.

Woolfolk, Alan. "Depth Psychology on the Surface." *Hitchcock at the Source: The Auteur as Adapter*. Eds. R. Barton Palmer and David Boyd. Albany: State University of New York Press, 2011.

Jennifer L. Jenkins

The Philosophy of Marriage in *North by Northwest*

> In America, where the romantic view of marriage has been taken more seriously than anywhere else, and where law and custom alike are based upon the dreams of spinsters, the result has been an extreme prevalence of divorce and an extreme rarity of happy marriages.
>
> —Bertrand Russell, *Marriage and Morals*[1]

FROM THE OPENING DIALOGIC EXCHANGE in Hitchcock's cross-country thriller *North by Northwest* (1959), marriage functions as a leitmotif. As Roger Thornhill (Cary Grant) emerges from the elevator of his Madison Avenue office high rise, *in medias res* and dictation to his secretary, he tosses "How's the wife?" to the elevator attendant Eddie, who replies "We're not speaking." Thornhill, clearly a serial multi-tasker in business and women, grins wryly, breaking neither stride nor stream of words. Without missing a beat, his next dictum to Maggie (Doreen Lang) affirms a piece of corporate one-upmanship, followed by instructions for a palliative gift of gilt-wrapped candy to a paramour who'll "think she's eating money" (Lehman 3). Thornhill handles both the corporate and the carnal transaction with the same ironic distance he showed toward

Eddie's domestic woes. There is no meeting of hearts or minds in any part of Thornhill's world, although he is clearly a skilled broker of business and personal unions. While not unaware of his responsibilities— "I've got a job, a secretary, a mother, two ex-wives and several bartenders waiting for me" (Lehman 129), he later announces to the Professor— Thornhill's relations are more facile than familial. Indeed, his dismissive attitude toward marriage is the stuff of midcentury jokes from Peter Arno's cartoons in *The New Yorker*, reflecting the urban sophisticate's casual attitude toward the trappings of postwar success, one of which was traditional marriage. Yet this film compulsively circles the subject of marriage, keeping it in view if not in center frame throughout. Positioned between *Vertigo* (1958) and *Psycho* (1960), *North by Northwest* was in pre-production when Alma Hitchcock was diagnosed and treated for cervical cancer (McGilligan 559). The potential loss of his artistic and life partner was a staggering blow to Hitchcock, and may well have shaped his portrait of marriage in his next feature film.[2] The Hitchcocks had a highly successful companionate marriage based on complementary but distinctive talents. While at the outset Roger Thornhill may be a man who doesn't believe in marriage, and Eve Kendall (Eva Marie Saint) may be an independent moral and double agent, Roger and Eve find their way by plane, train, and automobile to a partnership similar to that of the Hitchcocks. The philosophy of marriage in *North by Northwest* is a singularly democratic one: a volitional union of equals, hard-won by strife and commitment to an idea greater than themselves. A more perfect union, as it were.

In *Marriage and Morals* (1929) Bertrand Russell celebrated the post–World War I relaxation of nineteenth-century social and cultural mores. Russell advocated mutuality of relations, both sexual and social, between men and women as simple common sense in the modern world. His moral philosophy is grounded in utilitarianism. With reliable birth control to free both parties from obligatory marriage, the greater good is served by openness about human desire and companionability. Impartiality and self-awareness are cornerstones of this ethic, derived from Bentham and Mill, the goal of which might reductively be described simply as happiness. In his book, Russell notably endorses premarital sex or "trial marriage" between young men and women (of the same class, he cautions) to put an end to women's utter sexual ignorance and to steer young men away from prostitutes: "Sexual relations should be *a mutual delight*, entered into solely from the spontaneous impulse of both parties. Where this is not the case, everything that is valuable is absent" (152–53, emphasis mine). Among those values are equality, shared physical pleasure, and the ability to ask for and receive what's needed in a relationship. Indeed, Russell advocates marriage only if children are a consideration. Otherwise, he trusts adults to know their own hearts and minds and to seek happiness where they find it.

Russell claimed in his autobiography that the 1950 Nobel Prize was awarded him for this very work; certainly that prestigious award re-introduced the book into the midcentury cultural conversation (*Autobiography* 521). Russell had never been far from the minds of Americans, given his tours of U.S. colleges, lectures at Harvard, and his notorious un-hiring in 1940 by the College of the City of New York due to parents' moral objections. As a man with *three* ex-wives by 1952, Russell—like Roger Thornhill—had amply demonstrated his belief in marriage by his frequent participation in it. Russell's moral fitness was constantly questioned during his American sojourns, and yet his *Marriage and Morals* paved the way for the groundbreaking investigations into American relationships by Masters and Johnson and Betty Friedan that would challenge fifties conformity. He was a philosopher whom many disagreed with, but everybody read. Russell's work was omnipresent in 1958 as context for the motifs of *North by Northwest*, with its complex relations between men and women.

If happiness is the goal of Russell's philosophy of marriage, in his view love American style is not the ticket. Modern marriage, defined by American popular culture and psychology as a love-based, female homemaker–male breadwinner household was, rather, a ticket to disaster. Russell contends that unrealistic American romantic ideals about marriage led to serial divorce and widespread unhappiness, a perspective that is reflected in the world of the film. Neither Thornhill nor Kendall has achieved that putative ideal: he is twice divorced, and she introduces herself as "twenty-six and unmarried. Now you know everything." These interesting, autonomous, complex adults are the kinds Hitchcock audiences came to see and perhaps emulate. While *North by Northwest* can be viewed as a hero's journey away from mother and toward adult relationships, with Eve as the grail cup, this view minimizes the principals' agency within the context of midcentury re-negotiations of gender roles, relationships, and what twenty-first-century wags have termed "the work-life balance." A generation ago, Stanley Cavell identified the comedy of remarriage, and placed *North by Northwest* in that generic category. I would argue that the remarriage plot is one of repairing the partners, as we see in screwball comedies, rather than remaking the terms of marriage itself, as we see here. Russell frets about divorce as a cause of unhappiness, especially in America, but he and many Americans used it as a means to companionate happiness—a greater good being practicably served.

Marriage historian Stephanie Coontz notes that in the postwar period, American public intellectuals condoned divorce as a social corrective: "The influential sociologists Ernest Burgess and Harvey Locke wrote matter-of-factly that 'the companionate family relies upon divorce as a means of rectifying a mistake in mate selection;'" indeed, they viewed "divorce as a safety valve for the 'companionate' marriage" (Coontz *Marriage* 233). Film historian Virginia Wright Wexman notes that the postwar changes in gender dynamics and work hierarchies began to redefine gender roles in cinema around the same time: "By 1950 52 percent of women worked outside the home, part of a large-scale trend that was to continue as the century progressed. As a result, [onscreen] relations between the sexes became newly charged with issues of competition and dominance" (Wexman 168). Wexman cites *On the Waterfront* (1954), with Eva Marie Saint's good-girl Edie Doyle, as a film that portrays the ambivalence of gender roles in a changing midcentury world. Four years later, Saint's Eve Kendall would eschew the midcentury marriage model for much more interesting work outside the home.

Conformist domesticity of midcentury Middle America, stridently promoted in women's magazines, radio soap operas, and television, is wholly absent from the world of *North by Northwest*. It is replaced by a stylish world of sophistication, Cold War tensions, and independent moral agents. There is little place for cozy homemaker-breadwinner couples in the film's main locations: the U.N., mansions on Long Island and Mount Rushmore, posh hotels in New York and Chicago, the elegant Twentieth Century Limited, and the high-end Michigan Avenue auction house. Even the hospital and National Park Service cafeteria in Rapid City, South Dakota, seem inhospitable to couples. The female patient through—and from—whose room Thornhill escapes the hospital could well be one of Russell's dreaming spinsters. The families at Mount Rushmore are mere wallpaper to the complicated gendered showdown meant to separate Thornhill and Kendall, Kendall and Vandamm, and Vandamm (James Mason) and Leonard (Martin Landau). Couples therapy can occur only at the point of a gun, as in the cafeteria, the house atop Mount Rushmore, or on the face of the monument itself.

Freudians savor Roger Thornhill's apparent dependence on his mother at the beginning of the film and his suspension between secretary and mother, two surrogates for the wives he has lost (although not for the bartenders). In the Plaza drop-off scene, Thornhill and Maggie lean slightly toward each other as he ends his schedule review to exit the cab, barely hinting at but ultimately rejecting, of course, a kiss goodbye.

What Thornhill needs is not wife, mother, or secretary, but an equal partner. Yet Thornhill is not infantilized; he is fully adult, masculine, and in control even when he has been kidnapped. While he does use his one phone call from the Glen Cove Police Station to call Mother (Jesse Royce Landis), she certainly offers no sympathy or succor. After the court-mandated visit to the Townsend home and the charade of social niceties punctuated by Mother's dubious comments, she pointedly hints that he might want to grow up. As they leave the Townsend home amid Thornhill's protestations of his innocence, Mother says with exasperation, "Oh, Roger, *pay* the two dollars!" The drunk driving fine, as it happens, was also the cost of a New York State marriage license in 1958.[3]

North by Northwest challenges contemporary mores with such style that audiences accept the moral ambiguity of the principals as a temporary means to an end, anticipating a greater good for Thornhill and Kendall—and the free world, to boot. Their style and worldliness raise them above the home(l)y conformity of postwar America. Roger O. Thornhill transcends the executive uniform of the gray flannel suit, just as Eve rejects the looming, but in 1958 yet-unnamed, feminine mystique: neither would be functional in those quotidian midcentury gender roles. Whether or not they realize it at first, each seeks a fully companionate partnership, even as they spar over their respective independences: "I may have plans of my own, you know. And you have problems," says Eve to Roger in her Chicago hotel room. The ethic at play is that of one individual joined to another through choice rather than social convention or economic and familial pressure. As such, their relationship is not headed toward a fusty marriage as in *Shadow of a Doubt* or the stifling portraits of domestic life in *The Man Who Knew Too Much* and *Rear Window*. Russell would contend that Thornhill and Kendall's arrangement serves the utilitarian goals of a democratic society. Eve and Roger can only be pacesetters in terms of both a reimagined marriage ethic and personal style.

Much has been made of Roger Thornhill's bespoke Saville Row suits as an index of his status as urban sophisticate (Lehmann 470). Less attention has been given to Eve Kendall's clothing as sign, yet the costumes of the two lovers provide clues to their respective relations to marriage. Despite his two ex-wives (and presumably, in 1958, two alimony obligations), Thornhill does not wear a threadbare suit or last year's shoes. He makes no evident financial sacrifices for the vagaries of his love life. He has a pocketful of bills for tips to cabbies, messengers, valets, bribes to Mother and, presumably, two-dollar civil fees. He is sartorially perfect, and utterly independent. He cautions Eve that, "when I was a little boy, I wouldn't even let my mother undress me." Being "a big boy now," as she remarks approvingly, changes nothing (Lehman 119).

Married women—or women posing as married—dress in deep chocolate browns or muddy blacks. Vandamm's sister, posing as Mrs. Townsend (Josephine Hutchinson), wears a New Look–influenced black dinner dress with a peplum on the night of Thornhill's abduction and a brown sprigged day dress during the Glen Cove police visit the following morning. The dowager Mrs. Thornhill (Jesse Royce Landis) wears a chocolate brown Chanel-style suit with a luxuriant silver fox collar and a mink caplet. Both women wear pearls and have matronly auburn rinses on their "set" hair.[4] Their colors are drab and muddy, an indication of the miasmic state of marriage, even in the best of families.

By contrast, Eve's tailored black suit, wristwatch, and simple emerald pendant indicate a professional woman, dressed against type for a "Mata Hari" figure (Gilbert 10). Her hair is light blonde and simply styled, as befits a young woman of the world and a Hitchcock heroine. If we believe Eve's characterization of herself as, "twenty-six and unmarried" and an "industrial designer," she has had at least some engineering training. Her dark suit reflects that professionalism, whether it be industrial or international designs. Yet her suit blouse has a low boatneck rather than a conservative button collar or a severe bow, and her black handbag reminds us of Lisa Fremont's suggestive Mark Cross overnight bag in *Rear Window*. The moral index here is degrees of independence rather than degrees of sin, as Stephanie Coontz's research supports: "In movies as well, the images of acceptable female behavior narrowed, especially when it came to portraying women and work. Friedan's claim that during the 1940s and 1950s the career woman . . . increasingly stood for "ambition" rather than "adultery" (*Strange* 67). Eve Kendall is dressed for success in the man's world of espionage, rather than the midcentury marriage mart. As such, she is a free agent, governed by an ethic that is not yet readily apparent to Thornhill or the audience.

Ever the detail man, Hitchcock coded Eve's clothing to the stages of this moral journey. Meticulously chosen at Bergdorf's, Eve's clothes do indeed play against the emotions of the scenes in which she wears them, as Hitchcock had intended (McGilligan 567). When she runs hot, the clothes are severe; when she runs cold, they are colorful. However, and more important, Eve's clothes track her journey from New York to Chicago to South Dakota and from double agent to conflicted lover to soon-to-be-married woman. A New Look–style, full-skirted dinner dress in red and black replaces the business suit for the auction scene. As the red tones enter her wardrobe, so Eve's attachment to Roger becomes evident. The navy and mouse-gray day dress and hat that Eve wears at the Mount Rushmore cafeteria suggest an ingénue, a dependent role that the scene-within-the-scene is meant to reinforce with Vandamm. Still, her accessories hint at the changing circumstances: Eve wears a pearl choker and carries a brown handbag. Her traveling ensemble for the flight from South Dakota is a light cinnamon brown, with fawn accessories: she is heading toward a marriage commitment, though not that of the chocolate-clad matrons and not to the man she is about to join on the polar route to Moscow. Eve's costumes also make her visible against her various backdrops, marking her as utterly apart from domestic conformity.

Thornhill and Kendall meet in the train corridor of the Twentieth Century Limited while it is still in Grand Central Station. While we later learn that Kendall is on board to keep an eye on Thornhill, initially her response to his explanation of presence ("seven parking tickets") is a simple amused "Oh." It is worth noting that Ernest Lehman's shooting script denotes the space of their meeting as an "aisle." Hitchcock shoots the sequence like a wedding procession, with long shots down the aisle and reverse shots to show progress toward union. Thornhill enters the far end of the car in a limited vanishing-point long shot and moves center frame toward the camera. As he spots the police outside on the platform, frame right, he reverses course and heads back up the aisle toward the exit. The cut is to Kendall—at this point identified in the shooting script only as "GIRL"—in a medium shot, entering the car from the other end. She then moves toward the camera in a limited vanishing-point long shot that corresponds to Thornhill's. She advances up the aisle, small, measured, and feminine as a bride (although in black), until a reaction shot to Thornhill interrupts her progress. Despite being

Figure 13.1. Eve (Eve Marie Saint) walking down the train "aisle."

lit for day and timed for the bustle of train departure, this progress toward the camera recalls the slow, dreamy approach in *Vertigo* of Judy-remade-as-Madeleine toward the waiting, gray-suited Scotty. In *Vertigo*, this approach is Scotty's constructed fantasy of union; replayed in *North by Northwest*, it is a neutral meeting of—at this point—disaffected equals.

The exchange that this aisle leads to is not of vows. As the GIRL advances, Thornhill moves into frame left, and they perform a kind of *pas de deux*, neither giving way and neither leading. Lehman's shooting script describes their motions: "She steps to one side. But he steps to the same side. He moves to the other side—just as she does . . . They move to the center—but in unison. Again an impasse" (66). Their movements in concert anticipate the makeout scene in Kendall's train compartment, but the parallel movement and impasse in the aisle also suggest that they meet as equal agents. Thornhill doesn't appeal to Eve for help, nor does he kidnap her as a decoy. After a brief dinner interrupted by an unscheduled stop, they simply lie to and then with each other—a thoroughly modern encounter.

Russell's marriage ethic calls for a sexual morality predicated on measured self-control. Intentional action by independent agents is the goal of modern love. A morality based on fear of sin, of shame, of public condemnation can, for Russell, lead only to "thwarting of instinct" and unhealthy, unhappy liaisons (307). Given the Twentieth Century setting for this second stage of the plot—as well as Hitchcock's choice of final shot before the closing credits—Russell's metaphor seems fully apt:

> The use of self-control is like the use of the brakes on a train. It is useful when you find yourself going in the wrong direction, but merely harmful when the direction is right. No one would maintain that a train ought always to run with the brakes on, yet the habit of difficult self-control has a very similar injurious effect upon the energies available for useful activity. (Russell 308)

The "useful activity" at this juncture is Thornhill's pursuit of George Kaplan, and Eve's attempt to divert his energies from that quest. In the after-dinner train compartment scene, Eve and Roger negotiate the "unsteady" ("who isn't?") motion on the rails while exploring bodies and assessing characters. Their heavy petting is accompanied by witty, flirtatious talk characteristic of Hitchcock bedroom scenes. One needn't be a scholar of Elizabethan poetry to understand the sexualized references to death and ecstasy:

EVE: How do I know you *aren't* a murderer?

THORNHILL (to her neck): You don't.

EVE: Maybe you're planning to murder me, right here, tonight.

THORNHILL (working on her ear): Shall I?

EVE (whispers): Yes . . . please do. . . .

This time her hands do help him, and it is a long kiss indeed.

(Lehman 80–81)

Neither Thornhill nor Kendall hits the brakes very hard. Lest we miss the point, Hitchcock embeds a small sartorial joke in Eve's above-the-waist accessories: as Thornhill and Kendall neck in her low-light drawing room, her emerald pendant flashes a "green light." Later, when she tries to extricate herself from Thornhill in her hotel room in Chicago, her garnet choker and ring signal "red light" warnings. As Russell concludes, "Conventional morality has erred, not in demanding self-control, but in demanding it in the wrong place" (239).

The profile two-shots in the Twentieth Century drawing room indicate the separation between the two principals, despite their free agency and free love. Shot with Hitchcock's signature spiraling movement that stands in for sex in *Vertigo*, here the couple rather than the camera revolves, due to the close quarters of the compartment. When they finally settle on the edge of the bed and Thornhill leans in angularly for the kiss, Kendall contracts her torso to curve away from him. The only points of contact are hands and lips, a distance reinforced by her final bit of premarital pillow talk: ". . . you'll be sleeping on the floor" (Lehman 83). Those are the brakes of self-control. Unlike Marian Crane (Janet Leigh) in the following year's *Psycho*, Eve Kendall does not loll about her in underwear, and is not so desperate to marry that she'll "lick the stamps" on the alimony checks. Midcentury domesticity is decidedly not on Eve's agenda, whether the man in her life is Vandamm or Thornhill. Indeed, when questioned by police the next morning about her dinner with the fugitive, Eve refers to him as "Thornycroft"—the antithesis of the rose-covered cottage of domestic bliss. Yet the two have found more unison than impasse in their encounter, and Eve's note to Vandamm is, finally, not as sardonic as she would like. Hitchcock pulls up from practical eye-level to an existential high angle, as Eve acknowledges what has become for her a real dilemma: "What do I do with him in the morning?"

The Prairie Stop scene is notable for its dramatic editing and special effects, but in terms of the marriage plot it little serves the film narrative. After Thornhill's agile escape from the fireball of crop duster and oil tanker, he flees back to the city in a narrow bed pickup stolen from a farmer. He needs the truck, but the humble refrigerator in the back creates the joke. When Thornhill returns to his natural urban environment, the pickup and the "lonely" refrigerator stick out like a sore thumb, parked on Michigan Avenue near the posh Ambassador East in Chicago (Lehman 100). The refrigerator and the homely farm folk who stop to see the conflagration visually associate rurality with domesticity. These grangers look offscreen left as Thornhill backs out of frame right to steal the truck. They form a four-part tableau in profile, anticipating Thornhill's ultimate destination in the hunt for George Kaplan: Mount Rushmore.

The harrowing rural experience, capped by a homespun image of domesticity, leads directly to a reunion with Eve in a room that visually suggests a path to marriage. While George Kaplan's room 743 in the Plaza contained two single beds (he does have dandruff and a misshapen suit, after all), Eve's room 463 in the Ambassador East prominently displays an extra-large "matrimonial" bed as backdrop to Thornhill and Kendall's first reunion. The Asian décor also features two hybrid male-female Kannon figures on the credenza, poised between a rather nuptial arrangement of white carnations and gladiolus, and a television with remote control carefully positioned for watching in bed. This is not a spinster's room by any stretch of the imagination, even before we see the fully stocked bar and the commodious marble bathroom off the bedroom.

When Roger appears at her hotel room, Eve runs across to embrace him. We are meant to see the revelation of her attachment to him in her relief at his survival. Roger stands rigidly disengaged from her. While they stand erect, body to body, there is no sense of union or shared space. His sense of betrayal is palpable, and plural: sexual, physical, and emotional. He is unwilling to bend, blaming Eve for the elaborate wild goose chase for Kaplan and his own near-immolation. When he decides to change tactics, his posture loosens just as hers stiffens in the wake of the phone call from her "clients." Russell termed unmarried sexually active adults "emancipated" and "incontinent," evoking their uncontained natures more than their propensity for accidents. Thornhill and Kendall in this scene exhibit incontinent behavior, indeed. He attempts to re-seduce her, and she makes a point of shrugging off their intimate encounter: "We're *not* going to get involved. Last night was last night and that's all there was, that's all there is, there isn't going to be anything more between us. So please—goodbye, good luck, no conversation. Just leave" (Lehman 119). Her casual dismissal of the night of passion on the train is dismissed equally casually by Thornhill with "unh-uh." They both change tactics, she agreeing to dinner and he to freshening up. Fair is fair, as he says. The sexualized banter, spoken in front of the broad expanse of the bed, has a slight edge this time: "what could a man do with his clothes off for 20 minutes?" This line is nearly menacing in Roger's insistence on keeping Eve in the room. Yet Eve's take-charge—and decidedly not maternal—attitude toward Roger's undressing leads him to ask, coldly, "How does a girl like you become a girl like you?" Her flirtatious response elicits a barrage of condemnations that are in no way seductive: naughty, wicked, up to no good, tease. Sexual openness is not the problem, but lack of fair play among consenting adults is. That bed will remain made. Thornhill opts for the ruse of the cold shower while Kendall makes her escape to Vandamm, carefully tucking the auction house address in her evening bag alongside the usual feminine miscellanea: lipstick, compact, .25 automatic pistol. Kendall and Thornhill each relies on deception to evade the pull of the other, serving their own agendas after being mistaken in each other. Such is the case with emancipated adults in this Hitchcockian world: there are more things in heaven and earth than are dreamt of in Russell's philosophy.

The auction scene again places the couple in a setting imbued with domesticity—or its trappings, at any rate. Thornhill follows Kendall to Shaw and Oppenheim Galleries on Michigan Avenue, where an auction of high-end home furnishings is in progress. Purportedly "from the collection of Dr. Orlando Mendoza," the various lots suggest little that is Hispanic until Lot 105, the Pre-Columbian figure from Colima. When Thornhill enters the room to discover Kendall literally under the thumb of Vandamm, the melodrama plays out against the visual and aural backdrop of the auction. As the auctioneer announces a "magnificent pair of Louis XVI *fauteuils*," we see Vandamm's hand stroking Kendall's neck in an over-the-elbow medium closeup. In an unbroken pullaway and traveling pan shot, the camera moves toward Thornhill as he stands in the entrance to the auction hall, getting his bearings. He spots the spy tableau and crosses to them. As he approaches them, Thornhill compares Vandamm, Kendall, and Leonard to "a picture only Charles Addams could draw"—a domestic corruption altogether. Meanwhile, the auction proceeds. Each fine art piece in the catalog bears some metonymic relation to Eve, and thus fuels Roger's fury at finding her in the company of the man who has now twice tried to kill him. Her New Look–style petticoated dress is as "upholstered in pure silk damask" as the *fauteuils* and the "lovely Aubusson settee" that follows them onto the block. Lest we miss the association, as the Colima figure comes up and Vandamm directs Leonard to bid, Thornhill remarks, "(looking down at Eve) 'I'll bet you paid plenty for this little piece of—sculpture—'" (Lehman 115). Thornhill's sarcasm vents his anger at Eve's perfidy, but also betrays his nascent jealousy. Russell cautions:

> Among modern emancipated people the serious sense with which we are concerned is suffering a new danger. When people no longer feel any moral barrier against sexual intercourse, . . . they get into the habit of dissociating sex from serious emotion and feelings of affection; they may even come to associate it with feelings of hatred. (127)

The ethical position here is that sex without love *is* hateful, as Thornhill pointedly reminds the Professor once he is made to understand Kendall's double-agency. Eve and Roger will resolve these issues at Mount Rushmore, but not before revelations about Eve's mission realign their relationship as a high-stakes moral venture wholly apart from personal considerations.

The film's third act shifts the moral tenor from domestic relations to domestic security. This plot shift also diverts focus from the principals' distance from midcentury marriage mores. Their hitherto "emancipated" lives recede in the face(s) of national need. Eve says that the Professor's approach was "the first time anyone ever asked me to do anything worthwhile;" the same applies to Roger once he knows what is at stake (Lehman 142). Stephanie Coontz reports that contemporary resistance to the midcentury marriage ethic could be viewed as seditious in "the rigid Cold War atmosphere that associated questioning marriage or gender roles with support for communism" (*Marriage* 235). Kendall and Thornhill's elaborate performance for Vandamm's benefit leaves no doubt with the audience about their civic sentiments.

At Mount Rushmore, the philosophy of marriage temporarily defers to the philosophy of patriotism for both plot and ethical reasons. With the dead presidents as a backdrop, Kendall and Thornhill must set aside their personal agendas and work together for national security. Marriage models have no place in this scenario—there are no first ladies on a wall near Mount Rushmore. The site is dedicated to the ideals of the founding fathers for, as Russell sagely notes, modern men "wish to achieve greatness rather through their position in the State than through possession of a numerous progeny" (32). The spy plot plays out under the noses of historic leaders to emphasize the higher ethic. Once the nation is secured, the individual can sort out his and her relationship woes.

As noted, the cafeteria at Mount Rushmore is full of family groups and pairs of men and pairs of women: surprisingly few male-female couples populate the concession. This is fitting, given the shift from affairs of the heart to affairs of state. When Vandamm, Kendall, and Leonard enter the dining room, Thornhill pointedly refuses even to speak with Eve in the vicinity, raising the tension and the stakes for Vandamm and distilling the dramatic moment of this play-within-a-play. The medium-long establishing shot cuts to a medium two-shot of Thornhill and Vandamm after Eve stalks offscreen, offended by Thornhill's contempt. A quick cut to Leonard and back to Thornhill and Vandamm reminds us that this is a discussion among men. There is no place for gender equality in Vandamm's world: men are the deciders. This is just another indication of his corrupt evil, within the world of the film. With the goal of convincing Vandamm of his animus, Thornhill offers his deal: in exchange for not telling what he knows, he gets "the girl" to deliver to the police. Even when she returns to the scene, the geometry of the shot triangulates the major characters so that Eve is not coupled in frame with either man until the shooting is imminent. As Thornhill pulls her away from Vandamm out of frame left, Leonard holds Vandamm in place. The couples are defined by the level of risk they will embrace. The cut is to a leftward tracking pan of Thornhill leading Eve as she fumbles in her bag for her pistol. They move together, even more in unison than in the train aisle because they now share a higher purpose.

The staged shooting that concludes this play for Vandamm's benefit allows the personal and political to coalesce, clearly settling for the audience the question of the principals' loyalty. Freedom in adult relationships does not entail a sacrifice of principles in the world of the film, and the union of Kendall and Thornhill ultimately serves the greater good because they two alone can stop Vandamm and make the country free for democracy. Russell would view this kind of teamwork as the optimal relationship. Leonard and Vandamm skulk offscreen right, leaving Eve to her own devices and revealing their view of her as disposable—a view that is anathema to the film's moral and marriage philosophy.

The scene in the woods near Mount Rushmore places the couple alone, under watch of the monument, discussing their hurt feelings and disrupted relationship as a casualty of (Cold) War. Such bower scenes are a staple of the genre and lay the foundation for the spectacle of union that concludes the marriage plot: if they live, the plot is comic; if they die, like Romeo and Juliet, it is not. Here the dialogue is devoid of the flirty double entendres of the scenes on the Twentieth Century and in the Ambassador East, as both Eve and Roger know that their time is limited. Finally they are able to have a frank conversation about their circumstances. After Eve explains her past as a result of involvement with men like him "who don't believe in marriage," Roger can say, tenderly, "I may go back to hating you again. It was more fun" (Lehman 143). Thornhill can make such a quip now, because the danger that Russell predicted—paradoxically emancipated hurt feelings—has passed. The jealousy that colored the auction scene is dissolved, as is the question of divided loyalty.

The teamwork required of Roger and Eve in their escape from Vandamm reflects the *détente* they have reached in the cross-country process of sorting out their relationship. Despite her continuing with the charade of departure right up to the door of the plane, at the sound of gunshots Eve will snatch the "pumpkin" and flee with Roger, taking the microfilm-filled figure on their race across the faces of America. Their combined efforts allow each to be redeemed from their moral ambiguities in the process. As they begin moving across the heads of the monument, Eve falls into the gothic role of imperiled heroine, hampered by her shawl, then her jacket, shoes, and handbag. As they move closer to absolute interdependency, the feminine aspects of her costume fall away so that Roger and Eve can function as equals in the escape from Vandamm's henchmen. Lehman's shooting script refers to this shedding as a "striptease" (176), although its purpose is neither titillating nor provocative: Eve loses the encumbrances of her role as double agent, just as Roger was relieved of his gray flannel suit in the Rapid City hospital. Free of the respective personae they brought to the world of the film, the couple can now define themselves together as freedom fighters or outraged citizens or equal partners. Coontz traced public sentiment in the 1950s, finding that "[t]hroughout the decade, calls for partnership and mutuality in marriage alternated with public handwringing about whether people were taking these ideas to extremes . . . even 'near equality' must not be allowed to get out of hand" (*Marriage* 239). Partnership is the only defense against "the Vandamms of the world" (Lehman 144), but Roger and Eve have things well in hand, as the final sequence of the film reveals.

The flight across Mount Rushmore takes the pair across Jefferson's forehead, and down between the first and third presidents, charting a journey between Washingtonian federalism and Jeffersonian democracy writ large. As they clamber, slide, and slip between the American colossi, Roger and Eve negotiate a union of free agents that carries them from Washington's notion of "temporary alliances for extraordinary emergencies" (Farewell par. 41) to Jeffersonian principles of the collective good, "where every man . . . would meet invasions of the public order as his own personal concern" (Inaugural). As they cling by their fingers to the tiered side of the blasted rock, national and domestic concerns become aspects of same ethic. Here Thornhill and Kendall are alone together as they were in the forest scene, and able to discuss their situation with an honesty born of their state of suspension:

> THORNHILL: If we get out of this alive, let's go back to New York on a train together. All right?
>
> EVE: Is that a proposition?
>
> THORNHILL: It's a proposal, sweetie.
>
> EVE: What happened to the first two marriages?
>
> THORNHILL: My wives divorced me.
>
> EVE: Why?
>
> THORNHILL: I think they said I lived too dull a life.[5]

With the principals suspended between life and death, Hitchcock resorts to the marriage plot to resolve their situation. When Thornhill pleads with Leonard to help them up the cliff face, Leonard's response is to crush Thornhill's uphill hand, symbolically grinding the fingers under the sole of (Communist) oppression. This impasse can end only in violence, as the threat must be dispatched and the spectacle of union preserved. Vandamm loses both partners, Leonard and Eve, with one shot from a Park Service sniper. His corrupt model of emancipation cannot prevail once he plots to resolve his sexual jealousy "from a great height . . . over water" (Lehman 157).

Rather than ending with a saccharine taffeta wedding, Hitchcock opts for a match cut that sums up the relationship without exposition. As Thornhill struggles to pull Kendall to safety up the Mount Rushmore cliff, an extreme closeup of Thornhill against the deep blue South Dakota night sky unobtrusively becomes an extreme closeup of Thornhill against the blue Twentieth Century train compartment ceiling. He finally hoists "Mrs. Thornhill" to safety in the upper berth, thus satisfying the comic and dramatic plots in one short phrase. As they speed back to New York from the social and cultural parochialism of Middle America, Eve has traded her name and her costume for a new iteration of companionate

Figure 13.2. Thornhill (Cary Grant) and the new Mrs. Thornhill in their berth.

marriage. She hops into the upper berth, no longer dressed in either spy-girl jewel tones nor matronly mud colors. Hitchcock being Hitchcock, of course, reserves the last uxorious joke for himself. The train racing into the tunnel in the final shot ends the thriller with a knowing wink about the couple's legitimated sexual relationship. Hitchcock's philosophy of marriage, like Bertrand Russell's, espouses a union of equals serving the greater good of domestic security won through trouble and strife. And the wife, in this brave new world, is wearing pants.

Notes

    1. Bertrand Russell, *Marriage and Morals* (New York: Liveright, 1929; rev. ed, 1970), 76. Subsequent references to this work will be made parenthetically in the text of the essay.

    2. Thomas Leitch argues that these films are linked by their exploration of "personal disintegration" (189) in the stories of Scottie, Thornhill, and Norman Bates. They also, of course, form a triptych of portraits of untenable marriages.

    3. *The New York Times* of July 5, 1958, reports: "The $2 window at local race tracks caters to the more conservative gamblers in town. The stakes are somewhat higher at another $2 window, on the second floor of the Municipal Building, where *hopeful couples are licensed to play a realistic version of You Bet Your Life*" (emphasis mine). Note the sardonic tone worthy of Roger Thornhill. My thanks to Mary Feeney, University of Arizona Libraries, and the New York Public Library reference staff for confirming this amount.

4. Thomas M. Leitch associates "red, rust, and earth tones" (208) with mothers and mother-functions in the women surrounding Thornhill. He sees the film as a "comedy of homelessness" rather than a discourse on marriage, although Thornhill's journey home and his path to companionate marriage are ultimately the same. Eve, despite her name and womblike compartment on the train, shows no interest whatsoever in mothering Roger. Her industrial designs are not domestic.

5. This dialogue is transcribed from the film, as it varies from the Lehman shooting script.

Works Cited

Cavell, Stanley. "*North by Northwest.*" *Critical Inquiry* 7.4 (Summer 1981): 761–76.

Coontz, Stephanie. *Marriage, a History: How Love Conquered Marriage*. New York: Penguin, 2005.

———. *A Strange Stirring: 'The Feminine Mystique' and American Women at the Dawn of the 1960s*. New York: Basic Books, 2011.

Gilbert, Nora. "'She Makes Love for the Papers': Love, Sex, and Exploration in Hitchcock's Mata Hari Films." *Film & History* 41.2 (Fall 2011): 6–18.

Jefferson, Thomas. "First Inaugural Address." *The Papers of Thomas Jefferson* 33.17 (February to 30 April 1801). Princeton, NJ: Princeton UP, 2006: 148–52.

Lehman, Ernest. Shooting Script for *North by Northwest*. 1958.

Lehmann, Ulrich. "Language of the PurSuit: Cary Grant's Clothes in Alfred Hitchcock's 'North by Northwest.'" *Fashion Theory* 4.4 (2000): 467–86.

Leitch, Thomas M. *Find the Director and Other Hitchcock Games*. Athens: University of Georgia Press, 1991.

McGilligan, Patrick. *Alfred Hitchcock: A Life in Darkness and Light*. New York: Harper Collins, 2003.

Millington, Richard H. "Hitchcock and American Character: the Comedy of Self-Construction in *North by Northwest*." *Hitchcock's America*. Ed., Jonathan Freeman and Richard Millington. New York: Oxford UP, 1999.

Russell, Bertrand. *The Autobiography of Bertrand Russell*. Boston: Little, Brown, 1967. 3 vols.

———. *Marriage and Morals*. New York: Liveright, 1929; rev. ed., 1970.

Washington, George. "Farewell Address." September 17, 1796. https://www.senate.gov/artandhistory/history/minute/Washingtons_Farewell_Address.htm

Wexman, Virginia Wright. *Creating the Couple: Love, Marriage, and Hollywood Performance*. Princeton, NJ: Princeton UP, 1993.

14

Neil Sinyard

"The Loyalty of an Eel"

Issues of Political, Personal, and Professional Morality in (and around) *Torn Curtain*

Hitchcock's fiftieth film, *Torn Curtain* (1966), has had some bad press over the years, being vilified for its dull leading performances, its ponderous narrative. and its simplistic Cold War politics. Although the screenplay is credited to the distinguished novelist Brian Moore (for twenty years, Hitchcock's most prestigious literary collaboration), it is a matter of record that Hitchcock was unhappy with the script and brought in the writing team of Keith Waterhouse and Willis Hall to spice up the dialogue. This in turn led to a dispute over the final credit, with, according to Waterhouse, "Hitch campaigning valiantly for our names to be included on the final credits . . . we were campaigning just as vigorously to have our names kept right out of it" (Waterhouse 200).

The film has been seen as a rather tired addition to the vogue at that time for spy thrillers—falling between the two stools of James Bond and *The Spy Who Came in from the Cold*—and as an inferior version of the magnificent *Notorious* (1946) in its exploration of emotional deceit and betrayal in a treacherous political context. Yet, though I would not claim *Torn Curtain* to be one of Hitchcock's major achievements, the film is, in my view, more interesting and ambiguous than is sometimes contended. I want to discuss what seems to me the film's quite complex view of morality in both the personal and political sphere, and also to extend the discussion into a consideration of professional morality that led to a parting of ways between Alfred Hitchcock and his composer Bernard Herrmann, thus severing one of the greatest director/composer partnerships in the history of cinema.

The plot of *Torn Curtain* is deceptively simple. An American scientist (Paul Newman), with his reluctant fiancée (Julie Andrews) in tow, has defected to East Berlin so he can continue working on his "anti-missile missile project" (the film's MacGuffin) that Washington has refused to continue funding. However, his real goal is to ingratiate himself with a Professor Lindt—a brilliant East German scientist who seems to have solved the problem that the American has been working on—with the intention of discovering Lindt's formula and bringing it back to the West. There are two curious footnotes to this basic schema. The role of Lindt is played by Ludwig Donath, who was himself a victim of Cold War politics and was making his first (and last) appearance in a Hollywood film since being blacklisted in 1953. Also, there is an odd inconsistency in the hero's motivation, since if, as he claims, the purpose of the project is to bring peace and eliminate the effectiveness of nuclear weapons, why would he need to *steal* the formula in the first place, since both sides seem to be working to the same end?

The first part of the story is seen through the eyes of the hero's fiancée, a strategy that corresponds to Hitchcock's original inspiration for the plot: the defection of the two British diplomats Burgess and MacLean to the Soviet Union and Hitchcock's curiosity about the reaction of MacLean's wife. To whom should she now show loyalty? Had she ever suspected anything? Certainly Julie Andrews's heroine seems a little slow on the uptake. When she is told of the hero's destination, she utters the immortal line, "East Berlin? But that's behind the Iron Curtain!" (Keith Waterhouse pleaded with Hitchcock to cut that line, or at the very least cut the word "but," but to no avail.) Still, she is seeing the hero through a romantic haze and not wanting to believe the evidence of her own eyes. As well as underlining the hero's callousness toward her—we are to learn later that, unlike the East Germans, he does not even know her middle name—this perspective has the effect of allowing the director to subvert Julie Andrews's screen persona, so that her trademark goodness becomes synonymous with gullibility. Significantly, this is emphasized still more in the reconciliation scene when he tells her secretly of the real purpose of his mission. It is filmed as an inaudible long shot against a patently and expressively fake backdrop; and it releases a joy in her that the critic Gordon Gow shrewdly described as "a surfeit of false security," which the very artificiality of the mise-en-scene adroitly emphasizes (Gow 9). It is well known that Hitchcock did not want Julie Andrews in the role (he thought an audience would be expecting her to sing) and that indeed he was unhappy with both of his stars, not least because their huge salaries were eating into his budget and because, in his previous three films, he had been the star, so they were in a sense upstaging him. Given all this, I wonder whether Hitchcock secretly and perversely rather enjoyed undercutting the glamorous image of his expensive leading actors. If Miss Andrews is presented as a gullible romantic and ungallantly referred to at one stage as "excess baggage," this is nothing compared to what Hitchcock does with Paul Newman, who, as the man who knew too little rather than too much, gives quite the most unsympathetic characterization of his screen career.

Gordon Gow made an interesting observation on the character. "It is interesting to note," he wrote, "that science rather than politics is his motivation, and that his hero-quality is diminished by a blinkered, obsessive attitude to his work" (Gow 9). Rather like Gary Cooper's hero in Fritz Lang's *Cloak and Dagger* (1945), with which Hitchcock's film shares many intriguing similarities (the big set piece of both is a vicious and silent hand-to-hand fight to the death), he is a spy but does not really know what is involved. He is directly responsible for the only murder in the film (the murder of Gromek in the farmhouse), yet cannot even accomplish that efficiently on his own but needs assistance and has to implicate someone else in the deed. Even with the revelation that he is not really a traitor, his status as hero does not improve: if anything, it grows even more dubious. His mission, which in itself is ambiguous, begins to endanger more and more people, like those people on the bus who, in assisting his escape with his fiancée, are endangering their whole project of sneaking out East Berliners to the West; like the refugee (Lila Kedrova), who offers to help them if they will sponsor her trip to America but whom they leave in the lurch after she has served her purpose; and, finally, like the people in the theater, who scatter in terror when he deliberately provokes unnecessary panic in order to avoid arrest. It is striking how Hitchcock lingers on those moments of chaos that the hero's actions and presence have provoked, consciously drawing attention to them: for example, the bus passengers scattering in panic and running for their lives as the policeman opens fire; or Kedrova's refugee repeating "my sponsors . . ." as she lies injured on the stairs, having helped the Americans escape but being left by them to her surely unpleasant fate. One way of summarizing this would be to say that the American blunders in with his own self-serving agenda; does not have an exit strategy; and leaves chaos in his wake. In the modern political arena, that scenario has a familiar ring. Even at the time of the film's release, when Vietnam was looming ever larger on the nation's consciousness, Andrew Sarris was seeing the film as "at least partly a parable of American meddling in the world" (Sarris 58) In that context, it would not to be too fanciful to also recollect Brian Moore's admiration for his literary mentor, Graham Greene, and to see the screenplay as his variation, ten years on, of Greene's novel *The Quiet American* (1955).

Why is all this being done? Sarris was particularly struck by the absence of what he called the obligatory scene in which the hero is instructed that he is acting on behalf of national security. (There are such scenes in *Notorious*, for example.) Indeed it goes even further than just absence: the hero explicitly discloses that Washington, having abandoned his program, knows nothing about his mission behind the Iron Curtain. The reason for his supposed defection is to pick the brain of someone who is cleverer than he is from motives that are more personal than political and not altruistic so much as egotistical. Hitchcock seems to have viewed this character as a sort of Werner von Braun figure for whom the pursuit of science overrides all considerations of conscience, loyalty, and patriotism. One thinks of the famous Dr. Johnson maxim: "Knowledge without integrity is dangerous and dreadful."

The dubious morality behind what he is doing is particularly emphasized in the big scene between him and Lindt, where they are putting formulae on the blackboard and trying to tease out what the other knows—a kind of mathematical arm-wrestling, what one might call dueling egos. One of the striking things about the scene is that Lindt is not just one step ahead, which would at least offer the possibility of the American scientist eventually catching up, but at a strategic point he demonstrates a completely original approach that the hero, from his dumbfounded expression, would clearly never have thought of in a million years. After the initial shock, his response is to try and memorize it—not an act of patriotism but of plagiarism. This is a hero who lies to his fiancée, ignores and endangers others, and steals someone else's work to satisfy his scientific ambition. He would sell his soul, it seems, for ultimate knowledge: he is Faust.

The scene that, more than any other, clinches this connection is the scene at the ballet toward the end, when hero and heroine are in hiding from the police. (Parenthetically, one might recall that the film is designed by Hein Heckroth, Powell and Pressburger's designer on their 1948 ballet classic, *The Red Shoes*, which also has a subtext of plagiarism and Faust.) Our hero has stolen Lindt's secret formula but, as if

Figure 14.1. *Torn Curtain*—blackboard scene.

to underline the ignoble manner of his actions, his means of escape have become increasingly ignominious. No ingenious Bond-like inventions and contraptions for him—the hero's flight from danger is by bicycle, then bus, and finally basket, under cover of theatrical costumes, as if to emphasize his charlatanism. As he and the heroine wait anxiously in the audience during the ballet performance for their cue to escape, they are spotted by the star ballerina (Tamara Toumanova) in mid-pirouette. Until now, in a running joke of the film, she has always found herself upstaged at airport arrivals and news conferences by Newman's defecting, defective scientist, who, it could be argued, is even more of a prima donna than she is, since all of his behavior seems to have stemmed from his pique at Washington. With the police and Secret Service now advancing down the aisles looking for the fugitives, the hero has to act quickly. Looking at the stage as if for inspiration, he notices some simulated flames made out of *papier mâché*, and he leaps to his feet and shouts "Fire!," immediately creating pandemonium and the opportunity for escape amidst the ensuing panic.

On one level, this is Hitchcock's variation on the famous Royal Albert Hall sequence of *The Man Who Knew too much* (1956), when Doris Day's scream halts a concert performance and foils an attempted political assassination. In a film in which plagiarism is a major theme, it might seem appropriate or ironic that Hitchcock is, in a sense, plagiarizing himself (though he did always maintain that self-plagiarism is a form of style). What is particularly intriguing about that scene, however, is the choice of music. In his book on Hitchcock's use of music, David Schroeder makes no reference to this scene at all in his section on *Torn Curtain*, which is a curious omission given that this is the most striking and significant deployment of music in the film. Jack Sullivan mentions that Hitchcock toyed with using Ravel, Bartok, or Boulez for that sequence, but "finally settled for" Tchaikovsky's *Francesca da Rimini*, at which point, he rightly says, the film suddenly "comes to life" (Sullivan 287). Tchaikovsky's symphonic tone-poem was inspired by an episode from Dante's *Inferno* in which the souls of two lovers are swept into the flames of hellfire and has a dramatic appropriateness at this point in the film that the other suggestions do not have. But was the final choice Hitchcock's?

There is no doubt in my mind that the choice of music at that juncture was Bernard Herrmann's (it is the most Herrmannesque moment in the whole score) and would have been made before his spectacular falling-out with Hitchcock over his full score, on which more in a moment. My conviction on this point has been confirmed by correspondence with Herrmann's widow, Norma, who was also convinced that the choice would have been Herrmann's. "It makes sense anyway," she wrote in a letter to me in February of 1999, "because on the wall of Bernard Herrmann's study is an old engraving of Francesca . . . Benny bought it during the Depression as the music was a great favorite of his. He used to walk past it and stop and conduct in front of it, singing very badly." My feeling is that, just as Wagner's "Liebestod" from *Tristan and Isolde* was Herrmann's key to the mood and theme of *Vertigo*, he sensed that *Francesca da Rimini* fit the mood and theme of *Torn Curtain*, interpreting what Hitchcock had delivered, in other words, not as a tale of heroism and democracy but one of hellfire and damnation. One recalls the credits of the film: fire and smoke billowing out on one side of the screen, faces writhing in agony on the other, as if they are souls in purgatory. One might also recall the hero's angry response when he discovers the heroine has followed him to East Berlin: "What *in hell's name* are you doing here?" (my emphasis).

For many Hitchcock admirers, *Torn Curtain* has a primary significance that is not contained within the film itself but rather indicated by its absence—namely, that this is the film that marked the end of the collaboration between Hitchcock and his regular composer since *The Trouble with Harry* ten years before, Bernard Herrmann. One could argue that this was a far bigger blow than all of the other alleged deficiencies mentioned earlier, since their partnership had developed into one of the most celebrated director/composer partnerships in the history of the cinema, reaching its apex with that astonishing trio of films—*Vertigo*, *North by Northwest*, and *Psycho*—which are masterpieces of film scoring as well as direction. Their conflict also involves issues of morality, loyalty, and betrayal, on both a professional and personal level, which is the reason that a discussion of it is relevant here and is given added piquancy by the themes of the film.

The story has been told many times, but I hope to introduce some fresh perspectives that I do not believe have been raised before. Nevertheless, to understand what happened, it is necessary both to sketch in the background and to retread some familiar ground. Hints of a possible future division between the two had been surfacing even around the time of their biggest collaborative success, *Psycho*, as there had been issues of disagreement that were successfully resolved but might have left niggling feelings of disquiet. Famously, Hitchcock had originally not wanted music for the shower murder, while also recognizing that the whole film depended on the effectiveness of this sequence. Herrmann came up with those screaming violins—perhaps the most effective musical cue in film—and, in essence, proved Hitchcock wrong, which generally was not a wise thing to do. Still, one should give credit to Hitchcock for giving way on this point. Interestingly, Peter Bogdanovich is on record as saying that, when he was at the New York premiere of *Psycho*, the audience was screaming so loudly during the murder that he never even heard the music, so maybe Hitchcock was right after all. At one point Hitchcock was getting cold feet about the film and thinking of cutting it down to an hour to show as one of his television specials. It was Herrmann, particularly, who insisted he should not do that; and what particularly persuaded him was seeing the complete film with the score. In short, Herrmann was becoming very important, the danger of that being that he might be stealing some of the director's thunder (and of course Hitchcock was notoriously loath to give credit to his collaborators). In the end, with *Psycho*, everything worked out triumphantly, but when *Marnie* flopped, the partnership was put under stress as never before. Things came to a head over *Torn Curtain*.

There is no doubt that Hitchcock was under pressure from the heads of Universal and the MCA President, Lew Wasserman, to commission a score that was commercially exploitable, a feature of film scores at that time, as exemplified by the huge success of "Lara's Theme" from Maurice Jarre's score for *Doctor Zhivago* (1965). There was the widespread feeling in the industry that the conventional symphonic score of Hollywood's heyday was now a bit old hat. The pressure would have been intensified by Hitchcock's terror, as Herrmann's widow Norma has described it to me, of what he called "the whizzkids" and of being thought old fashioned and out of tune with the tastes of contemporary audiences. Before, he had always seemed ahead of the game, particularly with *Psycho*, which had been enormously popular and ahead of its time, confounding the studio and many of the critics, who had initially condemned the film but had been compelled to eat their words. Was he losing his touch? Was a new strategy required?

Initially, Hitchcock's decision to keep faith with Herrmann for the new film could be seen as being commendably loyal, particularly since Herrmann was a notoriously cantankerous individual who made no secret of his contempt for the studio's attitude to, and ignorance of, film music. I think it would be wrong to suggest that, as Clive Davis had contended in *The Times* (21 March 2006) when reviewing a concert of Herrmann's film music, that the relationship foundered during *Torn Curtain* because "Hitch's lordly ways had, it seems, been gnawing away at Herrmann for some time"—if anything, it was the other way round. Whatever the niggles over the *Psycho* experience, the swiftness and finality of their falling-out over *Torn Curtain* was a devastating blow to Herrmann and took him completely by surprise. Another mistake (reiterated in Howard Goodall's otherwise splendid 2006 program on Bernard Herrmann televised in the UK) has been the suggestion that, after the *Torn Curtain* debacle, Herrmann was seized on by Francois Truffaut to write the score for *Fahrenheit 451* (1966). In fact, Herrmann had been commissioned for the Truffaut film before the Hitchcock film; and indeed there is a letter by Truffaut to Hitchcock (November 18, 1965) that deepens the mystery of their subsequent split. "In London," Truffaut wrote, "I met Bernard Herrmann who will be writing the score for *Fahrenheit 451*. We had a long talk together about you and I feel that, in him, you have a great and genuine friend" (Truffaut 290). It should not be forgotten that the break-up was not simply a professional blow but, for both men, a severe personal loss. Herrmann was undoubtedly one of Hitchcock's closest friends in the film community, and vice versa; and both were experiencing emotional turmoil in their private lives at this time, so mutual friendship and support would have been particularly valued. Something seismic must have happened.

The exchange of telegrams between them about the upcoming score makes interesting reading (McGilligan 673–74). Although remaining loyal at this stage to Herrmann, Hitchcock had expressed his disappointment at the composer's recent score for the film *Joy in the Morning* (1965), which he had found repetitive and derivative, and demanded a different approach that recognized, as had European filmmakers, a new audience that was "young, vigorous and demanding" and required a score that had "a beat and a rhythm." "If you cannot do this," he concluded, "then I am the loser" (words that, one could say, would come back to haunt him). Herrmann seemed unfazed by this and responded with enthusiasm: "Delighted to Compose Beat Score for Torn Curtain. Always Pleased to Have your Views." Whether Herrmann quite understood what Hitchcock meant is a moot point. It is certain that Hitchcock was not satisfied with this reply, as he had a production assistant send a further cable to Herrmann saying that these were not Hitchcock's "views" but his "requirements." Nevertheless, were these requirements specific enough? He had told Herrmann that the score should be modern, and that, as he put it, "the main title should be exciting, arresting and rhythmic." Herrmann's main title music was all of these things: what it was not, however, was melodically memorable or evidently commercial. Herrmann went away and wrote the score. In March 1966, the Goldwyn Studios in Los Angeles were booked for two days for the recording of the score, with Herrmann conducting. It turned out to be the stormiest and most notorious recording session in Hollywood history.

Versions of what precisely happened that day have tended to differ. In broad terms, Herrmann started recording the score with the orchestra, and the recording was going well. Indeed, after the playback of the title music, the musicians had burst into spontaneous applause, a rare tribute from seasoned Hollywood musicians, who would have been accustomed to André Previn's cryptic summary of the film composer's perennial dilemma: "Do you want it good or do you want it Thursday?" However, as soon as Hitchcock appeared on the scene, the atmosphere changed. His first sight of Herrmann's orchestra would no doubt have startled him: twelve flutes, sixteen horns, nine trombones, two tubas, two sets of tympani, eight celli, eight double basses, and no violins. He must have wondered where his hit song would materialize from that combination.

Yet why was he there? Was it his usual practice to attend recording sessions? (I have been told that he was not at the recording sessions of *Psycho*, for example.) In his biography of Hitchcock, Patrick McGilligan writes that "Hitchcock kept an appointment with Herrmann in late March to listen to the first recording of the music" (McGilligan 674). However an article on the Herrmann website by Steve Vertlieb (2002) says that "Hitchcock who must have been warned by his spies about the performance, arrived unannounced on the stage accompanied by his assistant Peggy Robertson to listen to the newly recorded cues." It is not entirely clear whether Hitchcock was expected or not. Norma Herrmann has told me that, as a rule, Herrmann did not like directors turning up at recording sessions: his attitude was that, as they had done their job, he should be left to do his. If Hitchcock had been invited and expected, it seems strange that he was not there at the start of the session, particularly as he made specific requirements about the main title music. Also, if he had been invited, would Herrmann have started without him? Or was there another scenario unfolding?

A third version has it that Hitchcock's personal assistant, Peggy Robertson, had preceded his appearance at the session and had been disappointed that an intentionally humorous moment in the opening sequence (the scientists poking at their drinking glasses to break the ice) had not been scored that way (Schroeder 222). Hitchcock then arrived and, before she could express an opinion to him, Hitchcock listened to reel one, and said he had heard enough. Herrmann initially seemed to think that was Hitchcock's usual droll way of expressing approval, and then was thunderstruck when Hitchcock intimated the opposite. A row then broke out between director and composer in front of the other musicians, in which Hitchcock declared that this score was exactly the kind of score he had not wanted, cancelled the session on the spot, and walked out. (Norma Herrmann told me that, according to the principal horn player at the session, Alan Robinson, it was Herrmann who had stormed out first.) Hitchcock went straight over to the head office, apologizing for what had happened, confirming the cancellation of the next day's recording session, and offering to pay Herrmann's salary out of his own pocket to atone for his mistaken loyalty in hiring him in the first place. What has always struck me as extraordinary about that chain of events is that, for Hitchcock, it seems so out of character. Everyone who knew Hitchcock agreed that he was a man who hated confrontations; and yet in this instance, according to some accounts, he had gone out of his way to provoke a confrontation and to cause maximum embarrassment in the process. Surely there would been more tactful and sensitive ways of conveying to Herrmann that, in this instance, his score was unacceptable.

Later that day Hitchcock rang Herrmann, who was still at the recording studio in a state of shock. They resumed their argument, Hitchcock furious at Herrmann for disobeying instructions, as he saw it, and Herrmann angry with Hitchcock for, as he saw it, capitulating to the wishes of studio bosses. Hitchcock would have been additionally angry if he had known then that the composer had written music for a brutal murder scene when the director had expressly told him not to. This was a sensitive matter when one recalls that Hitchcock had originally not wanted music for the shower murder in *Psycho*—clearly he did not want to be proved wrong twice. And there is an odd subtext to this, for the music Herrmann used for this scene was the same as music he had used years before on the Hitchcock TV episode "Behind the Locked Door." Whether Hitchcock ever heard or recognized this musical cue is unclear, but if he had, it would certainly have made him even madder because it would have confirmed his belief that Herrmann was beginning to repeat himself. Herrmann, though, would most probably have said, as he had of his screaming strings in the *Psycho* shower murder: "If you don't like it, don't use it." In any event, according to Herrmann's biographer, Steven Smith, "Both voices were rising; and the conversation quickly ended. It was Hitchcock's and Herrmann's last" (Smith: 273). That last sentence, incidentally, is not strictly accurate, as I will shortly explain.

How, then, does one interpret what had happened? Had Herrmann betrayed Hitchcock's trust by ignoring his requirements and by going along with his own instincts rather than those of the director? Or had Hitchcock behaved with unpardonable insensitivity and rudeness toward one of his most loyal and prestigious collaborators? It has never been entirely clear whether Herrmann quit or was fired, and there are other mysteries associated with the event that seem to go beyond simply the question of creative differences. If Hitchcock was so insistent on requiring a modern or popular hit score, why had he asked Herrmann to do the film in the first place? This could have been loyalty to and confidence in his composer friend, but he must have known that it was a risk: Herrmann was a musician of extraordinary talents, but a commercial melodic gift was not the most prominent of them. Was Hitchcock deliberately setting up a confrontation? If so, why?

Also, even though he had been disconcerted by the sight of Herrmann's orchestra and had disliked the little of what he had heard, why did Hitchcock not at least listen to the whole score? This was the composer's own argument: the sessions have been booked, the musicians will still need to be paid, why don't we just carry on and finish, and if you still don't like it, then throw it out? (He might have added that, after all, audiences did not exactly leave the theater whistling the theme from *Psycho*, and yet there is no disputing the importance of the music to that film's success.) Hitchcock would not hear of it. His behavior was quite unprecedented. There is no other occasion I can recall when a director has halted a recording session in midflow after hearing only one section; berated the composer in front of the other musicians; and essentially rejected the complete score without hearing it. And all this from one of the foremost of all director/composer partnerships. Finally, after ditching Herrmann, why did Hitchcock replace him with John Addison, who was no more likely to come up with a popular score than was Herrmann? David Schroeder argues that, by this time, Hitchcock was cutting his losses and was prepared to settle for a fairly mediocre score (Schroeder 227), but, if that were the case, it seems utterly perverse to wreck an invaluable collaboration and a close friendship and then make do with something second rate—there must have been something more to it than that. More obvious choices to replace Herrmann would have been Dimitri Tiomkin, who was agitating for the job, had worked with Hitchcock before, and had a good track record of popular hits; or particularly, if available, Henry Mancini, one of the most popular composers of the day but who was also very adept at composing thrillers. Ironically, when he did employ Mancini to score his later film *Frenzy*, he was to reject that score as being too much like Bernard Herrmann. Anyone who has heard Mancini's score and compared it with Ron Goodwin's replacement might conclude that Hitchcock made the wrong choice—again.

In the television documentary, *Music for the Movies: Bernard Herrmann* (cited in Sullivan 283), a number of the interviewees, such as Claude Chabrol, see the break-up between Hitchcock and Herrmann as being entirely Hitchcock's fault and that indeed he may even have engineered the showdown. As the musicologist Christopher Palmer suggested, Herrmann was becoming too important to Hitchcock and getting too big for his boots; and Hitchcock, feeling as insecure as only a man with a massive ego can feel, was determined to demonstrate who was boss, and in as public a manner as possible. Hitchcock's most vociferous critic in the documentary was the composer David Raksin, who also seemed to suspect a setup. "He was determined to humiliate Benny," Raksin says, and describes Hitchcock as having "the loyalty of an eel," showing no gratitude toward the man whose music had so enriched his movies. As a composer himself and a close personal friend of Herrmann's, Raksin may well be a partial witness, but he was quite close to the event, Herrmann having showed him parts of the score prior to the recording ("I was amazed at the quality," Raksin told me) and Raksin seeing Herrmann and the leader of the cello section, Edgar Lustgarten, on the day of the recording session after the argument had occurred. In a personal letter to me (17 August, 1999), Raksin gave the following account of what happened:

> According to Eddie Lustgarten, when the Main Title Music was read for the first time, the orchestra responded with great applause, which I can understand, because Benny's music was so remarkable. But when Hitchcock appeared it was a different story. He listened to this extraordinary piece, and shortly thereafter demanded that the session be ended. Benny remonstrated, telling the director that since, in any case, the orchestra would have to be paid, why didn't Hitchcock let him continue the session, after which the director could make his decision. But Hitchcock, apparently determined to humiliate his longtime colleague, refused.

In this letter, Raksin went on to describe a dinner party set up that evening by Lustgarten, Raksin, and their wives on behalf of Herrmann, who had returned home from the session shaken, and had vomited. Herrmann had duly arrived with his dog, Twi, and when the conversation turned to that morning's events, according to Raksin, he had embarrassed everyone by offering a "loopy, obsequious" defense of Hitchcock. "Why are you defending that miserable sonofabitch," cried Raksin, "who really meant to hurt you?" As Raksin put it in his letter: "I don't really think that friends of victims have a right to act offended on their behalf, but I was outraged by the cold-blooded cruelty of that man. Had he no appreciation of what he owed Herrmann for years of exemplary work, music often superior to the contrivances of the director?" Intriguingly, Lustgarten had secretly recorded the entire conversation. It is a pity that, as yet, that recording has never come to light or come to the attention of Hitchcock or Herrmann biographers.

We might never know the full story of what happened that day, but who was in the right? Would Herrmann's score have made a difference to the film's reception and perception? As indicated in the earlier discussion of the use of *Francesca da Rimini* for the ballet sequence, Herrmann seemed musically to be seeking out the film's darker subtext and endeavoring to get behind these cardboard TV characters, as he called them, into something deeper. Would the film have been able to sustain that, or would the score have proved too heavy for the material? David Schroeder has argued that Herrmann completely misinterpreted the tone of the murder scene and that "everything about the scene suggests that Hitchcock not only wanted us to squirm but that the squirm should evoke macabre humour" (Schroeder 225). I have to say that I remain unconvinced by that. It would have involved a massive shift of tone from the somberness that had preceded the murder; the victim, Gromek, is arguably the most sympathetic character in the film (we learn more about him than we do about the hero, and indeed Hitchcock originally planned a later scene to include Gromek's brother to emphasize the hero's guilt and conscience); and in his interview with Truffaut, or anyone else for that matter, Hitchcock gives no indication that this was his intention. The rejected score survives and has been recorded in its entirety twice, which is more than the score that was actually used. It would be very interesting to see *Torn Curtain* in its entirety with the Herrmann music accompanying it, as has been done, for example, with William Walton's rejected score for the DVD release of *The Battle of Britain* (1969).

It has often been claimed that the two never spoke to each other again, and that Hitchcock actually hid behind his office door when Herrmann once turned up unannounced. However, Norma Herrmann (she married Herrmann in 1968) has told me she was actually present at an occasion when they met again, when Herrmann gave Hitchcock a recording of his opera *Wuthering Heights* on which he had been laboring for years. She has also shown me an inscription by Hitchcock to Herrmann on the latter's copy of Francois Truffaut's book-length interview with the director. The inscription is dated 1967—that is, after their falling-out over *Torn Curtain*—and reads "Fondest wishes." Herrmann was to continue to speak fondly and admiringly of Hitchcock even after the break-up; Hitchcock was never again, if it could be avoided, to mention Herrmann's name. In personal terms, the one who came off worse was definitely Herrmann. He was deeply wounded by the split; was genuinely shocked that it had happened; and hoped that his superb 1969 recording of orchestral suites from his Hitchcock scores might serve as an olive branch—to no avail. In professional terms, the loser was Hitchcock. While Herrmann was to be rediscovered by the Movie Brats, Hitchcock's final films were (with the exception of John Williams's charming score for *Family Plot*) indifferently scored. This is a personal opinion, and one with which Jack Sullivan does not concur, but I agree with Claude Chabrol in the *Music for the Movies* documentary when he suggests that the only decent musical moments in Hitchcock's last four films are those that sound like Herrmann.

In his book *The Alfred Hitchcock Story*, Ken Mogg makes the interesting point that Hitchcock wanted to end the film with the American scientist, now safe in Trelleborg, burning Lindt's formula in the fire. "But finally," Mogg wrote, "he bowed to commercial pressures"; and he contrasted this to Herrmann's attitude, where the break-up occurred, he wrote, "precisely because Herrmann had *not* compromised" (Mogg 173). If Hitchcock originally wanted the formula to be burnt at the end, this surely puts paid to any notion that the hero was meant to be seen as acting out of patriotic motives; and the hero's decision to burn the formula could be interpreted as an act of moral redemption. Rejecting this alternative ending, Hitchcock might have succumbed to commercial pressures, but he might also have been thinking that such an ending would negate the whole film and leave an audience wondering what all the fuss was about. Herrmann's score was certainly uncompromising, delivering what he thought was dramatically appropriate. Equally certain was it was not the kind of music Hitchcock thought he had asked for. The score must have seemed to Hitchcock like a provocation, a gauntlet thrown down by the composer to show that he knew better than the director what the film musically required. In the end, it was another case of dueling egos, like the two scientists at the blackboard, each looking to the other to deliver, but fundamentally at cross purposes. When Lindt furiously pulls down the blackboard like a curtain to prevent his American counterpart from reading any more, it seems almost analogous to Hitchcock's calling a halt to the recording session before Herrmann can complete his task. Frustration, anger, a sense of betrayal, ambiguity of motives, and a final sense of incompleteness: Hitchcock and Herrmann were acting out something of the emotional landscape of *Torn Curtain* itself, which is one of the reasons that, with all its faults, the film continues to fascinate.

Works Cited

Gow, Gordon. "*Torn Curtain*." *Films and Filming* (October, 1966): 9–10.
McGilligan, Patrick. *Alfred Hitchcock: A Life in Darkness and Light*. New York: HarperCollins, 2003.
Mogg, Ken. *The Alfred Hitchcock Story*. London: Titan Books, 2008.
Sarris, Andrew. "The Company Man." *Cahiers du Cinema* (May 1967): 57–58.
Schroeder, David. *Hitchcock's Ear: Music and the Director's Art*. New York: Continuum, 2012.
Smith, Steven C. *A Heart at Fire's Centre: the Life and Music of Bernard Herrmann*. Berkeley: University of California Press, 1999.
Sullivan, Jack. *Hitchcock's Music*. New Haven, CT: Yale UP, 2006.
Truffaut, François. *Letters*. London: Faber & Faber, 1989.
Verlieb, Steve. "Herrmann and Hitchcock: The Torn Curtain" (2002): htpp://www.bernardherrmann.org
Waterhouse, Keith. *Streets Ahead*. London: Hodder & Stoughton, 1995.

15

HOMER B. PETTEY

Hobbes, Hume, and Hitchcock

The Case of *Frenzy*

> Whatsoever therefore is consequent to a time of Warre, where every man is Enemy to every man; the same is consequent to the time, wherein men live without other security, than what their own strength, and their own invention shall furnish them withal. . . . and which is worst of all, continuall feare, and danger of violent death; And the life of man, solitary, poore, nasty, brutish, and short.
>
> —Thomas Hobbes, *Leviathan*

> The passion for philosophy, like that for religion, seems liable to this inconvenience, that, though it aims at the correction of our manners, and extirpation of our vices, it may only serve, by imprudent management, to foster a predominant inclination, and push the mind, with more determined resolution, towards that side, which already *draws* too much, by the bias and propensity of the natural temper.
>
> —David Hume, *An Enquiry Concerning Human Understanding*

Hell is a city much like London. The streets are paved with gold and all the maidens pretty. It's the modern Babylon, it's a kindly nurse and the great wen, that great cesspool. It's the epitome of our times. It has everything that life can afford and when a man is tired of London he is tired of life. It depends on one's point of view, none of the foregoing celebrated and hackneyed opinions being entirely true or entirely false.

—Arthur La Bern, *Goodbye Piccadilly, Farewell Leicester Square*[1]

༃

HITCHCOCK'S *FRENZY* (1972) EXPLORES a recurrent theme in his films of the wrong man trapped and imperiled by the power of the State. Blaney (Jon Finch), more fittingly and ironically "Blamey" in Arthur La Bern's novel, must negotiate an unjust world as both agent and acted upon, both free and restricted, and both at liberty and in fear. He wants his freedom and the exercise of his own desires, but at every turn he faces ethical obstacles, usually of his own making: accusations by his public house employer (Bernard Cribbins); disagreements with ex-wife Brenda (Barbara Leigh-Hunt); neglect by former friends, the Porters (Clive Swift and Billie Whitelaw); at times even suspicion from his lover, Babs Milligan (Anna Massey); and ultimately, when accused of serial murder, imprisonment by the State. In his more solemn alcohol-induced, self-pitying reflections, Blaney finds London society nasty and brutish, a world of ruthless competition and distrust. His self-preservation remains his foremost concern. At the same time, Blaney is his own worst enemy, acting out in anger, engaging in verbally violent confrontations with his ex-wife, and motivated almost exclusively by egotism. Clearly, passion controls him more than reason. In short, Blaney resides in a hostile Hobbesian social structure that he understands, like Hume, as unnatural and artificial, springing not from any sense of justice, but rather from self-interest. In *Frenzy*, Hitchcock places before the audience the philosophical dilemma of discerning moral justice in an apparently uncaring, unsympathetic, and overtly unjust world. Through the self-doubts of Chief Inspector Oxford (Alex McCowen), the film presents a philosophical inquiry on justice. The film's resolution, Blaney's retaliatory act of murder against the true serial killer, Robert Rusk (Barry Foster), further confounds the audience about the nature of human justice and morality. Of course, this confusion is precisely Hitchcock's point, to offer a counter theory to Hobbes's worldview and Hume's skepticism.

Frenzy offers a complex narrative of brutality and skepticism. It operates in a clever manner by means of a chiasmus structure, a crossing over of filmic repetitions to forge a connection between the protagonist and his obverse reflection, the psychotic "necktie killer." This chiasmus occurs in nearly every scene, whereby moral issues cross over to their opposite meanings, with the result being an uneasy moral experience for the audience. This obverse mirroring or criss-crossing of contradictory moral sentiments characterizes Hitchcock's cinematic strategy, which relies on sequences of repetitions that challenge the notions of causality and moral certainty.

Structurally in *Frenzy*, Hitchcock plays with the philosophical concepts of skepticism, causation, and moral judgment. While Hitchcock, a devout Catholic, would never embrace a Hobbesian skepticism or Hume's radical dismissal of cause-effect, he is willing to toy with these issues in order to manipulate his audience. The opening credits, with the magisterial helicopter fly-over shots up the middle of the Thames, serve as an homage to the great city, as well as an eye-of-God perspective on human civilization. The credit sequence is a long helicopter shot moving up the Thames to the County Hall across from the Houses of Parliament, where the film cuts to an outdoor political speech being delivered about proposed bills to cleanse the environment. This opening also undercuts any serious allegiance to government, particularly parliamentary rule, as evident by the foppish, ecologically faddish Minister of Health. His speech at County Hall is a perfect example of the irrationality of man trying to transform not only his own errors, but also Nature in the bargain. Cleaning up the Thames was part of the 1970s ethos of Earth Day, which took place one year before the production began on *Frenzy*. Although topical for the early 1970s political fetish for environmental reforms, this speech also makes for dark moral comedy by ironically commenting on the absurdity of man's efforts to transform Nature.

The Minister quotes Wordsworth as he begins his address: "When I was a lad, a journey down the rivers of England was a truly blithe experience—bliss was it in that dawn to be alive, as Wordsworth has it" (Shaffer 1). Of course, this poetic citation is taken completely out of context from Book X of Wordsworth's *The Prelude*, "Residence in France and French Revolution":

> O pleasant exercise of hope and joy!
> For great were the auxiliars which then stood
> Upon our side, we who were strong in love;
> Bliss was it in that dawn to be alive,
> But to be young was very heaven; O times,
> In which the meager, stale forbidding ways
> Of custom, law, and statute took at once
> The attraction of a Country in Romance;

> When Reason seem'd the most to assert her rights
> When most intent on making of herself
> A prime Enchanter to assist the work,
> Which then was going forwards in her name.
>
> (Wordsworth 196)

Here, Wordsworth is caught up in the youthful, hopeful zeal of a sense of a new world dictated by the Enlightenment of Pleasure and Reason, not staid politics and passé custom, but feeling, sensation, and experience. Still, Wordsworth writes of this bliss at the commencement of the transformation in France, before the unspeakable brutality of the September Massacres of 1792. The Minister's misuse of Wordsworth ironically and comically sets the narrative pattern of *Frenzy*, whereby hope is diminished by reality, reason succumbs to overwrought passions, and morality loses out to depravity.

The camera shifts away from the Minister to members of the crowd, who have turned to look into the Thames below, as the Minister's voice fades on a final word: "Let us rejoice that pollution will soon be banished from the waters of this river and that there will soon be no foreign bodies . . ." (2). The natural world of the Thames embankment is analogous to human nature in a very literal sense, since during these ecological platitudes a woman's strangled naked body—a real foreign body—floats toward shore and disrupts the speech. This moment is the first moral chiasmus in *Frenzy*. Having a human body polluting the Thames is certainly the ironic touch of the master's hand, a devious and derisive knock at the numerous riparian cleansings of the post-1968 era. Ameliorating social and environmental problems, however, come down to Hobbesian naked egotism. Upon seeing the body of a necktie-garroted woman on the edge of the Thames Embankment, the Minister drops all pretense of communal oneness and firm commitment to Earth-first rhetoric by instinctually resorting to bald self-interest, as he exclaims: "I say, that's not my club tie, is it?" Such a misplaced causal connection would have amused both Thomas Hobbes and David Hume.

The film then cuts to Blaney tying his tie before he heads down to the bar to steal an early morning brandy at the pub where he works. An ex-military flier, Richard Blaney's fame, glory, and sense of being are predicated on his past warlike state. In the civilian world, Blaney finds only obstacles, misfortune, and suspicion. He also finds it difficult to take any blame (hence, his ironic name in La Bern's novel), even though he is confronted with blame by nearly everyone around him. After being sacked for supposedly pilfering brandy from the bar, Blaney storms out and then wanders through Covent Garden, where he meets up with

Bob Rusk (Barry Foster), a fruit and vegetable dealer, who offers him the solace of a circling in the daily paper a sure-bet racing tip, a horse named "Coming Up," and a box of fresh grapes, neither of which Blaney will enjoy. Blaney's desire for immediate pleasure outweighs his contemplation of future benefit. Instead, he retreats to a nearby pub, orders a double brandy, and then scolds the bartender for not amply filling his glass. From these events, the audience observes a man clearly associated with antisocial behavior. The sequence of events establishes Blaney as a social outcast of sorts, and to the film's audience, a person assumed to be guilty of crimes. Certainly, Blaney is a man quicker to ire and outbursts than to reason. All circumstantial evidence from the outset of *Frenzy* points to Blaney as a man very capable of violent behavior.

In the pub, the causal link between the sexual murder of women and Blaney garners more credibility with the introduction of a conversation between a solicitor and a physician who have entered for a pint and some lunch. As the audience soon discovers, the London world of *Frenzy* is a brutal one for women and for the thoroughly unsympathetic, drunken protagonist, Richard Blaney. The necktie murders have reawakened a sinister, skeptical side to London society. As the two men discuss and make bad jokes about the necktie killings, the camera shots include Blaney in the background and then at the bar, while this visual, causal association, a contingent relationship between the murderer and Blaney, establishes itself for the audience. The scene is typical of Hitchcock's narrative pattern. At a moment when another director would insert cliché exposition, he often includes a scene of two seemingly inessential figures, usually male, who engage in what appears to be conversation unrelated to the main plot of the film, but which in fact resonates with the thematic structure and imagery at the heart of the matter. Such examples include the two police talking in Dr. Brulov's (Michael Chekhov) parlor about caring for one's mother and being ridiculed for it by his boss, Hennessey, thereby reiterating the Oedipal power struggle and problem of male impotency that are at the heart of *Spellbound* (1945) (Pomerance 80–82.) Here, the selection of solicitor and physician represents the dual forms of misjudgment in *Frenzy*, the legal and the psychiatric that will converge to convict an innocent man.

In this scene, the audience acquires some psychoanalytical assessments concerning the types of psychopath who commit rape-strangulation. In Shaffer's script, the doctor explains that these killers are "social misfits," who "appear as ordinary likeable adult fellows, but emotionally they remain as dangerous children," and in a very Hobbesian phrase, "whose conduct may revert to a primitive, subhuman level at any moment" (18). For Hobbes, such a description could well apply to all mankind, since by nature, self-preservation and self-interest are the "free-standing, primitive moral fact" (Lloyd 154). So, the doctor's argument is not limited to sexual sociopaths, especially when he admits that they are "being governed by the pleasure principle" (19). That pleasure principle, by the doctor's own admission, extends to sexual jokes and to the atmosphere of London itself. Overhearing their grim conversation, Maisie, the bar mistress, asks ("hopefully"), "He rapes them first, doesn't he?," to which the doctor responds with an unsettling, sardonic grin: "I suppose it's nice to know that every cloud has a silver lining" (18). London seems to thrive as a kind of hell filled with sexual psychopaths. A long history exists, from Jack the Ripper, who is mentioned in an exchange among crowd members observing the naked body in the Thames during the opening scene at the County Hall, to John Reginald Christie, who raped and strangled his numerous victims, not unlike the film's psychopath's *modus operandi*. "We haven't had a good juicy series of sex murders since Christie," the doctor mockingly regrets (20).

Of course, as Hobbes understood about human nature, if that pleasure principle is disrupted or threatened with pain, the reaction can prove to be quite dangerous. It should be noted the Blaney's childish fits of pique overshadow the scene following his departure from the bar, when Bob Rusk, whose name means twice-baked bread used for teething toddlers, shouts down to him from his flat window. In a retrospectively odd moment, Rusk introduces Blaney to his dear Mum, from which attentive audience members *should* recall the doctor's warning about psychopaths as "dangerous children." Rusk inquires about "Coming Up," his twenty-to-one winnings on the sure-bet, which Blaney has forgotten about, although he still has the newspaper. "Coming Up" is another ironic chiasmus in *Frenzy*, since Blaney's world, particularly at this moment, is falling down. As Blaney walks away, his facial expression becomes "savage," and he resorts once again to almost childish wrath, not reason:

> He throws the box of grapes onto the pavement, and stamps on them violently so that they spurt messily all over the place. He storms off up the street. A few yards further on he angrily throws his newspaper into the gutter . . . (22).

Hitchcock, of course, remains typically very playful with causal connections and intentional misdirections of impressions in his films.

As with the pub scene, Hitchcock continually creates visual associations between Blaney and the psychopath. Hume assesses ideas as responses to impressions; in fact, for Hume, no idea can exist that did not derive from a sensory impression or experience: "A blind man can form no notion of colours; a deaf man of sounds. Restore either of them that sense, in which he is deficient; by opening this new inlet for his sensations, you also open an inlet for ideas; and he finds no difficulty in conceiving these objects" (Hume *Enquiry*, 98). Hume's analogies are quite telling for film itself—the sight and sound experience producing the ideas, narrative, and thematic content of film. In *Frenzy*, sight and sound experiences form the basis for two essential diegetic details, both of which occur in types of flashbacks: one involving a montage of images when Rusk realizes that his monogrammed *R* tiepin is missing, and the other being the echoing sound of Blaney's accusations about Rusk that Inspector Oxford recalls as he remains in the courtroom after the verdict has been rendered. In both instances, the audience has already had the experience of the visual montage associated with Rusk's rape of Brenda Blaney and the shouts from Richard Blaney as he was led to the cells.

In order to understand the significant impact of these crucial moments in *Frenzy* from both an aesthetic and moral experience, it is necessary to work through Hume's ideas on perception and causation in relation to film construction. Hume acquired some of his initial conceptualizations of causation from Malebranche. As P.J.E. Kail points out with comparisons between Malebranche's *De la recherche de la Vérité* and Hume's *Treatise on Human Nature*, in particular, Hume reworked Malebranche's arguments on causation, occasionalism (all causes underwritten by God), and necessary connection in order to negate them.

Figure 15.1. *Frenzy*—Rusk's (Barry Foster) flashback post-murder.

Figure 15.2. Oxford's (Alec McCowen) aural flashback of Blaney's (Jon Finch) cries of innocence.

While Malebranche, not unlike Berkeley, locates all force, power, and connection in God's will, Hume defies such a necessity:

> The idea of necessity—which does not represent anything "in the object"—is nothing other than the psychological effect of repeated experience. A veridical impression of necessary connection would make it genuinely inconceivable that an effect not follow its cause, but we have no such experience. Instead association fools us into thinking that we have such an experience, and hence idea, of necessary connection. (Kail 69)

For Hume, the necessity of connection occurs not from a first experience of an event, but rather from its repetition, and even then, one can only make an inference from a memory or an idea, which results from a vague recollection of a sense impression. Hume contends that one cannot conceive of red without ever having seen the color; or, one cannot reason that one object necessarily leads to another's movement, as in a Newtonian motion, without having observed customarily that action. Hence, causal necessity is displaced or misplaced in a spatial region between cause and effect, not in the very objects themselves. For Hume, this amounts to an illusion of sorts, precisely because human beings wish to take from contiguous, associative, and conjoined objects a necessary cause and effect. Hitchcock understands that audiences possess this very same desire, and he exploits it.

Such precisely is the Kuleshov Effect by which audiences' desire necessary connections, relationships, reactions, and cause-effect conjunctions between one image and another. Not that there exists any necessary or sufficient connection, but rather a desire for a connection. Moreover, Kuleshov's Effect is based on the immediate, perceptual experience of the two images that produce the idea of a cause-effect connection when none whatsoever actually exists. As Kuleshov describes the discovery of this realization and its potential for cinema, he presents a case that very well could have come from Hitchcock:

> We went to various motion picture theatres and began to observe which films produced the greatest effect on the viewer and how these were made—in other words, which films and which techniques of filmmaking held the viewer, and how we could make him sense what we had conceived, what we wished to show, and how we intended to do this. At that time, it was wholly unimportant to us whether this effect was beneficial or even harmful to the viewer. It was only important for us to locate the source of cinematographic impressibility, and we knew if we did discover this means, that we should be able to direct it to produce whatever effect was needed. (44–45)

Such is the very basis of film shot selection, editing, and theory of montage. While Hume understands the illusion of cause and effect, Hobbes's philosophy depends on particular causality. Even if Hobbes views causation as multiple, complex, and often indecipherable, there must ultimately be a cause that effected an event, an action, and a result. Seeking that causal connection Hobbes sees as essential to the human predicament: "it is peculiar to the nature of Man, to be inquisitive into the Causes of the Events they see, some more, some lesse; but all men so much, as to be curious in the search of the causes of their own good and evill fortune" (*Leviathan* 12). Both Hobbes and Hume, then, concur that seeking out, inquiring into, and interpreting causes describe an all-too-human condition. In terms of his filmmaking, Hitchcock relies on this very human desire for making connections among a series of images, not only as a way to defer scenes of actual brutality, but also as a means for conditioning his audience to react to distinct images as though they were causally related.

For Hume, what we observe as cause-effect is contingent rather than necessary; that is, it is based on experiential perception, not *a priori* concepts, on a constant conjoining of perceptual experience, not from a transcendent idea of causation. Hume's description of this process corresponds to the theory of film montage: "... we then begin to entertain the notion of cause and connexion. We then *feel* a new sentiment or impression, to wit, a customary connexion in the thought or imagination between one object and its usual attendant; and this sentiment is the original of that idea which we seek for. For as this idea arises from a number of similar instances, and not from any single instance ..." (*Enquiry* 147). Sergei Eisenstein, according to David Bordwell, constructs his theory of *polyphonic montage* along similar lines as Hume's idea of constant conjunction (384). Hitchcock understood the emotional power of creating a moral reaction through the use of Kuleshov's and Eisenstein's editing practices, precisely because by the time of *Frenzy*'s release, audiences had already experienced such editing effects in their film viewing that they were accustomed to drawing cause-effect inferences.

In the case of *Frenzy*, Hitchcock relies on the illusion of cause-effect in order to persuade the audience into accepting the imaginative world of his film. In terms of Hume's concept of causation being an empirical experience, Hitchcock often structures his narrative according to these ideas from Hume. The accumulation of film experiences, the repetition of sense occurrences within the same film, produce the idea of cause and effect. Clearly, Hitchcock relies precisely on Hume's concept of repetition of sensate events to produce the chills and frights in his audience, not by some outlandish surprise, but rather by providing the audience with a sensory experience that later can be called upon as the basis for a series of cause-effect shocks. In *Psycho*, for example, Detective Milton Arbogast (Martin Balsam) enters the Bates's Gothic house, walks up the staircase, and in an overhead shot, the audience witnesses Mrs. Bates's violent knife attack on the all-too-trusting private detective. His tumbling backward, almost suspended in mid-air, intensifies the audience's reaction. Yet, the audience has already observed the incredible shower scene murder of Marion Crane (Janet Leigh) by Mrs. Bates. Arbogast's death, then, is hardly a surprise; rather, it fulfills a causational expectation. The key to much of the Master of Suspense's cinematic strategy lies in just this kind of imposed cause-effect that Hume demonstrated as acquired from repetition and custom. One can review any number of Hitchcock films and discover just this type of causational expectation, the formation of an idea of cause-effect, but really just an associative response to similar film moments.

In *Frenzy*, Hitchcock employs this causational association in several ways. The initial moment is the first necktie body in the Thames, followed by a quick cut to Richard Blaney tying his necktie in the mirror. This associative causation is not at all logical, since the body in the

Thames is not the effect of Blaney's actions. What Hitchcock works into the sequence is a sensory association of contiguous events, thereby making the audience falsely assume a cause-effect relationship. Perhaps in this connection an unconscious moral wariness, even condemnation occurs. By the time Blaney has intruded on his wife, Brenda, at her marital service office, raged against his misfortune so loudly as to alarm her secretary, Monica Barling (Jean Marsh), and later that evening, violently cut his hand at Brenda's ladies club, the audience certainly views Blaney as being less than a morally upright character. At this point in *Frenzy*, Hitchcock has used the accumulation of perceptual experiences to fashion a plausible causal link between Blaney and the violent necktie murderer, as well as to impart a moral denigration of Blaney in the audience's mind. Unlike other Hitchcock protagonists, Blaney's conduct appears reprehensible, not mysterious like the Lodger (Ivor Novello) in *The Lodger*, not heroic like Hannay (Robert Donat) in *The 39 Steps* or Barry (Robert Cummings) in *Saboteur*, not sympathetic like Manny Balestrero (Henry Fonda) in *The Wrong Man* or Father Michael Logan (Montgomery Clift) in *I Confess*, and certainly not comic like Roger O. Thornhill (Cary Grant) in *North by Northwest*. The key to *Frenzy*'s successful moment of disclosure of the real psycho-sexual killer's identity relies entirely on this series of misleading and occasionally false impressions about Blaney's questionable ethics and seeming indifference to morality.

Nearly midway through *Frenzy*, Hitchcock, still employing the same repetitions of sensory experiences, shifts the audience's moral offense from Blaney to Rusk. Hitchcock repeats the scene of violence in Brenda's office, substituting Rusk, the real psychotic killer, for the outraged, abusive husband, Blaney. The audience has already experienced this setting as a site for potential violence—emotional, verbal, and psychological—toward Brenda, which produced a moral distaste for Blaney. The rape and murder scene stands out among Hitchcock's films as his most controversial, but too often critics overlook its intent as his most effective scene for arousing moral outrage and disgust. Rusk enters Brenda's office surreptitiously and walks around in a somewhat domineering, although uneasily overpolite manner as he discusses the agency's refusal to find him a companion. Their exchange occurs through a series of reaction closeup shots. Although seated in a less powerful position, as she was during Blaney's tirade, Brenda does not coax or reason with Rusk, but reacts with an assertive and accusatory tone: "How shall I put it? Certain peculiarities appeal to you. . . . And you need women who submit to them." As Rusk tries to defend himself, that he likes flowers and the like, Brenda becomes more aggressive in her dismissal of his sexual desires, recasting her initial polite but firm stance into rightly moral intolerance by telling him to go elsewhere. At that point, Rusk leans over Brenda's desk and reasserts his dominance by pitching his type of uncomfortable woo: "But this one to me is the best because I like you." Then, in Rusk's most sinister moment, especially after Brenda's understated comments about his sadomasochistic perversity, he proclaims, "You're my kind of woman." At that moment, Brenda unwittingly makes a fatal error by voicing her complete moral contempt for Rusk: "Don't be ridiculous." As she attempts to make a call, in an effort to deflect Rusk's attentions from her, he cuts off the connection. He recovers his composure by standing over her desk and commenting on her frugal lunch as he bites into the apple she has before her. Rusk invites her out to lunch. She hastily agrees, but tries to leave the room with the excuse to wash her hands. At this moment, the rape begins.

Rusk pushes her up against the wall, twists her arms behind her back, calls her "wicked," and throws her down on the black leather couch. Brenda reacts by pushing her assailant off with her legs, but when she tries to flee, Rusk grabs her by the ankle and throws her down again on the office couch. The swiftness of this shot sequence and the focus on Brenda's legs adds to the peril of her predicament, but Hitchcock's focus here is more than mere sensationalism. He is establishing a visual association. When Rusk drags her by her feet back toward the couch, the camera does not reveal her face as she struggles toward the door. Instead, her legs stick out from her dress in a manner like Babs's legs from the potato bag in the lorry. Brenda's kicking Rusk will repeat itself later, in a darkly comic moment of repetition as retribution, with female legs extended from a potato bag smacking Rusk squarely in the face. Similarly, but more intensely graphic than the shower scene from *Psycho*, the rape and murder montage establishes yet another visual association that will produce the image of causation in this scene and later in Rusk's flashback. In seventy-nine shots in just over three minutes (nearly a shot every two and a third seconds), Hitchcock rapidly employs a fragmented series of cuts between Rusk's violence and Brenda's emotional and terrified reactions, conveyed primarily through closeups that accelerate and intensify the horrifying rape and murder. The two longest sequences during this ninety-second scene of penetration focus on Brenda's recitation of Psalm 91, as Stefan Sharff points out in his shot-by-shot analysis of *Frenzy*:

> Presently starts another, most intense separation. Shot 83 is a tight close-up of Brenda's head, looking to the side, she is reciting the ninety-first Psalm: "Thou shalt not be afraid for the terror of the night." In the background we hear the

> "lovely, lovely" mutterings of the rapist (10 ½ sec.). Shot 84 is a close-up of Brenda's bare breast (the same shot as we have seen before). She tries to cover it by pulling her slip. A small diamond studded medallion cross is seen on her chest (4 ½ sec.). Cut (shot 85) back to the close-up as in shot 83. She continues reciting. Rusk's shadow moving back and forth is seen on her right shoulder (11 ½ sec.). (Sharff 191)

By focusing on Brenda for this longest shot sequence of the assault, Hitchcock indelibly imprints the horrific effect of the rape on the victim with a sustained editing sequence, oddly lacking in any music, that includes obvious images (the cross) and sounds (reciting the Psalm) to invoke moral reactions in the audience. Part of the controversy about this rape scene in particular has been its apparent explicitness, even though, like the shower scene in *Psycho*, not very much is revealed. Rather, Hitchcock relies on the audience to draw the causal, and quite disturbing, connections among the sequences of fragmented closeups.

The actual strangulation murder contains forty-four shots in one minute and forty seconds and produces a startlingly brutal rapid sequence of extreme closeups that shift between Brenda's struggle for life and Rusk's horrid panting in near orgasmic pleasure. Many of the shots last less than a second. Again, the fragmented montage of the murder effectively allows the audience to create a cause-effect relationship between separate shots of Rusk and Brenda's face and throat. This technique is essential for the flashback that will occur later with Rusk. At that point in the film, Hitchcock has prepared the audience to imagine a causal sequence because of this previous, very disturbing perceptual experience. The unsettling shot of Brenda's tongue sticking out at a grotesque angle is not simply Hitchcock's invention, but part of Shaffer's script: "THE CAMERA PANS DOWN the face to the tongue which is now thrust out repulsively" (49). This ghastly image repeats with the revealing of the final victim in Rusk's bed, after Blaney unknowingly bludgeons the corpse and then pulls down the covers. Rusk staggers to Brenda's desk, rifles through her purse for money, as he takes another bite from the apple, before picking his teeth with his monogrammed "R" tiepin and departing. The sequence with the fruit and tiepin will also be part of the flashback scene, only done in reverse order.

The brutal rape and strangulation of Brenda Blaney in her office establishes a cause-effect expectation when Rusk invites Babs Milligan up to his second-story flat, and uses the key phrase as they enter: "You're my kind of woman." In a one-minute, self-contained shot, the camera follows Rusk and Babs from the foyer entrance, up the first short flight of stairs, for a few steps on the small landing, up the next short flight to the second story, where Rusk moves ahead of Babs and opens the door; then, the camera reverses the movement down the upper flight, across the landing, down the first story flight, through the foyer, and out the door. Using the editing trick from *Rope*, the cut takes place as an anonymous man walks by carrying a bag of potatoes, with the cut occurring on the potatoes, ironically enough! Heralded by many critics as a masterful touch by Hitchcock, a *tour de cinéma*, this one-minute shot, however, is vital to the construction of *Frenzy*'s narrative and thematic content. In reversing the ascent to a descent, the camera indicates a moral corruption and violation about to occur. The one-minute shot also functions as a kind of memory of the previous rape of Brenda Blaney. The audience never sees Babs's horrific rape and murder, but clearly understands that it will occur. Hitchcock brings the audience's attention to exactly this experiential cause-effect association, since the audience is led visually from the effect back to the cause. The reversal of the camera movement suggests just that idea. According to Hume's contentions about causation, the audience can make this association because it has already observed it before and it has all of the visual connections to formulate the result. In short, Hitchcock conditions his audience to make leaps from cause to effect, even though he need not reveal either in the process. Of course, moral disgust and fear occur as well.

The potato lorry scene constitutes one of Hitchcock' greatest gallows humor film sequences. Again, this scene relies on a series of experiential cause-effect associations and contiguities, as well as a series of repetitions. After depositing the body within the potato sack into the back of the lorry, Rusk returns to his flat, tosses himself on the black leather couch, pours himself a glass of wine, and chews on a piece of bread. The perversion of the bread and wine symbolism repeats the corruption of the Adamic symbolism with the apple in Brenda's office. As at the conclusion of Brenda's rape, Rusk picks his teeth, but discovers to his utter dismay, that his monogrammed "R" tiepin is missing. He scours the room, including opening the bottom dresser drawer and rifling through Babs's things, but to no avail. Hitchcock captures Rusk in a closeup of his face as he recalls Babs's murder in a montage flashback. In twelve seconds of twelve rapid shots, Hitchcock employs a similar technique as when he conveyed Brenda's murder. Because his audience has already experienced that fragmented montage of strangulation, Hitchcock can rely on the previous sensory experience to draw causal connections among the twelve extreme closeups that alternate between Rusk's homicidal action and Babs's defensive struggle. This time, however, the shots are of eyes, mouth, throat, hand, and finally, the tiepin as Babs's hand grabs it. Realizing what has occurred, Rusk rushes back to the lorry.

The repetitions in this lorry truck sequence function with bizarre humor to accentuate Hitchcock's twist on his own narrative convention, the near capture or discovery of an imperial hero, as occurs for Hannay in *The 39 Steps*, Barry in *Saboteur*, and of course, several close calls for Thornhill in *North by Northwest*. There are several dual incidents that bring out comic suspense to the scene: two times the lorry's rear gate is opened, the first when Rusk enters and the second when he comically tumbles out at the pull-out; twice the lorry's rear gate is closed, once when Rusk enters to retrieve his tiepin and later, when the trucker has to insure that no more of the load will spill onto the road; twice Babs's leg, in a grotesque slapstick, kicks Rusk in the face; twice he fears being caught as he sneezes from the potato dust; twice Babs's body becomes exposed to potential witnesses, the first when Rusk must cover her foot and his head from the trucker's view and the second when her leg sticks out from the back of the lorry, which arouses the suspicion of the police on patrol; and twice the lorry's load falls onto the road, first the potatoes, and finally, when Babs's naked body, with her upper torso and head still confined to the potato sack, topples out and is nearly run over by the pursuing police car. When the police uncover her, Babs's eyes are wide open and her mouth is open, almost expressing a hideous *risus sardonicus*, which further adds to Hitchcock's mixture of the frenzied and the humorous. Whenever a moment of dark humor arises, Hitchcock undercuts it almost immediately with a monstrous incident, such as the sound of Babs's fingers breaking as Rusk retrieves his monogrammed "R" tiepin. With these repetitions, Hitchcock forces his audience to anticipate the second, repeated occurrences by means of constructing a causal link. As with his previous scenes of rape, murder, and depravity, visual experiences lead to expected cinematic effects. Moreover, by placing the audience in a very uncomfortable position for the audience, between laughter and repulsion, Hitchcock forces them to question their moral assumptions.

This uneasy shifting of moral responses with humor typifies most Hitchcock films, but it also lays bare the alternating circumstances that produce the binary concepts of good and evil. In the sixth chapter of *Leviathan*, Hobbes catalogues pairs of foundational passions that accord with Hitchcock's emotional divisions in his films: desire and aversion, love and hate, joy and grief. In Hobbes's anatomical analysis of mankind, appetites and aversion do not remain constant, but as the body changes over time, so do they. His observation of the human body being "in continual mutation" leads Hobbes to dismiss the binary and rigid moral categories of good and evil:

> But whatsoever is the object of any mans Appetite or Desire; that is it, which he for his part calleth *Good*: And the object of his Hate, and Aversion, *Evill*; and of his Contempt, *Vile*, and *Inconsiderable*. For these words of Good, Evill, and Contemptible, are ever used with relation to the person that useth them: There being nothing simply and absolutely so; nor any common Rule of Good and Evill, to be taken from the nature of the objects themselves. (*Leviathan* 120)

This shifting dialectic of morality occurs because that is what occurs in nature—motion and change. Man, for Hobbes, is a natural being, and as such, responds to the world and society with a need for self-satisfaction and preservation. Hobbes thus rejects metaphysics in favor of a natural philosophy, as Gary B. Herbert contends: "The natural axiom of human behaviour is nothing more than that man, by natural necessity, desires his own good and shuns whatever is destructive of his well-being" (114). Rusk fulfills the Hobbesian view of passion, since he readily acts on appetite, an immediate satisfaction, and desire, an extended duration for satiability. Hitchcock portrays Rusk in this manner by associating him with the consumption of natural foods—raw fruits and vegetables. Symbolically, grapes, apples, and potatoes represent Rusk's desires, however morbid and twisted, as Dionysian frenzy, sexual temptation, and earthiness and filth. Food for Inspector Oxford, on the other hand, is always a form of aversion. As his wife (Vivien Merchant) brings him new courses, while he discusses the open case of the necktie murders, Oxford observes the *soupe de poisson* with apprehension, shudders at the discovery of a fish head, then eye, then skeleton in his bowl, and reacts visibly shaken when his wife informs him of the contents: "They're Smelts, Ling, Conger eel, John Dory, Pilchards, and Frogfish" (Shaffer 89). Oxford's reaction to the meal simulates the audience's reactions to the crimes—disgust, rejection, and aversion.

Like Hobbes in some respects, Hume has a naturalist or realist view of morality, especially the distinctions between good and evil, which arise from the senses and experience: "To approve of one character, to condemn another, are only so many different perceptions" (*Treatise* 67). In Book III: Of Morals in *A Treatise of Human Nature*, Hume maintains that "moral good or evil" arise from "*particular* pains or pleasures," which relate to "distinguishing impressions" of the senses and experience:

> To have the sense of virtue, is nothing but to *feel* a satisfaction of a particular kind from the contemplation of a character. The very *feeling* constitutes our praise or admiration. We go no

further; nor do we enquire into the cause of the satisfaction. We do not infer a character to be virtuous, because it pleases: But in feeling that it pleases after such a particular manner, we in effect feel that it is virtuous. The case is the same as in our judgments concerning all kinds of beauty, and tastes, and sensations. Our approbation is imply'd in the immediate pleasure they convey to us. (78)

Thus, Hume dismisses arguments purporting that Reason, which he believed was a slave to the passions, controls man's means or ends, thereby removing any theological grounding for morality. In the end, morality of good and evil is as artificial—that is, arising from custom, convention, and tradition—for Hume as it is for Hobbes. To be fair to both philosophers, their skepticism about the cause of morality—metaphysical, theological, natural, or teleological—does not mean that they promote immorality, or even amorality. For Hobbes, morality transforms into a necessary and willing submission to the sovereign or the State. For Hume, morality arises from sympathy, literally a similar feeling, that allows individuals to identify utilitarian ends according to the pleasure or pain they produce and to evaluate them by sentiment, that is, by the passion, not the process of reasoning, experienced.[2] In terms of *Frenzy*, Hume's sympathy and sentiment find their way into the disquieting doubts of Inspector Oxford. Contrary to Hobbes's reliance on the sovereign authority (read the court and the police) to rid society of discord, the State finds its antithesis in the Blaney case, whereby all judicial procedures were based in error, and the result is detrimental to the commonwealth.

Social justice imposed against the supposed serial killer is reversed by means of Inspector Oxford's skepticism, which is the narrative shift that parallels Blaney's escape and his subsequent murderous intent at the film's conclusion. In fact, it is the film's conclusion that requires the most careful examination in terms of assessing Hitchcockian morality. Hitchcock leads the audience to question Blaney's guilt in a moment of perceptual repetition, this time with sound. Court No. 1 of the Old Bailey, where Blaney's murder trial takes place, is given extensive description in La Bern's novel, including the judge's detailed instructions to the jury. Hitchcock, though, wishes to coax his audience into an aural framework that will relate to the visual repetitions of the two rapes. A guard posted outside the inner double doors of the courtroom opens them to admit a barrister, and in that brief moment, the audience can discern the judge's voice asking the jury for its verdict. The door then closes and silences the response. The audience waits in anticipation, listening as carefully for any clue, which occurs with the pronouncement of a sentence for which there will be no hope of release. Then, the door closes again. Blaney's shouts awaken the guard's curiosity, and he opens the door. Blaney screams several times, "Rusk did it!" as guards drag him from the box down the stairs to the cells, in a moment not unlike the reversal staircase scene of Babs's rape and murder. Blaney has been reduced to a Hobbesian man, for whom justice is utterly meaningless:

> To this warre of every man against every man, this also is consequent; that nothing can be Unjust. The notions of Right and Wrong, Justice and Injustice have there no place. Where there is no common Power, there is no Law; where no Law, no Injustice.
> Force and Fraud, are in warre the two Cardinall vertues. (*Leviathan* 188)

Blaney is not alone in questioning Justice. In an overhead shot, the camera observes Blaney thrown into his cell and then cuts to an overhead shot of Inspector Oxford alone in the empty courtroom. In a medium closeup of Oxford, Blaney's voice echoes his accusations against Rusk and his homicidal threats. This aural flashback functions in a similar mode to the visual flashbacks associated with the rapes and murders of Brenda and Babs. Here, instead of an inverted, perverse world dominating, Hitchcock offers a hope for a poetic justice of sorts.

Hume's causation critique and disparity between passion and reason in human understanding extend to dinner conversations between Inspector Oxford and his wife. It should be noted that none of these scenes with the Oxfords at home can be found in La Bern's novel; they are Hitchcock's comic relief, to displace the misogyny and degradation of the rapes and murders. Oxford's predicament, like everyone's for Hume, rests on an inability to make absolute causal connections, even though he *feels* that Blaney must assuredly be innocent. He explains this dilemma to his wife, while she prepares *pied de porc à la mode de Caen* and asserts that intuition not science would have solved the case from the outset: "A woman's intuition is worth far more than all those laboratories" (134). When Oxford confesses the lack of proof pointing to Rusk's guilt, in an exchange that Hume would applaud, the nature of human understanding becomes all too apparent:

> MRS OXFORD: Well, there you are. You told me the man's a sexual pervert. That's why he kept the clothes he put in poor Mr. Blaney's case.

OXFORD (V.O): We've no proof of that.

MRS OXFORD: It stands to reason.

OXFORD: Don't you mean intuition? (135)

In this comic domestic scene, Shaffer sums up Hume's attacks on *a priori* intuition and on the assertion by reason alone for causation. Both lead to inconclusive assumptions, no matter how earnest they may be for seeking out justice. That piece of evidence that Rusk sought from Babs's corpse is never discovered by the police in the film. Since Babs's body was already "deep in rigor mortis," Rusk had "to break the fingers of the right hand," which Hitchcock has Mrs. Oxford unconsciously repeat by snapping a bread stick in two, and then in two again (137). The audience already anticipates this comic repetition at the moment that Mrs. Oxford picks up the bread stick. Because the audience has endured the initial breaking of Babs's cold, dead fingers, this moment repeats, but relieves, that grotesquerie. Moreover, the Oxfords' domestic comedy reasserts normal, heterosexual relationships in a film that exposes the most deviant displays of sexual power. This scene also befits the comedy of errors that British justice has displayed and that made Blaney experience homicidal rage.

In some respects, Blaney has gone a bit mad and experiences a kind of frenzy in the courtroom. Certainly, Hobbes conceived of frenzy as "passions run amok, overvehement by our ordinary standards, and unguided by reason" (Lloyd 187). For Hobbes, madness derives from "conceit or of a sense of inferiority," which, in general, is contrary to "man's wish to take pleasure in himself by considering his own superiority" (Strauss 12). Hume's conception of madness, in part, derives from an inability to distinguish between impressions and ideas, because, like sleep or fever, "in spite of their strong force and vivacity, is that the external objects which the ideas represent are *not present*" (Wright 64). Certainly, to observers in the courtroom, Blaney's searching for the absent Rusk and threatening him with his own brand of justice must appear as a form of madness. Now, Blaney exists in a hinterland between all-out war against society's irrational and unjust conventions of jurisprudence and his own irrational sense to make present what is so wholly absent—justice in an unjust world. As he did in the film's opening sequences, Blaney reacts from passion, not from reason.

In terms of Hobbes's concept of obligation, especially to the State, Blaney is a counterexample in paradox: he wants to oblige authorities and, at the same time, realizes he cannot do so without risking his own life. Hobbesian self-preservation applies here, but not in order to sustain the State, but rather to show the façade which is the State, particularly the judicial system. Of course, Blaney is a Hobbesian man, who seeks no obligation except that which conforms to his concept of freedom, which is a "radically voluntarist doctrine" that is central to Hobbes's "commitment to individuality and individual self-making" (Flatham 71, 72). The problem for Blaney, in both a legal and moral sense, remains his ignorance of the predictable sociopolitical structure of a Hobbesian exchange of "natural liberty for a state of obligation" (Skinner 104). Hobbes himself makes clear in *Leviathan* that the *de facto* obligation to obey ceases when one is no longer protected by the State (Chapter 21). As Jeffrey R. Collins reiterates throughout *The Allegiance of Thomas Hobbes*, in the world of seventeenth-century revolutionary and reactionary politics, Hobbes's ideas on obligation could only be characterized as "an utterly static feature of his political theory, appearing without significant change in all of his writings" (Collins 120). In a Hobbesian world, which is often the world that Hitchcock critiques, even the natural liberty and innocence of the condemned man hardly affect the social construction of society, as Susanne Sreedhar contends:

> These individual acts of disobedience and resistance are unthreatening to the sovereign power, according to Hobbes. Indeed, one of the ways he argues for the true liberties of subjects is by appeal to the negligible consequences of their exercise. The condemned man is still put to death. His resistance, although justified, is political ineffectual, especially since, as Hobbes insists, the sovereign's right to punish the resistance is in no way jeopardized by the subject's right to resist. (160–61)

Blaney's resistance to the judge, as expressed by his repeated claims of his own innocence and his willingness to murder Rusk, have little effect on the imposing and the carrying-out of his sentence.

In fact, Blaney's escape from the prison hospital is inconsequential to the grand scheme of *res judicata*. Hobbesian reciprocity, which is the central axiom of moral reasoning, in the covenant between individuals and the State, hardly extends to Blaney's predicament. He served the nation as a military figure, but found nothing for him upon returning to society; he has a moral compass, but socioeconomic pressures test the boundaries of his commitment to conventional morality. Blaney certainly consents to his obligations to the State, although being accused of gruesome, sexual murders places him within a moral and social dilemma, even though he is not guilty of any of these horrific crimes. This dilemma is precisely Hitchcock's point: How can one obey the Law when the Law fails to seek justice? Or, put another way, how can one obey the Law when it appears to violate the very concept of Law itself? In order for Blaney to survive, he must counter all civil and social customs in favor of the instinct of self-preservation.

The conclusion leaves more questions than it answers. Blaney fakes a suicidal tumble down the prison stairs, lands in the prison wing of a hospital, escapes with the help of his fellow inmates and a swiped physician's lab coat, hotwires and steals a car, and arrives at Rusk's flat prepared to kill him. The causal links that could have produced such an elaborate scheme and execution of that plan remain missing from the narrative. In the ironic world of Hitchcock, Blaney uses his newly acquired tire iron to beat to death an already deceased woman, not his intended target—Rusk. Inspector Oxford arrives to find Blaney standing over the naked, beaten, and strangled woman. The reaction that spreads across Oxford's face perfectly illustrates false reasoning from effect to cause, for he appears to indict Blaney once again for crimes he did not commit while simultaneously realizing the error of his emotional judgment for supporting Blaney's innocence. Just at the moment of arrest, the thumping of a steamer trunk can be heard coming up the stairs. A panting Rusk enters, turns, and realizes to his shock that Blaney and Oxford have caught him red-handed. Oxford's words conclude the film: "Mr. Rusk, you're not wearing your tie." Hitchcock, however, leaves his audience with an ambiguous moral conclusion. Is the world relentlessly bent on aggression, meanness, deception, and self-interest? Is there little chance at proving guilt or innocence, right or wrong, good or evil in the world, without it having an adverse effect? In the end, Hitchcock leaves moral judgments to the audience, which may prove to be as unsettling in retrospect as the feelings induced by the rapes and murders.

Notes

1. Thomas Hobbes, *Leviathan*, ed. C.B. Macpherson (Harmondsworth, England: Penguin Books, 1974): 180; David Hume, *An Enquiry Concerning Human Understanding*, ed. Tom L. Beauchamp (Oxford: Oxford UP, 1999): 119; Arthur La Bern, *Frenzy* (New York: Paperback Library, 1971): 35; this novel was originally published in 1966 under the title *Goodbye Piccadilly, Farewell Leicester Square*. Hereafter these works will be cited in the text.

2. For a discussion of Hume's moral psychology, see Russell Hardin, *David Hume: Moral & Political Theorist* (Oxford: Oxford UP, 2007), in particular his sections on "The Limited Role of Reason," "Sympathy and Moral Sentiments," and "Natural and Artificial Virtues."

Works Cited

Bordwell, David. "Sergei Eisenstein." *The Routledge Companion to Philosophy and Film*. Eds. Paisely Livingstone and Carl Plantinga. Oxford: Routledge, 2009.

Collins, Jeffrey R. *The Allegiance of Thomas Hobbes*. Oxford: Oxford UP, 2005.

Flatham, Richard E. *Thomas Hobbes: Skepticism, Individuality, and Chastened Politics*. Lanham, MD: Rowman & Littlefield, 2002.

Hardin, Russell. *David Hume: Moral & Political Theorist*. Oxford: Oxford UP, 2007.

Herbert, Gary B. *Thomas Hobbes: The Unity of Scientific & Moral Wisdom*. Vancouver: University of British Columbia Press, 1989.

Hobbes, Thomas. *Leviathan*. Ed. C.B. Macpherson. Harmondsworth, England: Penguin Books, 1974.

Hume, David. *An Enquiry Concerning Human Understanding*. Ed. Tom L. Beauchamp. Oxford: Oxford UP, 1999.

———. *A Treatise on Human Nature* in *Moral Philosophy*. Ed. Geoffrey Sayre-McCord. Indianapolis, IN: Hackett Publishing, 2006.

Kail, P.J.E. "On Hume's Appropriation of Malebranche: Causation and Self." *European Journal of Philosophy* 16.1 (2007): 55–80.

Kuleshov, Lev. "Art of the Cinema." *Kuleshov on Film: Writings of Lev Kuleshov*. Trans. Ronald Levaco. Berkeley: University of California Press, 1974.

La Bern, Arthur. *Frenzy*. New York: Paperback Library, 1971. Originally published as *Goodbye Piccadilly, Farewell Leicester Square*, 1966.

Lloyd, S.A. *Morality in the Philosophy of Thomas Hobbes: Cases in the Law of Nature*. Cambridge: Cambridge UP, 2009.

Pomerance, Murray. *An Eye for Hitchcock*. New Brunswick: Rutgers UP, 2004.

Skinner, Quentin. *Hobbes and Republican Liberty*. Cambridge: Cambridge UP, 2008.

Shaffer, Anthony. *Frenzy*, July 21, 1971. Production No. 05110.

Sharff, Stefan. *Alfred Hitchcock's High Vernacular: Theory and Practice*. New York: Columbia UP, 1991.

Strauss, Leo. *The Political Philosophy of Hobbes: Its Basis and Its Genesis*. Trans. Elsa M. Sinclair. Chicago: University of Chicago Press, 1996.

Sreedhar, Susanne. *Hobbes on Resistance: Defying the Leviathan*. Oxford: Oxford UP, 2010.

Wordsworth, William. *The Prelude or Growth of a Poet's Mind* (Text of 1805). Ed. Ernest de Selincourt. Oxford: Oxford UP, 1933.

Wright, John P. *Hume's 'A Treatise of Human Nature': An Introduction*. Cambridge: Cambridge UP, 2009.

Bibliography

Abrams, Jerold J. "Cinema and the Aesthetics of the Dynamical Sublime." *Film and Philosophy*. 2003. 60–76.
Allen, Richard. "*The Lodger* and the Origins of Hitchcock's Aesthetic." *Hitchcock Annual* 10 (2001–2): 38–78.
———. *Hitchcock's Romantic Irony*. New York: Columbia UP, 2007.
Anderson, Lindsay. "Alfred Hitchcock," in *Sequence* 9 (August 1949), reprinted in *Focus on Alfred Hitchcock*, ed. Alfred LaValley. New Jersey: Prentice–Hall, 1972.
Aristotle. *The Basic Works of Aristotle*. Ed. Richard McKeon. New York: Random House, 1941.
Auiler, Dan. *Hitchcock's Notebooks: An Authorized and Illustrated Look Inside the Creative Mind of Alfred Hitchcock*. New York: Avon, 1999.
Baggett, David, and William A. Drumin. *Hitchcock and Philosophy*. Chicago: Open Court, 2007.
Baier, Kurt. *The Moral Point of View*. Ithaca, NY: Cornell UP. 1958.
Barr, Charles. *English Hitchcock*. Moffat, Scotland: Cameron & Hollis, 1999.
Becker, Howard S. *Outsiders: Studies in the Sociology of Deviance*. New York: Free Press, 1963.
Begg, Paul. *Jack the Ripper: The Uncensored Facts*. London: Robson Books, 1988.
Benjamin, Walter. "The Storyteller: Reflections of the Works of Nikolai Leskov." 1936; rpt. in *Illuminations*, ed. Hannah Arendt, trans. Harry Zohn. New York: Schocken, 1969: 83–109.
———. "What Is the Epic Theater? (II)," in *Selected Writings* Vol. 4 1938–1940. Trans. Edmund Jephcott and Others, Ed., Howard Eiland and Michael W. Jennings. Cambridge: Harvard UP, 2003, 302–09.
Borde, Raymond, and Etienne Chaumeton. *A Panorama of American Film Noir, 1941–1953*. Trans. Paul Hammond. San Francisco: City Lights, 2002.
Bordwell, David. *Narration in the Fiction Film*. Madison: University of Wisconsin Press, 1985.
Bordwell, David. "Sergei Eisenstein." *The Routledge Companion to Philosophy and Film*. Eds. Paisely Livingstone and Carl Plantinga. Oxford: Routledge, 2009.

Borges, Jorge Luis. *Ficciones*. New York: Grove Press, 1962.
Breuer, Josef, and Sigmund Freud, *Studies on Hysteria*. Trans. J. Strachey, in collaboration with Anna Freud. Basic Books, n.d.
Brill, Lesley. *The Hitchcock Romance: Love and Irony in Hitchcock's Films*. Princeton, NJ: Princeton UP, 1988.
Canguillhem, Georges. *The Normal and the Pathological*. Trans. Carolyn R. Fawcett and Robert S. Cohen, foreword by Michel Foucault. New York: Zone Books, 1991.
Carroll, Noël. *Mystifying Movies: Fads & Fallacies in Contemporary Film Theory*. New York: Columbia UP, 1988.
Cavell, Stanley. "*North by Northwest*." *Critical Inquiry* 7.4 (Summer 1981): 761–76.
Cerf, Bennett, ed. *Three Famous Murder Novels: Before the Fact, by Francis Iles; Trent's Last Case, by E.C. Bentley; The House of the Arrow, by A.E.W. Mason*. New York: Modern Library, 1941.
Chabrol, Claude. "Hitchcock devant le mal." *Cahiers du cinéma* no. 39 (1954): 18–24.
———. *Hitchcock: The First Forty-Four Films*. Trans. Stanley Hochman. New York: Ungar, 1979.
Chabrol, Claude, and Éric Rohmer. *Hitchcock*. Paris: Cahiers du cinéma, 1957.
Cohen, Paula Marantz. *Hitchcock and the Legacy of Victorianism*. Lexington: University of Kentucky Press, 1995.
Collins, Jeffrey R. *The Allegiance of Thomas Hobbes*. Oxford: Oxford UP, 2005.
Coontz, Stephanie. *Marriage, a History: How Love Conquered Marriage*. New York: Penguin, 2005.
———. *A Strange Stirring: "The Feminine Mystique" and American Women at the Dawn of the 1960s*. New York: Basic Books, 2011.
Copplestone, Frederick. *A History of Philosophy: 18th and 19th Century Philosophy, Volume 7*. New York: Continuum, 2003.
Currie, Gregory. *Image and Mind: Film, Philosophy and Cognitive Science*. New York: Cambridge UP, 1995.
Danto, Arthur. *The Philosophical Disenfranchisement of Art*. New York: Columbia UP, 1986.
———. *After the End of Art: Contemporary Art and the Pale of History*. Princeton, NJ: Princeton UP, 1997.
———. "The End of Art: A Philosophical Defense." In *History and Theory*, vol. 37, no. 4. Theme Issue 37: *Danto and His Critics: Art History, Historiography and After the End of Art*. December 1998.
———. *Philosophizing Art: Selected Essays*. Berkeley: University of California Press, 1999.
Deleuze, Gilles. *Cinema 1: The Movement–Image*. Trans. Hugh Tomlinson and Barbara Habberjam. Minneapolis: University of Minnesota Press, 1986.
———. *Cinema 2: The Time–Image*. Trans. Hugh Tomlinson and Robert Galeta. Minneapolis: University of Minnesota Press, 1989.
de Rougemont, Denis. *Love in the Western World*. Trans. M. Belgion. New York: Harper & Row, revised and augmented edition, 1974.

Deutelbaum, Marshall and Leland Poague. *A Hitchcock Reader*. Ames: Iowa State UP, 1986.

Dixon, Wheeler Winston. *The Early Film Criticism of François Truffaut*. Bloomington: Indiana UP, 1993.

Douchet, Jean. *Hitchcock*. Paris: Éditions de l'herne, 1967.

Durgnat, Raymond. *The Strange Case of Alfred Hitchcock, or, The Plain Man's Hitchcock*. London: Faber and Faber, 1974.

Ebert, Roger. "The Films of Buster Keaton (1923)." *Rogerebert.com*. November 10, 2002.

Ehrenberg, Alain. *The Weariness of the Self*. Montreal: McGill–Queen's Press, 2010.

Eliot, T.S. "Tradition and the Individual Talent," reprinted in *Perspecta: The Yale Architectural Journal*, vol. 19 (1982): 36–42.

Emerson, Ralph Waldo. *Essays by Ralph Waldo Emerson*. Intro. by I. Edman. New York: Thomas Y. Crowell Company, 1951.

Empson, William. *Milton's God*. New York: Praeger, 1979.

Flatham, Richard E. *Thomas Hobbes: Skepticism, Individuality, and Chastened Politics*. Lanham, MD: Rowman & Littlefield, 2002.

Freedland, Michael. *Gregory Peck*. London: W.H. Allen, 1980.

Freedman, Jonathan. "From *Spellbound* to *Vertigo*: Alfred Hitchcock and Therapeutic Culture in America." *Hitchcock's America*, ed. by J. Freedman and R. Millington. New York: Oxford UP, 1999.

Freud, Sigmund. "Three Essays on Sexuality." *On Sexuality*. Trans. James Strachey. London: Pelican Books, 1977.

Fried, Michael. *Menzel's Realism: Art and Embodiment in Nineteenth-Century Berlin*. New Haven, CT: Yale UP, 2002.

Gaut, Berys. "On Cinema and Perversion." *Film and Philosophy* 1 (1994): 3–17.

Gilbert, Nora. "'She Makes Love for the Papers': Love, Sex, and Exploration in Hitchcock's Mata Hari Films." *Film & History* 41.2 (Fall 2011): 6–18.

Goffman, Erving. *Relations in Public: Microstudies of the Public Order*. New York: Harper & Row, 1972.

———. *Gender Advertisements*. New York: Harper & Row, 1976.

Gottlieb, Sidney. *Hitchcock on Hitchcock: Selected Writings and Interviews*. Los Angeles: University of California Press, 1997.

Gow, Gordon. "*Torn Curtain*." *Films and Filming* (October, 1966): 9–10.

Gracq, Julien. *Reading Writing*. Trans. Jeanine Herman. New York: Turtle Point Press, 1980.

Gramsci, Antonio. *The Prison Notebooks*. London: Lawrence and Wishart, 1971.

Haeffner, Nicholas. *Alfred Hitchcock*. Essex: Pearson, 2005.

Hardin, Russell. *David Hume: Moral & Political Theorist*. Oxford: Oxford UP, 2007.

Hayes, John Michael. *Rear Window*, final white script, December 1, 1953.

Heath, Stephen. "Narrative Space." 1976; rpt. in *Questions of Cinema*. Bloomington: Indiana UP, 1981: 19–75.

Hegel, G.W.F. *Aesthetics: Lectures on Fine Art*. Trans. T.M. Knox. New York: Oxford at the Clarendon Press, 1975.
———. *Phenomenology of Spirit*. Trans. A.V. Miller. New York: Oxford UP, 1977.
Herbert, Gary B. *Thomas Hobbes: The Unity of Scientific & Moral Wisdom*. Vancouver: University of British Columbia Press, 1989.
Hichens, Robert. *The Paradine Case*. London: Ernest Benn Limited, 1933.
Hitchcock, Alfred. "*Rear Window.*" *Take One* 2, No. 2 (November–December 1968): 18–20.
Higham, Charles. "Hitchcock's World." *Film Quarterly* 16.2 (Winter 1962–63): 3–16.
Highsmith, Patricia. "The Trouble with Mrs. Blynn, the Trouble with the World," in *Nothing that Meets the Eye*. New York: W.W. Norton & Co., 2002.
Hobbes, Thomas. *Leviathan*. Ed. C.B. Macpherson. Harmondsworth, England: Penguin Books, 1974.
Holroyd, Stephen. *The Elements of Gnosticism*. Dorset: Element, 1994.
Hume, David. *A Treatise of Human Nature*. 2d. ed. Ed. L.A. Selby–Bigge. Rev. P.H. Nidditch. New York: Oxford UP, 1990.
———. *An Enquiry Concerning Human Understanding*. Ed. Tom L. Beauchamp. Oxford: Oxford UP, 1999.
———. *A Treatise on Human Nature* in *Moral Philosophy*. Ed. Geoffrey Sayre-McCord. Indianapolis, IN: Hackett Publishing, 2006.
Indick, William. *Psychology for Screenwriters: Building Conflict in Your Script*. California: Michael Wiese Productions, 2004.
Jacobs, Lewis. *The Rise of the American Film*. New York: Harcourt Brace and Co., 1939.
James, Henry. *The Portrait of a Lady*. New York: George Scribner and Sons, 1908.
Jay, Martin. *Downcast Eyes: The Denigration of Vision in Twentieth–Century French Thought*. Berkeley: University of California Press, 1994.
Jefferson, Thomas. "First Inaugural Address." *The Papers of Thomas Jefferson* 33.17 (February to 30 April 1801). Princeton, NJ: Princeton UP, 2006: 148–52.
Jonas, Hans. *The Gnostic Religion*. Boston: Beacon Press, 2001.
Kail, P.J.E. "On Hume's Appropriation of Malebranche: Causation and Self." *European Journal of Philosophy* 16.1 (2007): 55–80.
Kant, Immanuel. *Critique of Pure Reason*. Trans. Norman Kemp Smith. New York: St. Martins, 1965.
———. 1785. *Groundwork of the Metaphysics of Morals*, trans. H.J. Paton. New York: Harper, 1964.
Keniston, Kenneth. "Morals and Ethics." *The American Scholar* 34: 4 (Autumn 1965), 628–32.
Kierkegaard, Søren. *Fear and Trembling and the Sickness unto Death*. Trans. with intro. and notes by Walter Lowrie. Princeton, NJ: Princeton UP, 1968.
Klossowski, Pierre. *Sade, My Neighbour*. Trans. Alphonso Lingis. Evanston, IL: Northwestern UP, 1991.
Konkle, Lincoln. *Thornton Wilder and Puritan Narrative Tradition*. Columbia: University of Missouri Press, 2006.
Krohn, Bill. "Ambivalence (*Suspicion*)." *Hitchcock Annual* 11 (2002–3): 67–116.

Kuleshov, Lev. "Art of the Cinema." *Kuleshov on Film: Writings of Lev Kuleshov.* Trans. Ronald Levaco. Berkeley: University of California Press, 1974.
La Bern, Arthur. *Frenzy.* New York: Paperback Library, 1971. Originally published as *Goodbye Piccadilly, Farewell Leicester Square*, 1966.
Lasch, Christopher. *The Culture of Narcissism: American Life in an Age of Diminishing Expectations.* 1979; rpt. New York: W.W. Norton and Co., 1991.
Leff, Leonard J. *Hitchcock and Selznick: The Rich and Strange Collaboration of Alfred Hitchcock and David O. Selznick in Hollywood.* London: Weidenfeld and Nicolson, 1987.
Lehman, Ernest. Shooting Script for *North by Northwest*. 1958.
Lehmann, Ulrich. "Language of the PurSuit: Cary Grant's Clothes in Alfred Hitchcock's 'North by Northwest.'" *Fashion Theory* 4.4 (2000): 467–86.
Leitch, Thomas M. *Find the Director and Other Hitchcock Games.* Athens: University of Georgia Press, 1991.
Lloyd, S. A. *Morality in the Philosophy of Thomas Hobbes: Cases in the Law of Nature.* Cambridge: Cambridge UP, 2009.
Lowndes, Marie Belloc. *The Lodger.* Oxford: Oxford Popular Fiction, 1996. Originally published by Methuen in 1913.
McFarlane, Brian, ed. *An Autobiography of British Cinema.* London: Metheuen/British Film Institute, 1997.
McGilligan, Patrick. *Alfred Hitchcock: A Life in Darkness and Light.* New York: HarperCollins. 2003.
McGinn, Colin. *The Power of Movies: How Screen and Mind Interact.* New York: Pantheon Books, 2004.
Metz, Christian. *The Imaginary Signifier: Psychoanalysis and Cinema.* Trans. Celia Britton, Annwyl Williams, Ben Brewster, and Alfred Guzetti. Bloomington: Indiana UP, 1982.
Metzl, Jonathan M. "Voyeur Nation? Changing Definitions of Voyeurism, 1950–2004." *Harvard Review of Psychiatry* 12 (2004): 127–31.
Miller, Mark Crispin. "Hitchcock's Suspicions and *Suspicion*." 1983; rpt. in *Boxed In: The Culture of TV.* Evanston: Northwestern UP, 1988.
Millington, Richard H. "Hitchcock and American Character: the Comedy of Self–Construction in *North by Northwest*." *Hitchcock's America*. Ed. Jonathan Freeman and Richard Millington. New York: Oxford UP, 1999.
Mogg, Ken. *The Alfred Hitchcock Story.* London: Titan, 2000.
Mulvey, Laura. "Visual Pleasure and Narrative Cinema." *Screen* 16, no. 3 (Autumn 1975): 6–18.
———. *Visual and Other Pleasures.* Bloomington: Indiana UP, 1989.
Nagel, Thomas. "Sexual Perversions." *Mortal Questions.* New York: Cambridge UP, 1979.
Naremore, James. "Hitchcock at the Margins of Noir" in Allen and Ishii–Gonzales (eds.), *Alfred Hitchcock: Centenary Essays.* London: BFI, 1999.
Nelson, William N. *Morality: What's in It For Me?* Boulder, CO: Westview, 1991.
Nietzsche, Friedrich. *Beyond Good and Evil.* Trans. R.J. Hollingdale. Harmondsworth: Penguin, 2003.

Ortega y Gasset, José. *On Love: Aspects of a Single Theme*. Trans. T. Talbot. New York: Meridian Book, World Publishing, 1957.
Paglia, Camille. *The Birds*. London: British Film Institute, 1998.
Palmer, R. Barton. *Shot on Location: Postwar Hollywood's Exploration of Real Place*. New Brunswick, NJ: Rutgers UP, 2016.
Palmer, R. Barton, and David Boyd, eds. *Hitchcock at the Source*. Albany, NY: SUNY Press, 2011.
Pettey, Homer B. "Hitchcock, Class, and Noir." *The Cambridge Companion to Alfred Hitchcock*. Ed. Jonathan Freedman. Cambridge: Cambridge UP, 2015: 76–91.
Pinker, Steven. "A History of Violence," *The New Republic*, vol. 236, no. 4, 809. (March 19, 2007): 18.
Pippin, Robert. *Fatalism in American Film Noir*. Charlottesville: University of Virginia Press, 2012.
Pomerance, Murray. *An Eye for Hitchcock*. New Brunswick, NJ: Rutgers UP, 2004.
———. "'Finding Release': Storm Clouds and *The Man Who Knew Too Much*," in James Buhler, Caryl Flinn, and David Neumeyer, eds., *Music and Cinema*. Hanover, CT: Wesleyan UP, 2000, 207–46.
Praz, Mario. *The Romantic Agony*. Oxford: Oxford UP, 1970.
Pudovkin, V.I. *Film Techniques and Film Acting*. New York: Grove Press, 1960.
Rachels, James. *The Elements of Moral Philosophy*, 3rd ed. New York: McGraw-Hill, 1994.
Rieff, Philip. *The Feeling Intellect: Selected Writings*. Ed. and with intro. by J. Imber. Chicago: The University of Chicago Press, 1990.
———. *Freud: The Mind of the Moralist*, 3rd ed. Chicago: The University of Chicago Press, 1979.
———. *The Triumph of the Therapeutic: Uses of Faith after Freud*. New York: Harper & Row, 1968.
Rohmer, Eric, and Claude Chabrol. *Hitchcock*. Paris: Éditions Univérsitaires, 1957. Translated by Stanley Hochman as: *Hitchcock: The First Forty Films*. New York: Ungar, 1979.
Rorty, Richard. *Philosophy and the Mirror of Nature*. Princeton, NJ: Princeton UP, 1979.
Rothman, William. *Hitchcock: The Murderous Gaze*. Cambridge, MA: Harvard UP, 1982.
Russell, Bertrand. *The Autobiography of Bertrand Russell*. 3 vols. Boston: Little, Brown, 1967.
———. *Marriage and Morals*. New York: Liveright, 1929; rev. ed., 1970.
Ryall, Tom. *Alfred Hitchcock and the British Cinema*. London: Croom Helm, 1986.
San Juan, Eric, and Jim McDevitt. *Hitchcock's Villains: Murderers, Maniacs and Other Mother Issues*. Lanham, MD: The Scarecrow Press, 2013.
Sarris, Andrew. "The Company Man." *Cahiers du cinema* (May 1967): 57–58.
Schérer, Maurice. "A qui la faute?" *Cahiers du cinéma* no. 39 (1954): 6–10.
Schopp, Robert F. *Automatism, Insanity, and the Psychology of Criminal Responsibility*. Cambridge: Cambridge UP, 1991.

Schroeder, David. *Hitchcock's Ear: Music and the Director's Art*. New York: Continuum, 2012.
Shaffer, Anthony. *Frenzy*, July 21, 1971. Production No. 05110.
Sharff, Stefan. *Alfred Hitchcock's High Vernacular: Theory and Practice*. New York: Columbia UP, 1991.
Simpson, Helen. *Under Capricorn*. London: Angus & Robertson, 1983.
Singer, Irving. *Three Philosophical Filmmakers*. Cambridge: MIT Press, 2004.
Singer, Peter. *Practical Ethics*. Cambridge: Cambridge UP, 1979.
Skinner, Quentin. *Hobbes and Republican Liberty*. Cambridge: Cambridge UP, 2008.
Smith, Robert J. "The Psychopath as Moral Agent." *Philosophy and Phenomenological Research* 65 (1984): 177–93.
Smith, Steven C. *A Heart at Fire's Centre: the Life and Music of Bernard Herrmann*. Berkeley: University of California Press, 1999.
Smith, Susan. *Hitchcock: Suspense, Humour and Tone*. London: BFI, 2000.
Spivey, Nigel. *Enduring Creation: Art and Pain and Fortitude*. Berkeley: University of California Press, 2001.
Spoto, Donald. *The Art of Alfred Hitchcock*. New York: Doubleday, 1992.
———. *The Dark Side of Genius: The Life of Alfred Hitchcock*. Boston: Little, Brown, 1983.
Sprengler, Christine. *Hitchcock and Contemporary Art*. New York: Palgrave Macmillan, 2014.
Sreedhar, Susanne. *Hobbes on Resistance: Defying the Leviathan*. Oxford: Oxford UP, 2010.
Strauss, Leo. *The Political Philosophy of Hobbes: Its Basis and Its Genesis*. Trans. Elsa M. Sinclair. Chicago: University of Chicago Press, 1996.
Sugden, Philip. *The Complete History of Jack the Ripper*. New York: Carroll & Graf, 1994.
Sullivan, Jack. *Hitchcock's Music*. New Haven, CT: Yale UP, 2006.
Taylor, John Russell. *Hitch. The Life and Work of Alfred Hitchcock*. London: Faber & Faber, 1978.
Thomson, David. *The Moment of Psycho: How Alfred Hitchcock Taught America to Love Murder*. New York: Basic Books, 2009.
Truffaut, François. *Le Cinéma selon Hitchcock*. Paris: Laffont, 1966.
———. *Hitchcock*. Revised ed. New York: Simon and Schuster, 1983.
———. *Hitchcock by Truffaut*. London: Paladin, 1986.
———. *Letters*. London: Faber & Faber, 1989.
Twiggar, Beth. "Alfred Hitchcock, Master Maker of Mystery." *New York Herald Tribune*. 7 December 1941. Section 6, p. 3.
Walton, Kendall L. "Transparent Pictures: On the Nature of Photographic Realism." *Critical Inquiry* 11.2 (Dec 1984): 246–77.
Waterhouse, Keith. *Streets Ahead*. London: Hodder & Stoughton, 1995.
West, Nathanael. *Novels and Other Writings*. New York: Library of America, 1997.
Wexman, Virginia Wright. *Creating the Couple: Love, Marriage, and Hollywood Performance*. Princeton, NJ: Princeton UP, 1993.

Williams, Raymond. *Culture and Society.* New York: Columbia UP, 1983.
Williamson, George. *The Donne Tradition: A Study in English Poetry from Donne to the Death of Cowley.* Cambridge: Harvard UP, 1930.
Wilson, George. *Narration in Light: Studies in Cinematic Point of View.* Baltimore, MD: The Johns Hopkins UP, 1988.
———. *Seeing Fictions in Film: The Epistemology of Movies.* New York: Oxford UP, 2011.
Wollheim, Richard. *Art and Its Objects,* 2d ed. New York: Cambridge UP, 1980.
Wood, Robin. *Hitchcock's Films Revisited.* New York: Columbia UP, 1989.
Woolfolk, Alan. "The Horizon of Disenchantment: Film Noir, Camus and the Vicissitudes of Descent" in Mark T. Conrad, ed., *The Philosophy of Film Noir.* Lexington: University of Kentucky Press, 2006.
———. "Depth Psychology on the Surface." *Hitchcock at the Source: The Auteur as Adapter* in Palmer and Boyd: 129–37.
Wordsworth, William. *The Prelude or Growth of a Poet's Mind* (Text of 1805). Ed. Ernest de Selincourt. Oxford: Oxford UP, 1933.
Worland, Rick. "Before and After the Fact: Writing and Reading Hitchcock's Suspicion." *Cinema Journal* 41.4 (2002): 3–26.
Wright, John P. *Hume's 'A Treatise of Human Nature': An Introduction.* Cambridge: Cambridge UP, 2009.
Yacowar, Maurice. *Hitchcock's British Films.* Hamden, CT: Archon Books, 1977.

Alfred Hitchcock Selected Filmography

Films, as director (listed chronologically)

No. 13, 1922
The Pleasure Garden, 1925
The Mountain Eagle, 1926
The Lodger: A Story of the London Fog, 1926
Downhill, 1927
Easy Virtue, 1927
The Ring, 1927
The Manxman, 1928
The Farmer's Wife, 1928
Champagne, 1928
Blackmail, 1929
Juno and the Paycock, 1930
Murder! 1930
The Skin Game, 1931
Number Seventeen, 1932
Rich and Strange, 1932
Waltzes from Vienna, 1933
The Man Who Knew Too Much, 1934
The 39 Steps, 1935
Secret Agent, 1936
Sabotage, 1937
Young and Innocent, 1937
The Lady Vanishes, 1938
Jamaica Inn, 1939
Rebecca, 1940
Foreign Correspondent, 1940
Mr. and Mrs. Smith, 1941
Suspicion, 1941
Saboteur, 1942
Shadow of a Doubt, 1943

Lifeboat, 1944
Bon Voyage and *Aventure Malgache*, 1944
Spellbound, 1945
Notorious, 1946
The Paradine Case, 1948
Rope, 1948
Under Capricorn, 1949
Stage Fright, 1950
Strangers on a Train, 1950
I Confess, 1951
Dial M for Murder, 1954
Rear Window, 1954
To Catch a Thief, 1954
The Trouble with Harry, 1956
The Man Who Knew Too Much, 1956
The Wrong Man, 1957
Vertigo, 1958
North by Northwest, 1959
Psycho, 1960
The Birds, 1963
Marnie, 1964
Torn Curtain, 1966
Topaz, 1969
Frenzy, 1972
Family Plot, 1976

Television Series

"Alfred Hitchcock Presents," 1955–1965

Contributors

Jerold J. Abrams is associate professor of philosophy at Creighton University. His essays on film have appeared in such books as *James Bond and Philosophy*, *Star Wars and Philosophy*, and *The Philosophy of Film Noir*. He is also the editor of *The Philosophy of Stanley Kubrick*.

Richard Allen is Professor and Chair of the Cinema Studies Department at New York University. Along with Sidney Gottlieb, he edits the *Hitchcock Annual*. Allen is the author of many books on film and film theory, including *Hitchcock's Romantic Irony*.

Sidney Gottlieb is Professor of Media Studies and Digital Culture at Sacred Heart University, Fairfield, Connecticut. He has edited *Hitchcock on Hitchcock: Selected Writings and Interviews* and *Alfred Hitchcock: Interviews*, and is the co-editor (with Richard Allen) of the *Hitchcock Annual*.

Nicholas Haeffner is Senior Lecturer in Communications at London Metropolitan University. He is author of *Alfred Hitchcock* (Pearson Education, 2005) and is currently co-curator of a traveling new media exhibition featuring films, installations, and games inspired by Hitchcock's *Vertigo*.

Jennifer L. Jenkins teaches American literature, film history, and archival studies at the University of Arizona. Her study *Celluloid Pueblo: Western Ways Film Service and the Invention of the Postwar Southwest* is forthcoming from University of Arizona Press.

Thomas Leitch is Professor of English at the University of Delaware, specializing in film and cultural theory. Among his many books are *Find* *the Director and Other Hitchcock Games*, *The Encyclopedia of Alfred Hitchcock*, and *Crime Films*. Recently, he edited along with Leland Poague *A Companion to Alfred Hitchcock*.

Brian McFarlane, an Honorary Associate Professor at Monash University, Australia, and Visiting Professor at the University of Hull, United Kingdom, is the author of many articles on film and literature, and of books including *New Australian Cinema: Sources and Parallels in American and British Film* (Melbourne, Cambridge University Press, 1992), *Novel to Film: An Introduction to the Theory of Adaptation* (Clarendon, Oxford University Press, 1996), (as compiler, editor, and chief author) *The Encyclopedia of British Film* (Methuen/BFI, 2003, 3rd ed.), *Great Expectations: Screen Adaptations* (A&C Black/Norton, 2007) and (with Deane Williams) *Michael Winterbottom* (Manchester University Press, 2009).

R. Barton Palmer is Calhoun Lemon Professor of Literature at Clemson University, where he also directs the film studies program. Palmer is the author, editor, or co-editor of more than fifty books and a hundred book chapters and journal articles, including two volumes on film noir.

Graham Petrie is a British film critic and novelist living in Canada and teaching film at McMaster University, Hamilton, Ontario. Among his many books on film are studies of Francois Truffaut, Andrei Tarkovsky, and European directors working in the United States.

Homer B. Pettey teaches literature and film at the University of Arizona. His recent works include *Film Noir* and *International Noir* (Edinburgh University Press, 2014), co-edited with R. Barton Palmer. He is General/Founding Editor for two book series at Edinburgh University Press: *Global Film Studios* and *International Film Stars*.

Murray Pomerance is Professor in the Department of Sociology at Ryerson University and the author of *The Economist, Marnie, Alfred Hitchcock's America, The Eyes Have It: Cinema and the Reality Effect, Tomorrow, The Horse Who Drank the Sky: Film Experience Beyond Narrative and Theory, Edith Valmaine, Johnny Depp Starts Here, Savage Time, An Eye for Hitchcock,* and *Magia d'Amore*. He has edited or co-edited numerous volumes, including *Thinking in the Dark: Cinema, Theory, Practice, A Family Affair: Cinema Calls Home, City That Never Sleeps: New York and the Filmic Imagination, and Cinema and Modernity*. He is editor of the "Techniques of the Moving Image" series at Rutgers University Press and of the "Horizons of Cinema" series at State University of New

York Press, as well as co-editor, with Lester D. Friedman and Adrienne L. McLean, respectively, of the "Screen Decades" and "Star Decades" series at Rutgers.

Steven M. Sanders is Professor of Philosophy Emeritus at Bridgewater State University. His work on topics in film has appeared in *The Philosophy of Martin Scorsese* (2009), *Film Noir: The Directors* (2012), *A Companion to Film Noir* (2013), *Lonely Places, Dangerous Ground: Nicholas Ray in American Cinema* (2014), and *Michael Mann Cinema and Television: Interviews 1980–2012*, which he co-edited with R. Barton Palmer. He is completing a novel in which events in the lives of seventy major philosophers form the backdrop of a madman's memoir.

Neil Sinyard is Emeritus Professor of Film Studies at the University of Hull, UK. He is the author of twenty-five books on the cinema, including studies of directors such as Alfred Hitchcock, William Wyler, Billy Wilder, Fred Zinnemann, Woody Allen, Steven Spielberg, Jack Clayton, and Richard Lester. He is currently writing a book on the films of George Stevens.

George Toles, Distinguished Professor and Film Chair in the department of English, Film, and Theatre at the University of Manitoba, is Fellow of the Royal Society of Canada and collaborator on screenplays with Guy Maddin.

Alan Woolfolk is Provost of Flagler College. He has written extensively on contemporary culture, public intellectuals, and in recent years, film, including a preface to the second edition of R. Barton Palmer's *Hollywood's Dark Cinema* and a chapter on Godard in *The Philosophy of Science Fiction Film*. Woolfolk has twice been a National Endowment for the Humanities Fellow and is an advisory editor for *Society*.

Index

Abrams, Jerold J., 17, 211–236, 309, 319
Ackland, Rodney, 70
Addison, John, 281
Adorno, Theodor, 237
Aesop, 57
Alfred Hitchcock Presents (TV Show), 2, 39, 99, 204, 318
Alighieri, Dante, 276
Allen, Richard, 16, 48, 57, 118, 151–169, 308, 319
Allen, Woody, 1, 321
Anderson, Judith, 63
Anderson, Lindsay, 29, 31, 35, 309
Andrews, Julie, 272–273
Anthelme, Paul, 6, 11–12
Astruc, Alexandre, 3–4, 18
Augustus (Novel), 65

Bagdasarian, Ross, 136
Baier, Kurt, 127, 131, 309
Balsam, Martin, 296
Barr, Charles, 24, 28–29, 31–32, 35, 62, 65, 71–72, 309
Barrymore, Ethyl, 80
Bartók, Béla, 276
Bass, Saul, 71
Battle of Britain, The (1969, Guy Hamilton), 43, 283
Baxter, Anne, 10, 202
Baylor University, 37
Bazin, André, 3, 19

Becker, Howard, 175, 191, 309
Beeding, Francis, 195
Before the Fact (Novel), 38–39, 41, 45, 47–48, 51, 57, 310
Bel Geddes, Barbara, 239–240
Bell, Daniel, 181
Benjamin, Arthur, 186
Benjamin, Walter, 57, 178, 191, 309
Bentham, Jeremy, 254
Bergdorf's (Clothing Store), 258
Bergman, Ingmar, 1
Bergman, Ingrid, 81, 83, 85–87, 242
Berkeley, Anthony, 39
Berlin, Germany, 31, 131, 272–273, 276, 311
Birds, The (1963, Alfred Hitchcock), 8, 17, 37–38, 49, 51, 60, 63, 196–197, 212, 216, 230–231, 233, 314, 318
Blackmail (1929, Alfred Hitchcock), 38, 64, 70, 206, 317
Blake, William, 69, 135, 179
Boethius, 200
Bogart, Humphrey, 241
Bogdanovich, Peter, 217–218, 231, 233, 277
Boomerang (1947, Elia Kazan), 208
Borde, Raymond, 45, 56–57, 309
Boulez, Pierre, 276
Brean, Herbert, 209
Bridie, James, 81
Brill, Lesley, 36, 38, 57, 86–88, 310

323

Brillo Boxes (Art Installation), 213, 225
British Film Institute (BFI), 29, 58, 73, 88, 233, 313–315, 320
Brooks, Mel, 2
Buchan, John, 65, 194
Burr, Raymond, 143, 147, 161

Cahiers du cinéma, 3, 18–19, 193, 210, 285, 310, 314
California, 19, 24, 73, 114, 122, 131, 191, 210, 233, 285, 308, 310–313, 315
Call Northside 777 (1948, Henry Hathaway), 208
Calvert, Clay, 159, 169
Cameraman, The (1928, Edward Sedgwick), 219
Carey, Macdonald, 180
Carroll, Noël, 158, 223–224, 233, 310
Catholicism, 4–7, 67–68, 96, 173, 176, 179–180, 189, 289
Cavell, Stanley, 255, 269, 310
CBS (Columbia Broadcasting System), 204
Chabrol, Claude, 3–5, 7, 19, 29, 36, 173, 176, 191, 193–194, 202, 204–205, 210, 282, 284, 310, 314
Chaumeton, Etienne, 45, 56–57, 309
Chayefsky, Paddy, 207, 210
Chekhov, Michael, 291
Chicago, Illinois, 19, 131, 210, 251–252, 256–258, 261–262, 308–309, 314–315
Christie, John Reginald, 292
"Circles" (Essay), 249
Citizen Kane (1941, Orson Welles), 2
Clift, Montgomery, 9, 14, 69, 202, 297
Cloak and Dagger (1945, Fritz Lang), 273
Coburn, Charles, 78
Cohen, Paula Marantz, 164–165, 169, 310

Coles, Robert, 181
College of the City of New York, 255
Collins, Jeffrey R., 306, 308, 310
Consolation of Philosophy (Text), 200
Coontz, Stephanie, 256, 258, 264, 266, 269, 310
Cooper, Gary, 53, 273
Copernican Turn, 215
Cotten, Joseph, 15, 63, 66, 69, 81, 85, 118
Courbet, Gustave, 156
Covent Garden, 290
Crane, Ward, 220
Cribbins, Bernard, 288
Cronyn, Hume, 81
Cross, Mark, 258
Crowther, Bosley, 11, 18, 202
Culture and Society, 67, 73, 316
Currie, Gregory, 161–162, 169, 310

Dall, John, 120, 228
Daniell, Charles James, 209
Danto, Arthur C., 17, 211–215, 217, 219, 225, 233, 310
Darcy, Georgine, 136
Davis, Clive, 278
Dawson, Anthony, 120
Day, Doris, 275
De Banzie, Brenda, 183
de Certeau, Michel, 197, 210
De la recherche de la vérité, 293
Deleuze, Gilles, 215–217, 219–221, 233, 310
Demme, Jonathan, 2
Denby, David, 1, 19
D'entre les morts, 180
de Palma, Brian, 2
de Rochemont, Louis, 207–208
de Sade, Marquis, 59, 67, 71–72
Dewey, John, 1
Diagnostic and Statistical Manual (IV), 154, 169
Dial M for Murder (1954, Alfred Hitchcock), 50, 119–120, 318

Didion, Joan, 181
Dietrich, Marlene, 70
Donat, Robert, 297
Donath, Ludwig, 272
Donne, John, 149–150, 316
Dostoyevsky, Fyodor, 4
Double Indemnity (1944, Billy Wilder), 241
Douchet, Jean, 7–9, 19, 195–196, 200, 204, 209–210, 311
Dubos, René, 181
Durgnat, Raymond, 47, 53, 57, 311

East End (London), 23, 25, 28
Ebert, Roger, 219, 233, 311
Edgware Road, 25
Edington, Harry, 44–45
Eisenstein, Sergei, 31, 216, 296, 308–309
Eliot, T.S., 62, 73, 311
Elliott, Laura, 123
Embankment (London), 28, 30, 290
Emerson, Ralph Waldo, 8, 19, 249–251, 311
Enduring Creation: Art, Pain, and Fortitude, 112, 114, 315
Enquiry Concerning Human Understanding, An, 287, 307–308, 312
Evelyn, Judith, 145, 168
Existentialism, 7, 66, 69, 140, 182, 196, 199, 241, 262

Family Plot (1976, Alfred Hitchcock), 2, 50, 119, 284, 318
Faulkner, William, 4
FBI (Federal Bureau of Investigation), 208
Film Society (England), 35
Finch, Jon, 288, 294
Fincher, David, 65
Fonda, Henry, 173–174, 179, 195, 199, 206, 297
Fontaine, Joan, 38, 41, 43–44, 55
Foot, Philippa, 117

Foster, Barry, 63, 288, 291, 293
France, 5, 40, 289–290
Francesca da Rimini (Symphonic Poem), 276, 283
Freedman, Jonathan, 237–240, 242–243, 251, 311, 314
French New Wave 2
Frenzy (1972, Alfred Hitchcock), 4, 18, 50, 60, 63, 282, 287–293, 296–298, 300, 303, 307–308, 313, 315, 318
Freud, Sigmund, 17, 64–65, 152–155, 170, 197, 238, 242–244, 251–252, 256, 310–311, 314
Friedan, Betty, 255, 258

Gainsborough Pictures, 2
Gaut, Berys, 162, 170, 311
Gélin, Daniel, 183
Goethe, Johann Wolfgang von, 69
Goffman, Erving, 177, 179, 182, 191, 311
Goldwyn Studios, 279
Goodbye Piccadilly, Farewell Leicester Square, 60, 288, 307–308, 313
Goodwin, Ron, 282
Gottlieb, Sidney, 9, 16, 18–19, 62, 73, 119, 131, 133–150, 311, 319
Gow, Gordon, 273, 285, 311
Gracq, Julien, 98–99, 114, 311
Gramsci, Antonio, 70, 73, 311
Grand Central Station, 259
Granger, Farley, 94, 118, 120, 228
Grant, Cary, 38, 41, 43–45, 55–56, 69, 216, 253, 268–269, 297, 313
Greene, Graham, 4–5, 274
Griffith, D.W., 148–149, 216

Haas, Dolly, 6, 10
Haeffner, Nicholas, 15, 59–74, 311, 319
Hall, Willis, 271
Harrison, Joan, 41
Harvard University, 1, 36, 150, 191, 255, 309, 313–314, 316

Hasse, O.E., 10, 14
Hathaway, Henry, 207–208
Hays Office, 41, 45
Hazlitt, William, 91
HBO (Home Box Office), 1
"Hearts and Pearls" (Film within a Film), 220, 222
Heath, Stephen, 45, 57, 311
Heckroth, Hein, 274
Hedren, Tippi, 60, 216, 230
Hegel, G.W.F., 17, 211–212, 214, 225–226, 232–233, 312
Heidegger, Martin, 1
Hellinger, Mark, 209
Helmore, Tom, 17, 239
Herbert, Gary B., 302, 308, 312
Herrmann, Bernard, 18, 199, 272, 276–285, 315
Herrmann, Norma, 279–280, 283
Hichens, Robert, 76–80, 88, 312
Higham, Charles, 29, 32, 35–36, 312
Highsmith, Patricia, 101, 114, 195, 312
Hitchcock, Alfred, 1–9, 11–12, 14–19, 23–24, 28–29, 31–32, 34–39, 41, 53, 55–73, 75–84, 86–89, 92–99, 102–104, 108–114, 117–133, 135–154, 156, 158, 163–167, 169–170, 173–183, 185–189, 191, 193–199, 201–213, 215–225, 227–233, 237–238, 242, 248–255, 258–261, 263, 267–269, 271–285, 287–289, 291, 293, 295–321
Hitchcock's Notebook, 42, 57, 309
Hobbes, Thomas, 16, 18, 126–127, 129, 287–293, 295, 297, 299, 301–308, 310–313, 315
Hogan, Dick, 228
House on 92nd Street, The (1945, Henry Hathaway), 208
Hume, David, 18, 215, 233, 287–297, 299–308, 311–312, 316
Huston, John, 241
Hutchinson, Josephine, 258

I Confess (1953, Alfred Hitchcock), 5–7, 9, 11–12, 18, 63, 69–70, 176, 202, 209, 297, 318
Iles, Francis, 38–39, 44, 46–48, 51, 56, 57
Imaginary Signifier, The, 152, 170, 313
Indick, William, 64, 73, 312
Inferno, The, 276
Ingster, Boris, 43, 48
Ironsides (TV Show), 147

Jack the Ripper, 15, 23–24, 35–36, 292, 309, 315
James, Henry, 173, 178, 191, 312
James Bond Franchise, 271, 319
Jameson, Fredric, 9, 19
Jarre, Maurice, 277
Jeffersonian Principles, 266
Jenkins, Jennifer L., 17, 253–269, 319
Jourdan, Louis, 80
Joy in the Morning (1965, Alex Segal), 278
Jung, Carl, 69
Juno and the Paycock (1930, Alfred Hitchcock), 4, 317

Kafka, Franz, 103, 205
Kail, P.J.E., 293–294, 308, 312
Kapsis, Robert, 7, 19, 194, 210
Kazan, Elia, 207–208
Keaton, Buster, 212, 215, 219–221, 223, 225, 232, 233, 311
Keaton, Joe, 220
Keats, John, 51
Kedrova, Lila, 273
Keen, Michael, 33, 188
Kelly, Grace, 120, 137, 161, 221
Kelly, Mary, 24
Keniston, Kenneth, 181–182, 191, 312
Kierkegaard, Søren, 17, 238, 246–247, 250–251, 312
Killers, The (1946, Robert Siodmak), 241
King Kong (Character), 160

King's Cross, 25
Klossowski, Pierre, 67–68, 73, 312
Knight and Day (2010, James Mangold), 3
Krohn, Bill, 42–43, 46, 49, 57, 71, 312
Kuleshov Effect, The, 295–296, 308, 313
Kyrou, Ado, 5

La Bern, Arthur, 60, 288, 290, 303–304, 307–308, 313
Lady Vanishes, The (1938, Alfred Hitchcock), 3, 63, 317
Lancaster, Burt, 241
Landau, Martin, 256
Landis, Jesse Royce, 257–258
Lang, Doreen, 174, 253
Lang, Fritz, 273
Last Laugh, The (1924, F.W. Murnau), 31
Laughton, Charles, 78–79
Lector, Hannibal (Character), 65
Légar, Olivia, 10
Lehman, Ernst, 71, 253–254, 257, 259–264, 266–267, 269, 313
Leigh, Janet, 261, 296
Leigh-Hunt, Barbara, 288
Leighton, Margaret, 81, 86–87
Leitch, Thomas, 15, 37–58, 63–64, 73, 268–269, 313, 319
Leviathan (Book), 287, 295, 301–302, 304, 306–308, 312, 315
"Liebestod," 276
Life (Magazine), 206, 209
Liman, James, 3
Lodger: A Story of the London Fog, The (1927, Alfred Hitchcock), 15, 17, 23–36, 38, 45, 48–51, 54, 57, 60, 63, 188, 190, 297, 309, 313, 317
London, England, 12, 23, 28, 35–36, 57–58, 73, 88–89, 170, 184, 188, 190, 233, 278, 285, 287–288, 291–292, 309, 311–315, 319
Lorne, Marion, 123

Lowndes, Marie Belloc, 15, 23–24, 26, 28, 36, 48–49, 51, 313
Love and Death (1975, Woody Allen), 1
Lustgarten, Edgar, 282–283

MacGuffin, 11, 16, 95, 272
MacMurray, Fred, 241
Malden, Karl, 12
Malebranche, Nicolas, 293–294, 308, 312
Malice Afterthought, 39, 48
Maltese Falcon, The (1941, John Huston), 141
Mancini, Henry, 282
Mangold, James, 3
Mann, Delbert, 207
Man Who Knew Too Much, The (1934, Alfred Hitchcock), 37, 62, 317
Man Who Knew Too Much, The (1956, Alfred Hitchcock), 17, 182, 185, 187, 190–191, 196, 257, 275, 314, 318
Marnie (1964, Alfred Hitchcock), 8, 38, 50, 60, 277, 318, 320
Marriage and Morals (Book), 17, 253–255, 268–269, 314
Marsh, Jean, 297
Martin, Dean, 168
Marty (1955, Delbert Mann), 207
Mason, James, 256
Massey, Anna, 288
Masters and Johnson, 255
Matthews, Lester, 78
Mauriac, François, 5
MCA, 277
McCowen, Alec, 288, 294
McFarlane, Brian, 15–16, 75–90, 313, 320
McGilligan, Patrick, 38–39, 44–45, 48, 52, 57, 73, 96, 114, 195, 207, 210, 254, 258, 269, 278–279, 285, 313
McGuinn, Colin, 163, 170
McGuire, Kathryn, 220

Melville, Herman, 69
Merchant, Vivien, 302
Metz, Christian, 152
Metzl, Jonathan, 153–154, 170, 313
MGM (Metro Goldwyn Mayer), 39
Miles, Bernard, 182
Miles, Vera, 197, 206
Mill, John Stuart, 254
Milland, Ray, 120
Miller, Mark Crispin, 46–47, 57, 313
Milton, John, 65–66, 72–73, 311
Minciotti, Esther, 200
Mitchum, Robert, 241
Mogg, Ken, 45–46, 49, 57, 284–285, 313
Montagu, Ivor, 35
Moore, Brian, 181, 271, 274
Mount Rushmore, 256, 258, 262, 264–267
Movie Brats, 284
Mozart, Wolfgang Amadeus, 239–240
Mr. and Mrs. Smith (2005, James Liman), 3
Mulvey, Laura, 138, 150, 153, 164, 170, 313
Murnau, F.W., 31
Murray, Henry A., 181
Mystifying Movies (Book), 223, 233, 310

Nagel, Thomas, 155, 170, 313
Naked City, The (1948, Jules Dassin), 209
Nalder, Reginald, 184
Naremore, James, 69, 73, 313
Nelson, William N., 128–129, 131, 313
New Deal, 8
New England Universalism, 8
Newton, Robert, 80
New York, 19, 36, 57–58, 72–73, 88–89, 114, 131–132, 142, 150, 169–170, 174, 191, 197, 199, 203, 210, 213, 233, 251–252, 255–258, 267–269, 277, 285, 307–316, 319–320

New Yorker (Publication), 1, 19, 254
New York Times (Publication), 18, 195, 209, 267–268
Nietzsche, Friedrich, 1, 68, 70, 73, 102, 119, 135, 140, 228, 238, 313
North by Northwest (1959, Alfred Hitchcock), 17, 63, 71, 95, 212, 216, 218, 226, 230, 253–257, 259–261, 263, 265, 267, 269, 277, 297, 301, 310, 313, 318
Nos deux consciences (Play), 6, 11
Nosferatu (1922, F.W. Murnau), 147
Notorious (1946, Alfred Hitchcock), 38, 50, 61–64, 69–70, 83, 271, 274, 318
Novak, Kim, 17, 196, 239, 242, 249
Novello, Ivor, 31, 188, 297
Number 13 (1922, Alfred Hitchcock), 2
Nymph with Satyrs (Paintings), 156

O'Casey, Sean, 4
"On the Pleasure of Hating" (Essay), 91
On the Waterfront (1954, Elia Kazan), 256
Origin of the World, The (Painting), 156
Orr, John, 66, 69, 73
Out of the Past (1947, Jacques Tourneur), 241

Paglia, Camille, 230, 233, 314
Palmer, R. Barton, 1–19, 150, 193–210, 232, 252, 314, 316, 320–321
Paradine Case, The (1947, Alfred Hitchcock), 15, 75–76, 79, 87–88, 312, 318
Paradise Lost (Epic Poem), 65, 73
Paramount Pictures, 39, 204
Pearson, Roberta, 153, 164, 170
Percy, Esmé, 163
Perkins, Anthony, 63, 118, 216
Perry Mason (TV Show), 147
Petrie, Graham, 15, 23–36, 320

Pettey, Homer B., 18, 287–308, 314, 320
Pinker, Steven, 127–128, 131, 314
Pippin, Robert, 241, 251, 314
Plato, 117, 212
Pleasure Garden, The (1925, Alfred Hitchcock), 61, 151, 154–158, 166, 317
Pomerance, Murray, 16, 173–192, 291, 308, 314, 320
Positif, 5
Poussin, Nicolas, 156
Powell, Michael & Pressburger, Emeric, 274
Powerhouse, The (Book), 65
Praz, Mario, 65, 73, 314
Prelude, The (Epic Poem), 289, 308, 316
Presley, Elvis, 183
Previn, André, 279
Psycho (1960, Alfred Hitchcock), 37, 63–65, 71, 118–119, 131–132, 147, 196, 212, 216, 225–227, 230, 254, 261, 277–281, 296, 298–299, 315, 318
Psychology for Screenwriters (Textbook), 64, 73, 312
Pudovkin, V.I., 31, 223, 233, 314
Pullman, Philip, 65–66, 73
Puritan Ethic, 67

Quaife, Susan, 81
Quayle, Anthony, 200
Quiet American, The (Novel), 274

Rachels, James, 128, 131, 314
Rains, Claude, 61, 63–64
Raksin, David, 282–283
Raphaelson, Samson, 41, 52
Ravel, Maurice, 276
Rear Window (1954, Alfred Hitchcock), 16–17, 38, 49, 61, 63, 67, 70, 72, 119–120, 133–141, 144–145, 147–150, 152–156, 158, 160–161, 163–164, 166–167, 169–170, 212, 216–219, 221–227, 230, 232–233, 257–258, 311–312, 318
Rebecca (1940, Alfred Hitchcock), 38, 55, 63, 70, 317
Red Shoes, The (1948, Michael Powell & Emeric Pressburger), 274
Renoir, Jean, 2, 19
Reposessed (Art Installation), 59, 73, 96
Republic, The (Plato), 117, 212
Reville (Hitchcock), Alma, 41, 151
Rieff, Philip, 238, 241, 243, 251, 314
Ritter, Thelma, 72, 142, 166
Robertson, Peggy, 279–280
Rohmer, Eric, 3–5, 7, 19, 29, 36, 173, 176, 191, 193–194, 202, 204–205, 210, 310, 314
Roman, Ruth, 123
Romantic Agony, The (Book), 65, 73, 314
Rope (1948, Alfred Hitchcock), 17, 38, 50, 62–63, 70, 119–121, 124, 212, 216, 228–230, 300, 318
Rorty, Richard, 1, 19, 215, 233, 314
Rothman, William, 8–9, 19, 36, 314
Russell, Bertrand, 17, 253–257, 260–266, 268–269, 314

Sabotage (1937, Alfred Hitchcock), 38, 50, 64, 70, 76, 202, 204, 317
Saint, Eva Marie, 254, 256, 259
Sanders, Steven S., 1–19, 117–132, 232, 321
Saunders, Hilary Saint-George, 195
Schaefer, George, 48
Secret Agent, The (1936, Alfred Hitchcock), 76, 202, 204, 210, 317
Selznick, David O., 57, 78, 80, 88, 311, 313
September Massacre of 1792 (France), 290
Seven (1995, David Fincher), 65
Seventh Seal, The (1957, Ingmar Bergman), 1
Shadow of a Doubt (1943, Alfred Hitchcock), 12, 15, 38, 63–64,

Shadow of a Doubt (continued)
  66–69, 71, 118–120, 124, 130, 180,
  257, 317
Shaffer, Anthony, 289, 291, 299, 302,
  305, 308, 315
Shayne, Konstantin, 248
Sherlock Jr. (1924, Buster Keaton),
  212, 219–223, 225–226, 230, 232
Shinn, Roger, 181
Sickert, Walter, 24
Sight & Sound (Publication), 2
Simpson, Helen, 76, 81–83, 86, 88,
  315
Singer, Irving, 2–5, 7–9, 18–19, 118,
  132, 315
Sinyard, Neil, 18, 271–285, 321
Siodmak, Robert, 241
Sophocles, 57, 135
Sopranos, The (TV Series), 1
South Dakota, 256, 258–259, 267
Spellbound (1945, Alfred Hitchcock),
  69, 195, 237–238, 242–243, 251,
  291, 311, 318
Spivey, Nigel, 112, 114, 315
Spoto, Donald, 15, 24, 31, 35–36,
  44, 52, 58–62, 72, 80, 88, 179–180,
  191, 315
Spy Who Came In From The Cold, The
  (1966, Martin Ritt), 271
Stam, Robert, 153, 164, 170
Stannard, Eliot, 25, 28, 32
Sterritt, David, 4, 8, 19
"Storm Clouds" (Cantata), 186, 191,
  314
Strange Case of Jonathan Drew, The
  (1926, Alfred Hitchcock, alt. title),
  30
Strangers on a Train (1951, Alfred
  Hitchcock), 12, 16, 38, 50, 62–63,
  70, 91, 94, 98, 101, 119–120,
  123–124, 130–131, 179, 195,
  203–204, 318
Sugden, Philip, 23, 36, 315
Sullivan, Jack, 276, 282, 284–285, 315
Suspicion (1941, Alfred Hitchcock),
  15, 37–58, 69, 312–313, 316–317

Swift, Clive, 288

Taylor, John Russell, 24, 31, 35–36,
  44, 58, 70, 73, 81, 89, 315
Tchaikovsky, Pyotr Ilyich, 276
Tetzel, Joan, 80
Thames Embankment, 290
Thirty-Nine Steps, The (1935, Alfred
  Hitchcock), 38, 50, 201, 204, 297,
  301, 317
This is Spinal Tap (1984, Rob Reiner),
  162
Times, The (Publication), 278
To Catch a Thief (1955, Alfred
  Hitchcock), 207, 318
Todd, Ann, 78, 80
Todd, Richard, 70
Toles, George, 16, 91–114, 321
Torn Curtain (1966, Alfred
  Hitchcock), 18, 70, 181, 271–272,
  275–279, 283–285, 311, 318
Toumanova, Tamara, 275
Tourneur, Jacques, 241
Tradition and the Individual Talent
  (Essay), 62, 73, 311
Trail, The (Novel), 205
Treatise on Human Nature (Book),
  293, 308, 312
Tristan and Isolde (Opera), 276
Trouble with Harry, The (1955, Alfred
  Hitchcock), 4, 50, 180, 276, 318
Truffaut, Francois, 3, 24, 28, 31,
  35–36, 41, 44–45, 48, 58, 63, 73,
  76, 80, 89, 176, 180, 191, 193–196,
  205–208, 210–211, 214, 278,
  283–285, 311, 315, 320
Tussaud, Madame, 27
Twentieth-Century Fox, 206–207

Under Capricorn (1949, Alfred
  Hitchcock), 15, 75–76, 81, 83–84,
  86–88, 315, 318
Universal Pictures, 2, 39, 277

Vachell, H.A., 24, 28
Valli, Alida, 78

Valli, Virginia, 151
Van Sant, Gus, 2
Vertigo (1958, Alfred Hitchcock), 2, 17, 37, 51, 59, 63–64, 73, 119, 147–148, 180, 196, 207, 216, 237–244, 249, 251, 254, 260–261, 276–277, 311, 318–319
Vertlieb, Steve, 279
"Visual Pleasure and Narrative Cinema" (Essay), 138, 150, 153, 313

Wagner, Richard, 276
Walker, Robert, 16, 63, 94, 118
Walton, Kendall, 157, 160, 170, 315
Walton, William, 283
Warhol, Andy, 211, 213, 225, 232
Warner Brothers, 39, 193, 206–207
Wasserman, Lew, 277
Waterhouse, Keith, 271–272, 285, 315
Weiler, A.H., 195
Welles, Orson, 2, 19, 43
West, Nathaniel, 43, 58, 315
Wexman, Virginia Wright, 256, 269, 315
Whitelaw, Billie, 288

Who is He? (Novel/Play), 24
Wilder, Billy, 241, 321
Wilder, Thornton, 66–67, 70–71, 73, 312
Wilding, Michael, 81
Williams, Raymond, 67, 73, 316
Williamson, George, 149–150, 316
Wilson, George, 160–162, 170, 316
Wittgenstein, Ludwig, 1
Wollheim, Richard, 157, 170, 316
Wood, Robin, 5–6, 19, 45, 53–54, 58, 65, 67–69, 73, 85, 89, 210, 316
Woolfolk, Alan, 17, 69, 73, 237–252, 316, 321
Wordsworth, William, 289–290, 308, 316
Worland, Rick, 47, 58, 316
Wright, Teresa, 66, 122
Wrong Man, The (1956, Alfred Hitchcock), 5, 12, 17, 31, 50, 63, 173, 177, 182, 190, 193, 195–197, 199, 201–209, 297, 318
Wuthering Heights (Opera), 284

Zanuck, Darryl F., 207
Žižek, Slavoj, 106
Zodiac, 24

www.ingramcontent.com/pod-product-compliance
Ingram Content Group UK Ltd.
Pitfield, Milton Keynes, MK11 3LW, UK
UKHW021843140426
5217IPUK00022B/1574